Rooted

AMERICAN LAND AND LIFE SERIES

Wayne Franklin, Series Editor

Rooted

SEVEN MIDWEST WRITERS OF PLACE

BY DAVID R. PICHASKE *Foreword by Wayne Franklin*

UNIVERSITY OF IOWA PRESS, Iowa City

University of Iowa Press, Iowa City 52242

Copyright © 2006 by the University of Iowa Press

http://www.uiowa.edu/uiowapress

All rights reserved

Printed in the United States of America

Design by Richard Hendel

The University of Iowa Press is a member of Green Press
Initiative and is committed to preserving natural resources.

Printed on acid-free paper

Library of Congress Cataloging-in-Publication Data

Pichaske, David R.

Rooted: seven Midwest writers of place / by David R.
Pichaske; foreword by Wayne Franklin.

   p.   cm.—(American land and life series)

Includes bibliographical references and index.

ISBN 0-87745-978-9 (cloth), ISBN 0-87745-987-8 (pbk.)

   1. American literature—Middle West—History and
criticism.   2. American literature—20th century—History
and criticism.   3. Place (Philosophy) in literature.   4. Middle
West—In literature.   5. Middle West—Social life and
customs.   6. Landscape in literature.   7. Setting (Literature).
8. Authors, American—Homes and haunts—Middle West.
I. Title.   II. Series.

PS273.P54 2006   2005055921

810.9′327709045—dc22

06 07 08 09 10 C 5 4 3 2 1
06 07 08 09 10 P 5 4 3 2 1

for MICHELLE

CONTENTS

Although readers sometimes take it for granted that *place* is a fundamental element of literature, Mississippian Eudora Welty—more place-sensitive than many of her peers—notoriously proclaimed place to be "one of the lesser angels" in the literary heavens. She was both right and wrong. Writers often set the scene for a novel or a story with deft but fleeting attention to the local topography. Then they turn to the more important things: "character, plot, symbolic meaning, and so on," as Welty put it in her classic essay, "Place in Fiction." It is relatively uncommon for a writer to regard place seriously, and making place central to an extended work is rare indeed.

Does this mean that, despite our rootedness in nature, when we imagine the world we do not imagine it as *earth*, as landscape, but rather as a set of human relations? Not entirely. The frail imprint of place in much modern literature has a good deal to do with the institutional context within which literature, especially in its "high" forms, is produced and consumed. As a commercial product, modern literature is by definition metropolitan, and most writers display more allegiance to the literary market that gives their works economic and cultural value than to the actual places where they or their readers reside. If a work is too deeply implicated in some actual place, particularly the place in which the author herself or himself is personally invested, it often runs the risk of being dismissed as "merely regional" in character and interest. More to the point, it runs the risk of remaining in manuscript. Literature as a modern phenomenon deals with the fungible commonplaces of urban society, not with the idiosyncrasies of actual human environments.

Like films shot in California but set in some distinctly non-Californian place, most books ignore spatial plausibility. Quite unusual is the case in which place and plot coincide—unusual, but not unevidenced. Benjamin Franklin (Frank) Norris made credible use of San Francisco and the gold mining districts of central California in *McTeague*, published in 1899, but outdid himself—and most other novelists—in bringing that grim book to its dry, dusty close in Death Valley. There, what Welty called "symbolic meaning" was inextricably linked to place. When, twenty-five years after *McTeague*'s publication, Erich von Stroheim turned it into the film he called *Greed*, he shot the latter in San

Francisco and, rightly again, in Death Valley. Yet the fixation of novelist and director alike with the scorched desert was hardly that of native sons. Norris had been born and reared in Chicago, and did not see the West until he was a teenager. Almost as soon as his family relocated to San Francisco, he was packed off to Paris for schooling (he wanted to be a painter), where he began writing little medieval romances, a habit so hard to break that on his return to the United States and his matriculation at Berkeley in 1890 he set about writing a long poem, *Yvernelle, A Tale of Feudal France* (1892), that had virtually nothing to do with his immediate surroundings. When he soon found his proper topic and voice, it still bore the mark of his peripatetic upbringing: for it was the French naturalist Zola, whose work Norris encountered in California and then at Harvard, who provided the model for *McTeague*.

In the case of Vienna native Erich Stroheim, who added the noble *von* to his name upon his arrival in America in 1909, the wanderings pushed west rather than east but led to the odd convergence that made him attempt an almost literalistic transcription of Norris's novel for the screen. The result was a forty-odd-reel movie that was slashed again and again until it was merely a fraction of its now mostly lost original. The director had apprenticed under D. W. Griffith and became familiar with California at that time. But once he came across Norris's novel (reportedly in a tattered copy left behind in rented lodgings by a previous tenant, though one suspects that a 1914 film version, *Desert Gold* by Scott Sidney, must also have crossed his path) it was the realism of the novel's scenes more than any separate attachment Stroheim felt for his adopted region that led to his intense and intensive visualization. He boasted that not a single scene of the film was shot in the studio. He rented a house in San Francisco for the interiors and when the studio executives told him that he could shoot the desert scenes in Oxnard, a coastal town just north of Los Angeles which was the Hollywood stand-in for real desert, he refused, going instead to Death Valley: "Having read the marvelous descriptions of the real Death Valley as Norris had depicted them," Stroheim recalled in a letter to Peter Noble in 1950, "I insisted on the real Death Valley in California and Death Valley it was." It was hot there ("142 degrees Fahrenheit in the shade, and no shade," he humorously added), but Stroheim felt that the results achieved because of the heat and the physical suffering of the forty-two members of the crew and cast lent added weight and reality to the film.

In part, one gets the impression that for both Norris and Stroheim place verged on being a fetish, but the suspicion is a shallow one. Both men certainly took place seriously. Yet it is not clear that Norris spent any significant time in Death Valley (by contrast, we know that he had visited the Placer County mine of his friend Seymour Waterhouse while revising *McTeague* in 1897), so the powerful ending of his novel was a case of wonderfully contingent invention, stoked by reading and perhaps guided by the novelist's previous experience in the Transvaal in South Africa. So, if Stroheim was drawn to the "real Death Valley" as a result of the impact of Norris's prose, he was thus far tricked. He certainly took that place seriously, and made sure his crew and cast did so as well, but even his own poetic use of the desert amounted to something far more complex and indirect than a travelogue. The embedded quality of both works is not, in other words, as simple a thing as it seems.

Yet it remains true that most books and films are far less entangled with the world's actual places. Hollywood's "desert," Oxnard, reminds us of this point. Equally suggestive of the usual practice, especially in more recent decades, is the work of the contemporary Australian Jewish writer Morris Lurie, whose deft counterfeits of actual places are seductive illusions. Now living in Melbourne, Lurie has often set stories in other locations around the globe where he has spent extended periods, including Greece, Denmark, England, Morocco, and New York City. The globe-trotting, both personal and literary, is partly a function of the Australian literary market, which (like those of Canada or other small "Commonwealth" countries) often cannot adequately support native writers. Lurie's fellow Australian Patrick White, whose *Voss* probably owed something to *McTeague* (and/or *Greed*), sold modestly outside his homeland until the Nobel Prize started an international craze for his works. Barring such exceptional attention, if writers such as Lurie wish to make a living from their pens, they have to take an active interest in appealing to foreign readers. Hence Lurie's impressive spatial repertoire as a writer. Yet the Australian, whose work has often appeared in both *The New Yorker* and *Punch*, seems waggishly aware of how to defeat this game even as he plays it. Place is as often a joke in his work as a subject of reflection. In a tale that is a perfect embodiment of his typical practice, "Skylight in Lausanne," the title refers not to the splendid play of light in the sky over Lake Geneva but rather to a physical opening in a roof—a skylight, actually located in a building in Lausanne—up through which a character accidentally locked in a bathroom must make a frantic escape. That could happen anywhere.

David R. Pichaske is interested in the other kind of localism, the kind we may trace back to Norris (and some of his contemporaries, including Sarah Orne Jewett and Mary Austin). The seven modern Midwest writers explored in *Rooted*, not all of them natives of the particular part of the region about which they write (or, like Pichaske himself, even of the region at large), are doggedly committed to making their prose and poetry implicate their place. To some extent, the complexity of the modern American literary scene is such that they can afford to do so—as long as they do not expect the metropolitan market to support them. Much of what they write is locally published by regional or small presses, although in two cases (those of Jim Harrison and Jim Heynen) New York City is also an occasional, even regular, venue. Insofar as local production and consumption are norms, even ideals, their writings are a kind of frozen conversation, part of the rich local discourse through which human beings everywhere reify and organize their life in space, using speech to do what commercial literature, which in its search of readership is exogamous rather than endogamous, has so little interest in accomplishing. Here we are lucky to find the irreducible differences that make *this* place what it is. Whereas Willa Cather, Virginia-born and New Hampshire-buried, wrote very insightfully about the Great Plains, and especially its immigrant cultures, but did so largely for metropolitan audiences eager for some fresher, more distant sky, Pichaske's writers inhabit their spaces and what they have to say of them is heard first by other residents. If the metropole is aware of these things, it does not often admit it.

But in a world devastated by human arrogance, such local writings have a global application. It is of course fashionable in some circles to dismiss many of the questions I have raised as irrelevant or even wrongheaded. True, words are not things, and "setting" is not the same thing as place—so we cannot technically learn much about the material world by exploring verbal representations of it. Yet it is also true that human beings have long used language as a ready means to negotiate actual space—a tool for navigation, appropriation, cognition, and at last homemaking. If the earth is to be saved from the ravages of our species, we need to recover the intimacy of our longstanding verbal linkage to nature. The necessary change begins when any of Pichaske's writers inscribes on a blank sheet some territorial fragment, a whisper of inhabitance, whereby not just as writer but as person one is able to put down roots. The Midwest that these seven writers create (along with Pichaske, who possesses his own finely tuned instrument for registering the local) is a verbal territory we might all, wherever we are, wish to inhabit. It offers us a chance to begin restating our proper place in the world.

PREFACE AND ACKNOWLEDGMENTS

This is a book about the relationship between writers and place, about the way seven midwestern authors who came of age toward the close of the twentieth century grounded themselves and their work in terms of seven different places in seven different states. It is a book about the way place shapes thought and art, about the way art and thought shape place, about preserving, breaking, recovering, and transplanting roots. It is also a book about growing upward and away from roots, about the alter egos of seven writers of place, and thus about the subtle complexity of their lives and thought and work. This book suggests, although not always hopefully, a way out of the postmodern dissociation of personality and reflects I am sure the thinking of people like Wendell Berry on regaining our lost sense of community.

Not all of these writers are native to the landscapes with which they are most associated: Dave Etter was born not in small-town Illinois but in California; Norbert Blei first visited Door County, Wisconsin, at the age of twenty, did not move there permanently until he was thirty; Linda Hasselstrom arrived in Hermosa, South Dakota, at age three, moved to the ranch at age nine, left the ranch on a couple of occasions; Nebraska State Poet William Kloefkorn was born and raised in southern Kansas. Bill Holm, Jim Heynen, and Jim Harrison, all born in the rural Midwest, bugged out the moment they graduated from high school. All of these writers have one leg "elsewhere"; Jim Harrison is literally all over the globe. Well, it's happened before in American literature: Robert Frost was not a New Englander by birth, nor was Willa Cather a Nebraskan. Yet they all know their places intimately, and are tied in the minds of readers to very specific, identifiable patches of this planet. These seven writers know their places. They are more rooted than most Americans.

I myself was not born in my Minnesota place, was not even raised in the Midwest, yet something in the Midwest connected with something in my DNA (an encoded memory of the Baltic plains?) on that first Kerouacean bus ride west as an up-tight Springfield (Pennsylvania) High School senior, through the long night across the Appalachians, two hours of pinball at a rest stop in Wheeling, West Virginia (a dozen free games left on the machine when the Greyhound pulled out), then onto the Midwest flatlands, to Springfield, Ohio, and Wittenberg University. Sitting on the bus home two days later, I had already made up my mind: the Midwest was a good place, a better place, the right place for me. When my guidance counselor offered me the compliment of saying, "I think you should go to Princeton . . . in New Jersey," I looked him square in the eye and answered, "I'm going to Wittenberg . . . in Ohio."

I arrived in Ohio that freshman year, a little like Jim Harrison in New York City, with Joyce and Camus tucked ostentatiously under my arm. Then I put them away, pretty much for good, and spent four transformative years driving all over Ohio and Indiana as a member of the Tiger baseball team and sports editor of *The Torch*. Then I spent four years of graduate school in Athens, Ohio, and a decade teaching in Peoria, Illinois, and a quarter of a century teaching in western Minnesota, living first on a rented farm and then on a former nursery on the banks of the Minnesota River, days on end spent exploring the Midwest on every possible occasion, using every possible excuse, listening, watching, reporting, transforming myself further.

I began my academic career as a mediaevalist, teaching classes in Chaucer, *Beowulf*, Cynewulf, and the *Pearl* poet in the days when the English Department at a college of five thousand students could offer five sections of Shakespeare each term. When that department collapsed from thirty-three to something like fourteen, necessity nudged me in the direction of American literature, and spreading roots drew me toward midwestern writers. I invented a class called "Midwestern Literature," and began writing poems like "Hancock County, Illinois" with lines like "There is nothing here in this vastness. / The amplitudes absorb all that man throws against them." In 1977 I became editor of *Spoon River Quarterly*, a very little magazine which, owing to its location, favored midwestern poets, especially poets from Illinois. That bias was extended in 1979 when Spoon River Poetry Press began publishing books. When I moved to Minnesota in 1980, "Midwestern Literature" became "Rural-Regional Literature," part of the school's ambitious (and in 1980 virtually unique) Rural Studies Program. My focus was still midwestern writers, but my publishing operation realigned itself more toward the western part of the Midwest. My writing shifted as well. Instead of articles on Harry Bailly in *Chaucer Review* or Spenser's *Faerie Queene* in *Studies in English Literature*, I found myself writing on Dave Etter for *Indiana Review* and Meridel Le Sueur for *Minnesota English*

Journal. My interest in Bob Dylan—a life-long addiction—focused on Dylan's Minnesota roots. When the New York editor who had published *A Generation in Motion: Popular Music and Society in the Sixties* wanted another book, I offered *Late Harvest: Recent Rural American Writing,* an anthology which included several writers I had taught in class, published as a small press publisher, and hosted as participants in the week-long writers' festivals that Phil Dacey and I organized at Southwest Minnesota State University. By this time, of course, the writers, the academics, and the publishers were all pretty close. We have, in a way, grown up together.

We have, in a way, grown old together. Writing entries for the *Dictionary of Midwestern Literature* in the 1990s, I noticed that I was doing the first serious scholarship on several authors, especially those who could claim no entitlement of gender or ethnicity. These were major writers; they had published a dozen books; several were retired or approaching retirement in academic oblivion. I found almost no criticism beyond a newspaper article or a book review. The whole concept of a *Dictionary of Midwestern Literature (DML)* was unusual in an era of postmodernist theory and cultural diversity which privileged every culture except the one outside the front door; the dictionary was a throw-back to the thirties, when so much more attention seems to have been paid to American regions. But the *Dictionary* was itself part of another shift in literary scholarship, the rise of "bioregionalism" in the 1990s, as Michael Kowalewski's learned essay on "Contemporary Regionalism" for *A Companion to the Regional Literatures of America* shows. Gradually some of my brief *DML* entries became full-fledged articles in major journals. Several books published first as Spoon River Poetry Press or Ellis Press titles were reprinted by prestigious university presses. European conferences—which in the 1980s and early 1990s had emphasized race, gender (not so much class), and postmodernist theory—turned their attention to region, and I found myself sponsored by the U.S. Embassy or State Department to lecture on midwestern writers in Poland, Norway, Latvia, Germany, England, Hungary, and Austria.

I offer all this as an explanation of the essays which follow. *A Generation in Motion* is in many ways the song of youth told in the voices of musicians under thirty; its motto is the destination on Ken Kesey's famous bus: "FURTHUR." This book is the song of age told in the voices of writers twice thirty; its motto is "roots." I'm not saying one book is truer than the other, but they make an interesting set of bookends. This book grows out of a great deal of life experience; out of two, in some cases three decades of reading, thinking, teaching, and writing; and out of a very close relationship with most of the writers. Scholarly distancing has clearly been compromised, but there are offsetting gains, and I think I have been honest in my handling of my subject. In one respect this book is like the community which emerges among people whose daily lives are so entangled in each other and in their shared place that even quibbles and quarrels become acts of charity and support. In another respect, I want to model a way for the literary critic to begin not with French deconstructionist theory—or with any theory at all—but with text, landscape, and biography—a way to privilege writers over theoreticians. This approach is especially important in discussing memoir and autobiographical fiction and poetry.

In any event, I owe a great debt of gratitude to many people, especially those who have worked the fields of midwestern literature before me, including Thomas McAvoy's *The Midwest: Myth or Reality*, Lucien Stryk's *Heartland: Poets of the Midwest* anthologies, Clarence Andrews's *A Literary History of Iowa*, Ronald Szymanski's *America in Literature: The Midwest*, Gerald Nemanic's *A Bibliographical Guide to Midwestern Literature*, Robert C. Bray's *Rediscoveries: Literature and Place in Illinois*, Richard Boudreau's *The Literary Heritage of Wisconsin*, John E. Hallwas's *Illinois Literature: The Nineteenth Century*, Alfred Kazin's *A Writer's America: Landscape in Literature*, Ronald Weber's *The Midwestern Ascendancy in American Writing*, Wayne Franklin and Michael Steiner's *Mapping American Culture*, Mark Vinz and Thom Tammaro's *Imagining Home: Writing from the Midwest*, Diane Dufve Quantic's *The Nature of the Place*, and Charles L. Crow's *A Companion to the Regional Literatures of America*. Thanks also to John Judson, whose Juniper Press and *Voyages to the Inland Sea* series gave voice to so many Midwest writers; David D. Anderson for the Society for the Study of Midwest Literature and *Mid-America* journal—and, indirectly, for *Dictionary of Midwestern Literature* (Indiana University Press, 2001); to Joseph Amato and David Nass for their roles in building the Southwest Minnesota State University Rural Studies Program; to editors Ken Stuart for *Late Harvest* and Greg Britton for *A Place Called Home*; to the U.S. State Department and the Fulbright Commission for connections to Poland and Latvia and Mongolia, and thence to Norway, Germany, England, Austria, and Hungary; to Agnieszka Salska of the University of Łódź, Poland, for many opportunities to teach and write; to the Illinois Arts Council, the National Endowment for the Arts, and Southwest Minnesota State University for their support of my publishing operations; to Jon Wefald and Robert Carothers, "the good presidents"; to my students, some of whom have taught me more than I taught them; to Sandy Mosch for proofreading; to the editors of *Journal of Modern Literature, Western American Literature*, and *Studies in American Fiction* for permission to reprint here, in altered and expanded form, material first published in those places; and most of all to Dave Etter, William Kloefkorn, Norbert Blei, Bill Holm, Linda Hasselstrom, Jim Heynen, and Jim Harrison—and many other writers whose stories I have yet to write about—who with their books made possible this book about their books.

For permission to reprint material quoted in this book I would like to thank the following writers and publishers:

Dave Etter for excerpts from *Go Read the River* (copyright © 1966), *The Last Train to Prophetstown* (copyright © 1968), *Well, You Needn't* (copyright © 1975), *Central Standard Time* (copyright © 1978), *Open to the Wind* (copyright © 1978), *Riding the Rock Island Through Kansas* (copyright © 1979), *Cornfields* (copyright © 1980), *West of Chicago* (copyright © 1981), *Boondocks* (copyright © 1982), *Alliance, Illinois* (copyright © 1978, 1983), *Home State* (copyright © 1985), *Live at the Silver Dollar* (copyright © 1985), *Selected Poems* (copyright © 1987), *Midlanders* (copyright © 1988), *Electric Avenue* (copyright © 1988), *Carnival* (copyright © 1990), *Sunflower County* (copyright © 1994), *I Want to Talk about You* (copyright © 1995), *How High the Moon* (copyright © 1996), *Next Time You See Me* (copyright © 1997), and *Looking for Sheena Easton* (copyright © 2003); and Spoon River Poetry Press for material published in 1980, 1981, 1983, 1985, 1987, 1988, 1990, 1994, 1996, and 2003. Quotations from the works of Dave Etter are reprinted with permission of the author and of Spoon River Poetry Press.

William Kloefkorn for excerpts from *Alvin Turner as Farmer* (copyright © 1974), *Uncertain the Final Run to Winter* (copyright © 1974), *loony* (copyright © 1975), *ludi jr.* (copyright © 1976), *Stocker* (copyright © 1978), *Cottonwood County* (copyright © 1979), *Not Such a Bad Place to Be* (copyright © 1980), *Let the Dance Begin* (copyright © 1981), *Platte Valley Homestead* (copyright © 1981), *Honeymoon* (copyright © 1982), *Houses and Beyond* (copyright © 1982), *A Life Like Mine* (copyright © 1984), *Collecting for the Wichita Beacon* (copyright © 1984), *Drinking* the Tin Cup Dry (copyright © 1989), Where the Visible Sun Is (copyright © 1989), Dragging Sand Creek for Minnows (copyright © 1992), Going Out, Coming Back (copyright © 1993), The Coldest Christmas (copyright © 1993), Burning the Hymnal (copyright © 1994), Treehouse: New and Selected Poems (copyright © 1996), This Death by Drowning (copyright © 1997), A Time to Sink Her Pretty Little Ship (copyright © 1999), Welcome to Carlos (copyright © 2000), Loup River Psalter (copyright © 2001), Sergeant Patrick Gass, Chief Carpenter (copyright © 2002), Restoring the Burnt Child: A Primer (copyright © 2003), Shadowboxing and Other Stories (copyright © 2003), Fielding Imaginary Grounders (copyright © 2004), and Sunrise, Dayglow, Sunset, Moon (copyright © 2004); and University of Nebraska Press for material from This Death by Drowning/Prairie Schooner, reprinted from Prairie Schooner, volume 29, number 2 (summer 1995) by permission of the University of Nebraska Press, © 1995 by the University of Nebraska Press. Excerpt "Not Such a Bad Place to Be" from Treehouse: New and Selected Poems, copyright © 1996 by William Kloefkorn, reprinted with the permission of White Pine Press, Buffalo, New York. Quotations from the works of William Kloefkorn are reprinted with permission of the author and University of Nebraska Press.

Norbert Blei for excerpts from The Watercolored Word (copyright © 1968), The Hour of the Sunshine Now (copyright © 1978), The Second Novel (copyright © 1978), Door Way (copyright © 1981), Adventures in an American's Literature (copyright © 1982), Door Steps (copyright © 1983), Door to Door (copyright © 1985), The Ghost of Sandburg's Phizzog (copyright © 1986), Paint Me a Picture/Make Me a Poem (copyright © 1987), Neighborhood (copyright © 1987), Meditations on a Small Lake (copyright © 1987), Chi Town (copyright © 1990, 2003), Chronicles of a Rural Journalist (copyright © 1990), What I Know by Heart So Far (copyright © 1995), Winter Book (copyright © 2002); and December Press for excerpts from The Second Novel (copyright © 1978); and Ellis Press for material published in 1981, 1982, 1983, 1985, 1986, 1987, 1990, and 2002. Quotations from the works of Norbert Blei are reprinted with permission of the author and of December Press and Ellis Press.

Linda M. Hasselstrom for excerpts from The Muse Is Blue (copyright © 1965), The Book Book (copyright © 1979), Caught by One Wing (copyright © 1984); Going Over East (copyright © 1987), Roadkill (copyright © 1987), Windbreak (copyright © 1987), Land Circle (copyright

© 1991), *Dakota Bones* (copyright © 1993), *Roadside History of South Dakota* (copyright © 1994), *Bison: Monarch of the Plains* (copyright © 1998), *Feels Like Far* (copyright © 1999), *Bitter Creek Junction* (copyright © 2000), *Between Grass and Sky* (copyright © 2002); and Barn Owl Books (distributed through Windbreak House, P.O. Box 169, Hermosa, SD 57744) for selections from *Windbreak* (copyright © 1987); and High Plains Press for "Rhubarb Pie" from *Bitter Creek Junction* (copyright © 2000); and Spoon River Poetry Press for material published in 1987 and 1993. Quotations from the works of Linda Hasselstrom are reprinted with permission of the author and of Barn Owl Books, High Plains Press, and Spoon River Poetry Press.

Bill Holm for excerpts from *Boxelder Bug Variations* (copyright © 1985), *The Music of Failure* (copyright © 1985), *Coming Home Crazy: An Alphabet of China Essays* (copyright © 1990), *The Dead Get by with Everything* (copyright © 1990), *A Landscape of Ghosts* (copyright © 1993), *The Heart Can Be Filled Anywhere on Earth* (copyright © 1996), *Eccentric Islands* (copyright © 2000), *Playing the Black Piano* (copyright © 2004); and Milkweed Editions for material published in *Boxelder Bug Variations* (copyright © 1985), *Coming Home Crazy: An Alphabet of China Essays* (copyright © 1990), *The Dead Get By with Everything* (copyright © 1990), *The Heart Can Be Filled Anywhere on Earth* (copyright © 1996), *Eccentric Islands* (copyright © 2000), and *Playing the Black Piano* (copyright © 2004). Quotations from the works of Bill Holm are reprinted with permission of the author and of Milkweed Editions and Plains Press.

Jim Heynen for excerpts from *Notes from Custer* (copyright © 1976), *How the Sow Became a Goddess* (copyright © 1977), *The Man Who Kept Cigars in His Cap* (copyright © 1979), *A Suitable Church* (copyright © 1981), *You Know What Is Right* (copyright © 1985), *The One-Room Schoolhouse: Stories about the Boys* (copyright © 1993), *Being Youngest* (copyright © 1997), *Cosmos Coyote and William the Nice* (copyright © 2000), *The Boys' House* (copyright © 2001), *Standing Naked: New and Selected Poems* (copyright © 2001); and Minnesota Historical Society Press for material reprinted from *The Boys' House* (St. Paul: Minnesota Historical Society Press, 2001). Excerpt from "Our Farm/Our Family" from *Standing Naked: New and Selected Poems*, copyright © 2001 by Jim Heynen, reprinted with permission of Confluence Press. Excerpt from "Butcherdog" from *How the Sow Became a Goddess*, copy-

I explored some of the ideas in chapter 1, "Midwestern Literature," in an essay called "So What's Midwestern about Midwestern Literature?" delivered as a conference paper and published in *Local Colors of the Stars and Stripes*, Torun, Poland: Polish American Studies Association, 2002.

A shorter version of chapter 2, "Dave Etter: Call It Cornbelt Baroque," appeared in *The Journal of Modern Literature*, 23.3/4 (summer 2000), pages 393–427, under the title "Searching for Our Lost American Souls," and is used here with permission of Indiana University Press.

A shorter version of chapter 3, "William Kloefkorn: Looking Back Over the Shoulder of Memory," appeared in *Western American Literature*, spring 2003, pages 4–29, and is used here with permission of the editor.

A shorter version of chapter 4, "Norbert Blei: Portrait of the Artist as an Outsider," appeared in *Studies in American Fiction* 32.2 (autumn 2004), pages 215–40, and is used here with permission of the editor.

Rooted

Midwestern Literature

1

*"Would you say that the search for identity is primarily an
American theme?" novelist Ralph Ellison was once asked by
an interviewer. "It is the American theme," he replied.*
—Thomas Cooley, Preface *to the* Adventures of
Huckleberry Finn

*Iowa, for example, is not only a state in the union but also a
state of mind in the American consciousness—a metaphor
accentuating an amorphous traditionalism deployed in
the "family"; a largely unreflective patriotism; an ethic
of hard work and democratic-socialist egalitarianism;
community spirit of the action-oriented, "barn-raising"
sort; a commitment to "basic values"; moral, spiritual, and
educational fair-dealing and loyalty to one's employer; a
parsimony on principle; a verbal commitment to the myth of
the family farm even in a period of agribusiness takeover; an
international export-ethic and aspiration to multinational
prowess; a healthy local skepticism about all such claims;
and the social practices surrounding American rural
and small-town life, particularly those of the community
potluck supper, the church social, and the county fair.
Contradictions abound here without entirely disrupting.*
—Cheryl Herr, Critical Regionalism and Cultural Studies

*When I explain myself
I'll be talking geography.*
—Pablo Neruda, Extravagaria

Literature boils down, mostly, to three basic questions: Who am I? What made me what I am? What might I become? It is the answers to those questions that make poetry, stories, novels, and history worth reading—and writing.

There are many answers. Who am I? "Oedipus, who bear the famous name." "Call me Ishmael." "I'm 'wife'—I've finished that / That other state." Call me an *Invisible Man*. Call me *A Son of the Middle Border*.

What made me what I am? "Divine am I, inside and out." "If you really want to hear about it, the first thing you'll probably want to know is where I was born, and what my lousy childhood was like." "Mad Ireland hurt you into poetry." "I was born on the prairie and the milk of its wheat, the red of its clover, the eyes of its women, gave me a song and a slogan." "I see now that this has been a story of the West, after all—Tom and Gatsby, Daisy and Jordan and I, were all Westerners."

What might I become? "Think thou on hell, Faustus, for thou art damned." "All right, then, I'll *go* to hell." "Du musst dein Leben ändern." "I left the woods for as good a reason as I went there. Perhaps it seemed to me that I had several more lives to live, and could not spare any more time for that one." "The town of Winesburg had disappeared and his life there had become but a background on which to paint the dreams of his manhood."

Nosce teipsum.

It is true that all human beings share certain possibilities, if not propensities or characteristics—I might have been you, and you me. There may be a little of you in me, and me in you. It is also true, as Kent C. Ryden argues, that literary fiction (he is speaking of Faulkner) "reaches beyond the particular into the universal" (49); it at least attempts to transcend the particular for universal truths, which, like all generalizations, can then be applied again to particulars. But between the universal great truth—if such truth there be—and each individual lie various levels of generalization. What is important is to understand that generalizations offer only likelihoods, to assess the correct degree of probability implied in any generalization (not to overgeneralize), to find the right level of applicability for each generalization.

So we understand ourselves in the context of generalizations about those around us, in whom we identify similarities and differences. Out of the similar we fashion a Self. "In general," write Clayton and Onuf, "human beings construct individual identities through identification with other people with whom they believe they share similar values" (43).

The dissimilar becomes a not-Self, an Other (or Others), against which we define the Self. It is good to encounter the Other, but it is not good to be absorbed into the Other, to become decentered. Programs of Multicultural Studies were intended, by the ethnic minorities who created them and mainstream allies who supported them, to construct a female or black or Native American Self in appropriate terms, terms distinct from those of the dominant Other. In the 1980s and '90s those programs became quite popular inside the academy. Inevitably their content was commodified by and disseminated among non-ethnics, with practical support from General Studies requirements and theoretical support from sundry European philosophers, to the extent that the Other annihilated the Self. Jim Harrison writes satirically of Elizabeth, an undergraduate who "had spent the school year pretending to be Jewish and observing Jewish holidays. The year before, she had become a Native American. Bob said the black students were cringing over the idea that they might be next on her schedule of adoptions" (*Julip* 193). Many academics these days find themselves completely decentered, and on the T-shirts of students one reads slogans like "If you don't stand for something, you'll fall for anything."

Late twentieth-century theories on the formation of Self—and programs using literature to focus the study of identity—emphasized race, ethnicity, gender, and sexual preference as forces more powerful in shaping personality than religion, age, geography, diet, birth order, or—two things almost nobody considers—athletic prowess or physical appearance. Generally speaking, they privilege the Other on the margins over the traditional Self. Universities these days might offer Women's Studies, Black Studies, Gay Studies, Islamic Studies, but probably not Protestant Studies, Old Person's Studies, Homely Person Studies, or, usually, Midwest Studies. But places too can be marginalized, reduced to "flyover country." And any de-emphasis of place strikes me as historically aberrant in what has always been a nation of regions[1] and in a discipline which takes as a given that a good writer "uses the literary substance which he knows best, the life of his own neighborhood, of his own city or state—the material about which he is most likely to be able to write with meaning" (Frederick xv). The postmodernist orientation of literary scholarship in the eighties and nineties probably distorted the thinking of a whole generation of graduate students. The propensity of many postmodernist writers to float upward to placeless abstraction gave us wit without wisdom (pedantry), but it is the tendency of other writers to skip blithely from neighborhood to fashionable neighborhood, home and abroad—some never even visiting the places about which they write—that creates the real poison in the system. Someday a true Montana patriot will inventory the clichés, misrepresentations, and general inanities of *The Horse Whisperer* and its progeny.

A course correction is underway, triggered by general dissatisfaction with the media-generated non-place reflected in titles like Joshua Meyrowitz's 1985 *No Sense of Place* and James Kunstler's 1993 *The Geography of Nowhere*. Michael Kowalewski suggests,

> Contemporary evocations of place in America often seem embattled, unsettled, and besieged: at odds—often overwhelming odds—with attitudes and economic, technological, and social forces that threaten the local distinctiveness of the American landscape, both rural and urban. Overscheduled and overstimulated Americans, the feeling goes, have grown numb to the importance of place in their lives. Members of an "attention deficit disorder" society, . . . Americans are increasingly surrounded by a Velveeta landscape of sprawling, look-alike suburbs, traffic-choked expressways full of drivers on cellphones, and huge, corporate superstores with acres of parking lots. The spiritual as well as physical "macadamization" of contemporary America has eroded the distinctiveness of individual places and pre-emptively discouraged people from caring about them. (12)

Kowalewski goes on to suggest that both individuals and communities come to consciousness "*through*, not apart from, the natural environment they inhabit" (16). He echoes Peirce Lewis, who suggested in 1979, "If we want to understand ourselves, we would do well to take a searching look at our landscapes" (Meinig 2). In 1988 Michael Bradshaw noted in the realm of American Studies a developing emphasis on regional units "bringing together literature, the visual arts and historical accounts in terms of 'regional images'" (3), including a basic understanding of "the ways in which geographical space affects social practice and acts as an essential medium for it" (172). Defining "bioregionalism" in 1999, Dan Flores advanced the argument that the "evolutionary trajectory" of human beings for 99 percent of their time on earth "has been spent as gatherer-hunters living in bands of 125 to 150 that were deeply conversant with small pieces of the world. . . . If our social lives for the bulk of our time as primate species teach anything, it is that staying in place and interacting in small communities is what evolution has prepared us for" (181).

Gradually we have come also to understand "place" as meaning not only geography, biosphere, and climate but also "an emotional complex of associations, both generative and restrictive," including human communities with their unique values and histories (Tammaro and Vinz vii). Larry McMurtry draws the connection between social awareness and landscape in his popular and insightful *Walter Benjamin at the Dairy Queen*: "My social awareness was formed in a place that had been virgin land only a few decades earlier. Emptiness, space, vast skies, long horizons, and few people were my first facts, and for long, the dominant facts" (45, 46). Given such an expanded understanding of place, we might rank place as the number one force in shaping personality. In fall of 2004, Enkhee Dagva, a Mongolian student doing graduate work in Budapest, e-mailed her homesickness, her inability to understand Central Europeans, and her dissatisfaction with grad school theories of personality: "Bioregionalism, or whatever, that talks about landscape affecting character is better than this gender bullshit. I miss the Gobi, the simplicity of life and ordinariness of the people there . . . so much that it actually hurts to think about it on a morning like this, among people such as these."

Place is important to literature for several reasons. For one thing, many American place names have a ring all their own. A litany of place names lends that music—and mystique—to a poem or story: Ashtabula, Kankakee, Chicago, Wapakoneta, Yellow Medicine County, Missouri, Ohio, Mississippi. Place also provides concrete, recognizable markers of geography: names of towns and rivers, species of plants and animals, descriptions of streets and buildings and restaurants, even details of river water that let us know precisely where we are. "When it was daylight, here was the clear Ohio water in shore, sure enough, and outside was the old regular Muddy! So it was all up with Cairo" (Twain 77). In many cases, these markers are significant metaphors, like Robert Bly's "great sweeps of snow that stop suddenly six feet from the house" (*Selected* 148).

Place also provides recognizable markers of language, so that in Twain's words regarding the literary offenses of Fenimore Cooper, the talk shall sound like human talk, and not like the voice from anywhere. Frederick C. Stern claims that no "unifying linguistic materials" have been found for any geographical region of the country, including the South (16), but dialecticians and other scholars (and writers) disagree. In an essay titled "Tradition and Innovation in Twentieth-Century Illinois

Poetry," Dan Guillory writes, "In practical terms, the use of tradition has meant an adherence to two kinds of icons: icons of place and icons of voice" (43). Guillory defines voice as "a set of attitudes and postures ... a subtle appropriation of reality through unique stops and starts, syntactical leaps, and idiosyncratic phrasing" (47). These markers may be dialect, like the several dialects used so carefully by Twain in *Adventures of Huckleberry Finn*. They may be something as simple as vocabulary preferences: "bucket" or "pail"? "Sun up" or "sun rise"? "Soda," "pop," or "Coke"? "Over at" or "over to"? "Dinner" or "supper"? Linguistic markers of place may be idiomatic grammar or usage, like Sherwood Anderson's "I ain't so queer. I guess I showed him I ain't so queer" (201); Louise Erdrich's "I never really done much with my life, I suppose" (230); Larry McMurtry's "Reckon you and her would have got it all straightened out if I hadn't butted in?" (*Last Picture Show* 270). Many writers believe that even the sounds of language reflect geographical place: Kansas-born William Stafford remarked on the "mossy, deadened sound" of the Northwest (Kowalewski 22); Ohio columnist Tim Hardin suggests that the nasality of New Yorkers comes from lack of oxygen in the Manhattan sky-scrapers (*American Tongues*); Paula Nelson quotes a homesteader who reported in a letter to folks back home that people in South Dakota "talked very loudly. She discovered that the constant wind forced conversation into high volume" (xxi). Howard Mohr made an entertaining career from a book called *How to Talk Minnesotan*, a "language system" built primarily on Guillory's icons of geography and icons of voice.

And place provides a characteristic manner of acting and reacting—a behavioral language, if you will—which locates a character in time and space. John Steinbeck went so far as to say, "There is no question in my mind that places in America mark their natives, not only in their speech patterns, but physically—in build, in stance, in conformation. Climate may have something to do with this as well as food supply and techniques of living; in any case, each of us can detect a stranger" (quoted in Stryk, *Heartland* ix). In an essay titled "The Ancient People and the Newly Come," Meridel Le Sueur writes, "The body repeats the landscape. They are the source of each other and create each other" (17). Jane Smiley used the line as an epigraph to her novel *A Thousand Acres*, and Kent Meyers echoed her sentiment: "He formed the place. The place formed him. They were part of each other" (*Witness* 17). Even William Goyen—in many respects a postmodern language poet—has said, "I don't think anyone ever recovers from the place he was born" (Gibbons 325).

We recognize intuitively that Faulkner's characters, as much as they reach toward universals, would not be Faulkner's characters in Yoknapatawpha County, Iowa. And we recognize the behavior of Scandinavian immigrants Nelse and Signa in Willa Cather's *O Pioneers!* (1913) and Garrison Keillor's family from *Lake Wobegon* (1985) as exhibiting characteristically midwestern behavior:

It is supposed that Nelse Jensen, one of the six men at the dinner-table, is courting Signa, though he has been so careful not to commit himself that no one in the house, least of all Signa, can tell just how far the matter has progressed. Nelse watches her glumly as she waits upon the table, and in the evening he sits on a bench behind the stove with his *dragharmonika*, playing mournful airs and watching her as she goes about her work. When Alexandra asked Signa whether she thought Nelse was in earnest, the poor child hid her hands under her apron and murmured, "I don't know, ma'm. But he scolds me about everything, like as if he wanted to have me!" (Cather, *O Pioneers!* 86)

Eight of us sat around the bed that first afternoon, taking turns holding Grandma's hand so that if she had any sensation, it would be one of love. Four more came that evening. We talked in whispers, but didn't talk much; it was hard to know what to say. "Mother always said she wanted to go in her sleep," my mother said. "She didn't want to linger." I felt that we should be saying profound things about Grandma's life and what it had meant to each of us, but I didn't know how to say that we should. My uncles were uneasy. The women saw to Grandma and wept a little now and then, a few friendly tears; the men only sat and crossed and uncrossed their legs, slowly perishing of profound truth, until they began to whisper among themselves—I heard gas mileage mentioned, and a new combine—and then they resumed their normal voices. "I wouldn't drive a Fairlane if you give it to me for nothing," Uncle Frank said. "They are nothing but grief." (Keillor 8)

Ted Kooser connects Midwest place and Midwest character in his poem "An Old Photograph," capturing perfectly the midwestern emotional restraint and the reasons for it:

This old couple, Nils and Lydia
were married for seventy years.
Here they are sixty years old
and already like brother

and sister—small, lustreless eyes,
large ears, the same serious line
to the mouths. After those years
spent together, sharing
the weather of sex, the sour milk
of lost children, barns burning,
grasshoppers, fevers and silence,
they were beginning to share
their hard looks. How far apart
they sit; not touching at shoulder
or knee, hands clasped in their laps
as if under each pair was a key
to a trunk hidden somewhere,
full of those lessons one keeps
to himself. (5)

More significant, however, are the writers' own subtle habits of
thought and attitude: Willa Cather and Sinclair Lewis, Langston Hughes
and Toni Morrison, N. Scott Momaday and Adrian C. Louis, Jim Harrison and Wright Morris seem to bring a certain midwestern frame of reference even to material that is not specifically midwestern.[2] Morris himself said as much: "The characteristics of this region have conditioned
what I see, what I look for, and what I find in the world to write about. So
I believe in shearing off, in working and in traveling light. I like a mini-
mum of words arranged for a maximum effect. . . . As the writer of the
South inclines toward the baroque, and strives for the symbolic ornamental cluster, the writer on the plains is powerfully inclined to shear the
ornament off" (xii).

The Midwest did set, or find itself at the forefront of several cultural
and literary trends early in the twentieth century, and its landscape best
accommodates the quintessential late twentieth-century American landscape symbol, the superhighway. Nevertheless, the Midwest has lost
much of its social, political, and literary clout in the past three decades
. . . including pages in the *Norton Anthology of American Literature*. Certainly the Midwest is no longer the literary capital of the Republic, as
H. L. Mencken thought it was in 1920 when he wrote,

Where, then, is the good writing that goes on in the Republic done? In
New York? Not much of it. New York is the home of literary artisans,

not of literary artists. . . . [C]onsidering its population, the big town produces very little literature of genuine significance. . . . Draw a circle of two hundred miles radius around Chicago, and you will enclose four-fifths of the real literature of America—particularly four-fifths of the literature of tomorrow. (13)

As James Shortridge points out (12–26, 82–96), the Midwest has been historically difficult to locate geographically. Annie Dillard argues that "Pittsburgh is the Midwest's eastern edge" (*American* 214), and while "high plains" would seem to offer a great deal of latitude in defining a western border, it does not: that point at which seed caps yield to Stetsons, work shoes to cowboy boots, and planted crops to cattle range is a narrow, fifty-mile band of America from Canada down to Texas. People who live there pretty much agree that the Midwest—admittedly a region of many subregions—is roughly the region between the Missouri and the Ohio Rivers, an area of fewer "authored landscapes" than either the East or the South, but more populated than the Wild West. Its dominant features of big sky and open fields give a feeling of emptiness. The Midwest is the region of big wind, and Big Windy. And of big waters, predominantly the Great Lakes, the Mississippi, and its tributaries. "I think that the river / Is a strong brown god," wrote T. S. Eliot in "The Dry Salvages," "sullen, untamed and intractable, / Patient to some degree, at first recognized as a frontier" (130).

There is, however, a significant human component to the Midwest, a population dispersed across the amplitudes in settlements of larger or smaller size, and it is these villages which most define the region. "The tendency to ignore the place's urban reality and industrial strength, which has been apparent in the popular literature since the 1920s, had not lessened at all by 1980," notes Shortridge (80). The Midwest still pictures itself as a patchwork of "lost Swede towns," to use a phrase Carol Bly borrowed from F. Scott Fitzgerald (1), a network of agricultural-based villages. "A dissonance of parts and people, we are a consonance of Towns," wrote William Gass in 1958 (186).

To think of the Midwest more as Main Street than as "hog butcher for the world" implies a view that may be nostalgic myth, as Herr and others argue, a will to recover that place in which "so many millions found some real substance to the American Dream" (Meinig 168). Perhaps this view of the Midwest is an opposition to some Eastern, Western, Southern, urban Other. James Shortridge writes, "I will argue here that pastoralism and industry were segregated mentally: the former was as-signed to a regional 'box' called Middle West; the latter, to one called East" (41). Perhaps the Midwest's traditional view of itself as a village is an indictment of the city: John Knoepfle claims that "the cities of Amer-ica are, like taxes, designed for the movement of goods, and not for the comfort of people in their social and festive nature, so that they long for a courtesy in space that they do not find in the street and the boulevard" ("Crossing" 148).[3] Perhaps the Midwest's traditional view of itself as a village is defensive reaction to a national prejudice identified by Dana Gioia: "In most industrialized countries there is also a pervasive urban bias against agricultural areas. In America that prejudice is focused on the Midwest which is seen as flat, characterless, and provincial. . . . To the outsider there is less obvious local color—no accents, no dramatic social problems, less various scenery although ironically it is this same uniformity that gives it an unusually distinctive cultural identity" (92).

Open skies, open fields, straight roads from one lost Swede town to the next, reducing the prairie to a checkerboard. That's my Midwest, and the Midwest of the writers I will discuss in this book.

Typically, Midwest writers begin with space. As Franklin and Steiner suggest, they are not alone among American writers in this regard (3), but opening with landscape is a gambit so common as to be a cliché. Asked how to write the midwestern poem, Dave Etter told James Haz-ard, "Just drop Keokuk, Kalamazoo, Milwaukee, Chicago into the poem. But of course that's superficial. You have to capture the people, the flavor of the area. You have to capture the expanse of it; you know, the highways here go on forever. There are no mountains to block the view, the vision" (31). "There was nothing but land," Jim Burden remembers in Willa Cather's *My Ántonia*; "not a country at all, but the material out of which countries are made" (8). Rolvaag, like Cather in both *My Ántonia* and *O Pioneers!*, opens his own pioneering novel *Giants in the Earth* with the big picture: "Bright, clear sky over a plain so wide that the rim of the heavens cut down on it around the entire horizon. . . . Bright, clear sky, to-day, to-morrow, and for all time to come. . . . And sun! And still more sun!" (3). Wright Morris begins his classic *Ceremony in Lone Tree* with the view from the window, which is nothing but space: "Come to the window. The one at the rear of the Lone Tree Hotel. The view is to the west. There is no obstruction but the sky" (3).

Meridel Le Sueur opens with space, before moving to character: "Most of all one was born into space, into the great resonance of space, a magnetic midwestern valley through which the winds clashed in lassos of thunder and lightning at the apex of the sky, the very wrath of God" ("Ancient People" 17). Even literary critics begin with the lay of the land:

> The essential picture of rural Illinois today is from the air. A mile above McLean County, descending to Bloomington, the land is a farmscape of rectangular geometry: square-mile sections of land enclosing soft modulations of hills, veined tracings of streams, and, early in April, dark brown fields furrowed to hypnotic effect. Receding parallels lead the eye toward a vanishing point on the distant horizon. Everything in the scene suggests a latitude, a limitless prospect of prosperity, and pastoral loveliness. So the picture has been for a very long time. (Bray, *Rediscoveries* 14)

Amplitude presents both threat and opportunity. As Roderick Frazier Nash shows in *Wilderness and the American Mind*, most settlers in the pioneering era came to the landscape intent on transforming it, and the great expanses of empty space were an opponent against which humans struggled for identity and their sanity. Even tourists, who came for rest and relaxation, felt the gloom. In his 1835 *A Tour on the Prairies*, Washington Irving noted, "There is something inexpressibly lonely in the solitude of a prairie. . . . We have the consciousness of being far, far beyond the bounds of human habitation; we feel as if moving in the midst of a desert world" (175). Baron E. de Mandat-Grancy, visiting western Minnesota in the 1880s, found the landscape "gloomy in the extreme" (8). Washington Irving and the French count were tourists; they could leave. Per Hansa's wife was a settler and could not leave. She went crazy. "It is hard for the eye to wander from sky line to sky line, year in and year out, without finding a resting place!" Rolvaag notes (413); "asylum after asylum was filled with disordered beings who had once been human." "It is like an iron country," writes Cather of the Divide in winter, "and the spirit is oppressed by its rigor and melancholy" (*O Pioneers!* 187). "In the Midwest, around the Lower Lakes, the sky in the winter is heavy and close, and it is a rare day, a day to remark on, when the sky lifts and allows the heart up," writes William Gass in mid-twentieth century (173).

On the other hand, as Nash also shows, Americans have always found something restorative in the amplitudes: a new Eden, a grace in the wild, space for personal growth and freedom. N. Scott Momaday writes, "There is something about the heart of the continent that resides always in the end of vision, some essence of the sun and wind. That man knew the possible quest. There was nothing to prevent his going out; he could enter upon the land and be alive, could bear at once the great hot weight of its silence. In a sense the question of survival had never been more imminent, for no land is more the measure of human strength" (101). Open space may offer restoration, protection, a release from the dark anxieties and complexities of "civilization." This is the function of the Mississippi in *Adventures of Huckleberry Finn*, of the prairie in Paul Gruchow's *The Necessity of Empty Places*, and of open water in Hemingway's "The Big Two-Hearted River": "Nick did not want to go in there now. . . . In the swamp the banks were bare, the big cedars came together overhead, the sun did not come through, except in patches; in the fast deep water, in the half light, the fishing would be tragic. In the swamp fishing was a tragic adventure. Nick did not want it" (180).

Attention to landscape inevitably emphasizes weather because, as Diane Dufva Quantic points out, "In a region where there are no natural barriers the great expanses exacerbate the weather's natural violence, and the land's products continue to influence the quality of life, no matter how far removed one imagines oneself to be from the land" (xii). Drake Hokanson writes in his 1994 *Reflecting a Prairie Town*, "No one who has been around Paterson [Iowa], or anywhere else in the Midwest, very long, would deny that this climate is formed by great and dramatic weather" (35). Patricia Hampl, after suggesting that "landscape plays a key role in the formation of the imagination. . . . it is the primer coat under all we can paint for ourselves and others" (125), recalls that her landscape as a young girl in St. Paul, Minnesota, "was all weather and not much else" (126). Watching his marriage fall apart, Terry Reese in a Dave Etter poem subtitled "Boom Boom on B Street," takes a shotgun to his old Oldsmobile:

> It was the two feet of snow that did us in.
> Man, what a blizzard that baby was
> Lois, eyes hard as icicles, kept saying
> she was finished with me, kaput,
> was going home to Mother, getting out for good.
> "Bitch, bitch, bitch, bitch, bitch," I said,
> as I had been saying for weeks and weeks,
> knowing we were cracking up this winter,
> what with all the snow, the goddamn snow. (*Alliance* 1983, 109)

Susan Allen Toth titles her 2003 memoir of Midwest weather *Leaning into the Wind*, and in his 1891 *Main-Travelled Roads*, Hamlin Garland writes of wind: "But the third [wind upon Chicago] is the West of Southwest wind, dry, magnetic, full of smell of unmeasured miles of growing grain in summer, or ripening corn and wheat in autumn. When it comes in winter the air glitters with incredible brilliancy" (207). The wealth of wind and weather in the songs of Bob "Blowin' in the Wind" Dylan is one reflection of his Minnesota origins (Pichaske, "Some Notes" 59).

Whatever the weather, those who stick with big sky—or big water—seem historically to develop a certain vision. In a passage of *The Music of Failure* quoted by Toth, Bill Holm writes,

> There are two eyes in the human head—the eye of mystery, and the eye of harsh truth—the hidden and the open—the woods eye and the prairie eye. The prairie eye looks for distance, clarity, and light; the woods eye for closeness, complexity, and darkness. The prairie eye looks for usefulness and plainness in art and architecture; the woods eye for the baroque and ornamental. Dark old brownstones on Summit Avenue were created by a woods eye; the square white farmhouse and red barn are prairie eye's work. Sherwood Anderson wrote his stories with a prairie eye, plain and awkward, told in the voice of a man almost embarrassed to be telling them, but bullheadedly persistent to get at the meaning of the events; Faulkner, whose endless complications of motive and language take the reader miles behind the simple facts of an event, sees the world with a woods eye. One eye is not superior to the other, but they are different. To some degree, like male and female, darkness and light, they exist in all human heads, but one or the other seems dominant. (17)[4]

Kent Meyers corroborates Holm's testimony: "Students of Native American art have noted that when Indian tribes—the Lakota/Dakota for instance—moved out of a woodland habitat onto the plains, their artwork changed. Woodland art tends to be composed of curving lines and animal figures, whereas plains art consists of straight lines and geometric figures. Surely this is the influence of the land on the imagination, the straight line of the prairie exerting itself" (*Witness* 88). The prairie attracted settlers with a prairie eye, and further trained their children, and their children's children, in a prairie sensibility: distance, clarity, and light.

With all its space, the Midwest is probably America as something commensurate with man's capacity for wonder. Momaday picks up this theme in the line which follows the passage quoted earlier: "neither had wonder been more accessible to the mind nor destiny to the will."

Yet the Midwest's combination of amplitude and population brings landscape directly to bear on social and cultural institutions. Its fertile soil, and easily traversed landscape were ideally suited to homesteading: 160 acres—one-quarter of a square mile of land—free to any native or immigrant willing to invest five years living upon and "improving" (i.e., cultivating) the claim. Homesteading gave the Midwest that grid of mile roads—so recognizable from the air—four farm sites to the square mile, house and barn surrounded by a square grove and rectilinear fields. The railroad companies which (subsidized by generous government grants) brought the settlers gave us the familiar pattern of a village every seven miles—three or four miles being a reasonable day's ride for a farmer in a horse-drawn buckboard—villages far in excess of what the landscape really needed, chartered more as points to collect grain and sell lumber than as social or cultural centers. While most of these villages are smaller today than they were fifty or one hundred years ago,[5] the Midwest remains "a consonance of Towns" (Gass 186).

The harmonic combination of space and population produced what Wallace Stegner calls "an American faith: that a new society striking boldly off from the old would first give up everything but axe and gun and then, as the pioneering hardships were survived, would begin to shape itself in new forms. Prosperity would follow in due course. A native character would begin to emerge, a character more self-reliant and more naturally noble than any that could be formed in tired and corrupt Europe, and new institutions would spring from the new social compact among free and classless men. After an appropriate interval this society ought to find its voice in unmistakably native arts" (288). In an essay "Midwestern Poetry: Goodbye to All That," Lisel Mueller also draws a line from landscape through society to aesthetics:

What I am left with by way of definition is a body of poetry that owes its life to the heart of the heartland: the vast stretches of farmland, the rolling hills with their many shades of green, the great rivers and thousands of small lakes, the forests of Michigan, Minnesota, and Wisconsin, the towns with their rectangular layouts, their elm-shaded porches, their Elks' Clubs, and their dreary Main Streets.

Ultimately, it owes its life to a population of nineteenth century settlers, predominantly Protestant, predominantly British, German, and Scandinavian, whose society was founded on such principles as egalitarianism, individualism, and self-sufficiency. The farmers, craftsmen, and merchants who settled the land carried out an experiment in grass-roots democracy that would have caused considerable misgivings among our skeptical and aristocratic Founding Fathers. Without any authority other than their practical reason and a belief in individual human dignity, they set up self-governing communities which functioned well in the decades before industrialism changed the premises on which the society was based. There was no colonial charter, no theocracy to govern public and private conduct; there was no elite of rank and culture nor, in the beginning, of money. Hardship and isolation were accepted as the price for stability and, in many cases, eventual prosperity. For these people, experience was the touchstone of knowledge. As a result, the society was characterized by considerable anti-intellectualism and a distrust of "impractical," abstract thinking. (It is unimaginable that, for example, transcendentalism or the art-for-art's sake movement could have arisen in the Midwest.) This was the region of log-cabin presidents. There was— and still is—pride in poverty turned success, obscurity turned accomplishment. (2, 3)

Mueller argues that free verse in the Midwest was "not a European import," because the region's "bias toward naturalness and against formalism was entirely consistent with the egalitarian heritage" (7). The midwestern mentality described by Mueller transcends urban/rural and racial distinctions. Cyrus Colter—Afro-American, urban, late twentieth century—confirms the fact that midwestern thought is practical rather than theoretical: "Chicago is robust," he writes. "It's less academic, precious, and mandarin—less Byzantine [than New York]. That's how I see it, but also how (more important) I feel it, as a writer" (Gibbons 331).

As David Marion Holman notes, the characteristic midwestern literary mode has always been realism (49).[6] The Midwest was, as it were, the mother lode of realism in America. "Realism in America would have been nothing without Chicago; Chicago was nothing without realism," observes Alfred Kazin in A Writer's America (183); the city "would never be altogether right for an avant-garde" (184). This was true even before Chicago was Chicago. In 1834 Dr. Daniel Drake told the Union Literary

Society of Miami University that the future literature of the West would be "rough rather than elegant," and "pragmatic" (Flanagan 208). In the years between 1834 and Garland's *Crumbling Idols* (1895), "perhaps the most important quality shared by the western writers . . . was their slow but perceptible trend toward realism. . . . From the very beginning, the more serious middle western writers were conscious of the need for verisimilitude" (Flanagan 210–11). In *A Son of the Middle Border*, Garland formulated the principle in seven words: "truth [is] a higher quality than beauty" (374); he was simply repeating Joseph Kirkland: "Let only the truth be told" (Bray, *Rediscoveries* 6). Writers of the Chicago Renaissance—Masters, Sandburg, Dreiser, Dell, Anderson, even Vachel Lindsay—are remarkable not for complex theories borrowed from the Continent, but for their insights into human nature and social and economic conditions. They are not philosophers, but observers. The same could be said of Garrison Keillor. A century after Garland, midwesterners are still mostly mud-on-the-shoes realists, prone to draw a dichotomy between style and content and to favor content over style. They are practical people. A Polish graduate student entangled in theory at an urban university remarked to me a few years ago, "People where you live always have their hands on something real—an ear of corn, a chainsaw, a cow's teat. Many people in this city have never in their lives had their hands on anything more substantial than the stems of their cocktail glasses." In a talk at Southwest Minnesota State given on September 12, 2000, visiting fellow Paul Nielson (raised on a farm, PhD from the University of Chicago) observed, "aesthetics versus practicality has always been an issue on the farm, where the ugliest buildings are often among the most useful. Sentimentalists want family farms to be lovely in a Terry Redlin way, with no mess and no fences to keep the cows in. We had visitors to our farm from the cities who asked why we didn't mow the hay fields more, to keep the grass down."

The reformist component of Midwest literature bears special comment. Holman sees the two as related: "Realism—the 'democratic' mode—is appropriate for the region the midwest writer depicts because the history of the Midwest and its inhabitants is inextricably entangled with populist idealism. . . . Implicit in the idea of the Midwest is the belief that it is a region that holds the promise of Jacksonian democracy" (51). While the Heartland has a reputation these days for social and political conservatism, leftist or progressive politics have until recently been a tradition in the region: the Knights of Labor, the Farmers' Alliance, the Granger Movement, the People's Party, the Nonpartisan League, the International Workers of the World, Milo Reno's Farm Holiday Movement, Minnesota's Farmer-Labor Party, Michigan's Students for a Democratic Society, the National Farm Organization, even Iowa Governor Terry Branstad's activation of the state foreclosure moratorium law during the farm crises of the 1980s. Writers especially have been social activists. After publishing *Main-Travelled Roads* Hamlin Garland, whose political populism and literary "veritism" were inextricably linked, barnstormed the Midwest, reading stories and speaking at gatherings of the Grange and the People's Party. Sinclair Lewis incorporated into *Main Street* the observations of Miles Bjornstam, "the Red Swede," and an overheard conversation among local farmers:

> There you got it—good market, and these towns keeping us from it. Gus, that's the way these towns work all the time. They pay what they want to for our wheat, but we pay what they want us to for their clothes. Stowbody and Dawson foreclose every mortgage they can, and put in tenant farmers. The *Dauntless* lies to us about the Nonpartisan League, the lawyers sting us, the machinery-dealers hate to carry us over bad years, and then their daughters put on swell dresses and look at us as if we were a bunch of hoboes. Man, I'd like to burn this town! (223)

In *O Pioneers!* Lou Bergson suggests that if Carl Lindstrum and his buddies had any nerve, they'd "get together and march down to Wall Street and blow it up. Dynamite it, I mean" (112). Robert Bray argues that author William Allen White, "while much better known as a stalwart of the Republican party, devoutly wished to be remembered as a progressive in his fiction" (*Rediscoveries* 4). The socialist perspective permeates the work of Carl Sandburg, who rode the "Red Special" in 1908 with Eugene V. Debs and in 1910 became personal secretary to Emil Seidel, Socialist mayor of Milwaukee, Wisconsin. It colors the poems of Edgar Lee Masters and Vachel Lindsay ("Why I Voted the Socialist Ticket," "Bryan, Bryan, Bryan, Bryan"), and the work of Meridel Le Sueur (whose father was the Socialist mayor of Minot, North Dakota), Tillie Olsen, and Sioux City's Josephine Herbst who, John Knoepfle recalls, described the Communist Party scene in New York "as a tempest in a pisspot . . . that meant nothing to farmers and laborers in the Midwest" ("Crossing" 137). Section 3, part 4 of Thomas McGrath's *Letter to an Imaginary Friend, Part I* is a hymn to the memory of a local wobblie:

> As tough as whang-leather, with a brick-topped mulish face,
> A quiet talker. He read *The Industrial Worker,*
> Though I didn't know what the paper was at the time.
> The last of the real Wobs—that, too, I didn't know,
> Couldn't. (17)

Robert Bly's antiwar activism grew out of this tradition, and echoes can be heard in the writing of other midwestern poets, including Dave Etter, John Knoepfle, and Bill Holm:

> It's not that I'm unhappy being a Democrat, it's that I would be a whole lot happier being a Populist—a real bumping, jumping, thumping Populist. (Etter, *Selected* 149)

> some damn odin
> eats us up dont you think
> one by one by one
> he holds us upside down
> by our ankles and what
> can we do with him
> nothing I can tell you (Knoepfle, *poems* 83)

> My dad told me how
> the sheriff would ride out to the farm
> to auction off the farmer's goods for the bank.
> Neighbors came with pitchforks
> to gather in the yard:
> "What am I bid for this cow?"
> Three cents. Four cents. No more bids.
> If a stranger came in and bid a nickel,
> a circle of pitchforks gathered around him,
> and the bidding stopped. (Holm, *Dead* 28)

In the Midwest, Mueller argues, social justice and humanism were social traditions before they were literary traditions ("Midwestern Poetry" 7). Garland, whom even Herr credits as "voicing the moment when the Heartland was being constructed in its current formulation" (94), wrote succinctly, "The merely beautiful in art seemed petty, and success at the cost of the happiness of others a monstrous egotism" (*Son* 374). This quest for social justice is found even in writers who write far from the villages and towns—say, Richard Wright, Studs Terkel, Kurt Vonnegut, Kenneth Patchen, and James T. Farrell. James Seaton writes that though neither Charles J. Sykes's *Profscam* or Allan Bloom's *The Closing of the American Mind* appeals to regional prejudices, "the Midwestern origin of their authors betrays itself in their muckraking" (204).

There are corollaries. Midwesterners are traditionally skeptical of theory, look to experience as the touchstone of knowledge, react with simple pragmatism. "How the devil do I know / if there are rocks in your field," writes Iowan James Hearst in a poem called "Truth"; "plow it and find out . . . the connection with a thing / is the only truth that I know of, / so plow it" (Stryk 79). In *High Water*, Richard Bissell humorously constructs the "theory" of an accident on the Illinois River:

> "Why did that barge dive, Kid? Why did that goddam old number 36 decide to sink on us?"
>
> "Well, I'll tell you," says the Kid, taking out a stick of Beeman's Pepsin Gum, "I've got a theory about that."
>
> "I'll bet it's a killer," I said. "So go ahead, pride of Alton, Illinois, and tell us the theory. . . ."
>
> "Well to make a long story short my theory is like this: I figure the river was to blame. I think some water got in that barge somehow and she sunk." (132)

In Tim O'Brien's novel *Northern Lights*, one of the older locals chides a youngster for forgetting common sense when lost in the woods:

> "Don't know how you coulda got lost in the first place," the man was saying. "But I sure would've built me a big fire, first thing."
>
> "We did that."
>
> "A *big* fire. . . ."
>
> The man shook his head. "Stupid," he finally said.
>
> Perry nodded again. "Pretty dumb."
>
> "Stupid, that's what." (288, 289)

The midwestern style is plainspeak. John T. Flanagan notes in Midwest writers "a definite lack of artistry, of polish. . . . The English write better, but the Americans have something to say" (232). The midwestern narrator is rarely flamboyant or self-celebrating. Usually he is reticent, unpolished, apologetic, ambivalent, confused, unpretentious. "You don't know about me, without you have read a book by the name of 'The Adventures of Tom Sawyer,' but that ain't no matter," says Huck Finn. Narrator, author, and central characters are often dubious, lost, confused. "I have missed something," Sherwood Anderson's George Willard thinks to himself; "I have missed something Kate Swift was trying to tell me" (166). John Knoepfle notes, "Carol Kennicott's own difficulty in defining herself and the difficulty Lewis had in deciding whether she was to be a heroine or another object of satire are as much a part of the image of Gopher Prairie as the goings on at the Thanatopsis Club and the Jolly Seventeen" ("Crossing" 109). The midwestern narrator is nothing unusual: "I am in other respects / like everyone here," announces Knoepfle's own "Princess Candidate, Sangamon County Fair" (*poems* 95). Sings Bob Dylan,

> I'm just average, common too
> I'm just like him, the same as you
> I'm everybody's brother and son
> I ain't different from anyone
> It ain't no use a-talkin' to me
> It's just the same as talking to you. (128)

Midwest humor—it exists—is wry, understated, offhand, the humor of Mark Twain, James Thurber, Garrison Keillor, and Langston Hughes's Jessie B. Simple stories. Also, midwestern writers contain their stylistic and structural experiments within a relatively narrow range. Imagism, surrealism, mysticism, and *Field of Dreams* magical realism—all of which can indeed be found in midwestern literature—are usually so alloyed with realism as to slip by almost unnoticed. Even a Robert Bly deep-image poem begins with "Those great sweeps of snow that stop suddenly six feet from the house" (*Selected* 148) or ends, having "given up all ambition," with the flake of snow that has just fallen on the horse's mane (*Selected* 34).

So the midwestern style: realism bordering on naturalism, with elements of humanism and social critique. Plain, colloquial speech, with elements of self-conscious doubt. Guarded experimentation. Limited theory.

Of course it is a commonplace these days that Americans know little of their country's geography, that they are innocent of America as a landscape of rivers, mountains, towns, and thus places. And place is missing from a great deal of writing done in the Midwest these days, especially the work of academic writers or folks associated with literary centers like The Loft in Minneapolis, and the Fiction Collective in Normal, Illinois. Don DeLillo's much-celebrated novel *White Noise* is set in some midwestern town so lacking in recognizable markers of place that it's hard to identify a state, let alone a town. Charles Baxter's Five Oaks, Michigan—which has the sound of a developer's pipedream—totally lacks recognizable character. The town's vanilla flavor may be intentional. Jill Gidmark observes that "Baxter's use of the Midwest signifies neither conventional nostalgia nor rootedness. . . . The reader is never certain just where the center lies" (Greasley 55). But in a story like "The Next Building I Plan to Bomb," Baxter offers not a single identifying feature, nothing to particularize it, no building, street, or habit of speech that would distinguish Five Oaks from any vanilla-flavored suburb anywhere in the United States. Five Oaks is the Midwest town as non-place. So too is Prairie Junction, the setting for Jane Hamilton's much-ballyhooed *A Map of the World*. No feature of landscape or voice lets readers know they're in Wisconsin, not Missouri, New Hampshire, or, for that matter, western Poland. Hamilton's characters speak and act like the urban transplants they are, dine on Chicken Almond Ding, buy a dairy herd of Golden Guernseys because Howard is "a philosophical and poetical farmer" who "liked their color and the way 'Golden Guernsey' floated off his tongue" (3, 4).

Editors Kevin Stein and G. E. Murray proudly claim that *Illinois Voices: An Anthology of Twentieth-Century Poetry*—a collection depressingly different from Lucien Stryk's two famous *Heartland* anthologies—"offers a gloss for that of the nation at large" (xxiii), a panorama of "didacticism, modernism, Imagism, surrealism, Objectivism, Deep Imagism, Confessionalism, feminism, Afro-American, Latino/Latina, and Asian American voices, gay and lesbian poetry, New Narrativism, New Formalism, LANGUAGE and 'performance' poetry" (xxii). The anthology is no more Illinois than the New York Yankees. Poet Julie Herrick White, whose work is included in Elton Glaser and William Greenway's (more impressive) anthology *I Have My Own Song for It: Modern Poems of Ohio*, lived in the state barely a year. "I never really got to know Steubenville," she admits ingenuously; "Thirteen months were not enough" (93). "The development of writing workshops in the universities has been a disaster," Robert Bly wrote way back in 1975; "The poetry out of the workshops is worse and worse every year. . . . There are exceptions, but most of it is daydream-head poetry" ("Writer's Sense" 75).

But writers like these have always been among us, and they have never lasted very long. In *Lake Wobegon Days*, Garrison Keillor remembers a humanities class at the University of Minnesota, taught by an instructor "who sounded to be from someplace east of the East," and a composition instructor who, while urging students to write from personal experience, "said it with a smirk, suggesting that we didn't have much, so instead I wrote the sort of dreary, clever essay I imagined I'd appreciate if I were him" (22). Keillor gives up the clever essays (and the university), returns to Lake Wobegon, and writes a book that people read. The writing from the Midwest, which has survived, and will survive, is harmonious with midwestern society, which is itself a result of an almost Darwinian process of natural selection as the environment tests and sorts newcomers, and as newcomers adjust to their environment.[7]

The weight of historical evidence suggests that the Midwest supports some cultural values while being subtly unsuited to others because, while landscape and society engage in reciprocal interaction, geography is more powerful and ultimately proves inexorable. In public lectures, essayist Paul Gruchow was fond of warning that social systems which have not been in harmony with the natural system, which have demanded more of it than it could deliver without undue stress, or that have taken from it more than they returned, have not, historically, survived for any great length of time. We might press Gruchow's thought further: philosophical systems that are not in harmony with the social, economic, and natural landscapes will not survive for any great length of time in that geography. Historian Paula M. Nelson titled her 1996 study of West River country in South Dakota *The Prairie Winnows Out Its Own*. Frederick C. Stern, after arguing for ten pages against the Midwest as an identifiable literary region, does a 180-degree about-face beginning with the section heading "And Yet . . . and Yet and Still . . ." (20). Landscape, he decides, "*does* have an influence on the way the mind and feelings work" (22, italics his).

Dave Etter, William Kloefkorn, Norbert Blei, Linda Hasselstrom, Bill Holm, Jim Heynen, and Jim Harrison are perfectly conscious of the media, academia, and the national (and international) literary scenes— although their native pragmatism may make them skeptical and therefore light in the theory department. Harrison especially offers a paradigm of the midwestern writer lured by the bright lights of New York,

Hollywood, and Paris, who had to find his way home mentally and stylistically. The others traveled as well, in geography and style, and as I will suggest, the writing of each contains profound dislocations and ambivalences. All seven, however, write within the tradition I have been describing: they grow out of and extend that tradition, modifying it when pressured by necessity or opportunity. Each has, like the author of this book, one leg in his or her place and the other leg somewhere else. You need to know the world, Cather once observed, to see the parish. The rootedness of each of these authors in a particular place, and the ways they alternately break and preserve those roots, is the subject of the chapters which follow.

Dave Etter

Call It Cornbelt Baroque

I too am drifting and sinking
in the slow autumn weather
of Kane County Illinois

But I know now I know now
it is first love of this place
I want to hang on to
—*Dave Etter,* Go Read the River

"Dave Etter is the poet who speaks for the Midwest these days," wrote A. G. Sobin, in 1970; "Roethke, Sandburg, Wright and now Etter write of a place that exists outside the awareness of most of us. . . . They cut us a window" (27). In the following decades, Etter emerged as one of the Midwest's premier poets. He won both Midland Authors and Carl Sandburg awards; his poems appeared in a hundred anthologies and eight foreign countries, including translation into German, Japanese, and Polish; and *Alliance, Illinois* was endorsed by Raymond Carver as "hands down the most impressive long work of poetry I've read in years."[1] Like Robert Frost, another native Californian who successfully rerooted himself in a foreign soil, Dave Etter has been valued more for his witness to a geography and an idiom than for the art of his poetry. Etter's work is a photograph of village life in the Midwest circa 1970.

It is the particulars of Etter's rural Illinois landscape—details of setting and language—which first catch a reader's attention, directed, as it were, by Etter's titles: *The Last Train to Prophetstown, Boondocks, West of Chicago, Midlanders,* and *Home State.* He underscores the titles with epigraphs that emphasize not only his midwestern material but also the primacy of matter over manner: "In the end a man can expect to understand no land but his own" (Vachel Lindsay for *Alliance, Illinois*); "I was born on the prairie and the milk of its wheat, the red of its clover, the eyes of its women, gave me a song and a slogan" (Carl Sandburg for *West of Chicago*); "A windmill, a junk heap, and a Rotarian in their American setting have more meaning to me than Notre Dame, the Parthenon, or the heroes of the ages. I understand them. I get them emotionally" (Thomas Hart Benton for *Sunflower County*). The epigraphs he underscores with pronouncements, sometimes tongue-in-cheek, such as "Of course I'm a regional writer. How arrogant it would be to think of myself as either national or international" ("Notes on Regionalism," *Home State* 58). The pronouncements he underscores with epigraphs, such as that in "Emmylou Oberkfell: Fifth Grade Poem on America": "America / is / a big / Christmas / pie: / the Middle West / is berries, / the rest / is / just / crust" (*Alliance* 202).

Early reviews focused on Etter's matter more than his style and encouraged the poet's proclivities toward Midwest realism. "In *Go Read the River*," wrote Etta Blum, "Dave Etter celebrates the *place* which, for him, is the American Middle West. . . . Usually the poem is built up through detail on detail in almost staccato fashion, giving the overall impression of a photograph" (342). "[Etter] is a chronicler of Midwest prairie towns and the disappearing race of semi-rural people, with their inarticulate dreams and dark secrets," wrote Lisel Mueller in reviewing *Last Train to Prophetstown* for *Poetry* magazine (326). In 1971 Mueller identified Dave Etter—along with Robert Bly, Tom McGrath, William Stafford, John Knoepfle, James Wright, and James Tate—as representative of and heir to the tradition of midwestern poetry, "poetry that owes its life to the heart of the heartland" (4). Across the Atlantic, Walter Hübling traced the tradition of small-town midwestern literature from Zona Gale to Dave Etter in "From Main Street to Lake Wobegon and Half-Way Back: The Ambiguous Myth of the Small Town in Recent American Literature."

Etter's most acclaimed work, *Alliance, Illinois*, is usually appreciated in terms of character (voice) and geography (place). It is a collection of mostly dramatic monologues somewhere between Masters and Anderson: "I had the idea of this town thing so strongly from *Winesburg*, and *Spoon River Anthology* and *Raintree County*," Etter recalled in 1987 (Follstad). "I thought of maybe one book of 64 pages." The project grew almost exponentially over a quarter of a century from the brief character sketches first published in *Voyages to the Inland Sea* (1971) to a 75-page fictional village *Alliance, Illinois* (Kylix, 1978), enlarged via shorter collections like *Cornfields* (1980) and *West of Chicago* (1981) to a 222-poem *Alliance, Illinois* (Spoon River, 1983; Northwestern University Press, 2004), then further enlarged via *Midlanders* (1988) and *Electric Avenue* (1988) to the 400-page *Sunflower County* (1994). Those 400 pages detail at once a unique fictional creation and an archetypical midwestern village comparable to Anderson's Winesburg, Lewis's Gopher Prairie, and Garrison Keillor's Lake Wobegon.

"Alliance comes complete with a verbal map," notes James T. Jones (93). Geographical coordinates are set by north-central Illinois locators mentioned in the poems themselves, including Prophetstown, Sycamore, Rochelle, DeKalb County, I-55, and the Kishwaukee, Illinois, and Fox Rivers.[2] Just across the Chicago and North Western tracks a sign announces, "ALLIANCE, pop. 6428." In the collection's opening poem, George Maxwell rumbles into town in an eighteen-wheeler, past another sign that reads "Alliance Chamber of Commerce Welcomes You to the Hybrid Corn Capital of America," past the "bruised bodies of billboards" advertising Lichenwalner's Department Store, Carl's Mainline Cafe, Hotel Tall Corn and Bob's Texaco Station. He thanks the driver for the lift, and turns to confront the fact that "nothing has, nothing could have / really changed since I went away" (2).

Alliance supports at least four churches—Episcopal, Baptist, Congregational, and Catholic—and five bars: Farley's Tap, Jake's Tap, Arne's Pub, Gene's Bar and Grill, and the Dew Drop Inn. An Amoco and Mobil station, the Sunset Bowling Lanes, the Paradise Theater, the Holiday Funeral Home, the White Star Pharmacy, an American Legion Hall, the Masonic Temple, Franklin School, a public swimming pool, Gust Reinhart Realty, the office of the *Alliance Gazette*, the Spot-Lite Diner, and the Elite Cafe. Like banks across the Midwest, the Alliance Farmers National Bank is spelled without an apostrophe. In the tradition of midwestern villages east of Minnesota and Iowa, the heart of Alliance is a courthouse square with a band shell, a canon, and a statue of a Union soldier. The old red train depot is no longer in use; the opera house is razed on page 352 of *Sunflower County*. Alliance contains a Lincoln Street, as well as Grant, Pershing, Garfield, Illinois, Liberty, Union, Prairie, River, Park, Old Mill, and of course Main Streets. And the ubiquitous tree streets, including Elm and Mulberry. Also, in that failure of imagination which seems to have characterized all midwestern village planners, running north-south throughout the town, First, Second, Third, Fourth, Fifth, Sixth, on up to Tenth Streets. In "Stubby Payne: Stocking Tops," Etter presents a familiar photograph of two-story "business district" buildings: shops below; lawyers' and doctors' offices and an occasional rented room above. Dentist Nathan Ackerman rents office space above Western Union in the

McFee Block. In a room above the shoe store lives Bee, the town's over-worked "bumbling barfly" (*Alliance* 29).

Toward the edge of town, by the railroad tracks and the grain eleva-tor, are a pool hall and a roller rink. Outside of town there are Blackberry Hill Cemetery, the cannery, and Willow Creek Road, Blue Hollow Road, County Road K, and Potawatomi Road, along with Jake Cotton's old barn with "Chew Mail Pouch Tobacco" peeling off its weathered sides, and, before it was torched by a drunken arsonist, Kentfield's new red barn with "Jesus Saves" painted on its side.

The Alliance High School basketball team is nicknamed "the Corn-huskers," and the school colors are orange and black.

The features of this village will be familiar to anyone who ever spent time in the Upper Midwest; to echo Sinclair Lewis, the town would look the same in Ohio or Montana, in Kansas or Kentucky or Illinois. Like most midwestern villages, Alliance of the 1980s is locked inside the 1970s, if not the 1960s. The town's food franchises are the older chains such as A & W Root Beer and Dairy Queen. There is no McDonald's, Godfather's, Pizza Hut, or Subway; there is a Walgreen's, a Rexall Drugs, and a Western Auto store, but no Wal-Mart, True Value, SuperAmerica, or Kinko's. Many businesses still bear the names of their owners: Greer's Feed and Grain, Guthrie's Feed and Grain, Feldkamp's Lumberyard, Bert and Larry's Liquor, Peacock's Hardware Store, Ludwig's Jewelry Store, and Moo Chow's Chinese Restaurant, now reduced by the loss of its blue neon "h" to Moo Cow's. This characteristic of Alliance, too, will sound familiar to residents of the Midwest's smaller villages.

In other ways Alliance reflects an older tradition. Etter's language, a high-spirited romp through the midwestern idiom, likewise dates to the fifties and even the forties: "bamboozled," "vamoose," "rube," "keen," "hooch," "snazzy." [3] The idioms sound old: "sweet on," "over to," "where you was at," "got mad on me," "used to had me a dog like him," "some such like that." Cultural references like Dick Tracy, Woody Herman, and Groucho Marx seem dated. [4] The trademarks that litter Etter's poems have an antique air: Lionel trains, Nehi grape, Studebaker cars, Zenith and Philco radios. [5] "Etter's work is like an antique shop in which one can see the advertisements of another era," Victor Contoski writes (54).

This time disjuncture, a reflection as much of Etter's subject as his style, seems to disconcert urban- and suburbanites, who take it for the nostalgic clichés which seem, almost by definition, to taint local color writing. But Etter does not traffic unconsciously in clichés, and some

Alliance poems actually parody the cliché-ridden speech of semi-conscious midwesterners, as in the talk outside the Western Auto store recorded by "Woody O'Neill": "Feel 'em, fuck 'em, forget 'em, is what I say"; "Now you take your average Arab girl . . ." (*Alliance* 139). "The Talk at Laclede's Landing" (*Live* 60) is basically a collation of forty clichés and St. Louis idioms, as is the fatherly advice offered by Leonard Massingail:

> You don't know beans about girls
> and you are going about half-cocked.
> It will always be a wild-goose chase
> until, by hook or crook,
> you break the ice with her. . . .
> Look, either fish or cut bait,
> or you will always eat crow.
> Damnit, take the bull by the horns! (*Alliance* 222)

Invariably Etter proves dead-on accurate in details of place and language. "If anyone writing poetry in America today has a more sensitive eye or ear than does the man from Elburn, Illinois," writes William Kloefkorn, "I don't know who that poet is" ("Man from Elburn" 69).

Visitors to Etter's western Illinois towns confirm both the language and some of the time gone backward. In closing an essay titled "Lost in Elburn," Norbert Blei describes a scene right out of *Alliance*:

> The tavern we turn into [sic] doesn't even have a sign or a light in the window; it is *that* dead in Elburn on a Saturday night. Even Etter thinks the joint is closed. We sit at a dark bar with three customers (one of them the bartender), nursing a final drink, staring at dusty pennants on the wall, watching TV.
>
> I steal a glance at Etter, lost in the lascivious antics of Benny Hill on the tube, and suddenly feel old. Etter looks old. The bar is past its prime. Elburn is on the road to nowhere, the Midwest is history, and we've even bequeathed our imaginations to places lost in time. (*Door to Door* 55–56)

If Alliance has an antique air, perhaps that is because in Alliance, as in most rural villages, the old outnumber the young, and many adult inhabitants of Alliance are locked in a distant or recent past, backing into the future, if they are moving forward at all. Abraham Lincoln casts a long shadow over Alliance, as do other Illinois historical figures, usually liberals like Altgeld and Stevenson, and the three great poets of the

Chicago Renaissance: Masters, Lindsay, and Sandburg. The young have sex; the old have memories. For Sylvester Billings and his son Jess, the Civil War remains The War, a subject worthy of extended analysis. Remembering takes up too much time of too many adults in Alliance. Warren Eggleston, in an *Alliance* poem subtitled "Nostalgia," admits, "I live only in the past, boy. / The present is a flat beer / I poured down the kitchen sink / and the future is a loaded shotgun" (*Alliance* 154).[6]

But Etter is no blindered romantic. As James T. Jones points out, "In Dave Etter's poetry, nostalgia does not imply excessive sentimentality. What he sees, he sees with a cold, clear eye" (88). Many residents of Alliance are as broken as the town they inhabit. Some are insane and dangerous: murderers, arsonists, child abusers. Others, like the grotesques in Anderson's *Winesburg, Ohio*, have clearly been twisted one turn too tight. Amateur painter Maury Chase stocks up on Days Work tobacco, the choice of Thomas Hart Benton, figuring it will help him realize his life's ambition to become a famous painter. An honor roll student at Alliance High School cashes in his collections of seashells, beer cans, and matchbook folders to specialize in acorns. Rex Agee, on the advice of Sherwood Anderson, has canceled his newspaper subscriptions and reads only the labels on canned tomatoes. Yale Brocklander (a character based on Freddie Kodanko, a resident of Door County, Wisconsin, described in Norbert Blei's *Door Way*) drives his Farmall tractor into town because "some lady judge up at the Courthouse" suspended his driver's license for driving drunk into a tree (87).

The hard times of the 1970s have hit Alliance hard: half the townspeople seem to be out of work. One farm has been lost to foreclosure; another farm has been lost to a federal highway. "I am an empty burlap bag now," muses unemployed Michael Flanagan, sitting at his rolltop desk and drawing tiny Ferris wheels on a Trailways timetable (*Alliance* 37). Recently fired Crystal Gavis watches a black ant drag a bread crumb across the kitchen floor, thinking, "That's something else I can't do" (*Alliance* 126). Recently retired Guy Hansen stares at the rain through the steamy window of the Spot-Lite Diner: "So this is retirement, this empty nothing?" (*Alliance* 182). Under-employed Heidi Koenig stares blankly at the window:

The raindrop
on the right
would have

overtaken
the raindrop
on the left
in the match race
down my
windowpane
but
the raindrop
on the right
ran smack into
the blood bug
of the week
so
the raindrop
on the left
won
easily. (*Alliance* 178)

Communication is a problem in Alliance, between sexes and generations, inside a family. Although Etter has denied that his town is "all
ill,"[7] characters in *Alliance* are more *"allied"* than integrated. (How seldom, one notices, do Etter's characters bring their love to a satisfying
and permanent fruition!) In a house on Union Street, the mother "who
has read all the Latin poets" ignores the children, "who have read all the
Oz books," who ignore the father, "who has read all of Ring Lardner,"
who ignores the college boy, "who has read all of Marx" (*Alliance* 70).
Unlike Masters's *Spoon River Anthology*, Etter's *Alliance, Illinois* contains
only two instances of characters escaping their own poems to reappear
in someone else's world, and one of those poems is "Kate Pinchot:
Public Library."

The loss in Alliance, however, goes beyond age, unemployment, mis-
communication, and isolation. Like Americans everywhere, its citizens
have lost their nerve. "Spider webs are wrapped around / Alliance,
around Illinois, / around the whole U. S. of A.," muses Sonny Baxter
(*Alliance* 66). In a letter of March 27, 1999, Etter himself complains,
"*Sunflower County* is a *dark, brooding book* [italics Etter's] not something
for the comedy stage." In the penultimate poem to the 1983 *Alliance*,
Walter Ingram has given up racing his big blue Buick up the back

country roads or just creeping along to look into windows of village homes, to pass out, drunk on gin, in his overstuffed chair:

Damn, it is hard to stay sober here
when one day yawns into the next
and there is little nerve left
to scale the fence, fly the coop. . . .
I am being buried half alive
among the tired smiles of used-car salesmen
in the middle of the Middle West. (*Alliance* 238)

Exactly what the loss is, most citizens of Alliance probably could not say. The emptiness in Alliance is certainly more than economic, and in poems like "Moe Ott: Deathbed Words of a Life Insurance Salesman" Etter even suggests that certain kinds of employment may have caused the loss: "The boss said, / 'You must / sell yourself, / my boy.' / So I did, / and soon / sold myself / for life" (*Alliance* 213). What's missing is more abstract: quality of life, vision, integrity—concerns that elude the conscious consideration of most Etter characters.[8] They remain inert, sometimes nostalgic, sometimes drunk, usually inarticulate, lost, and confused. "We are living in the middle of nowhere," realizes a bewildered Gretchen Naylor (*Alliance* 134). "She says I'm bored because I'm boring. / I say I'm bored because she's boring," explains a bitter Donald Guest (*Alliance* 189). "I have an empty house to go to / and cold thoughts to rattle in my head," admits Melissa Jenkins, staring into winter (*Alliance* 21). "Too many things are busted here," concludes Iris Exley (*Sunflower* 286).

To say that Etter's characters are old, broken or, like their creator, have a love-hate relationship with the town is not to say they lack psychological complexity or validity. A postmodern sensibility accustomed to neurotics, psychotics, transvestites, Neo-Nazis, punks, pederasts, pushers, pornographers, and pedophiles may find Etter's villagers one-dimensional, but layers of psychological subtleties underlie the dramatic monologues of *Alliance, Illinois*, condensed, usually, to a single page of surface data and speech. (The retrospective gaze of village elders is itself a reflection of the psychological truth that for most of us modes of perception, speech, and behavior change little after we leave high school.) Barbara Totherow has created a full high school English class unit on "family constellations" based on Etter's "Aaron Ficklin: Brother."[9] Describing the unit in *English Journal* she details layers of family dynamics buried inside Etter's poem, supporting her analysis with material from psychologists Dreikurs and Grey on "'family constellation' in which birth order, sex of the child, and the age differences between the children have an enormous effect on personality development" and material from psychologist Haim Ginott on "jealousy, envy, and rivalry" (80). Interestingly, Totherow concludes that the poem speaks well to today's teenagers, to whom "the complexities of modern family life perhaps give . . . a much more experienced view of family relationships than those of us from simpler, more traditional family backgrounds can ever know" (81).

Another complex emotional relationship can be found in "Stubby Payne: Stocking Tops" (*Sunflower* 55) where a middle-aged speaker nurses wouldof, couldof, shouldofs over drinks at Arne's Pub. "Yes, I should have bedded down with you myself, / said so what if you were a bumbling barfly, / every drinking man's little honeybush," Payne tells himself (*Alliance* 29), knowing as we do that were Bee to buzz one more time through Alliance, he'd find one excuse or another. In Stubby Payne, Etter depicts the paralysis of inhibition, the preference of some males for a safe voyeurism over stepping across the line and, at the risk of rejection, actually *doing* something. Bee, of course, is Stubby's polar opposite: savvy, self-directed, independent, manipulative, and free enough of guilt to get herself to Prairie du Chien, Wisconsin, to comfort an aunt "full of money . . . and dying of cancer." In the tradition of village realists from Anderson and Lewis to Keillor and McMurtry, promising youth leave town and paralyzed age remains, nursing a long beer at the local tap. Against both older human players, Etter poses the rich, organic sensuality of Nature: "Stiff tassels shake in the sexual sun. / There's a dust of pollen in the air." Layers of gender, age, and psychological conflict underlie this tale of regret from an Alliance pub.[10]

Similar multilayered interchanges can be found everywhere in *Alliance*: Zachary Grant meditating ruefully on the ugly-ducking daughter he never got along with; virgin Valerie Mayhew spinning tales of wild times down in Macomb; Stella Lynch warning her friend May away from the loud-mouthed, bean-brained creep she clearly wants to date herself; blizzard-crazed Terry Reese threatening wife and dog with his shotgun, pumping, finally, five shells into the old Oldsmobile before collapsing into a snow bank next to Lois and the dog.

The kids of Alliance are a more variegated group. Some have been warped at an early age. "Flodeen greets all trains, / all Greyhound buses, / and winks at good lookin' strangers. / DeWayne draws naked ladies, / fools with mice and matches, / and picks scabs at church meetin'," Holly Jo Anderson admits (*Alliance* 194), concluding that "things they start out bad / and they just stay bad" (*Sunflower* 336). Aaron Ficklin, having killed his older brother in a hunting accident, has appropriated his boots and sold his law books, spends Halloween evening drinking bourbon on his grave. However, most Alliance children do well emotionally, and in poems like "Tracy Limantour," "Jerome Holtsapple," and "Booth Schofield" Etter draws a sharp contrast between expressive youth and dour old age. "Trudy Monroe: Saturday Afternoon on Elm Street" is another such contrast:

> In the green-shuttered Victorian house
> the birthday party boys and girls
> are playing pin-the-tail-on-the-donkey.
>
> But the real jackass on Elm street
> is the vacuum cleaner salesman next door
> who has locked his keys inside the Plymouth,
> the headlights burning, the radio on,
> the slain deer still tied to the hood.
>
> The salesman's face is three shades of blue.
> He walks around and around the car,
> turning his shapeless hat in his hands.
>
> The donkey is full of laughing pins. (*Alliance* 82)

Preadolescent Jamie McFee, having problems understanding her older sister, wonders "if it was a good thing / to grow up and be grown up / and not like anything anymore" (*Alliance* 23), but adolescence is not really a problem in Alliance. Hormones—male and female—rage as freely there as in America's cities or suburbs, and Etter blesses adolescent sex as he blesses childhood innocence. Roxanne Russell and her friend Dee Dee Watson wrestle naked on the rec room rug. Hazel Jordan and girlfriend Brenda wrestle in the bushes. Kyle Trowbridge climbs a tall pine to watch Amy Scott sunbathe with her halter off. Lamar Wockenfuss's blonde girlfriend runs her hands under his gold shorts, asks if they could go to the movies tonight and does he have enough money for hot buttered popcorn. Peddling her bicycle to work at the cannery, Joni LeFevre meditates on boys: "Roger's stiff cock / when he walked away.

Milo's muscles. Curly weeds. / Pubic itch" (*Sunflower* 424). Tom Randall and Barbara Allen are just plain in love, and "The whole damned Middle-West / is looking / up" (*Alliance* 68).

In balance, however, Etter is interested more in warped and eccentric age than in cute kids or even sexually active teenagers. It is precisely the break, the warp, the scratch—qualities of the present, not the past—which interest Etter. In "Avery Lucas: Apples," Etter uses a metaphor to explain his fascination with the inhabitants of Alliance:

> . . . then come at last
> to an abandoned orchard
> of six scrawny trees.
> Here, I gather the ugliest
> apples you've ever seen:
> puny, lopsided, bird-pecked,
> yet possessing a special
> flavor all their own. (*Alliance* 102)

These apples come from trees planted by Sherwood Anderson in *Winesburg, Ohio*:[11]

> In the fall one walks in the orchards and the ground is hard with frost underfoot. The apples have been taken from the trees by pickers. They have been put in barrels and shipped to the cities where they will be eaten in apartments that are filled with books, magazines, furniture, and people. On the trees are only a few gnarled apples that the pickers have rejected. They look like the knuckles of Doctor Reefy's hands. One nibbles at them and they are delicious. Into a little round place at the side of the apple has been gathered all of its sweetness. One runs from tree to tree over the frosted ground picking the gnarled, twisted apples and filling his pockets with them. Only the few know the sweetness of the twisted apples. (36)

Anderson's apples represent Doctor Reefy's grotesque implosion into himself; Etter's apples stand for all the characters and caricatures of Alliance. Like the trees (not the apples), Etter's characters are rooted, and Etter appreciates their rootedness. Not nostalgia but affection, as well as dark brooding, is contained in the poet's relationship with Alliance . . . and Illinois, and the U. S. of A. "I don't like this idea that a small town is some place you have to get *out* of," Etter observed in 1981 (Pichaske,

"Etter's Alliance" 21).[12] In 1987, he elaborated on his affection for small towns to Steve Follstad, emphasizing the need for continuity: "There's a difference between a suburb and a town like the one that I live in, where people are there for generations. You take Glen Ellyn, for instance, this is a bedroom town. A guy gets transferred to Chicago, they say, 'Where can we live?' They say, 'You can live north, northwest, south, you can go out west, they got a train going out there. Wheaton, Glen Ellyn, Lombard.' They're there six years and transfer to Baton Rouge, Atlanta, Los Angeles, someplace. And they don't expect to be there long. They have no ties with it. No one has ever lived there with their families. No one."[13]

In that same interview, Etter remembered his own childhood neighborhood and that of Norbert Blei, lamenting the loss of many lovely, ingenious things, and celebrating what survives:

> I proofread [Blei's] *Neighborhood*, and it is absolutely a classic. It has things in there that these people themselves will never preserve . . . they don't keep diaries, journals. . . . A lot of the things that he talks about are like people I used to know, like scissors grinders and people that fix shoes, heels and soles. And they do it themselves, not on machines. . . . and there can't be too many stories and books about this type of thing. It's vanishing . . . and he has preserved this. I was fascinated by that, because I didn't grow up in [his] neighborhood, but I grew up in another neighborhood that touched on these things: the bread man, the milk man, and of course the Good Humor man. We have a guy comes around in our town, Elburn, Illinois, and he plays the same tune, something from the past, I think it's an old Union tune, and he comes around, and I love those things. Because anything that will say, "It used to be, and it still is," really peps me up. Because most of it is gone, and you can sit there and look forever, and you won't see it. Like a scissors grinder, these old guys, the junk men that come down the alleys. When I was in Evanston they used to come by . . . coal men. I miss coal smoke. I love it!

For Etter, the decaying past is preferable to the new, antiseptic present. His affection is for tradition maintained, even in slightly reduced circumstances. "I am at home among the dead, / the deformed, the discolored," he writes in "Forgotten Graveyard" (*Selected* 44). "Beyond the empty crossroads store . . . we fish for our lost American souls," he writes in "Green-Eyed Boy After Reading Whitman and Sandburg" (*Selected*

123). The moment of decline, of late afternoon hours and lengthening shadows, is often the point at which he constructs his affirmation:

Howard Drumgoole: Hotel Tall Corn

You know, I sorta, kinda like it.

It's not very tall at all,
and the only corn about the old place
is dispensed by the night desk clerk,
who's been around since Alf Landon
stopped being presidential timber.

The beds are soft, the plumbing works.

If you miss the last bus out of town,
that's where you go to get some sleep.

One cold, gloomy December evening
I slopped through half-frozen slush
to attend a wedding reception,
held in the swankiest suite they had.
The next morning the groom was found
hanging by his farmer's red neck
in a round barn west of Rochelle.

Woody Herman's band played there once,
a real "Woodchopper's Ball."

I hope it stays alive a little while.

It's the kind of rube hotel
Sherwood Anderson would hole up in
to write about the beauty of horses,
the faded dreams of small-town girls,
and the lives of love-sick millhands.

You know, I sorta, kinda like it. (*Alliance* 55)

This poem enumerates every quality Etter values in his lost Illinois village: comfort, history, rest, humor, functionalism, and the ghost of Sherwood Anderson writing psychological realism. He loves not what is lost, but what remains, even if what remains is only a shadow of its former self—or perhaps because what remains bears the nicks and scratches of time. Time is a test of quality, and here, if anywhere, begins the reconstruction of our lost American souls. Etter's art preserves those flavoring elements which, even while making the village stereotypical, make its region unique: the Midwest before that "uniformity of life all over the country [that] makes it easy for us to change houses and neighbors as we change cars and clothes" (Mueller, "Midwestern Poetry" 3). Etter emphasizes those qualities that make the town different from urban-renewed Chicago and St. Louis, from sanitized suburbs like Schaumburg and Carol Stream and Hoffman Estates.

In preserving the old names, old stores, old language, old characters, old ways, Etter is in one sense encouraging the sense of community that Americans seem to have lost somewhere around 1970, with the national ascendancy of a postmodern sensibility. He offers a directional marker for a culture which he senses took a wrong turn somewhere in the 1950s, possibly earlier with the loss of rail transportation, stable farm communities and the Populist agenda (see *Home State* #13). In another sense, Etter is merely providing a balanced report, commingling the positive and the negative. "It speaks for contemporary writers like Carol Bly, Louise Erdrich, and Garrison Keillor, as well as poets like John Knoepfle, Dave Etter, and Bill Kloefkorn that they continue to be critical of the weaknesses of small-town society while also acknowledging its positive aspects," notes Walter Hübling (57). "Here in Alliance, Illinois," says Henry Lichenwalner in *Sunflower County*'s third poem, "I'm living in the middle, . . . believing in the middle way, . . . in the true-blue middle / of middle America, / in the middle of my dreams" (4). Balance. "If there is such a thing as a tone which is both amused and elegiac, Etter's poems have it," Robert Bray notes (*Rediscoveries* 159). Balance. "If nostalgia is the force that generates these poems," Lisel Mueller notes ("Versions" 326), "it is balanced by a fine, dry wit and matter-of-fact— sometimes almost grudging—speech." Balance.

Mueller's observations appeared in *Voyages to the Inland Sea* number 1, an issue that also contained her own poems and poems by John Knoepfle and Dave Etter himself. Published in 1971, the book antedates the Kylix Press *Alliance* by seven years, although Etter had already experimented with truncated dramatic monologues in *Go Read the River* (1966) and *The Last Train to Prophetstown* (1968), which Mueller certainly knew, and in the Juniper Press chapbook *Strawberries* (1970), which Mueller may not have seen. Her observations of 1971, so relevant to *Alliance*, apply as well to Etter's early work. The dominant characteristics of *Alliance*—character, geography, idiom, loss, rural sensuality—are found in Etter's first books. The little red brick town in the title poem of *Go Read the River* long ago "went to pot," and thick dust blows against beer signs in the village. In Argyle, Wisconsin, the city limits sign is black with bullet holes, and the windows of the hotel are broken. On shore leave in an old county seat, a deck hand downs a cucumber sandwich and a bottle of Grain Belt, then heads upstairs for a "fooling around session / with Penelope Jane" on the four-poster bed. In the wheat fields west of Hays, Kansas, "the fat thighs of a farm girl" are clamped around the loins of a midwestern youth. "The Hometown Hero Comes Home" describes the mixed feelings of a discharged Vietnam War veteran, returning home to Dubuque, where no brass bands will greet him. He looks at the woman beside him, longing to "go off with her to some lost / fishing village on the Mississippi / and be quiet among stones and small boats" (*Go Read* 2).

Skelly Gas, Pabst Blue Ribbon, Grain Belt beer, Old Crow whiskey, and Elsie, the Borden cow, provide cultural markers. Etter's geographical markers—Vandalia, Prophetstown, Nauvoo, Argyle, Galena, "old, hunchbacked Dubuque," Waterloo, Keokuk, Chillicothe, Wichita, Guttenberg, Dixon, Hannibal, and Hays—are dead and dying towns, gray, musty pawn shops still doing business (*Go Read* 51). "Springfield, Illinois, / has no Altgeld," Etter laments, and "no Vachel Lindsay, / no Stevenson" (*Go Read* 42). "The Land of Lincoln," opening poem in *Last Train to Prophetstown*, extends the litany:

> Lindsay gone. Masters gone. Sandburg gone.
> Abe gone. Darrow gone. Altgeld the Eagle gone.
> Little Giant Douglas gone. Stevenson gone.

Etter's idiom, as usual, is familiar with a hint of gone: "old codger," "splat," "kerplunk," "smack dab," "whooped," "cotton to," "dad-blamed," "take a leak." There is Maple Street, Elm Street, and Cedar Street, Third Street and Main Street and Water Street, Frampton's Drugs, Hotel Tall Corn, Jake's Tap, and the Burlington tracks.

A decade before *Alliance, Illinois* we are in the town of Alliance, Illinois. "The world of Dave Etter's poetry is essentially that of the small Middle Western town," reads the jacket of *The Last Train to Prophetstown*, "with its meandering river, railroad tracks, graveyard, courthouse, corner drugstore, gossipy barbershop, front-porch swings, backyard vegetable gardens, school children, and eccentric old men—surrounded by endless cornfields. His themes are typically American and his language is the everyday speech of his environment."

Home State, which followed *Alliance, Illinois* in 1985, gives a similar impression—at least initially. James T. Jones claims it is a better book than *Alliance, Illinois*, "even in Etter's terms." The style of Garrison Keillor is "crossed with that of Charles Bukowski [*HS* #83 carries an epigraph from Bukowski]. . . . Etter takes his readers on a postmodern tour of Illinois, a tour which, lacking the nostalgic gloss of *Alliance*, finds the incongruities not only amusing, but essential aspects of midwestern life" (93). *Home State* is an unpaginated compilation of one hundred short prose poems describing the cities, towns, grain elevators, county courthouses, scarecrows, windmills, Burma Shave advertisements, dogs, politicians, highways, baseball, weather, cultural achievements, and citizens (most importantly, Etter's half-mythical, half-real companion, "Doreen") of the poet's adopted home state. The book places us immediately in familiar territory:

> Tonight, coming out of the Paradise theater, after taking in a double-feature plus Bugs Bunny cartoon, with lots of popcorn, strawberry soda pop, and Milk Duds, we walk down Prairie Street to the town square, kicking and crunching the fallen maple leaves. Through the blue-gray fog that drifts up from the river, we can see the lit-up courthouse clocks. (*HS* #1)

Etter's geography expands to DuQuoin, Beardstown, Pittsfield, Quincy, Waukegan, Cairo, Galena, Danville, Decatur, Peoria, Monmouth, Joliet, Rockford, and of course the City by the Lake. His reverence for things old produces encomiums on courthouse clocks, horse races (the Hambletonian Championships, formerly run in DuQuoin), tall-grass prairies, freight trains (*HS* #17 is little more than an extended list of Etter's favorite rail names), the state fair, barns, roadside produce stands, the Hiram Walker Distillery (girlfriend Doreen's "alcohol alma mater"), cornfields, dandelions, sunflowers, "real farmers," Stan Kenton, and Thelonious Monk. Celebrated Illinois writers include Anderson, Dreiser, Ade, Ben Hecht, Finley Peter Dunne, Mike Royko, John Knoepfle, and of course Lindsay, Sandburg, and Masters. Celebrated artist: Olaf Krans, who taught Etter that "what you leave out is equally important as what you put in" (*HS* #60). Celebrated politicians: Lincoln, Altgeld, Bryan, Lovejoy, Black Hawk, Grant, Harold Washington, and

Adlai Stevenson. Prairie populist Dave Etter contrasts past Illinois great-ness and recent Illinois mediocrity:

> Adlai Stevenson is by far the greatest man Illinois produced in the twentieth century. . . . Men of his high standards seldom appear on the political scene. If you doubt this, look around for yourself, and be sure to take a long look at the jackass who currently occupies the gov-ernor's chair in Springfield. Like many other good citizens of Illinois, I am looking forward to the day when "Big Jim" Thompson is no longer making a shambles of the state I love. (*HS* #50)[14]

Etter's preference for the village leads him to savage Chicago in a piece that opens with a brilliant parody of Sandburg's famous poem:

> City of the bent shoulders, the bum ticker, the bad back. City of the called third strike, the blocked punt. City of the ever-deferred dream. City of the shattered windshield, the loose wheel, the empty gas tank. City of I remember when, of once upon a time. City of not "I will" but of "I wish I could." (*HS* #10)

In an argument over which side of town is the best side—the West Side, the North Side, the South Side—Etter votes for the East Side: Lake Michigan.

"I write about small people living small lives in small towns," poet Dave Etter tells Cousin Arlene (*HS* #27). "Had I liked Ernest Heming-way *more* and Sherwood Anderson *less* when I was starting out to be-come a writer," he muses (*HS* #97), "I might be living in Paris now in-stead of Elburn, Illinois. But I'm sure I have found my right spot on the planet, and if it is my fate to stay here for the rest of my life, I will have no complaints whatsoever. In the end, the true art of living is to belong to one place, a place that is always 'home.'"

But closer examination shows that *Home State* is not a prose *Alliance*, or even an *Alliance* with extended geographical range. It is scarcely as comprehensively conceived or executed as *Alliance*, and it is prose, not poetry. More significantly, Etter and his companion Doreen[15] give the book the unity created by George Willard in *Winesburg, Ohio*. Across a dozen *Home State* appearances, Doreen emerges as a mythical earth goddess, Etter's imaginary but constant companion, "like Harvey, the invisible rabbit who goes everywhere with Mr. Elwood P. Dowd" (*HS* #1). Doreen is clearly more idea than reality, representative of every-thing green and golden in the poet's history, an image who alternately beckons and waves goodbye, receding at the very moment she seems most attainable. At other moments Doreen is a lost love akin to Gatsby's Daisy Fay: "The most painful thing in this painful world is to say, 'I love you' and know she can't hear me" (*HS* #77). But Doreen is also a very physical presence, at various moments Etter's young daughter (*HS* #63, #91), Etter's first sexual experience (*HS* #52), a teenager in braces (*HS* #26), a recovering alcoholic graduated from Hiram Walker U (*HS* #35), a 210-pound pro wrestler (*HS* #78), and Etter's live-in companion born in Cody, Wyoming (*HS* #82). She is filled with the vitality and sexuality which Etter gave in *Alliance* only to the landscape and to teenagers:

> "I know," she said, and she slipped down the zipper on her tall grass-stained blue jeans. (*HS* #4)

> Barefoot, wearing skin-tight jeans cut off high on her tan thighs, Doreen bursts between two wind-crazed sunflowers. She is breathing hard. Her round, firm breasts rise and fall under her yellow T-shirt which carries the words: *Maid for Wrestling*. (*HS* #25)

> "Let's do it," she said, and began to take off her clothes. (*HS* #52)

> I wear neither pajama tops nor pajama bottoms. You wouldn't either if you slept with Doreen. (*HS* #99)

"She is a person of much energy, unpredictability, and passion," Etter told Follstad. "Nine out of ten guys would have to admit that she is too much woman for them." But Etter uses Doreen for more than sex: she provides him with a practical perspective, a witty retort, a snap ending, an occasional hard sock in the stomach and an occasional verbal left to the jaw:

> "I'm going to start a tallgrass prairie plot," I said to Doreen before hitting the hay on a warm and windless night in mid-May. "I'm going to plant big bluestem, little bluestem, Indian grass, prairie coneflower, purple coneflower, sloughgrass, false sunflower, downy sunflower, compass-plant, rattlesnake-master, and prairie dock." "Sounds like a good idea, but who's going to do all the work, and especially who's going to do all the weeding?" she said, pulling the spread off the bed. (*HS* #4)

Streetwise, stacked, and sassy, Doreen is the most fully realized character in all of Etter's work, the poet's alter ego and his equal.

The poet—his *persona*, his real self, his political and social opinions—is more present on the surface of *Home State* than of any previous Etter book, partly because the work's prose nature permits Etter such luxuries as including a roster of the artists who have most influenced him (*HS* #9), a list of his favorite books (*HS* #39),[16] and a lovely yarn about fishing in Door County with writer friend Norbert Blei.

> The talk turned from fish to other topics—magazine editors, critics, forgotten novelists—and then at last to the mystery of words: words like "erstwhile" and "equivocate," like "myriad" and "mellifluous." And the talk turned to obscure nouns and strange verbs, to ridiculous adjectives and comical adverbs. The poles were put back in the boat. We no longer tried to fish for fish. We were after words now. It was a good day. Yes, a mighty fine fishing day. Each of us had caught a mess of words. (*HS* #23)

The normally bemused, amusing Etter displays in this book a dark, disillusioned, even bitter side heretofore absent or at least concealed. Out of work and under-appreciated, he vents his anger at a world controlled by imbeciles, academics, and literary elitists. Discovering in the mailbox a postcard saying that *Paris Review* cannot find the poems he sent nine months ago, a letter announcing that Shell Oil has canceled his credit card, a postcard saying the Illinois Arts Council will not be funding his grant, an expiration notice for his subscription to *Down Beat*, and an invitation from some New York literary agent who would be pleased to read anything he has written that takes place in outer space, Etter explodes: "The mail is slow, is it? Don't make me laugh. Hey, United States Postal Service, you're doing just fine. Keep all those cards and letters coming—as slow as possible" (*HS* #16). At a downstate poetry reading, Etter declines the request of a "middle-aged woman, dressed like she was still living in the 1960s," who has giggled her way through his performance. "That nice William Stafford would never act like that," Etter imagines her telling her friends; "nor Howard Nemerov either" (*HS* #87). At Monmouth College, Etter takes a few jabs at his Bennington-educated aunt, who "can't write poetry worth a hoot, so she turned critic—what else?" (*HS* #27). At another downstate reading, a fictive question receives a very real answer:

> *Question*: "After twenty-five years of writing and publishing your poems, can you give me one word that would sum up your relationship with the general American public?"

> *Answer*: "Alienation." (*HS* #87)

With politicians, especially Illinois Governor James Thompson and President Ronald Reagan, Etter displays even less patience. Feeling the economic pinch of the Reagan depression, Etter rails against Republicans and suggests that we especially "take a long look at the jackass who currently occupies the governor's chair in Springfield" (*HS* #50). A clean-shaven man snoozing under a sycamore tree in a Quincy public park is probably "another victim of the Reagan Depression (brought about by the carefully crafted campaign to help the rich and screw the poor)" (*HS* #92). Assessing Governor James Thompson again, Etter writes, "I agree with Theodore Roethke's statement: 'A considerable section of influential American public men are simply hillbillies who have learned to count'" (*HS* #50). "Robert Frost said he had a 'lover's quarrel with the world,'" Etter notes (*HS* #48), adding, "I, too, have had a lover's quarrel with the world, but it has gone on much too long and I have decided to sue for divorce."

Home State presents an Etter still in love with the Illinois village and the small people living small lives, but retreating into populist rage and into imagined (or remembered) sexual fantasies from a country, which in the 1980s had indeed lost its American soul. The poet seems trapped in some crisis of confidence, or of art, or of midlife. In *Home State* Etter is often physically lost in fog, dreams, memories, or surrealistic reveries. Enveloped in fog on Interstate 80, Etter tells a state highway patrolman, "I don't know what day or month it is, or even what year it is" (*HS* #84). Absorbed in fruits and vegetables at a roadside produce stand, Etter drives off without his grandmother, last seen "picking out some rutabagas and trading one-liners with an old guy in a grubby hat who said he was originally from Moose Jaw, Saskatchewan" (*HS* #96). In the local graveyard, Etter and Doreen contemplate a tombstone inscribed, "HERE LIES THE BODY / OF AN OLD POET NAMED / ETTER / HE TRIED TO BE BEST / BUT HE JUST NEVER GOT / BETTER" (*HS* #85).

In other ways *Home State* appears to move Etter in a new direction. The landscape of "A Beardstown Dream" looks like something from the other side of the looking glass:

I watched some mighty fine catfish types come out of their catfish houses and walk along East Catfish Street. I saw them eating catfish burgers and sipping catfish colas at the Catfish Drive-In. . . . Later, after I checked out of the Catfish Motor Court, I pulled into the Catfish Amoco filling station and was told I need two quarts of Catfish oil.

"I don't believe this Beardstown," I said to the gas-pump jockey with the blue catfish tattoo on his arm. "Believe it," he said, and handed me my change: three crisp catfish dollars and two shiny catfish dimes. (*HS* #7)

Words and phrases are used for their sound value as much as for their cognitive value, mere verbal material to be manipulated in an almost abstract manner:

But it does snow. It snows heavily. It snows on tulip tree, on picnic table, on telephone pole, on trailer truck, on swimming pool, on storage tank, on super market, on water tower, on coal pile, on courthouse dome, on Catholic church, on school bus, on green-house, on lumberyard, on pet shop, on drugstore, on filling station, on factory parking lot, on silo, on windmill, on cow, on horse, on pig, on corncrib, on apple orchard, on graves of pioneers, on Doreen, on me. (*HS* #74)

The unusually nondescript nature of Etter's material (picnic table, telephone pole, cow, horse, pig, and corncrib) suggests an interest not in sense but in sound—and sound not quite in Guillory's sense of an icon of voice, of "unique [Midwest] stops and starts, syntactical leaps, and idiosyncratic phrasing." The passage might well be subtitled, "Jazz Improv on Prepositional Phrases Beginning with the Word *On*," opening with the tri-syllabic long-short-long pattern (*tulip tree, swimming pool, trailer truck, courthouse dome, storage tank*), adding occasional shorts for rhythmic variation (*picnic table, telephone pole, super market*), slipping subtly into bisyllabic double stress complements (*school bus, green-house, pet shop, drug store*), restating of the original motif (*lumberyard*), before ending with explorations of longer phrasal riffs (*factory parking lot, graves of pioneers*) and shorter, monosyllabic complements (*cow, horse, pig*).

Home State, then, is not so much a rural-regionalist photograph of Illinois as a multiperspective collage of disjointed public and private fragments, handled in a manner that emphasizes style more than content. Rural realism in the Garland-Anderson-Lewis mode is not even the dominant aesthetic of this book, as Etter makes abundantly clear in his list of twenty major influences on his work. Only nine are writers. Three are American painters, and five are jazz musicians. Concluding the list, Etter offers a revealing comment:

The man on my list who has been doing the most for me lately is Thelonious Monk. In his music Monk has shown me a great deal about form, rhythm, harmony, rhyme, tone, mood, precision, where to break the line, the importance of simplicity, how to structure a poem and develop a theme, how to put things in the right places, and (perhaps most vital of all) the absolute necessity of never compromising but to always do everything my own way, no matter how misunderstood the result may be to many people. Yes, Thelonious Monk has been and no doubt will be the principal influence on my poetry. (*HS* #9)

This is an odd statement to be coming from the spokesman for Midwest villagers and farmers who, as Etter admits in "Real Farmers," "have never heard of Coleman Hawkins and Ornette Coleman" (*HS* #33), or Thelonious Monk either. The "How High the Moon" combination of back porch, dew-wet grass, walnut and willow trees, crickets and katydids with "radio jazz" and a long string of jazz musicians is unlikely in Elburn, Illinois. Nor would most Illinois villagers agree with Etter that "the most significant revolution in the arts in the twentieth century was the bebop revolution of the 1940s" (*HS* #66).

This revolution, according to Etter, was "how to use notes differently," an aesthetic which places the poet squarely in the middle of the modernist and postmodernist traditions[17] and their obsession with experimentation. Apparently the apologist for native Midwest realism has his left foot in the European home of modernism. Tracking elements of *Home State* back in time to *Alliance* and earlier work, a reader comes to appreciate an entirely new dimension in Etter's work: a conscious familiarity with and embodiment of many trends in modernist and postmodernist art, including such diverse qualities as neorealism, experimentalism, imagism, surrealism, class and ethnic pluralism, oral poetics, collage or pastiche, self-reflexiveness, new formalism, and the absorption of elements of American popular and commercial culture into serious literature. His poems are possibly as postmodern as many of those contained in *Postmodern American Poetry: A Norton Anthology*, whose introduction by Paul Hoover provided the qualities listed in my previous sentence, save *neorealism* and *new formalism*.[18] Examined from this perspective, Etter is as much craftsman as village reporter, as attentive to manner as to material. The most interesting question becomes not whether his language and material betoken a retrogazing sentimentality, but whether his artistry comes second-hand from models (imagist and surrealist writers, painters, and musicians), first-hand from his own experiments in exploring and shaping language, or as part of his natural midwestern heritage, which is both consonant with and different from European models. The answer is probably all three: as Mueller points out, "Since Masters and Sandburg, Midwestern poets have, of course, been exposed to a great diversity of theoretical and practical influences. Naturalness has gone through assorted sieves" ("Midwestern Poetry" 7). Etter is especially successful at melding form and content, masking artistic experiment beneath the surface of a simple story simply told, and thus synthesizing—insofar as many characteristics of modernism and postmodernism are foreign imports—the European and American traditions.

Of the many recent trends reflected in Etter's work, the one most consonant with his Midwest realism is, of course, neorealism. The term is not much discussed among American academics, but Italo Calvino links Italian neorealism with "largely marginal" voice and place, the precise combination identified in Etter by Guillory and Mueller:

> Actually the extraliterary elements stood there so massive and so indisputable that they seemed a fact of nature; to us the whole problem was one of poetics; how to transform into a literary work that work which for us was *the* world. "Neorealism" was not a school. (We must try to state things precisely.) It was a collection of voices, largely marginal, a multiple discovery of the various Italys, even—or particularly—the Italys previously unknown to literature. Without the variety of Italys unknown (or presumedly unknown) to one another, without the variety of dialects and jargon that could be kneaded and molded into the literary language, there would have been no "neorealism." But it was not provincial, in the sense of the regional *verismo* of the nineteenth century. Local characterization was intended to give the flavor of truth to a depiction in which the whole wide world was to be recognized: like the rural America of those 1930s writers whose direct or indirect disciples so many critics accused us of being. Therefore language, style, pace had so much importance for us, for this realism of ours which was to be as distant as possible from naturalism. (vii–viii)

Calvino could not more accurately have described Etter's early work, with its icons of Illinois voice and place. Etter's catalogs of trademarks and brand names, his idiomatic speech patterns, his geographical markers may all be understood as part of neorealism, a movement that celebrates fidelity to locality if not local color. While Etter is not as prone to theoretical analysis as Calvino, his signed *Encyclopedia Britannica* article on John Berryman suggests a conscious decision to explore aspects of neorealism in his own poetry: "Here [in *The Dream Songs*], the poet, using a jazzy, colloquial idiom, discovered his own authentic American voice" (533).

Imagism and surrealism, constant in Etter's work since his first book, are also areas in which rural Illinois life and international literary trends coincide. Etter's imagism has been frequently commented upon by both readers and the poet himself. "I've got two [senses]," Etter told Follstad, referring to his ear and his eye; "the other three I have to work at." Taste and scent images are (to indulge in an Etteresque pun) strong in his first book, *Go Read the River* (for example, "a river wind laced / with fresh paint and dead carp"—"Old Dubuque," 51), although visual images predominate even there. Victor Contoski notes that "Etter is particularly sensitive to color" (60), especially to the bold primary colors that fill his poems and color the jackets and covers of his books: bright green (*Selected Poems*), dark blue (*Electric Avenue, How High the Moon*), pure purple (*Live at the Silver Dollar*), stop-sign red (the Kylix *Alliance, Midlanders*), and especially gold / yellow (*Riding the Rock Island, Open to the Wind*, the Spoon River *Alliance*, and *Sunflower County*). "Theme in Yellow" (*Go Read* 44) is a perfect surrealist poem not only in the color imagery, but in the spaces between images:

A cold wind from Waterloo
loosens the yellow apples.

They fall in the front yard and roll
to where an old willow tree
breathes through her thin hair.

The street light moves
on a yellow hair ribbon.

My mother died in a yellow nightgown.

It sweeps the worn kitchen floor
on windy, sleepless nights.

Many of Etter's early poems reduce to a single visual image: a yellow school bus on a winter-white landscape, a red cardinal in the green cornfield, a pale moon over October cornfields, an old red bicycle propped against the screened porch of the clapboard house. Even *Alliance, Illinois*, primarily a book of condensed dramatic monologues, contains many imagistic poems, including "Jane's Blue Jeans" and "Kim Austin: Art Class," a one-image, color-contrasting sentence strung by Etter to a tall cornstalk of a poem of thirty-eight single-syllable lines: "Because there was too much blue sky in my real life picture of Sunflower County I painted the tallest cornstalk there ever was anywhere anyplace" (*Alliance* 142).

Etter described imagism to Steve Follstad as "pure poetry," although by "pure" he did not necessarily mean unalloyed, as in the manner of some William Carlos Williams poems. Etter may begin a poem with a simple image—"A gorgeous, smiling girl in a sky-blue dress and cute white hat" ("Reception," *Carnival* 16)—and then move to narrative. An image, partially converted to metaphor, may be spliced into the middle of a catalog of lonesome midwestern railroads:

> The black branches of mulberry trees
> are writing my name on the backs of barns. ("House by the Tracks,"
>   *Go Read* 79)

Or in the middle of a dramatic monologue commemorating unconsummated desire:

> Toward the End of July
> Sunflower County cornfields turn blond.
> Still tassels shake in the sexual sun. ("Stubby Payne: Stocking
>   Tops," *Alliance* 29)

An image right out of Williams may appear in the middle of a monologue on loss and return:

> The Jewish woman who sits next to me
> sheds tears for a son, dead in Viet Nam.
> Her full lips are the color of crushed plums. ("The Hometown
>   Hero Comes Home," *Go Read* 2)

So images, although prominent in Etter's poetry, are not ends in themselves, or even poetic experiments. The best, like the shadows of mulberry tree and the stiff corn tassels, are components of Etter's rural landscape so naturally integrated into the poem that there is indeed no idea but the thing of landscape, the rock of experience.

Jay Paul believes that Etter's interest in color "reflects a larger interest—surrealism, with its luminous imagery and dreamlike discontinuities," which he sees as "the most pervasive influence on Etter's poems" (385). He recognizes a kinship with James Wright and Robert Bly, and behind them Vallejo and Neruda. "Vivid, discontinuous images and ecstatic declarations [reflecting the surrealistic tradition] abound in Etter's first two books," he argues (385). Much of Etter's work does indeed suggest surrealism. Two persistent characteristics are the dreamlike nature of reality and dissimilar images joined in a single phrase or line. In "Wedding Day" (*Go Read* 3), a poem analyzed at length by Paul (385–86), the speaker drifts off in a cupola bedroom toward marriage with a strange girl, and into oblivion. "The five statements of 'Wedding Day' float outside sequence and logic," Paul points out, "making the spaces between them as important as the statements themselves." We are as in a dream. Jones offers "Barn Dreams" as an example of "the surreal element that runs through Etter's poetry" (91): wandering "in a daze of remembrance" into an Illinois barn, Etter discovers the girl he lost at the Illinois State Fair ages and ages ago, sitting quietly on a bale of hay. "Booth Schofield: A Dream of Old," a dark narrative in which the word *old* tolls a total of forty-three times, becomes surrealistic as the town's playful children grow suddenly antique:

> I shake a boy's hand and it crumbles to dust.
> A girl in old calico has flies caked to her nose.
> What is this all about? What have I done?
> Startled, I scream, then I begin to weep.
> The children's faces spring to old smiles. (*Alliance* 100)

In "Chalk Lines" he awakens from a drunken stupor to find himself in a Clint Eastwood movie:

> I dreamed I had
> too much to drink
> and passed out on
> the kitchen floor
> and then the cops
> came in and drew
> chalk lines around
> my body and
> began looking
> for clues certain
> I was victim

of homicide
and I came to
and said can't a
guy get stewed in
his own house and
be left alone
to sleep it off
and a squint-eyed
detective who
looked very much
like Clint Eastwood
said lie still and
shut your fat yap
this is police
business and you
are a dead man (*Live* 22)

In poems separated by three decades, "all the sad young girls" Etter ever knew hang upside down from the bare limbs of his tattered and tossed childhood ("All the Sad Young Girls," *How High* 20), and all the children of the poet's youth rise from the dead to stand by their own gravestones ("The Poet Dreams of His Youth," *Go Read* 21). Elsewhere in the poet's work Picasso dines with the Etters on sweet potatoes and baked ham; Tess of the D'Urbervilles rises from the Ausagaunaskee River to greet Ivan Loomis (*Alliance* 158); the statue of a Civil War soldier on Alliance's courthouse square scratches his crotch in full view of townsfolk (*Alliance* 60); Bonnie Parker jots down poems when she knows Clyde is otherwise occupied; animal crackers laugh themselves to crumbs over the anteater (*Midlanders* 28); Etter converses at some length with a scarecrow (*Sunflower* 70); a beer can tossed out of the pickup window in Pittsfield, Pike County, Illinois, bounces 200 miles to the front door of a narrator just deserted by his girl (*Alliance* 143); and a female wrestler throws her opponent right out of the television screen and onto the rug in front of Etter and his surprised son (*Live* 12).

Etter's debt to surrealism—and to international modernism in general—may be gauged from his references to writers and painters. Although not richly allusive, Etter's poetry includes mentions of, or epigraphs from Joyce, Kafka, Apollinaire, Villon, Mallarmé, Lorca, Pasternak, Neruda, Rilke, Böll, Moravia, Umbral, Lawrence, Henry Miller,

Dylan Thomas, Gottfried Benn, Charles Bukowski, Antonio Machado, William Faulkner, e.e. cummings, Theodore Roethke, William H. Gass, William Carlos Williams, Chagall, Miró, Matisse, Van Gogh, Toulouse-Lautrec, Picasso, Modigliani, Wyeth, Pollock, Hopper, and Grant Wood.[19]

The degree to which Etter's surrealism reflects the influence of artists and writers is difficult to determine. In a brief reminiscence titled "The Road to the Poem: An Autobiographical Fragment," Etter recalls exploring poetry in the off-hours while working a desk job in the army: "I also became attached to several foreign poets, especially Dylan Thomas, Federico Garcia Lorca, Boris Pasternak, and the French Surrealists" (17). Elsewhere he writes, "My knowledge of surrealism came from books by the French surrealists (Breton, Eluard, Desnos, et al.)"; "also from *Age of Surrealism*, by Wallace Fowlie, and from books on surrealist painters — all of which I have. Surrealism was a very small and very brief influence" (Letter). Some borderline surrealism in Etter's world may derive as much from his place as from theory or models. The title poem of *Live at the Silver Dollar*, subtitled "Another Late-Night Fantasy," has Etter broadcasting poems over Minnesota Public Radio from the Silver Dollar Bar in Ghent, Minnesota (*Live* 64). Etter did once, in fact, read his poetry at the Silver Dollar Bar in Ghent, Minnesota, but not on radio. However, so-called "Cornstock" poetry readings from Ghent (not including Etter) were in fact broadcast on South Dakota (not Minnesota) Public Radio. We may ask whether the poem is a surrealist fantasy, imagination, or lightly edited truth. Is the title poem of *Electric Avenue* symbolism, surrealism, or merely everyday life in Elburn?

> The tattooed man next door ran across the lawn
> carrying a fish tank, the fish still in it,
> and slammed it down on the stained and marked cement.
> "Okay, let it begin right here," he screamed.
> I watched from behind my snorting power mower,
> trying to decide whether to smile or snicker.
> "What's going to begin here?" my wife said.
> It was then the rock hit the art-glass window. (*Electric* 11)

An American colleague teaching in Poland, Tom Sammet, once remarked to me that a Fulbright year in Central Europe, 1989-90, had led him to consider Franz Kafka a "pedestrian realist." Dan Guillory writes, "Even today a poet living in the urban sprawl of Chicago can gain access to the *prairie* by a short drive on the interstate highway. Once there, the poet encounters a world of *surreal* emptiness" (44, italics mine). After discussing color imagery in early Etter and noting the poet's preference for yellow, Etta Blum catches herself: "there's no getting away from it— the sun is a large fact of life in cornfield land" (342). If free verse, Midwest style, is less a European import than an introduction of everyday common speech patterns into the province of poetry, as Lisel Mueller argues, and if the midwestern bias toward naturalness and against formalism is mostly a reflection of the Midwest's egalitarian heritage, then perhaps the surrealism in Etter's poetry may be pedestrian realism describing life in a different time zone. Norbert Blei's description of a 1984 visit to the Etter home in Elburn reads in places like an Etter dialogue poem, with Etter lost in his own world and the grandmother lost at the roadside produce stand come home to haunt:

> "We were worried you guys might not find your way back," says Emily, "but George says you're used to driving the Door County roads at night with a bottle of Jack Daniel's between your knees." "Somehow George has the wrong impression," I say. "How do you want your steak?" Peg asks. "What do you say we have a drink?" someone suggests. Dave's mother-in-law says she wouldn't mind a little bourbon but says, in an undertone toward me, Dave won't get it for her. Dave returns with drinks for all but neglects to fill his mother-in-law's request. "See, what did I tell you," she says to me. "I'll get your drink, mother," says Peg. (*Door to Door* 54)

In addition to imagism and surrealism, Etter shares with many postmodernists a fondness for verbal play and puns, although his are rarely based on etymology or classical or literary allusions. "Birds" and "Batman" play off each other from the beginning of lines at opposite ends of "Two Beers in Argyle, Wisconsin" (*Go Read* 27); bad local news and a string of passing railroad cars leaves Etter "Erie-Lackawanna" in "A House by the Tracks" (*Go Read* 79); a woman named Bee is a "bumbling barfly, / every drinking man's little honey bush" in "Stubby Payne" (*Alliance* 29). "The girl's name is April, born in May," Etter writes in "Hard Rain" (*How High* 21). "When it came to being nuts," observes Selma Skogland (*Alliance* 180), Dad "was the whole tree." "She was a good egg who liked to get laid," Etter writes in "Chicken-Fried Steak" (*Live* 29).

A more prominent aspect of Etter's word play is his fascination with language as sound, the range of snazzy, swanky, persnickety, screwball chitchat used by Midwest rubes and whippersnappers. These words he usually sets like garnets in settings of the most commonplace American English, which has, of course, a vigor all its own. In a letter to John Bartlett, written in 1913, Robert Frost suggested, "The best place to get the abstract sound of sense is from voices behind a door that cuts off the words. Ask yourself how these sentences would sound without the words in which they are embodied: You mean to tell me you can't read? I said no such thing. Well read then. You're not my teacher" (80). Remembering her youth in Pittsburgh, Annie Dillard writes,

> One Sunday afternoon Mother wandered through our kitchen, where Father was making a sandwich and listening to the ball game. The Pirates were playing the New York Giants at Forbes Field. In those days, the Giants had a utility infielder named Wayne Terwilliger. Just as Mother passed through, the radio announcer cried—with undue drama—"Terwilliger bunts one!"
>
> "Terwilliger bunts one?" Mother cried back, stopped short. "Is that English?"
>
> "The player's name is Terwilliger," Father said. "He bunted."
>
> "That's marvelous," Mother said. "'Terwilliger bunts one.' No wonder you listen to baseball. 'Terwilliger bunts one.'"
>
> For the next seven or eight years, Mother made this surprising string of syllables her own. Testing a microphone, she repeated, "Terwilliger bunts one"; testing a pen or a typewriter, she wrote it. If, as happened surprisingly often in the course of various improvised gags, she pretended to whisper something else in my ear, she actually whispered, "Terwilliger bunts one." Whenever someone used a French phrase, or a Latin one, she answered solemnly, "Terwilliger bunts one." (*American Childhood* 110)

Many of Etter's best lines come to us from behind the door, or drifting in from a radio broadcast, complex patterns of alliteration, assonance, rhythm, and pitch. Sometimes Etter seems to play only with the sound of language as language, of word as word, improvising upon its sound value, in the manner of a jazz musician. If paint can be only paint, and notes can be only sound, words can be valued as much for their tonal qualities as for their meaning. Lines like "Yes, bacon and grits, bacon and grits. / I'm in a rut with bacon and grits" ("All Morning Long," *How High* 55) are interesting more for the sound of the phrase—the rhythm, the pitch, the tonal qualities of vowels and consonants—than the taste of the food. The same is true of the opening lines of "Chicken-Fried Steak" (*Live* 29):

"Chicken-fried steak," I said.
"Chicken-fried steak," the waitress said.

"Chicken-fried steak," the cook said.
Iowa: a chicken-fried place.

Etter might test a microphone with *chicken-fried steak*, or answer a remark in Latin with "baconandgrits." Sometimes he reproduces pure sound:

Bam, bam, bam went the baseball bat
    ("Delbert Varney,"*Alliance* 103)

ga-ga-ga-ga, goin-goin-goin-goin,
ga-ga-ga-ga, goin-goin-goin-goin.
    ("Anthony Fasano," *Alliance* 124)

SPLAT: four ripe ones smack
some old codger's Chevy
    ("As You Travel Ask Us," *Go Read* 23)

"Klook-a-mop-flop
    ("Farewell to Sand Dune Beach," *Looking* 30)

Etter's interest in word-as-sound extends to rhyme, which he uses with surprising frequency:

Statement

The roasted,
oat-toasted aroma
of this old Corn Belt
mill town,
which spreads
its commercial
oatmeal shanks
over both banks
of a brown river,
has sickened me
much too long,

as have blue memories
of the peanut man
who kept a small
tumbledown stall
by the railroad tracks
all summer long,
then one day
in early May
flung himself
under the wheels
of an eastbound freight,
so it's more than
just likely,
or even fate,
that come next fall
I'll leave this town
like Danny did,
and Phil and Sid,
and maybe not
come back at all. (*Selected* 125)

Alliteration is an oft-observed and oft-commented upon feature of Etter's poetry, and the source of much of his celebrated music. His patterns of alliteration, rhyme, sound, and pitch are as subtle and complex
as the chords and harmonies of jazz, infinitely beyond the handful of
types Eduard Sievers worked out for alliterative Anglo-Saxon poetry.

Etter trained his ear listening to jazz, an element of modern American
culture far less compatible with the world of Elburn, Illinois, than neorealism, imagism, and surrealism. Jazz influences were apparent early
in Etter's work: Thelonious Monk, John Coltrane, Eric Dolphy, and Sonny
Rollins. They became especially prominent in the twelve jazz poems collectively titled "A Long Walk with Thelonious Monk" in *The Last Train
to Prophetstown* and published, with additions, in the chapbook *Well, You
Needn't.* Jazz influences and references are abundant in the later poems
of *Live at the Silver Dollar,* the second section of *Carnival* (1990), and
Looking for Sheena Easton (2003). Jazz is the dominant influence on *How
High the Moon,* reflected on the book's cover (an interracial night club
scene from Thomas Hart Benton's "A Social History of Missouri" mu-

ral at the Missouri State Capital). The book contains "Jazz Junkie," with its list of trumpet players; "Double Exposure," with its list of blues singers; and "Gardenia," in which Etter does what he has done time and time again: repeat and three-peat the word and phrase, with constant variations of tone and pitch:

"We're going now," my girl said.
"We're going now," I said.
Had my dad's Ford out front.
Helped her in, closed the door.
"Off to the dance," I said.
"Going, going, going," she said.
She sat close to me, sat real close to me.
"Thanks for the lovely flower," she said.
"It sure looks nice," I said.
We drove down Prairie Street.
We drove down Illinois Street.
"Going, going, going," she said. (*How High* 93)

There is plenty of jazz in *Alliance, Illinois,* too. "What do you study at college?" Arnold Wheeler's father asks his son (225); "Thelonious Monk," the boy answers.

"What is your favorite subject?" Mother says.
"Thelonious Monk," I say.
"Just what *do* you get out of school?" Father says.
"Thelonious Monk," I say. (*Alliance* 225)

Also on display in *Alliance, Illinois* is Etter's incorporation of jazz techniques, "form, rhythm, harmony, rhyme, tone, mood, precision, where to break the line, the importance of simplicity, how to structure a poem and develop a theme, how to put things in the right places":

Lester Rasmussen: Jane's Blue Jeans

Hanging alone on a blue-rain clothesline,
hanging alone in a blue rain,
hanging alone:

a pair of torn blue jeans,
a pair of faded blue jeans,
a pair of Jane's blue jeans.

Blue jeans in the shape of Jane,
Jane now in another pair of blue jeans,
blue jeans that also take the shape of Jane.

Oh, Jane, my rainy blues blue-jeans girl,
blue jeans without you inside
is the saddest blue I've seen all day. (*Alliance* 34)

This memorable and winsome love poem, built on a single visual image seen every summer day in small-town America, is more than anything Dave Etter's "Jazz Improv on the Consonants *J* and *B*, Long Sad Vowels, and the Word *Blue* (With Occasional Allusions to the Letter *R*)."

Jazz taught Etter the technique of repeating, and repeating with variation, which is so much a part of his poetry. There is the simple repeat, or the repeat with slight variation:

turning and whirling
dancing dancing like Monk.
   ("Dancing Like Monk," *How High* 32)

"My god," I said. "My god!"
   ("Denny Grimes: Winged Seeds," *Sunflower* 231)

Then the grass burned brown.
Yes, the grass turned brown.
   ("Lonnie Evans: Diminuendo in Green," *Sunflower* 69)

And in two days it rained hard,
and it rained hard for two days: ("Milo Ferris: A Damned Pretty
   Rain," *Alliance* 107)

There is the three-peat of word, consonant, or phrase:

"Don't let it touch the ground.
Don't let it touch the ground.
Don't let it touch the ground." ("Kevin Pruitt: Taking Down the
   Flag," *Alliance* 121)

Etter's favorite is probably the three-peat with variation:

I mowed the front-yard grass,
I mowed the side-yard grass,
I mowed the back-yard grass.
   ("Melvin Tikoo: Rocking," *Sunflower* 68)

He said, "yes, sir,
no, sir, yes, sir." ("Oliver Briggs: Night Work," *Sunflower* 16)

The four-peat of word or phrase or rhyme:

"Chow, cow, plow, sow," he says. ("Phyllis Nesbit: Chinese
Restaurant," *Alliance* 161)

beyond a hollow stump filled with black water,
beyond the boarded-up schoolhouse,
beyond a worn-out sofa on a worn-out porch,
beyond three broken wine bottles ("Nicholas Hobson: Juney Love,"
Sunflower 35)

The five-peat:

"Bitch, bitch, bitch, bitch, bitch," I said. ("Terry Reese: Boom Boom
on B Street," *Alliance* 109)

Etter's interest in words-as-sound is further apparent in his "talk poems"—the "I said/he said" dialogues[20] and the poems that are collages of juxtaposed fragments of midwestern speech.[21] In these poems Etter seems more interested in the sounds of words than in the messages communicated, emphasizing the talk itself, as in "Hamilton Rivers: Noon at Carl's Mainline Cafe" (*Alliance* 232), which begins and ends with couplets disparaging the content of village chatter and specifically directing attention to the act of talking.

Talk of septic tanks, sheep dip, soap powder.
Talk just to be talking, saying something; . . .

Damn, I wish I hadn't heard all that nonsense.
I don't even remember what the hell I ate. (*Alliance* 232, 233)

Each line of the poem contains at least one recognizably Midwest element of vocabulary, usage, or idiom, from "Arbor Day" and "wienies" and "gonna" to "south the highway bridge" and "all them boxes" and "we used to get us." While this poem accurately records the noontime chatter heard in any small town cafe, our focus in the poem (as in the cafe) is mostly on the American idiom, and on the social function of talk for the sake of talking. In other poems Etter plays jazz variations on attributives—the "he said," "she said"—which he uses mainly for their sound value as elements in a jazz improvisation. Note the complex variations and balances in phrase and positioning of the attributives (as well as the rhymes, alliterations, and Midwest usages) in "Lance Boomsma: Wedding Reception."

"Hey, go kiss the bride," I said to my brother Ben.
"I already done that already," Ben said.
"Where is it you're to honeymoon at?" Mother said.
"Galena," my bride said. "Up to Galena."
"You ain't sore she was once your girl?" I said to Ben.
"That's the way life goes," Uncle Ted said.
"Galena?" my sister said. "Why Galena?"
"Cold up there this time of year," Aunt Flo said.
"We'll be back in a week," my bride said.
"Better take plenty of sweaters," Mother said.
"We're going via Rockford and Freeport," I said.
"How about that? First class all the way," Ben said. (*Alliance* 160)

Finally, the sound collages of most Etter poems are, like the rhythms and harmonies of jazz, not to be described, but to be played: the pattern of F's, T's, and long E's, subtheme of K's and soft A's in "Well, You Needn't," the pattern of J's, B's, and long sad vowels in "Jane's Blue Jeans." Etter's rhymes, alliterations, and repetitions create a rich collage of sounds drawn from Midwest slang, idiom, and diction, blended into a jazz-based improvisation.

The other side of sound-as-sound is sign-as-sign. Etter's fascination with verbal icons is evident in poems that are predominately catalogs, especially catalogs of trade names.[22] Ours is a culture of names and trade names. Writers have been slower than other creators of culture to recognize this fact, but having come finally to understand the iconic power of the words "Coca-Cola" and "Big Mac," new realists have made strong currency of names. In this regard, Etter has always been ahead of the pack, although he is more likely to conjure us with "Nehi," "Philco" and "C&NW" than with "Evian," "Nokia," and "Hummer." Sometimes Etter seems to be telling us, "No ideas but in sounds"; other times he insists, "No ideas but in things." In both regards, he is squarely in the modernist tradition . . . as he is in experimental verbal usages like "moonshine horselaughed his scarecrow face" (*Sunflower* 70) and "A blue light bulb blues the porch" (*How High* 52). Etter even experimented briefly with dropping the apostrophes from *won't* and *don't* and *can't*.[23]

In two other respects Etter's work reflects developments in mainstream American literature since 1960. His work can profitably be examined in terms of both the self-referentialism that marks much American poetry of the 1990s and the so-called New Formalism which marks much American poetry of the 1990s. Since lyric poetry is by definition the expression of the poet's emotional self, it is not surprising to find Etter's presence in his work, but Etter's credibility as a rural journalist requires objectivity and detachment. "What do you mean / you heard I was / a poet and / therefore can't be / relied upon / to tell the truth?" Etter demands in mock outrage in "The Poet as Witness" (*How High* 69). Similarly, the dramatic monologue and the narrative poem, Etter staples, do not lend themselves *as poetic forms* to self-indulgent self-expression. In contrast to the grand masters of postmodernism, Etter appears to be a modest fellow. He is, however, a performer, both part of, and in charge of, his own act:

> If any of you want me to read
> a certain poem, forget it.
> Look, I read what I want.
> These are *my* poems. (*Next Time* 19)

Etter the poet appears surprisingly often in Etter's work, even outside of *Home State*, describing his own enthusiasms and prejudices, asserting control (or lack of control) over the immediate situation, revealing his presence as author and human being. Since his enthusiasm for jazz is atypical of residents of out-of-state Illinois villages, when Etter begins "Gabe Ingels: Jazz Night" with the lines "I had five friends of mine / from Du Page County / over to the house last weekend / to hear some new jazz" (*Sunflower* 64) the person of speaker approximates closely the person of Dave Etter. Etter's characters also share their maker's reverence for Lincoln, liberal Democratic politics, and all that is battered and bruised, lost, discarded, used up, cracked or broken, neglected, rejected, discharged, forgotten, misplaced, displaced, retired, or rendered obsolete. Prominent as well is Etter's fondness for alcohol (especially Jack Daniel's), hard sex (including prostitutes and strippers), and American painters, including Thomas Hart Benton. Etter's friends, relatives, acquaintances, and pets frequently appear in his poetry: David and Barbara Clewell in "Henry Krenchicki: Tallgrass Township" (*Sunflower* 39), Sarah Kohlmeyer in "Black Russians" (*Carnival* 5), Doreen Mitchell in "Why I Don't Go to Parties Anymore" (*Open* 30), and Dave Etter in "Poet

Working Late" (*Open* 31). That's Etter's daughter Emily on the cover of *Live at the Silver Dollar*, Etter's cat on the cover of *Selected Poems*, and Etter himself, in the bow tie, on the cover of *Midlanders*. "I am IN every poem I have ever written," Etter writes. "Some very much so, some barely" (Letter). Two poems Etter is very much in are "Gregory Dawson: Sick [on bad booze] Before Supper" (*Alliance* 205) and companion poem "Home Cooking," which concludes with a scene out of Bukowski:

> Mr. Etter leaning against a green snow-fence.
> Mr. Etter bending over a clump of weeds.
> Mr. Etter sick as a dog in Tennessee. (*Selected* 129)

The young Dave Etter is very much the speaker of "Arnold Wheeler: Ambition"; an older Dave Etter is very much the voice of "Kind of Blue":

> He says he's tired of sending his work
> to the Mickey Mouse quarterlies,
> the sad academic journals.
> He wants his poems in *Yellow Silk*. (*How High* 26)

Etter's own biography is reflected in the "Chicago Romance" of "Matt Rollins":

> I was twenty-one, a wage slave
> loading trucks five nights a week
> at Marshall Field's warehouse
> over on Harrison Street.
> We were crazy in love, real gone
> as the forties swingers would have it. (*Sunflower* 77)

The poet's experience in the warehouse of McDougal, Littell, and Company is contained, even less refracted, in such *Sunflower County* poems as "Beverly Lomax: Shipping Clerk" (324), "Wendell Magee: Second Shift at the Printing Plant" (310), "Christine Andrews: Company Lunchroom" (383), and "Luke Hennessey: Time Clock" (41):

> Brothers and sisters
> of the long warehouse week,
> comrades of conveyor belt,
> lunchroom, and time clock,
> we're going home again.
> And isn't it about time?

Etter's blue-collar poems contribute significantly to analyses of class conflict in modern America, as his poems on interracial sex (especially in *How High the Moon*) contribute to discussions of race and sex in the 1980s.

In the manner of postmodernists, Etter-as-writer sometimes intrudes on his own work, and the poet performing the poem becomes the poem: "I don't like / to read my / poetry / in public / anymore / unless I / have a good / microphone / in front of / me because / I really / like the sound / of my voice / better when / amplified" (*How High* 34). Etter's personal self constitutes an especially strong presence in *Home State*, *Electric Avenue*, and *Carnival*. While Dave Etter is not really the primary subject of Dave Etter's books in the manner of a Charles Bukowski, Etter is present enough through all his work to leave an indelible impression of his authorial self, and for Jones to offer an extended explication of the author's photograph on *Electric Avenue* (69).

In one other respect Etter's work reflects developments in mainstream American literature since 1960, and that is the matter of form.

We have heard almost as much about the New Formalism lately as we've heard about the New Realism. After a period of free verse deteriorating to prose, traditional and ad hoc poetic forms have reappeared, and the concept of giving some shape to a poem—measured lines, measured syllables, measured pulses—has been firmly re-established. An interesting debate concerns which is more avant-garde: improvisation, undirected random, or tight form. Etter has been a formalist since *Go Read the River* in 1966. While most of his poems are, in the architecture of phrase and line and stanza, as improvisational, provisional, and complex as the jazz music which has influenced them, many reveal a simple design apparent at first glance. This architecture is achieved not with traditional meters and rhyme schemes (the ballad, the couplet, the quatrain, the sonnet), but by counting and arranging lines in stanzas, by counting syllables, and by sandwiching or mirror-imaging poetic elements (phrases, images, lines).

The simplest method of creating an ad hoc poetic form is to design stanzas containing the same number of lines of similar length. Several poems in *Go Read the River* do precisely this, including "Where I Am" (15):

My wife draws a scarlet kangaroo
where once we hung Toulouse-Lautrec.

The baby dreams in her crib of eyes
and runs from Humpty Dumpty.

Beyond the crawling tomato vines
an owl digs my grave on the moon.

This imagistic poem consists of three stanzas, two lines per stanza, each
stanza a declarative sentence, one image per line, nine syllables in the
first line, and seven or eight in the second line. The poem facing
"Where I Am" is shaped into four stanzas of two lines each, syllabic
count 4/5 5/4 5/4 4/5. Other poems are looser on the matter of syllabic
count, but settle for two, three, or four lines per stanza. "Homesick in a
River Town" (*Go Read* 75) contains stanzas of 3 : 1 : 2 / / 2 / / 2 : 1 : 3 lines
each, each stanza ending in a period. "Romp" strings one declarative
sentence to thirty-three lines of one one-syllable word each. "Picnic"
contains three stanzas of 1 : 18 : 1 lines each. The first and last lines run,
respectively, "And here's the way it was" and "And that's the way it goes":
a middle is sandwiched between two slices of bread. Etter often expands
this technique to several mirror-imaged lines:

Last night at Tony's
as I sat by the jukebox
I thought about you
and thought about you
and thought about you
I drank boilermakers . . .

and I got pretty drunk
and thought about you
and thought about you
I thought about you
as I sat by the jukebox
last night at Tony's. ("Jukebox," *How High* 27)

The stanzas of "Summer Sequence" make use of irregular rhymes:

Beyond the barn
sweet red clover
is robbed by bees
with amber knees

Sunflowers
mock the sun

in fields where
rabbits run (*Go Read* 57)

In later work, Etter largely abandoned rhyme, but refined syllabic count and arrangement of lines to create the shapes which many of his poems assume. He has written poems of lines counting one syllable per line, two syllables, three syllables, on up to at least eight syllables. In "Jack's Place" (*Looking* 53), Etter shapes a poem of nineteen lines counting 1, 2, 3, 4, 5, 6, 7, 8, 9, 10, 9, 8, 7, 6, 5, 4, 3, 2, 1 syllables per line. *Alliance, Illinois*, in addition to poems of six-, five-, four-, three-, and two-line stanzas, includes poems in the following lines per stanza:

3 : 1 : 3 : 1 : 3 : 1 : 3 ("Ursula Zollinger")
2 : 1 : 3 / / 2 : 1 : 3 / / 2 : 1 : 3 ("Tom Randall")
1 : 5 : 1 / / 2 : 7 : 2 / / 1 : 5 : 1 ("Howard Drumgoole")
4 : 3 : 2 : 1 ("David Moss")
3 : 2 : 1 ("Helen Albright")
1 : 4 : 1 : 4 : 1 ("Garth Light")
4 : 2 : 2 / / 4 : 2 : 2 ("O. E. Mooney")
3 : 1 : 3 : 1 : 3 : 1 : 3 : 1 : 3 : 1 : 3 : 1 : 3 : 1 : 3 : 1 ("Roger Powell")
1 : 10 : 1 : 10 : 1 ("Clarence Fowler")
2 : 4 : 2 : 4 : 2 : 4 : 2 ("Abigail Taylor")
3 : 4 : 1 / / 3 : 4 : 3 / / 1 : 4 : 3 ("Stubby Payne")

"Stubby Payne" (*Alliance* 29) is further patterned by subject and governing images into a mirroring structure: A : B : C : D / / C / / D : C : B : A. First and last stanzas are governed by the bush image and strong images of smell and taste (orange and honey). The second and second-to-last stanzas, both containing four lines, are governed by parts of the body: legs and arms. Both one-line stanzas are divorced from Etter's primary subject (a romance in Arne's pub), and describe instead the natural sensuality / sexuality of Sunflower County. The three-line stanzas sandwiching the central quatrain describe trips. The central quatrain picks up the theme of the two one-line stanzas, describing blond, sexual Sunflower County cornfields. The poem is extremely conscious of its form:

Stubby Payne: Stocking Tops

In June the syringa bushes bloom,
and I swear I can smell oranges there.
That was your smell, Bee. I knew it well.

And I think of you today in Arne's Pub,
where all winter long you sipped Gordon's gin,
legs crossed, showing a bulge of creamy thigh
above those tantalizing stocking tops.

Green summer again. Rain. The warm earth steams.

You left town on a Burlington day coach
to visit an aunt in Prairie du Chien.
"She's full of money," you said, "and dying of cancer."

Toward the end of July,
Sunflower County cornfields turn blond.
Stiff tassels shake in the sexual sun.
There's a dust of pollen in the air.

How many bags of potato chips?
How many trips to the can?
Oh, how many quarters in the jukebox, Bee?

August heat. The girls go almost naked here.

Like some overworked Cinderella,
you always took off just before midnight
on the arm of Prince or Joe or Hal or Smith,
bound for your place above the shoe store.

Yes, I should have bedded down with you myself,
said so what if you were a bumbling barfly,
every drinking man's little honey bush?

Similar close structural analysis could be profitably applied to any number of other Etter poems, including "Looking for Sheena Easton" (*Looking* 1), a poem structured 2 : 2 : 1 : 1 : 4 : 1 : 2 : 6 : 1 : 14 : 1 : 6 : 2 : 1 : 4 : 1 : 1 : 2 : 2. The mirror-imaging technique is central to one of Etter's most popular "talk poems," "Hamilton Rivers: Noon at Carl's Mainline Cafe" (*Alliance* 232) in which twenty-three couplets of apparently pointless remarks are mirror-imaged around central couplet number 12, so that the subjects of 11 and 13, 10 and 14, 9 and 15, on out to 1 and 23 echo or complement each other. Similar mirror-imaging can be found in the lines of "Connie Carpenter: Gold" (*Sun-*

flower County 321) or in the central stanza of "Aunt Alice Is Dead" (*Live* 44):

> Old Aunt Alice
> full of malice
> lived in a palace
> down in Dallas
> old Aunt Alice
> down in Dallas
> died in a palace
> full of malice
> old Aunt Alice.

Etter's books themselves give ample evidence of careful arrangement, and reward careful attention to structural details, from interrelated poems on facing pages[24] to opening, middle, and closing poems in extended collections.[25] So Etter is a jazz aficionado and a formalist; what Monk taught him is, finally, to be a careful craftsman.

Etter's work, finally, is broadly bipolar: he is a rural American realist jealously guarding (and extending) what he perceives to be a native, midwestern tradition.[26] But he is certainly cognizant of modern and postmodern writers and trends, many of which he exemplifies and, in a non-theoretical way, helped to create. Etter often denigrates the modernist-postmodernist traditions in both art and literature, which he often (and correctly) presents as a less than salutary transatlantic threat to nativist American art.[27] T. S. Eliot is dismissed as a fantastic tennis player of the cold-mutton school (the allusion is to Frost's remark, quoted earlier in the prose poem, about free verse being like playing tennis with the net down) who "bores me to death" (*HS* #27). A museum director who assures Etter "with an uppity smirk" that the rural art of Grant Wood and John Steuart Curry is "out of fashion and not worth his time" discovers that he has hung a Jackson Pollock canvas upside down, that his new imported shoes carry the scent of dog shit. Given the bipolar nature of American literature in the second half of the twentieth century, presenting the two traditions as mutually exclusive contrasts is one poetic possibility. The confrontation is most evident in Etter's poem "Picasso" (*Live* 17), in an American child's reaction to the "art treasure" Picasso has fashioned from an old bicycle pump, a Mobil oil can, some baling wire, and two green parrot feathers: "What the hell is that?"

However, Etter's poems rarely present a naked split. One alternative possibility is transfer, what Etter does in "'Round Midnight," the last poem in *Well, You Needn't*, creating a surreal Iowa jazz party conjoining, from the American side, Tube City beer, scotch and sodas, and a topless mother-in-law with, from the European side, Bulgarian girls, foreign cars, and a surrealist river-rat from Lansing shouting sonnets at the parakeet.

A third option is to adapt the best of the external traditions to the Midwest quotidian, not as a down-home Iowan in European surrealist blackface, but as a new shoot of an old tree. While the distinction between synthesis and adaptation is subtle, Etter's best work is adaptation. Any number of individual poems come to mind, but "Failing" (*Live* 1) is one significant poem that demands attention.

A failing bank in a failing town,
the president of the bank shot dead
for foreclosing on a failing farm,
the farmer, turned fugitive, not caught yet.

The slow hound sleeps away his last days
on the railroad ties of no trains.

A big old boy they call C. W.
says to me in the Harvest Moon Cafe,
"You done using that there ketchup?"

Folks sipping coffee in the back booth
talking on what used to be in town
but isn't any longer in town.

There's the bank president's daughter out there.
She strolls down the broken sidewalk,
cool and prim as a dining-car rose.
She married safe money in another town.

The jukebox snuffs out locals' local chatter.
The jukebox plays Eddy Arnold's
(ah, yes, yes) "Make the World Go Away."

C. W. puts plenty of Heinz ketchup
in his bowl of broccoli soup,
crumbles plenty of crackers on top.

"Don't tell me about no Reaganomics
and nothing about Reagan, neither."

The banker's casket is in the ground now.
Not too many friends came around.
The day is hot and dry, corn withers.
The weather has failed and failed again.

The matter of this poem comes not from Illinois but from a story Etter heard during his 1984 residency at Southwest Minnesota State University. A Ruthton, Minnesota, man lost his farm in one of the many 1980s foreclosures and moved with his family to Texas. Two years later he and his son returned, lured the banker and his assistant back to the farm by posing as prospective buyers, killed both with an M-16, then disappeared into the fog-shrouded back roads.[28] Etter alters the story slightly, shifting attention from the murder to the Reagan recession and its effect on the chattering locals and the town they inhabit. "A failing bank in a failing town" is prime Etter material, as are the rotting railroad ties, the Harvest Moon Cafe, Eddy Arnold, the jukebox, the broken sidewalk, and all that "used to be in town / but isn't any longer in town." C. W. and his bowl of broccoli soup supplemented with crackers and ketchup are an invention of genius. The idiom is recognizably Midwest: "shot dead," "a big old boy," "that there," "talking on," "came around," the double negatives of "Don't tell me about no Reaganomics," the metaphor of "cool and prim as a dining-car rose." Etter is an accurate reporter.

He is also a careful architect, placing the banker in the first, fifth, and ninth stanzas (the four-line stanzas), C. W. in mirrored third and seventh stanzas, the locals with their chatter in mirrored stanzas four and six, the old hound and the old president in mirrored stanzas two and eight. Both the first line and the last line contain the word "failing"— twice, as if for emphasis.

Etter is also, as always, the jazz musician, playing alliterative tunes on the letters F, B, and K, with a subdominant R in mirrored stanzas 2 and 8. He repeats ("ah, yes, yes," "farm" / "farmer," "Reaganomics" / "Reagan," "local's local," "jukebox" / "jukebox") and he three-peats ("failing" in stanza 1).

The poet is present, a subtle part of the collapse, one of the local locals in the Harvest Moon, prominent mainly in his value judgments. He invites the dog and train tracks into this poem, and selects the oh-so-significant Arnold song and the very significant (unattributed) line of local chatter: "Don't tell me about no Reaganomics." He provides the remark about "safe money in another town," and the judgment it implies, and the metaphor of the dining-car rose. Etter makes the final judgment about the weather failing twice. The poem, finally, is more about Etter's perception of America in the 1980s than about the farm murder.

In a subtle manner, the poem works because of implied color, especially red: the rose, the ketchup in the broccoli soup. The soup is an unforgettable, mildly amusing, and vaguely surreal image. In fact, stripped of its poignancy, the whole scene sounds like something out of *Deliverance*: fugitive farmer-murderer, C. W. and his bowl of broccoli soup, Eddy Arnold, rich bitch banker's daughter, sleeping hound. The cafe scene might be a grotesque parody of some impressionist painting of dinner in a Parisian cafe. Or a rural, noontime "Nighthawks."

But Etter's place is not Paris and Etter's poem is not European. Realistic at its core, it incorporates elements of imagism, surrealism, and jazz. Reflecting the proletarian politics of Sandburg, the formalism of Lindsay, and the free verse of Masters, it achieves a level of art more sophisticated than that achieved by any of the three. The poem represents the best of Etter, and the best of midwestern American poetry of the late twentieth century, a poetry that is both regional and international in the best senses of both terms.

William Kloefkorn

Looking Back over the Shoulder of Memory

*Which leads me into my own handy-dandy definition of
what a poem honest and truly is . . . words nibbling at the
edge of something vast.*
—*William Kloefkorn*, Voyages 35

As a teenager in the 1950s, I flew upward into the abstraction of ideas. Nudged as a child in that direction by life in the Protestant parsonage, with its emphasis on *logos*, and bored with late-fifties suburbia, I was further encouraged by success in school: grade school, high school, college, and graduate studies. I ascended finally to a PhD in mediaeval British literature . . . as far away from Springfield, Delaware County, Pennsylvania, as a guy could get.

Even then, however, I felt occasionally the tug of gravity: Canadian spruce and lakes, bass and perch on family vacations to Papineau Lake in Ontario; the heft of trash cans and the smell of road tar while working a summer job for the county highway department; the satisfying thunk of leather baseball struck by wooden bat; and later the hills of southeastern Ohio, and the prairies of western Illinois; the pleasant exhaustion of cultivating my own garden, mowing my own lawn, painting my own house, and shingling my own roof. Gradually I descended into physical labor and my own small acreage, giving up ambition and learning, to paraphrase Robert Bly, to see with clearer eyes the flake of snow on the horse's mane.

And I developed a theory, or a sequence of theories. Where I had first aspired to a thousand points of *light*—stars, very distant and very high—I came eventually to believe in *line* determined by two points: earth and sky, thing and idea, here and eternity. Mere headwork seemed frivolous, and writing divorced from place seemed slack and self-indulgent. Two years in post-Soviet Poland transformed the theory of line to the theory of triangle: the Self is best measured against an Other, and from the particulars of one's own place and labor, defined in part by its baseline opposite, one rises more surely to abstraction. The longer the baseline (the more distant the Self and Other), the higher and more fixed the triangle.

With the addition of the dimension of time—backwards from the baseline of Self and Other—the base became a triangle and the edifice a pyramid, the most stable of geometric constructions, a three-dimensional version of metaphor. From a base of triangulated Self, Other, and Past, the writer most surely ascends to idea.

William Kloefkorn arrived at approximately the same conclusion, although probably via a different route. Kloefkorn is quintessentially a poet of place, of the Kansas-Nebraska Plains with their unique particulars of geography and voice. Kloefkorn is also very much a poet of self: much more than Dave Etter's poetry, Kloefkorn's work records personal experience and family history. Repeatedly Kloefkorn explores the community, especially a dark side of the Great Plains psyche that we might call the Rural Id, or Other. Repeatedly he triangulates Self, Other, and Past, to ascend into the larger concerns of ideas: "Whatever complex metaphysical speculations my poems might occasionally explore," he writes, "I hope they do so on the heels of, or in the midst of, an authentic place and situation and people; I hope they are tied to the physical" (Letter 12).

Nebraska State Poet William Kloefkorn was born, ironically, in Kansas, in 1932, to Katie Marie (Yock), who never completed high school, and Ralph Kloefkorn, who never started high school. The first two years of his life he lived with parents and older sister Janet and two cows on a rented quarter section north of Attica, on the far side of Sand Creek. Then the family moved—with one of the Jerseys, two of the pigs, and several of the chickens—into town. Kloefkorn describes Attica as "a small ramshackle town" (*Going Out* 85), "population more or less seven hundred, half a dozen churches, and a town ordinance extremely unfavorable to anything not white or Protestant" (*This Death* 10). The town was not much more than "an overgrown farm with a good crop of churches, a couple of filling stations, a depot and a pool hall and a cafe and Mr. Ely's elevator" (*This Death* 46). The family, increased by one with the birth of John, moved a dozen times inside the city limits; Ralph Kloefkorn worked for the county and the WPA, then tried a series of businesses including a filling station, a grocery store, and a cafe that bore his initials. Kloefkorn's mother sold Avon products and worked at the cafe and, later, for Alvin Corser, editor of the town newspaper, the *Independent* (*Going Out* 46).

Kloefkorn's childhood was in some respects something out of *Tom Sawyer*: skinnydipping in the pond at Ely's Sandpit or fishing with a cane pole for turtles and bullheads in Heacock's Reservoir; hopping short rides on the slow freights of the Atchison, Topeka, and Santa Fe Railroad, Panhandle Division; spending Sunday mornings with his German-born maternal grandmother at the Evangelical United Brethren Church, supplemented with home Bible study and an occasional tent revival; and gathering eggs and milking cows on summer and holiday visits to the paternal grandparents' dairy farm. As an adolescent, Kloefkorn worked a paper route delivering *The Wichita Eagle* and the Hutchinson *Herald* (eighty cents a month, sixty-seven subscribers) and mowed lawns, for which he was paid in movie theater passes. Later he helped the fathers of friends with planting and harvest, and even worked on the railroad. He drank malts and played pinball at Doc Bauman's Rexall Drugstore, collected comic books, fell in love with Betty Grable on the screen of the Rialto and with a sequence of local girls in town, played football and basketball, and threw the javelin in track.[1] Kloefkorn's senior year, the Attica Bulldog basketball team went 3–17 (*Collecting* 31, 40).

This idyll was clouded by a series of tragedies and near-tragedies. Ralph Kloefkorn's jobs provided only a subsistence living—even with the cow and chickens—and Janet, to whom young William was attached, boarded for a year with her grandparents. In 1936 Ralph Kloefkorn lost two middle fingers of his right hand in a work-related accident; he was later debilitated by a floating kidney and a double hernia. In 1939 William nearly drowned after chasing a grasshopper into Harold Simpson's cow-pasture pond; in 1944 John Kloefkorn nearly bled to death after cutting an artery on the broken window of an old Hudson sunk at the bottom of Ely's Sandpit pond two miles east of town. The troubled marriage of Katie and Ralph Kloefkorn finally broke apart in 1951. Several school chums died young. Kloefkorn also remembers burning down the family outhouse, possibly with a misdirected match used to light firecrackers; singeing his hand and face with another firecracker held a split second too long; biting his brother on the arm, clear to the bone; and at age eleven torching the family house with a box of Diamond matches while playing war games. These early years constituted for Kloefkorn, as for Twain, a touchstone experience that "leaves an imprint on one or more of the senses so indelible that it significantly influences a large portion of what the individual thinks and does and writes for the rest of his lovely and tormented life" (*This Death* 6). The kitchen fire especially stamped itself in Kloefkorn's mind: "The flames, to my surprise, were unbelievably hot, so hot that even today I measure hotness by the hotness of our burning kitchen. So how hot might hell be? Well, hotter than our burning kitchen. Jesus. Can you imagine?" (*Restoring* 13).

In contrast, Kloefkorn's college years do not figure much in his writing. From 1950 to 1954 he attended Emporia State College, where he majored in English, washed dishes in the college cafeteria, and worked as a disc jockey for station KSTW. After graduation he entered the Marine Corps: boot camp and officer's training in Quantico, Virginia, then two years at Camp Pendleton, California, a lieutenant in command of an anti-tank assault platoon.[2] He taught briefly at Ellinwood (Kansas) High School, and then returned to Emporia State for an MS. In 1958 he joined the English Department at Wichita State University, moving in 1962 to Nebraska Wesleyan University, where he taught until his retirement in 1999.

Kloefkorn's writing reflects his academic life in occasional poems about teaching and in appropriate echoes of and references to canonical British and American authors,[3] but he is no academic poet in the Pound-Eliot tradition. From the Greats, he learned mostly "rhythms and philosophies":

I didn't learn much from the Brits and Europeans, not systematically. But I learned a lot from them by way of osmosis; I took a hodgepodge of courses that focused on Brits and Europeans, but I didn't pay very strict attention. Even so, I found myself mumbling lines like "There is a pleasure in the pathless woods," and I reckon that any number of lines like this one insinuated themselves on the most impressionable section of my neocortex. Rhythms and philosophies. I detest sermons, but I appreciate philosophies, as do the Brits and in general the Europeans. So perhaps I learned to appreciate the well-phrased insight from them. (Letter)

As important stylistic influences, Kloefkorn credits Chaucer, Faulkner, and Twain among the older writers, James Dickey, Dave Etter, and Gary Gildner among his contemporaries (Cicotello 280–81). Kloefkorn's poems contain several references to students at the university or in lower level schools, which he visited frequently during the 1970s as a poet in the schools:

Taking the test
she bubbles her gum
without one time bursting the bubble,

each time retrieving the pink glistening sphere
as if a delicate flycatcher.
Her nails are the color of the gum,

her dark hair
windblown.
She is telling me

more than I'll ever care to know
of Neoclassicism ("Taking the Test," *Drinking* 42)

Despite serving all that time in a college environment, Kloefkorn has maintained contact with farm and village, the parameters within which most of his imaginative life is lived. In 1978 he won the state hog-calling championship at Nebraskaland Days (June 18–25) in North Platte. He spent a sabbatical semester in early 1981 holed up for several months (with intermittent conjugal visits) in a cabin near the Platte River between Lincoln and Omaha, reading Nebraska writers (Willa Cather, Wright Morris, Mari Sandoz, John Neihardt, Bess Streeter Aldrich, and Loren Eiseley), listening to country music on KRUN, and writing the poems of *Platte Valley Homestead*. He spent a few weeks (officially teaching a writing course) on the *Delta Queen*, traveling upriver from New Orleans to Cincinnati, recovering Mark Twain's Mississippi River. Each summer for over thirty years he and a group of friends have floated the Loup River, through territory described by Jim Harrison in *The Road Home*, in a twelve-foot jonboat named *Our Lady of the Loup*. In many poems and his memoir *This Death by Drowning* he describes family outings—children, their spouses, Kloefkorn's grandchildren—on "Maggie's Pond, in south-central Kansas north and west of my hometown" (146).

Kloefkorn's contact with life outside of academia and his memories of farm and village life are more important to his work than literary influences. He is not an untutored or unconscious writer, but he is a poet more of place than of high culture. Because the Midwest is so central to his writing, and because he is stylistically outside of the postmodern tradition, Kloefkorn is frequently described as a regionalist. In fact, reviewing *Treehouse: New and Selected Poems*, Tom Hansen admits, "It is easy to dismiss Kloefkorn's work, even as one admires it, for being insistently regional" (176). It is just as easy to praise this regionalism:

> These lines are the real thing because Kloefkorn deals with real-life situations and real people. The man is onto life in the Great Plains like a duck on a June bug. A poet cannot write really well until he reaches the point where he is completely at home with his material, until he knows much more than he can ever use. When he knows a place and its people well, he can forget the book-knowledge references, the pedantry, the soap-bubble esoterica. He doesn't need them, he doesn't want them. (Etter, "William Kloefkorn" 20)

"When you spend a lot of time in / one place," Kloefkorn as Carlos observes, "one place / spends a lot of time in you" (*Welcome* 79). That place is "the Great Plains," which Kloefkorn defines in an essay of the same title as "a town of about 700 semi-warm bodies in south-central Kansas" (343). This fictive town very much resembles Attica, Kansas: the Atchison, Topeka, and Santa Fe Railroad tracks mark the south border (with the shack of a Mexican gandydancer on the far side), and the combination grade school-junior high school-senior high school marks the northern border. "Throw a rock out of the window of the music room on the third floor of the school," Kloefkorn claims, "and it will land in buffalo grass on the west side of the football field" (343). Downtown consists of Butch Mischler's pool hall, Urie's barber shop, and Doc Bauman's Rexall Drugstore serving malted milks to football players turned from practice to pinball. The east side of town is a nest of unpainted clapboard houses; the west side of town is a cemetery containing everything from Methodists to Pentecostals. "Reshape any or all of this," Kloefkorn concludes, "and you have something of the Great Plains in the poem that you hope moves beyond and rises above the boundaries of railroad tracks, school-house, shanty, cemetery" (344).

Kloefkorn's geographical markers are the first Great Plains feature to catch a reader's attention. Some are drawn from personal history, others chosen for verisimilitude, connotation, or sound value: Butler County and Barber County, Kansas (*Uncertain* 19, 40); Otoe (*Uncertain* 6), Sheridan (*Visible* 62), Cherry (*Dance* 19), and Sarpy (*Burning* 50) counties in Nebraska; Medicine Lodge, Spivey, Sharon, Attica, Kiowa, and

Cunningham in Kansas (*Uncertain* 3, 11, 13, 29, 31); Oshkosh, Ogallala, Scottsbluff, and North Platte in Nebraska (*Uncertain* 14); "Wahoo. Swedeburg. Wisner. Scribner. Laurel"—a north-south line rising from Lincoln and U.S. 77 (*Uncertain* 42); Sweetwater, Mud Creek, Ravenna, Mason City, Ansley, Hazard, Cairo—strung along Nebraska 2 (*Cottonwood* 8); Huntington Street in Lincoln, Nebraska (*Cottonwood* 3); The Old Brown House Doll Museum at 15th and F in Gothenburg, Nebraska (*Burning* 58); and Ole's Big Game Lounge in Paxton, Nebraska (*Not Such* 27). And the waterways, especially the Platte, the Elkhorn, the Niobrara, and the Loup in Nebraska, and Sand Creek in Kansas.

Kloefkorn's poems are also rich in landscape markers: "sumac, / trumpetvine, raspberry, hosta, rose / . . . tiger lily, . . . magnolia" (*Fielding* 36); "yellow daisies, prairie / clover, wild indigo more purple than / passion," (*Loup* 92); "sumac, honeylocust, walnut, willow, / ash, chinaberry, maple, / hickory, elm" (*Fielding* 66); "lespedeza" (ubiquitous); "egret and gull, heron and warbler and shrike" (*Loup* 59); "Cricket and cottonwood and/cicada" (*Dragging* 8); "catfish and carp and a covey of quail" (*Not Such* 89); "Kansas creeks puffed white with sand, / Parching, twisting, waiting for water" (*Uncertain* 9). Like Etter, Kloefkorn is a master of the catalog, selecting markers both for their sound value and as a reminder of the primacy of thing:

> Bur oak. Syca-
> more. Green ash.
> Hackberry. Black
> walnut. Kentucky
> coffeetree. Col-
> umnar white pine.
> Snowdrift flower-
> ing crabapple.

> Ginkgo. ("Learning the Names of Things: Trees," *Life* 53)

"The vocabulary of Kansas," Kloefkorn calls this landscape in "Driving Back to Kansas to Watch a Wedding" (*Drinking* 60): "rock and chalk and Jayhawk, / high sky, I tell her, / for losing your deepest thought in, / and space enough / for barley and wheat / and burial." "The landscapes should be familiar," writes Mark Barnett in reviewing *Welcome to Carlos* for *The Wichita Eagle* (April 16, 2000); "They are the landscapes of south-central Kansas."

They are also, in another of Kloefkorn's phrases, "the acreage / of our own small understandings" (*Welcome* 23), and they are also the landscapes, vocabulary, and acreage of that state to the north in poems like "The Exquisite Beauty of Southeastern Nebraska," "Nebraska: This Place, These People," and "Song: These Nebraska Skies."

Kloefkorn attends to much in the landscape that others might overlook, things that are "lost, neglected, absent, weathered, or dead" (*Uncertain* 47). Frequently his poems catch the countryside at sundown, when the long, low light of late afternoon magnifies and celebrates every tree, every barb on every wire, every ear on every cornstalk, every hair on every person in the county:

The flesh of soil is vast and cool,
bulged,
wound like a gift
with wire whose barbs burst
against a low sun's light ("Midlands Profile: November,"
  Uncertain 42)

Plenitude legitimizes Kloefkorn's claims that both human and natural landscapes are "Fat, now, and quietly proud" (*Uncertain* 42), or "blaz[ing] like firebushes" (*Not Such* 90). While admitting drawbacks of temperature and rainfall, certain shortcomings of temperament and behavior, Kloefkorn is approving, and even affectionate:

True, the wind in the elms
is sometimes enough almost
to tip the scales
in the wrong direction,
and when the water gathers itself
into an onslaught down the big branch,
even Christkiller Burhman
goes to his knees in the pool hall,
pleading for fins.
And the soil:
true, it often takes back
more than a portion
of that which it gives,
it being in cahoots, one suspects,

with the water and the wind.
Which leaves us with
the daily vexation of fire:
how it can warm to madness
that very same skull
it enlightens.

Even so,
it's not such a bad place to be.
At certain moments
an element swells the lungs
with something akin to faith (*Not Such* 9)

"It is there like a postcard," a friend announces in the opening lines
of "The Exquisite Beauty of Southeastern Nebraska," and after invento-
rying winesaps at Nebraska City, corncribs south of Bennett, and the
lowdown price of hogs everywhere, Kloefkorn allows himself to concur:
"Enough almost by god to make a fellow / Not ashamed to worship"
(*Uncertain* 34).

Brand name markers are as important to Kloefkorn's poetry as his
geographical markers: Folgers coffee, Bull Durham and Prince Albert
tobacco, Monarch and Schwinn bicycles, Batman and Wonder Woman
comic books, Brylcreem and Sweet-Pea talcum, Tube City beer, Lava
soap, Ludens cherry drops, Juicy Fruit gum, Red Ryder and Daisy BB
guns, Maytag washers, Barlow knives, Nehi grape soda, Diamond
matches, Philco radios, Ticonderoga pencils, and Louisville Slugger
baseball bats.

So too is the vocabulary: "pshaw!" (*Alvin Turner* #4, #12), "gumbo"
(*Alvin Turner* #8), "nosireebob" (*loony* 8), "a real dilly" (*loony* 8), "nutty"
(*loony* 37), "buckaroo" (*Dragging* 17), "skedaddle" (*Going Out* 40), "pis-
mires" (*Sunrise* 9), "doohickey" (*Life* 25, *Restoring* 12, *Sunrise* 15), "shit-
forbrains" (*Burning* 86), "cattywumpus" (*Welcome* 36), "vamoose" (*Welcome* 2), "britches" (*Loup* 99), "numbnut" (*Loup* 87, *Sunrise* 99),
"flapdoodle" (*Loup* 77), "peckerhead" (*Loup* 62), "heebie-jeebies" (*Loup*
28), "hotshot businessman" (*Restoring* 57). Like his acknowledged mentors, Etter and Frost,[4] Kloefkorn has an ear attuned to the rhythms, idioms, and vocabulary of idiomatic, spoken English. "Poems of voice,"
Jack Brown called them in reviewing *Covenants* (*Nebraska Territory* 25),
and he was not referring only to that particular collection.

Voice, of course, is a function of place, the special vocabulary of a specific place—"Late afternoon. Early evening. We call it dusk" (*Restoring* 8)—and even the sound of speech. For Kloefkorn, sound is as important as sense, and in the process of acquiring culture, appreciation of voice may precede comprehension of meaning. In an essay for *Voyages to the Inland Sea*, Kloefkorn writes, "The uneasy business of understanding a poem can (and probably should) begin very early in one's life—at a time, say, when the individual is too young to respond to anything but the way a poem sounds" (33).[5] In *This Death by Drowning*, Kloefkorn recounts his early fascination with language:

> "Look at those fingers," he [Kloefkorn's father] said, and I did. "Work for the county long enough," he said, "and you'll end up strung out in bottles all the way from hell to breakfast."
>
> I remember wondering, What does that mean, *all the way from hell to breakfast?* I tried to imagine my body parts in jars of formaldehyde strung out *all the way from hell to breakfast*, but I had trouble forming a clear and coherent image of hell. (5)[6]

These expressions and others (some profane) Kloefkorn picked up from his parents and friends, but also from gospel preachers (see *Restoring* 39), and from customers in his father's businesses:

> My mother is fond of homely expressions, and many of them, I'm sure, wore off on me. But equally influential were the endless hours and days I spent in those little businesses I mentioned above watching and listening to the banterings of farmers and idlers and merchants and pissed-off mechanics. I hung on their words like ugly on a Republican; I couldn't get enough. And it was their devising variant versions of an old expression that most impressed me. "I'm so hungry I could eat a horse" became eventually "I'm so hungry I could eat a horse's ass," which evolved from horse to skunk, with some gravy tossed in: "I'm so hungry a skunk's assend would taste like gravy." Ah, such improvisation! And there seemed to be no end to it, and there isn't. And, too, I learned the occasional surprise value of understatement. Thus "Drier than a popcorn fart" became "Drier than a popcorn emission," and "O kiss my dead ass, Marvin," became "O kiss my long-gone nether eye, Marvin." Once the door to such possibilities is opened, it remains open. (Letter)

The well-turned phrase—usually working class, sometimes rhyming or alliterative, often profane, occasionally biblical, always recognizably midwestern—is an important component of Kloefkorn's recognizably Great Plains voice. Some phrases are so familiar that we barely recognize them as idiomatic vernacular: "wasn't born yesterday" (*loony* 8), "hauling ass" (*Platte Valley* 25), "come hell or high water" (*Restoring* 22), "one screw loose" (*loony* 61), "Between you and me and the gatepost" (*Sunrise* 58), "you have made your own bed" (*Honeymoon* 40), "a month of Sundays" (*Going Out* 24), "shit from shinola" (*Drinking* 34), "Fuck him. And the horse he rode/into town on" (*Fielding* 21), "I'm a monkey's uncle" (*Drinking* 21), "where in the dickens I'm going" (*Going Out* 87), "I hope you're satisfied" (*Life* 26), "more eggs than you can shake a stick at" (*Dragging* 6), "when push comes to shove" (*Covenants* 30).

> If you think
> I'm going to fix that
> sonofabitch before
> supper you have
> another think
> coming. (*Where the Visible Sun Is* 7)

Other phrases are more flamboyant: "tough titty" (*Fielding* 9), "don't make a fat rat's ass" (*loony* 21), "eat shit and bark at the moon" (*loony* 48), "the whole kit and caboodle" (*Welcome* 38), "blown a gasket" (*loony* 61), "got your fat ears lowered" (*Uncertain* 28), "good riddance to bad rubbish" (*Sunrise* 72), "two-timing, piss-complected son of a bitch" (*ludi jr* 39), "hell, I got things to do, / places to go / people to screw" (*ludi jr* 59), "dressed fit to slaughter" (*Houses* 46), "both a card and a caution" (*Honeymoon* 47), "disaster with a dress on" (*Welcome* 41), "ass over appetite" (*Covenants* 29, *Welcome* 16), "shit on the pump handle, Smiley" (*Houses* 42), "Jesus Christ on a popsicle stick" (*Loup* 43), "the width of a blonde pubic hair" (*Where* 24), "have a Chinaman's chance" (*Where* 25), "give two hoots in Halifax" (*Life* 25). Here is American vernacular at its most inventive.

Kloefkorn can adapt and rewrite sayings and proverbs, usually with an ear toward alliteration, assonance, and rhythm: "a youngster who didn't yet know starboard from port, feces from Shinola" (*Restoring* 126), "if it isn't one damn / thing it's a dozen" (*Life* 4), "don't let the bastards ever (do you hear me?) / wear you down" (*Loup* 54), "the sun / for all its magnitude / don't shine on some dogs' asses / ever at all" (*Drinking* 10), "To err, Carlos says, is that which / constitutes Divine" (*Welcome* 72), "the brand that both our mothers / hang their bonnets on" (*Welcome* 24), "Piss on the messenger and on the / horse that will bring him" (*Welcome* 3), "Give a river rat enough rope / and having hanged himself / he'll ask for more" (*Loup* 51), "how many pool sharks / can play 8-ball / on the head of a pin" (*Stocker* 10), "whose third of three wishes / is that in the long run / the long run keep its / curious distance" (*Where* 8).

Kloefkorn can create proverbs of his own: "The only free cheese is in the mouse trap" (*Going Out* 73), "If you ever get hit with a bucket of shit / be sure to close your eyes" (*Welcome* 5), "The yellow sand plum, / someone says, is better off / jelly" (*Loup* 90). And—like Etter—he can parody clichés:

She's six of one, half a dozen of another,
According to Stocker:
Not a bad looker, for a widowwoman,
But her face is so knobbed with indecision
You'd swear she has hemorrhoids.
Heard of another case just like her,
He said,
Who starved to death in a grocery store,
Comparing labels.
Always and forever between a rock and a hard place—
Not fishing, quite,
And not cutting bait. (*Stocker* 5)

Kloefkorn's metaphors deserve mention. The symbolic rock in *Alvin Turner as Farmer* made clear that this poet operates on the bilevel of metaphor. Another early poem, "No Longer Believing in Wind" (*Voyages* 54), expands that symbol (which will become recurrent), reflects Kloefkorn's double vision, and announces one of his most recurrent themes:

From the airborne dust we learn alliances:
at the most unlikely moments
we too settle among the veins of old leaves,
cozy into the corners of unsung barns.
Less solvent than snow,
we fill the hollows of our forebears,
those slow rocks of the fields.

Our flights are fancies
no more enduring than the movements
of small wings.
Always there is the pull
of something deeper than our thrust,
of something loftier even
than our wild propulsions.

And so it is we find ourselves
reduced to birth:
brother to brother descended,
in league with the center of the earth.

Most Kloefkorn symbols and metaphors are less weighty than field rocks. The ingenuity so admired by modernist critics in the metaphysical poets is not for Kloefkorn. His metaphors emerge organically from the landscape. From *Alvin Turner*: "The baby is solid as a tractor lug" (#11), "Her voice clean as mopped linoleum" (#12), "I love the boys like they were fanbelts" (#14), "Working my ears like a watchdog" (#16), "belly full as a tick" (#19), "Like a bull sideboarded for market" (#28), "Straight as a rakehandle" (#31), "Clapping like a congregation" (#35), "grinning like a gopher" (#47), "Clinging like cotton underwear" (#50), and "heavy as a sashweight" (#53). With maturity, Kloefkorn added humor: "no more teeth in it / Than Prohibition" (*Uncertain* 41), "smells like the inside of a new Chevy" (*loony* 19), "phony as a three-dollar bill" and "crooked as a dog's hind leg" (*Drinking* 28), "spicy as a sophomore kiss" (*Where* 35), "grinning like a gopher" (*Restoring* 69), "like a housefly hangs around honey" (*Time* 7), "drier, Carlos says, / than a popcorn fart" (*Carlos* 59), "Blue as the Dutchman's britches" (*Loup* 99), "clean as a Presbyterian's hands" (*This Death* 11), "narrow as a virgin," and "dry as a Presbyterian" (*Time* 5). Thus Kloefkorn's metaphors become, finally, a matter as much of voice as of meaning.

Moreover, Kloefkorn can fine-tune his voice as occasion demands to sound like a thirteen-year-old male, a twenty-year-old newlywed wife, a befuddled husband, or a middle-aged farmer:

. . . he honestly believes
that someone as lovely and as trim
as Wonder Woman would care

for such a slob, who has
acne, too, like him. (*Life* 14)

You dummy, Doris says,
you blind incorrigible fool!
When are you ever going
to grow beyond the confines
of your jackstraw world? (*Honeymoon* 9)

Jesus Christ, honey, I say,
I never said you couldn't, (*Honeymoon* 15)

I want a dozen pancakes,
Ma'am,
A ton of sausage,
Half a crate of eggs,
Some oatmeal and a loaf of toast. (*Alvin Turner* #11)

In the subtle modulations of voices, Kloefkorn is vaguely postmodernist: ironic, multivocalic, almost a language poet. In person, the poet speaks in the voices of his personae; personae speak the wisdom and the language of the poet . . . or the poet's younger selves, or, as I shall point out, of the poet's alter egos, his submerged dark side. Especially in the later work, and in letters and readings, personae and poet merge so that it is impossible to tell the dancer from the dance.

Focusing on the poet's midwestern voice redirects attention from place to the second point of Kloefkorn's base triangle, the Self. This Self can be either personal or communal, sometimes both at the same time. Russ Stratton, reviewing "The Poetry of William Kloefkorn," divides the books into "(1) the biographies, (2) the autobiographies, and (3) the remainder" (8). Throughout his career, Kloefkorn has written often and extensively not only about himself, but about his extended family and friends: in the dedication of *Uncertain the Final Run to Winter*, he suggests that his brother John "knows none of these poems / by rote, but many of them by heart." Occasional poems abound, especially love poems to Eloise, his children, and grandchildren. Kloefkorn's first book, *Alvin Turner as Farmer*, is based on the life of his paternal grandparents, and the words of Alvin Turner are "pretty much from my paternal grandfather, whose voice as I remember it was at once both firm and gentle. He had enormous respect for the land, for the pitiful quarter section on which he eked out his and his family's existence" (Letter). In *This Death by Drowning*, Kloefkorn describes the actual farm:

> He had farmed a more productive quarter section just north of my hometown, but lost that section for some reason or other and was forced to settle for whatever he could afford, which then was next to nothing. I am certain that the man he bought it from had given it up as a lost cause. Occupying a scraggly chunk of Chautauqua County southwest of Cedar Vale, this farm had precious little to recommend it—except perhaps its price. But my hard-working grandfather and my tight-lipped grandmother moved their mortal necessities into an unpainted cracker box on the side of a hill and began their lives as tillers of the soil all over again.
>
> Both house and outbuildings were equally run down—lopsided granary, chicken house with chicken-wire windows askew, an open-faced lodgepole barn, a ramshackle two-holer outhouse with a maverick osage orange sprawling above it, in season dropping its fruit dense as cannonade onto the shake-shingle roof. (39, 40)

The extent to which Kloefkorn's first book, *Alvin Turner as Farmer*, incorporates the life of his paternal grandparents can be gauged by comparing the poems with Kloefkorn's memoir, *This Death by Drowning*: from hill and rock and gumbo, Grandfather C. A. Kloefkorn, alias Alvin Turner, creates a home and a farm: he repairs buildings (*This Death* 39, *Alvin Turner* #19, #26), installs a complex system of downspouts leading to a cistern below the house (*This Death* 41–43, *Alvin Turner* #12, #17), excavates a pond with a horse-drawn scoop (*Death* 48–51, *Alvin Turner* #8, #55), picks rocks (*This Death* 51, *Alvin Turner* #1, #2, #35, #41, #60), plants the acreage in lespedeza (*This Death* 51, *Alvin Turner* #13), and sets about dairy farming (*This Death* 44, *Alvin Turner* #5, #29). With his wife Martha Anderson, Turner lives a life full of chores, church (*This Death* 53–55, *Alvin Turner* #28), children Robert and Andrew (*This Death* 49, *Alvin Turner* #14, #16, #37), birth and death (*Alvin Turner* #38, #40, #53, *Burning* 29–35), and perseverance:

> To say *There is always the rock*
> Is not to forfeit the harvest.
> Below, beside each hard place
> Lies the Land. (*Alvin Turner* #60)

Many poems in *Cottonwood County* (1979) recreate episodes from Kloefkorn's childhood, like his grandmother cheating at Parcheesi (4) or Doris Higgenbottom's death from epilepsy (14). *Houses and Beyond* (1982) chronicles Kloefkorn family history during the 1930s, starting with life on the farm: "the First House" (1), the milk cow killed by bottle flies (3, 4), "the Next House" (5), Bill burning down the outhouse (6), the third house (11), Janet living with the grandparents (18, 29), life with brother John (9, 19, 21, 22, 31, 49), Bill's near-drowning experience (26, 54), mother's work at the R & K Cafe (51), and father's floating kidney (51). The poems describe battles between brothers, punishment for swearing, farm and household chores, practice for the eighth-grade spelling bee, and a pet run over by a dumptruck.

Kloefkorn's paper route, high school sporting events, World War II, and various buddies and romances are recreated in the first two sections of *Collecting for the Wichita Beacon*, in which Kloefkorn describes a dozen small-town characters and Aunt Flora and Uncle Glen (17), Grandmother Moulton (23), and Uncle Elmer, Aunt Vivian, and their gift of a souvenir pocket knife from Niagara Falls (11).

In *A Life Like Mine* (1984), obviously autobiographical, Kloefkorn resurrects in poetry his mother's onion soup cure for bronchitis, the daily Depression ritual of carrying a bottle of milk to Janet, an automobile breakdown on a Christmas trip, walking the paper route when his bicycle tire went flat, building model airplanes, riding freight trains, shooting snooker with John, taking piano lessons, hypnotizing a chicken at his grandmother's farm, working in a gas station with his father, and watching a friend steal a comic book:

I see Bubba Barnes
sneak a comic book
from the rack in
the Rexall drug-
store and the next
day at recess
I tell him. He
says Prove it. ("Prove It," *Life* 20)

Kloefkorn's fictional companion Carlos appears in two poems in this collection.

Where the Visible Sun Is and *Drinking the Tin Cup Dry*, both 1989, retrace familiar territory—father's floating kidney and missing fingers,

Bill's paper route, Aunt Vivian and Uncle Elmer, the Nebraska Sand Hills, and Kansas's Sand Creek—but add Kloefkorn's marital problems and a series of adolescent sexual experiences, actual or imagined. *Dragging Sand Creek for Minnows* (1992) returns to Carlos and old man Fenton, the father's kidney, the R & K Cafe, the lespedeza on grandpa's farm, high school football, and the occurrence at Ely's Sandpit. Kloefkorn adds wonderful stories of a youthful get-rich-quick scheme of breeding and selling rabbits, of nearly burning the house down while playing with kitchen matches, and of pitching hen eggs against the barn door.

Going Out, Coming Back (1993) elaborates on the paper route deliveries, describing as well the hometown softball and professional baseball games of his youth (especially the Dodger-Yankee battles), Janet's homemade dress ("not much fancier than a feed sack," 19), and staking out the cow at age ten. Two recent collections of poetry—*Welcome to Carlos* (2000) and *Loup River Psalter* (2001)—return to Attica, Kansas, and the Loup River in Nebraska, with references to Sand Creek, Simpson's Pond, Doc and Josephine's Rexall Drugs, the Rialto Theater, AT&SF, Urie's Barber Shop, sister's stint at grandma's, grandpa's lespedeza and cistern, young William's accident at Harold Simpson's cow pasture pond, and the on-river adventures of the brothers Kloefkorn.

An early series titled "Special Problems" was based on the poet's Marine Corps experience. It was discontinued because Kloefkorn felt his experience was incomplete ("It was a matter of not having enough foundation there to sustain that series"), and published only in 1994, in *Burning the Hymnal: The Uncollected Poems of William Kloefkorn* (16–21). In that same book, Kloefkorn describes another series, *Important Phone Numbers*, abandoned because "I [didn't] think I was relying enough on my own experience" (24).

Kloefkorn's memoirs *This Death by Drowning* and *Restoring the Burnt Child* usually verify the names and stories in the poems, but sometimes research suggests caution: "The father in this poem ["Plowing"] was actually my best friend's father when I was growing up," Kloefkorn told Genoways (*Burning* 66). Younger brother John became "my older brother" in "Saying It Once Again" (*Covenants* 20), and he appeared as Franklin in the poems of *Houses and Beyond*. The floating kidney is assigned to Kloefkorn's uncle in the poem "1943" (*Treehouse* 146). "Most of the people in my books are semi-real," he writes in a letter of July 21, 2001; "I have a character in mind, an actual figure, but the figure becomes changed as the writing moves along—sometimes only a little, sometimes drastically" (9). Kloefkorn has also mentioned "a couple of old telephone books" he keeps handy. "Hearsay and fabrication," Kloefkorn writes in *This Death by Drowning*; "what I don't remember I attribute to someone else, and when that fails I fabricate" (1). So we will never really know if it was indeed Zelma Lee Crenshaw who "was the only one / to go all the way" at young Kloefkorn's first homemade peepshow (*Uncertain* 4), or whether it was somebody else, or whether the peepshow was one of Mark Twain's "stretchers." Likewise we will never know if the townsfolk named as Billy's customers in *Collecting for the Wichita Beacon* were in fact Billy's customers of 1945, or how the game against Kiowa was won.

Ultimately the point is moot, because in a Kloefkorn poem personal experience is usually only expanded to communal experience: athletics, farm chores, fishing and hunting, swimming and boating, repairing old cars and cruising the town, smoking Folgers coffee, tipping over outhouses on Halloween, and flushing firecrackers down the toilet in the Baptist church. As Kloefkorn noted in a talk given at South Dakota State University on March 14, 2001, "When a writer fails to write about where we've all been, then he is writing a private poem." Kloefkorn is a private poet, but his details of geography and voice make him a public poet. In addition to recounting family history, his books form a communal history of the Midwest, beginning with exploration (*Sergeant Patrick Gass, Chief Carpenter: On the Trail with Lewis and Clark*), through settlement (*Platte Valley Homestead*) to the Great Depression (*Alvin Turner as Farmer*), World War II and the fifties (*Houses and Beyond; Collecting for the Wichita Beacon; Going Out, Coming Back*), and into the present (*Loup River Psalter*). Tom Montag makes this point in an early review of *Alvin Turner*:

> And yet, for all this, reading and re-reading *Alvin Turner as Farmer*, I see life and truth for our own age suggested by another time and place, I see the figures of my own grandfather and great uncles silhouetted against the rolling horizon, I see half-dreams and memories of my own: if Kloefkorn has not lived as Alvin Turner, his grandfather did, and my grandfather, and countless other men who have struggled against "the rock," who have juggled the price of hogs and the cost of corn, who have buried a wife and daughter in the land they loved, and who have been buried there themselves. The world that comes through *Alvin Turner as Farmer* may not be Kloefkorn's

personally, but it is still somehow his, and mine, and our fathers' and uncles' and brothers.' (60)

In fact, some of Kloefkorn's material comes not from family history but from imagination based on research. Kloefkorn's *Sergeant Patrick Gass, Chief Carpenter: On the Trail with Lewis and Clark* (2002) is based entirely on research into the journals of the person to whom Kloefkorn gives voice; the poems in this collection are a complex interweaving of public history and bifocal private vision. Here is another example of research incorporated into *Platte Valley Homestead*:

> April, and at the edge of the lower forty
> the falling river leaves what looks to be
> the tailgate from an ancient wagon,
> and I tell Anna how it must have escaped
> the cholera of eighteen-fifty,
> four people dead to every mile
> of river roadway traveled.
> Wood so precious the pioneers
> broke down their wagons
> for the building of coffins,
> the tailgate first to go,
> the last of all their rolling cares,
> the most expendable. (23)

In this book, a kind of 1880s antecedent to *Alvin Turner as Farmer*, pioneers Anna (loosely Kloefkorn's maternal grandmother) and Jacob (more loosely her brother) shape their land, give birth to (and in two cases bury) their children, survive flood and fire, plant their crops, and raise their livestock. They are archetypical Midwest farmers surviving the hardships that confronted both Kloefkorn's grandparents and all Great Plains settlers. The list in Kloefkorn's memoir *This Death by Drowning*—"locust, typhoid, kangaroo rate, grasshopper, cholera, smallpox, tick, blizzard, colic, distemper"—is not much different from the list in *Platte Valley Homestead* poem 33: "Locusts. Typhoid. Bottlejaw . . . Grasshoppers. Cholera. Smallpox . . . Blizzards. Cholic. Distemper." This list is communal history. Jacob's major problem is water—alternating flood and drought—as Alvin Turner's major problem is rocks. As personal as water and rock obviously are, and as symbolic,[7] they are also facts of Great Plains history like the quarrying of ice in the days before electricity:

> Because twelve weeks ago
> the river was moved away
> in blocks of ice
> to cool the produce
> in the boxcars of the Burlington.
> William worked for a time
> for wages then,
> one day bringing home a polygon of ice
> with a carp frozen
> squarely at the center. (56)

As the nineteenth century melts into the twentieth, the Kloefkorn family history becomes Great Plains family history in the experience of farm crises, Depression, World War II, social and religious experiences, stages of growth, and customs of courtship. Kloefkorn's grandfather's experience was the Depression quotidian: "debt and depression / and a bumper wheat harvest / lost in a maelstrom of greed / and deceit" (*Fielding* 4). In many places Kloefkorn goes out of his way to universalize what might otherwise have been a particularized and personal experience. Alvin Turner, for example, inherits at age thirty his hard-scrabble farm from a dying father (*Alvin Turner* 7, 21, 24) rather than moving to it after losing a better section, as did Kloefkorn's dad. Kloefkorn brings the outside world, in the form of a political or historical event, into a personal memory. The events of World War II often function in this capacity, especially Hiroshima, and especially in the poems of *Collecting for the Wichita Beacon*, where the juxtaposition of larger and smaller worlds creates a contrast between innocence and experience:

> Grandmother Moulton heavy against a crutch
> receives her copy of the paper
> as if a blessing, her lips
> thanking God incessantly
> for most everything—for
> her grandson John's diving, not jumping,
> into that crater at Omaha Beach,
> burst of bullets shattering

only the right ankle,
for the end of the war by whatever means,
and I am not halfway around the route
before Hiroshima becomes a word
I was born with never to understand. (23)

Honeymoon, which looks backward to courtship and forward to married life from the perspective of Doris and Howard's honeymoon at Niagara Falls, seems very much a paradigm: making out at "Put Out Point," milking cows, begetting and birthing children, planting a garden, snapping beans, taking a beer out of the refrigerator, or emptying a dishwasher. The Protestant-Catholic animosities and the Protestant denominational squabblings described by Kloefkorn are public history in the Midwest, and Alvin Turner's on-going battles against rabbits and rocks, drought and low hog prices and the interminable wind are communal farm experiences. Kloefkorn's oft-mentioned antipathy for the New York Yankees, and affection for the Brooklyn Dodgers, were shared American values in the 1950s, and remain so today.

And sometimes Kloefkorn writes outside of his own history, in the first person of experiences that belong not to his youth but to some kind of Great Plains everyman:

Later I'll blame it on the low August sun,
say, God Almighty it fried my sunflower brain,

but at the moment, chasing this young cottontail
slow-motion across a quarter-section of topsoil

soft as a featherbed, I want more than anything
to prove my boyhood, to see this animal hanging

upside down, my fingers pulling its warm pelt
downward from hind leg to belly to throat,

but heaven help us all I have to catch it first (*Going Out* 41)

"Life in a prairie town breeds its own sorts of characters," observed Mark Barnett in reviewing *Welcome to Carlos*; "The hopes, the fears, the rhythms and contours of our places mark us and make us who we are" (4D). The teachers and clergymen and shopkeepers and eccentrics who fill his books are Great Plains small-town types, what Laura Rotunno calls "a rich array of land-sown characters" (15). Tom Hansen argues that in readings Kloefkorn himself represents one such character, a persona, "a slightly larger-than-life small-town 'character,' as if he were one of those quirky but likable people that he has so often written about" ("Kloefkorn's 'Easter Sunday'" 159). Especially in *Uncertain the Final Run to Winter*, although also in *Collecting for the Wichita Beacon* and some poems of *Not Such a Bad Place to Be*, Kloefkorn appears to toy with the idea of creating a whole fictional village along the lines of Etter's *Alliance, Illinois* or Masters's *Spoon River Anthology*, a village with the complete midwestern range of midwestern experiences and attitudes: Fannie Young, Cory Batt, Old Man Kinzer, Ruby Shoemaker, Shorty Cleveland, Mabel Cleveland, Fuzzy and Josephine Bauman, Mutt Moody, Roper Joe Endbody, cheerleader Tootsie Slocum, beer-drinking Floyd Fenton, indecisive Elsie Martin, brain-dead Ruby, railroad foreman Rhodes, mechanic W. P. Hanson, banker's daughter Mavis Cunningham, R. K. Bonham talking aloud to the near end of a hoe handle, Russell Calvert driving out of his way to run over animals, and Mrs. Wilma Hunt, "twisted one notch too tight" (*Uncertain* 41).[8]

To the cycles of family and Great Plains history may be added another series of Kloefkorn poems, and another series of Kloefkorn books — those exploring alter-egos personal and collective: *loony, ludi jr, Stocker*, and *Welcome to Carlos*. "I just try to explore as many sides of myself as I can," Kloefkorn told J. V. Brummels in 1983 (30), but these collections constitute a systematic, focused exploration of a dark-side alter ego. The poet posits a yin to every yang, a shadow to every sunbeam, a wrong side of the tracks to every right side of the tracks, a reptilian corner of the brain to every God-fearing Baptist and Pentecostal. In the last lines of the opening poem of *Alvin Turner* Kloefkorn mentions "That part which I cannot see," the part that is omnipresent although covered up, the part that even when ignored "threatens to reduce him" (1). In *Dragging Sand Creek for Minnows* it is a "lizard brain," singing its river hymn in the night:

Say that for a few moments
the brain reverts to become the lizard's,
and belly slick against the wet late-night grass
I hear the wind in the cottonwoods
singing an old hymn. (29)

In "That Voice from a Brain Evolved to Dream," dedicated to Loren Eiseley, Kloefkorn has himself and his brother crawling on their bellies down the slope of a tunnel into a hand-dug cave, into "Earth, dark earth," reverting to croak and claw (*Houses* 35). A similar descent into darkness, possibly spun from the same childhood experience, is described in "Returning to Caves":

It is the only way to repair,
to get things done:
to crawl like a child
from what seems almost certain
to what is dark and moist,
quiet and enclosed and unknown. (*Not Such* 53).

This shadow self—associated with sexuality, crime, drink, "the body's / myriad hungers" (*Covenants* 15)—has its own seductive wisdom, usually the inverse of orthodox Christianity. At the very least, "Going somewhere forbidden to do something terrifying has a charm that defies total explanation" (*This Death* 29).

Like Sherwood Anderson and Dave Etter, William Kloefkorn offers glimpses of the dark side of small-town life in poems suggesting, for example, his parents' quarrels (*Drinking* 6, 13), Urie's alcoholism (*Sunrise* 69), and small-town crimes like pinching comic books, shooting swallows in the haymow, or peeping at naked girls. This dark-side behavior also appears in short stories, including Kloefkorn's tale of a little girl who wants a talking moose for Christmas and, when the vocabulary of the moose Santa delivers is too limited, throws a little girl snit and kicks him "on the place where he had been sitting." "I didn't like that little girl very much anyway," Santa decides; "Too spooky. And when she sends me a letter asking for something else, I am going to throw it away" (*Coldest Christmas* 41). In the first story of *A Time to Sink Her Pretty Little Ship*, Velma Cleveland is murdered and raped "in that order" (11) by one of the local adolescents who has never been quite right in the head; in the second story an elderly Mr. Gunderson is arrested for pissing in public ("third violation this week"—19); in the third story a clearly demented Cora Hill "baptizes" the shirt of her dying husband Clarence, who refuses to come to the Lord on his own, intending to wrap his body in the shirt of salvation and maybe sneak him into heaven via the side door. The book's title story describes small-town suspicion of German-Americans during World War II. Upset over the 1943 combat death of a hometown hero he clearly admired just a little too much, adolescent Kevin Anderson plots his revenge, deciding finally "not to murder Anna Koeppen, but, instead, to firebomb her garage. A Molotov cocktail. John Wayne rising from a slit trench with the pin of a grenade clenched in his teeth" (53). Which is just what Kevin does, to his own satisfaction.

Four times Kloefkorn has expanded this dark-side alter ego into a fully developed character. In the case of college professor and Nebraska State Poet William Kloefkorn, the "Animal at the Far Edge of My Mind" (*Not Such* 66) is, variously, an autistic savant (*loony*), a hormonal adolescent (*ludi jr*), an overgrown small-town knownothing (*Stocker*) and, most recently and most successfully, the son of a Mexican railroad worker (*Welcome to Carlos*). *Stocker* (1978) never grew larger than a chapbook, but the other three expanded into perfect bound books. *Loony* (1975)—who shares with his creator an affinity for the Brooklyn Dodgers (37), pinball at the Rexall Drugstore (7), and even a drowning experience (6, 42)—is a village idiot who allows Kloefkorn to reduce to their purest essences the experiences of seeing, feeling, and tasting, and who therefore "knows what he knows" (8). What he knows is a mini-*Alliance* of small-town dark-side behavior: theft, bootlegging, drunkenness, window-peeping (and window-performing), shoplifting, pyromania, automobile wrecks, lust, sadism, sodomy, and the old Catholic-Protestant animosities. "The blackness keeps on coming," loony observes, "sometimes even when the sun / is like an unspent coin / atop the bank building" (32). Kloefkorn's language is not exactly small-town Protestant church or 1970s college classroom: "shitfire" (37), "bigwig fisheater" (48), "dipstick" (61). Most interesting, however, in this early attempt at describing the Other is that some of the names (Urie, Thelma Hunt, Shorty Coleman) appear in other Kloefkorn books, so that loony lives among us. Further, Kloefkorn states, loony is "all of us, it seems, / full of wrath and worms and vinegar, / all slightly disconnected in the head / and needing mercy" (29).

Even more than loony, ludi jr (1976) is every one of us—or more precisely, every adolescent male. In *ludi jr* Kloefkorn extends his range of wordplay, suggests even more clearly than in previous poems sex as valid form of salvation, and introduces the street wisdom that will mark Carlos. Like loony, ludi jr and his creator have a lot in common, noticeably place locators, an underwater adventure, a paper route, skill at hypnotizing chickens, and a working familiarity with T. S. Eliot, William

Shakespeare, and the Pentecostal religious tradition. Like loony, ludi is a primitive: his mind is filled with "the mating of worms / the call of the coyote / the pecking of small birds" (1). The fatherly advice which he assiduously ignores suggests that ludi has dabbled in certain behaviors not acceptable to the Pentecostal church or the affirmative action officer:

do not shoot the rabbit
through either its good eye
or the one that most offends you

do not sit too easily
in the lap of you
know who I mean

return the air freshener
the comicbooks the lifesavers
to the drugstore

remember one of the following:
father mother

do not neglect
the days of the calendar

that bar of soap
you carved the other night:
shred it like ripe cabbage
into the throat of the drain

do not want the words
that the unkind give you

do not tell betty jean's mother
what under betty jean's underwear
is growing

remember this trinity
to keep it holy:
blood is sour

and verily verily
when the dark asks you
say *no.* ("ludi jr sits quietly through the passing along of his father's
advice" 17)

From window-peeping in the dark ludi has fashioned a wisdom of his own: "no matter what my father said / blood for blood / is sweetest" (22). To kill, skin, roast, and eat the beautiful flesh of the world's greatest catfish is "in this scheme of things / the only way to reign: / to be the very last / and thus the highest / of the world's greatest catfish / fishermen" (6). The mind of ludi jr spins with those impossible, ridiculous, and often dark imaginings of all teenage boys: "with his spyglass ludi jr discovers cindy kohlman" (25), "ludi jr bounces his basketball on an anthill in a crack in the sidewalk inflicting heavy casualties" (29), "ludi jr walks barefoot through a stickerpatch without saying ouch" (40), "ludi jr kills one cow, seven frogs, and fourteen toads to make a fur piece to adorn the shoulders of his lady fair" (73), "ludi jr turns cartwheels and backflips from one end of the gymnasium to the other" and as he does,

in his nose the aromatic mist of
floor polish and sawdust

sweat flickering from his forehead and chin
like water off a saltlick

and all the time the chosen one
not missing a single beat

hell you know he's plenty good
you can tell it in the way
the muscles at his back
and on his legs
are bunching. (51)

"Who is that unmasked feller not on a white horse not riding away into the sunset? why that's ludi jr, buster, hanging around to claim his fair share of the reward" (82). Ludi is "a young fellow trying to tell the truth," Kloefkorn claims; "Thus he is roughly the first half of ludicrous" (Burning 38).

Ludi is also well on his way to becoming Carlos in Welcome to Carlos (2000). Carlos, Kloefkorn claims, is modeled largely on a childhood chum, Nick Mora, four years older than the poet, with elements of Jess Charles, Jack Giggy, and Carter Leroy Hays (Letter). In this book Kloefkorn's narrator, though not wealthy, lives on the respectable side of town; Carlos, whose father is a gandydancer for the railroad and whose mother takes in laundry, comes from south of the tracks. "The character of

Carlos emerges in these poems as both comrade and foil to Kloefkorn's persona," observes Ted Genoways (*Burning* 75). Carlos is Kloefkorn's shadow side, the Other to whom Kloefkorn over long seasons has "confided . . . almost everything" (*Welcome* 49).

Carlos attends the Baptist church, but only so he can watch the Anglos make fools of themselves. In a secret night-time ritual, Carlos and the narrator burn the hymnal, page by page, singing hymns as they go. Carlos's true church is the Church of the International Pick-up Truck, which he keeps running with a trinity of his own: screwdriver, pliers, box-end wrench. He shoots pool and plays pinball, carries a Trojan in his billfold right next to the photo of Betty Grable, sneaks into movies without paying, drinks wine, steals melons, smokes Folgers coffee, requites verbal assaults with physical blows, shoots homemade arrows at mourning doves, and douses owls with gasoline before setting them afire. He chooses "the overgrown path, / the alley, the less-traveled road" (65). In an adventure out of Kloefkorn's youth (*This Death* 127–29, where it is attributed to Carter Hays), Carlos sneaks into the basement of the Baptist church and flushes a lighted firecracker down the toilet. By his own admission unloved by the Lord, Carlos goes to the tent revival with the express purpose of not being saved. Carlos is, in the book's final poem, "the bad penny," which represents "whatever the body does / when it's not deceiving" (81). He is, in other words, the narrator's flip side.

But Carlos, "self-taught to read between the / lines" (2), is "more honest than / the night is long" (49). He preaches a worldly gospel, a kind of anti-doctrine, or the doctrine contained in those interesting parts of the Bible that don't get read much in church:

Believe, Carlos says, what you believe
  late at night when what
  you have been told to believe
  has washed itself from the soft skin
  of your stoutest face. (79)

This code of dark truth, which links Carlos to ludi jr and loony before him, advises self-protection, self-preservation, and self-advancement. "I don't want to die, Carlos says, / on the tracks that day by day my father / dies on" (18). Sin is "whatever the body has to do / to keep itself sufficiently / aroused" (15). Sex without love is just "wading with your socks on" (45). To err is "that which / constitutes Divine" (72). And always, "Deny everything. / Make the bastards prove it" (22).

Carlos's theology reflects Kloefkorn's theology. In *This Death by Drowning*, he identifies the religious affiliation he long ago dropped as "[m]iddle Protestant. . . . It began as United Brethren, then became Evangelical United Brethren, then was absorbed lock stock and barrel by the Methodists" (68). This heritage came mainly from his paternal grandmother who belonged "to an order that believed in not believing: she did not believe in dancing, in drinking, in swearing, or in wearing makeup—nor did she believe in practicing any of these, or any of a hundred other human indulgences, even in moderation" (*This Death* 53). She did believe in a bountiful dinner table, familial love, an occasional reward in the form of a silver dollar, and the Word of God. The price of enjoying the first three was studying the third, and becoming conversant in the great gospel songs (many involving rocks and water) which appear quoted, paraphrased, or as epigraphs in many Kloefkorn poems: "Shall We Gather at the River?" "Jesus Is the Rock in a Weary Land," "Are You Washed in the Blood of the Lamb?" "Down Deep in the Sea." Kloefkorn claims to have memorized most of Ecclesiastes, and knows enough of the Old and New Testaments to quote or paraphrase both in countless poems.

As a teenager he explored the more interesting portions of the Old Testament, including Second Kings ("I will cut off from Ahab him that pisseth against the wall") and Deuteronomy ("He that is wounded in the stones, or hath his privy member cut off, shall not enter into the congregation of the Lord"). In *Restoring the Burnt Child* and in several poems Kloefkorn describes at length the tent revivals of his early adolescence: the singing, the preaching, the performances, the words. For a time, he recalls, "I was hooked on Sister Hook" (*Restoring* 31). Young Kloefkorn, faced with his mother's home-boiled onion syrup for croup, can pray, "dear God / take this cup from me" (*Life* 1). An older Kloefkorn can testify in the voice of a revivalist preacher, although more to the church of baseball than to the church of Christ: "Yes, I was very much a Dodger fan—because Urie the barber was a Dodger fan, and it was Urie who claimed that in the beginning God created first the National League, then the Dodgers. Created Pistol Pete Reiser. Roy Campanella. Gil Hodges. Jackie Robinson. Pee Wee Reese. Created he them. Yes, and created Ralph Branca, too; and just because he lost the game to the Forces of Evil does not mean that come Armageddon the Forces of Evil shall prevail. Not by a long goddam shot" (Letter). Old habits are difficult to break, and in a poem titled "Prayer" Kloefkorn admits "Much of the time / when I'm not belittling prayer / I'm praying" (*Fielding* 77). The poem "Grandmother Comes Back from the Grave to Tell Me Not to Forget to Go to Sunday School" concludes,

> O God of Rote and Ritual,
> get thee behind me!
> And you who move now
> at the center of this world
> I move in,
> grant me the strength to break,
> and break again,
> all dear and soulless vows
> that must be broken! (*Let the Dance* 8)

But Kloefkorn is no mainline Midwest Christian, or even a Midwest Christian socialist like Vachel Lindsay. The revivals were performances; remembering the theology, Kloefkorn recalls mostly "its horrors, its / elusive promises, its utmost threats" (*Fielding* 85). Like Carlos, he disapproves of a religion in which damnation is "more awful, more visible, than mercy" (*Collecting* 19). He dislikes sermons that present easy solutions to complex dilemmas. In his poems, young Kloefkorn frequently mock-baptizes a pet or a friend or a girlfriend. In his metaphors and adapted idioms, Kloefkorn deliberately conjoins the sacred and the profane. Kloefkorn as Alvin Turner sometimes dozes off during the sermon, and in *Honeymoon* #8 Howard informs his young bride that "she believes too stoutly in God." The poem "Sacramental Meditation #6" begins, "The text for today / is neither Genesis nor Revelation / But is instead Demure, / Embodied by the third girl (from / The right) on the front row" (*Burning* 22). Ted Genoways argues that while Kloefkorn can be a poet of "conventional religious thought [arranged] in an unconventional way" (*Burning* 22), he is a poet of the sacred body as well as the immortal soul. "In the Old Bible Bookstore," he happens upon "a young couple / kissing, one of his hands / deep into her blouse, one of hers / kneading a lump / beyond an unzipped zipper" (*Where* 66). Tom Hansen calls Kloefkorn "a mystagogue":

> Though presented in comfortable, down-home terms, the radical nature of Kloefkorn's religious stance in this poem ["Riding My

Bicycle without Hands Down Huntington Street"] is by now evident. As Joseph Campbell explains in *Creative Mythology*, in Christianity as in Judaism and Islam, the link between the human and the divine is one of relationship. One must achieve and maintain a proper relationship with God—as both "God" and "proper" are defined by the particular sect whose authority one accepts. In contrast, the oriental and Neoplatonic concept noumenal reality beyond all perception [sic] is such that the link between creation and creator is essentially one of identity. Divinity, no longer relegated to a transcendent never-neverland, is experienced as being immanent, indwelling within every natural object. ("Kloefkorn's 'Easter Sunday'" 160)

So Kloefkorn, although not a mainline Christian and certainly one acquainted with the night, is affirmative in the broadest context. His affirmation is based on his acceptance of both ends of those lines which stretch from backyard swings in Attica to the moon in the heavens, from the cave of the lizard to the Baptist church.

His affirmation is based on knowledge of another line as well, the line that connects time present and time past. Time is really Kloefkorn's major theme, and has been for most of his career. The agrarian idyll of interdependent small towns and farms is irretrievably lost for Kloefkorn, as for Etter and the other writers discussed in this book, and for all of us in the Midwest, in America. Although all of these writers depict rural life in harsh, realistic terms, the loss is huge, although not exactly news these days. In reviewing Mark Sanders's *The Plains Sense of Things 2: Eight Poets from Lincoln, Nebraska* (1977), Bruce Nelson writes,

These poets mainly come from small towns to which they cannot return. They stay in Lincoln as reluctant captives only because they have nowhere else to go. The Nebraska of their collective childhood is gone. Though he is a Kansas native, Nebraska State Poet William Kloefkorn perhaps said it best in "Leaving the Home Place:"

[G]oodbye, hello, come back, don't
for Jesus

    Christ's sake ever
      leave me;

you are the only one on earth who
understands. (21)

However, in the warp of time/space, Kloefkorn finds the redemption of Sanders's "suffering-loss-redemption archetype" (21). For an epigraph to *Drinking the Tin Cup Dry*, Kloefkorn selected a line from Faulkner, which he has quoted on other occasions: "The past is not dead. It is not even past." In *Restoring the Burnt Child*, Kloefkorn writes, "I'll say it again: Chronology has at best a habit of collapsing, of becoming quickly smaller, like the leaky bellows of the old red-and-black accordion as my grandfather squeezed it—or at worst frankly not giving a damn" (153). In the poetry, this is most certainly true. "A sort of lyrical eternity recurs throughout the book," wrote Mark Sanders in a review of *Going Out, Coming Back* (115). Many collections and several individual poems slip easily between past and present. Especially in his second book of prose memoirs, *Restoring the Burnt Child*, Kloefkorn jumpcuts in prose, in a manner that reflects *Beowulf* and anticipates Linda Hasselstrom's memoir *Feels Like Far*:

> We were all of us in the living room. . . . A duofold rested along the west wall; commodious and covered with well-worn leather, it would be the bed my grandmother would die on, refusing all forms of medication insofar as she had the strength. Grandfather would sleep on a pallet of quilts on the floor beside her. He would be thankful that she died in her sleep.
>
> But at the moment she was sitting in her own rocker not far from the doorway to the kitchen. (120)

The poems of collections that trace a personal or communal history—*Alvin Turner as Farmer* or *Honeymoon*—are often in chronological disarray, so that in our end is our beginning, and our end comes even before our beginning. In *Honeymoon*, Howard and Doris name and raise their children even before they're conceived. In "By Lamplight," one of his more surreal poems, Kloefkorn becomes his grandfather, making love to his grandmother, testing her breasts "by touch and by taste" (*Covenants* 47). Memory, and something beyond memory, annihilate time: revisiting the R & K Cafe, now a library, Kloefkorn reads a book of poems at about the place where the pinball machine used to stand:

It's

funny isn't it

how those blinking lights can't stop
blinking, how the salt

> from that first
>
> kiss keeps on working. ("Back Then," *Covenants* 8)

"Writing poetry," Kloefkorn concludes, "is chiefly the process of connecting and interconnecting moments both real and imagined" (Letter).
Probably this interconnectedness is the reason many of Kloefkorn's
books read as unified collections, one poem melting into the next, until
a hundred pages of eighty poems become one long page of one long
poem.

The river is a traditional metaphor for time thus conceived. Water is
"the tactile touchstone by which I measure all degrees of submersion,"
Kloefkorn writes in *This Death by Drowning* (6), "and I respect this touchstone as [Matthew] Arnold respected a glorious handful of lines from the
masters." Water, argues Mark Sanders in an essay on Kloefkorn's use of
symbols, carries associations of life's passing, of strange and terrible
death, and of purification ("Rocks, Water, and Fire" 21). Kloefkorn himself identifies water as a counter-symbol to the rock:

> The river, you see, is the Biblical flip-side of the rock. I grew up
> singing hymns loaded with rock and water metaphor, so, having
> toyed with the rock in *Alvin Turner*, I sooner or later had to give equal
> time to water. There are many other differences, but this is a funda-
> mental one. Alvin Turner learns to live with the rock, to plow around
> it rather than through it; the narrator of *Platte Valley Homestead*
> learns that water can purify as well as destroy. (Brummels 32)

"One of my favorite [hymns]," Kloefkorn writes, is "'Down Deep in the
Sea': 'My sins have been cast in the depths of the sea, / Down deep in
the sea. / So deep they can never be brought against me, / Down deep
in the sea'" (*This Death* 75). Later in *This Death by Drowning*, Kloefkorn
refers to "the on-going lotus of the river" (105). This is a remarkable passage, really, for Kloefkorn conjoins the Pawnee creation myth, his granddaughter, his grandmother, stones, and water into a pattern of loss into
water and recovery from water. Awakening from her nap in a sleeping
bag, Kloefkorn's granddaughter Michelle "emerges as if from a soft co-
coon," and sets about a child's game of "assembling and dissembling,
gathering and yielding, collecting and giving away." First she makes a
small mound of carefully selected stones, "a cairn," which she then
throws, one rock at a time, into the river. Pausing for a few sips of Country Time lemonade, she then wades into the shallow river to retrieve those

rocks, studying each one carefully "to determine if it is in fact one of those that she had thrown—one she had gathered and stacked and designated as family—or an outsider wanting to weasel its way in." Back on shore she dries and names each rock, allowing them in her child's imagination to move and play and grow old, at which point she gathers them again into a heap and "returns them back to the on-going lotus of the river" (105).

This pattern of regeneration by water appears frequently in Kloefkorn's work. On a very simple and non-symbolic level, water heals, and Kloefkorn would concur with Jim Harrison, that other devotee of western Nebraska rivers, when he told Eleanor Wachtel in a 1998 interview, "if you're willing to say try it sometime, sit down on a stone or a cushion or just on the bank of a river for two solid hours. And you find, if you're willing to give up everything, or open up a bit, the river does absorb rather nonchalantly your poisons" (DeMott 180). For all the problems it posed in, say, *Platte Valley Homestead*, the river is ultimately benign: in "Benediction," a poem which opens *Let the Dance Begin*, river redeems owlcall and darkness:

> Somewhere deep in the grove of cottonwoods
> an owl with its dark split tongue
> pronounces an end to day,
> and the river,
> that great brown hussy, that gadabout,
> moves on,
> its motion its wisdom,
> its wayward parts at last becoming one,
> its crooked path as seen from the proper height
> the soft deflections of a tireless line. (5)

Loup River Psalter, not surprisingly, references Loren Eiseley's *The Immense Journey*, Kent Meyers's *The River Warren*, and Norman MacLean's *A River Runs through It* in making a nearly biblical case for the magic and mystery of rivers. Its final poem uses the river as a summary image of redemption through the warp of space-time:

> He rises
> to stand watching
> cold water rise
> to flow out of its
> trough and out

of the spring house
to lose itself
in a clean and
relentless stream.
And so it goes:
our story's never done. (101)

For Kloefkorn, as for Faulkner and Eliot, all place is eternally present, and the past isn't really past. It hasn't even happened yet.

A Kloefkorn poem, then, is likely to scale whatever metaphysical heights it achieves from particulars of Place, Self, and Other. In this respect, "Summer in Southcentral Kansas" is typical:

Saltshaker in hand
I climb the greenest tree
in old man Fenton's orchard.
Lost in a darkening of leaves
I sink the keen edge of my Barlow
into an apple tart as anybody's flesh.

*

Mother meanwhile flips a mean flapjack
on the grill of the R & K Cafe,
where sooner or later the bulk of the town
will treat itself to something special—
a wedge of pie, apple maybe,
mouths active with hearsay
flaky and sweet.

*

Cricket and cottonwood and
cicada,
until at last the grownups
retire,
my girl and I then swinging on the porch,
her long hair flowing dark as a moonless branch,
my hand on its own reaching out to touch
what the thief for all his reptilian nerve
can't bring his curious heart
to steal away. (*Dragging* 8)

This complex and tightly knit poem reaches, literally and figuratively, both below and above. It begins with autobiography: the theft of an apple from Old Man Fenton's orchard, the ubiquitous Barlow knife, the R & K Cafe, Kloefkorn, and his girlfriend. It localizes itself in the communal experiences of small town life (gossip at the cafe, smooching on the porch swing), in the markers of Midwest landscape (cricket, cottonwood, cicada), and in markers of language ("flips a mean flapjack," "treat itself to something special"). It extends to myth in the biblical allusions associated with the apple and the snake, and in the universal experience of entanglement in something dark and mysterious (in a tree, in hair, in a sexual encounter) while reaching (climbing, swinging) toward something higher. Behind the balances between orchard and town, nature and society, individual and community, young and old, Kloefkorn suggests the balance between innocence and a dark, reptilian experience ("sink the keen edge of my Barlow/into an apple tart as anybody's flesh"). So situated, the poet offers a profound and somewhat startling insight: we reach out instinctively for something we dare not take, which is itself both a blessing and a curse.

Norbert Blei

Portrait of the Artist as an Outsider

*Knowing that as long as I consider myself a writer, I am
doomed to live a life separate and apart, somewhere halfway
between home.*
—*Norbert Blei*, Door Way

*A mission of one. The single, solitary writer who happens to
find himself with no history of his own to speak of . . . no
family, no traditions, no ancestral name on the plat map to
call the land my own.*
—*Norbert Blei*, Door to Door

I wanted to be a loser from the beginning, you see.
—*Norbert Blei*, The Second Novel

Norbert Blei—"the conscience of Door County, Wisconsin" (*Meditations* 37)—was born in a Bohemian American enclave of Chicago, at 26th and Pulaski, "The Little Village," where "Czech women on Sundays wore beautiful Old World costumes as they waltzed and danced the polka to the music of buttonbox concertinas. The men drank beer, told stories, and played pinochle in the shade of trees" (*Chi Town* 9). In the early forties, Blei's maternal grandparents left the Village for a Michigan farm, described in the first chapter of *What I Know by Heart So Far*. In the late 1940s Blei's parents also left the Village for another Bohemian enclave in Cicero, which was then Chicago's western suburbs.[1] Father George Blei worked in the Continental Bank of Chicago, from age sixteen to his mandatory retirement at age sixty-five. Mother Emily Papp Blei worked at the Western Electric plant.

The writer's childhood, although not exactly that of a bank official's son, was tamer than that recounted by Miroslav Blazen in the opening chapter of *Adventures in an American's Literature*.[2] Blei was educated in a Catholic grammar school and at one time considered becoming a priest, attracted to church ritual and the Latin mass (*Adventures* 23, *Neighborhood* 165–74). Blei attended a public high school, J. Sterling Morton High.

"I came from a culturally deprived environment by anyone's standards," Blei recalls in the essay "Me and My Watercolors" (*Paint* 40); "I don't think we had a dictionary in the house. Who needed one except people who maybe wrote a letter? As for art, I think there was a Woolworth painting of an Indian on a cliff hanging on a dark wall. . . . The Art Institute was the building downtown that had the lions outside. I entered it for the first time after my twenty-first birthday—when I was sure it was legal for me to do just about anything" (40–41).

Blei's early dislike of high school ("especially the first two years"—*Chi Town* 44) was changed by "a few exceptional teachers," the newspaper columns of Sydney J. Harris (recommended by his father), and increasing maturity. After graduation he enrolled at Morton Junior College in Cicero, "The 'Bohemian Harvard' some called it. Or 'Czech Tech'" (*Chi Town* 366). He then transferred to Illinois State University and in 1957 completed a BA in education. The institution and the degree he later described as "a nothing degree" and "a nothing college" (*Second Novel* 109), where he played the role of a serious, alienated, cool, fifties intellectual. College memories recounted in *The Second Novel* include Putnam's Book Shop, a coffeehouse named Coen's (later Jack's Place), a professor identified as Old Fielding, and a campus visit by Jeff Jones (substituting for Mark Rudd) of the Students for a Democratic Society. In *Adventures in an American's Literature* Blei tells the story of body painting a couple of coeds with his friend Richard Alger (in the novel *Addur*).

Upon graduation Blei married Barbara (they divorced in 2001)[3]; the couple had two children, Christopher (October 28, 1963) and Bridget (April 21, 1967).

In the fall of 1957 Blei took a job as a cub reporter with the City News Bureau of Chicago at $35 a week, and enrolled in the MA program at the University of Chicago. His studies lasted not even a semester: he decided he would rather be doing the writing than studying the writing. The job at City News Bureau "was an incredible system of tutelage in the best school of journalism anywhere," he recalled in *Chi Town* (273): a systematic progression from ink monkey to checking morgue reports to Teletype to the position of gofer on the night shift, to accompanying seasoned reporters on their beats to working one's own part-time beat to full-time status to working the rewrite desk in the newsroom. Blei left after half a year, never reaching the level of a reporter with his own beat. "I pulled back for fear I'd never be able to write what I truly wanted to write, even though I was uncertain what that really was or what form it would take," he explains (*Chi Town* 45). Besides, teaching offered a better salary.

From 1958 to 1960 Blei taught at East High School in Aurora, writing fiction and poetry (no journalism), and feeling for direction. In *Chi Town* he remembers himself at this time as "a young man from Cicero, in love with Chicago, unhappy with himself and the world, mostly in school or between jobs, mostly wanting to become a writer but too ignorant to begin, too insecure to reveal his desire to anyone, mostly riding the El back and forth to the Loop unexplainably, wandering Chicago's streets, searching for the city's literary past and present, hanging around the main public library on Randolph and Michigan, reading the Chicago papers at Pixley & Ehler's across from the library each morning and often at night" (*Chi Town* 261). In 1960 he spent a few weeks alone in New York City's Greenwich Village "trying to act like a writer" (*Second Novel* 79).

Blei taught the 1960–61 year at Villa Park High School, then quit in the spring to travel, with Barbara, to Europe: London, Paris ("where Great Artists are supposed to be"—*Second Novel* 4), Sweden, Denmark, Italy, Portugal, Yugoslavia, and Greece. Blei was semi-consciously tailoring himself to fit the stereotypical description of a writer, and licensing himself to preach knowledgeably on the Continent: "Europe humanizes a person. It puts one in close touch with beauty, tradition, nature, and other people" ("Europe in Chicago," *Chi Town* 57). The couple left the States in July, returned after Christmas. Blei lived with his in-laws in Berwyn, worked as a mail carrier and a substitute teacher, continued to write, considered a return to the City News Bureau. Instead, he accepted a job at Lyons Township High School in La Grange, Illinois, where his old friend Ralph Rausch had moved. There he taught small honors sections of academically gifted students. His friendship with Ross LewAllen dates to this period, although LewAllen left Lyons before Blei.

The material in *Adventures* reflects, although it does not necessarily recount, Blei's own teaching experiences. He describes at length two classes, the first at an "East Campbell High," in which Miroslav Blazen, a first-year teacher, is visited unexpectedly by his department chair. Unprepared as usual, Blazen ("Hassock") decides to give a quiz:

"Okay, please carefully copy each question as I give it. Leave enough space between questions, and when I'm through dictating them, you can go back and answer the questions in the blank spaces."

"I don't understand." "We never did it this way before." "What did he say?" "What was the question?" "He didn't give no questions yet, you dope."

"Did everybody hear me?"

"No. What was the question?"

"I didn't ask any questions yet. I'm merely giving directions."

"What's 'merely' mean?" Laughter.

"Okay, number one: Who is the author of this essay?"

Moans, groans, snickers . . . a whisper. "Do you know?" Shoulders shrugging, heads turning . . .

"Okay, Cass, close your book." Laughter. Very funny, Cass, you sonofabitch.

"Number two: What kind of essay is this?"

"You mean what's it about?"

"No, I mean what type of essay is this. Remember, we talked about the various types of essays. What type is this one?"

"Rotten."

You bastards. (59)

The day ends with Hassock, who cares too much about life and truth, confronting his class, which cares not at all about life, truth, or anything else:

> "And when you act like this, completely oblivious to what I'm try-ing to tell you, you're all a bunch of damn idiots to me! You don't want a teacher. You want a cop like Reckelson. Or some old maid you can crap all over. Well, I don't want to be either one. I give up. You can sit here on your dead-asses for the rest of the year for all I care. You can write FUCK YOU on my blackboard every day. I don't give a shit. I don't owe you anything!" (64)

This harangue is heard by Hassock's principal, who is standing right outside his door, and at year's end Miroslav Blazen is "allowed to resign."

Much later in the novel Hassock—mellowed out by a near-death experience in Mexico and a nervous breakdown in Yugoslavia—confronts a North Highland High class that is much smaller, much more intelligent, and much more uptight than its teacher:

> "Lock the door, Marvin. Let's everybody take a look at *Adventures in American Literature* and see what's to be done with it. Turn to the section on the colonial period and tear out everything by Taylor, and Sarah-baby-Knight. Then . . ."

"Hassock?"

"Emma?"

"Are you kidding?"

"No."

"Literally 'tear out' these pages?"

"Literally, figuratively, tear out all those goddam pages that are boring as hell, speak no adventure, and have nothing to do with who we
are and what we might become. Yes. Rip out Sarah Baby, Johnny
Edwards, William the Byrd. Franklin, Henry, Paine, Jefferson, etc.
Suit yourself. They're all right—but they're all history. We're looking
for literature." (140–41)[4]

While teaching, Blei wrote extensively, mornings and nights, in a
sequence of retreats described in *The Second Novel*: his father's attic
in Cicero, which "had the aura of a Greenwich Village loft" (72); a pan-
eled ex-porch/bedroom in his first apartment in Cicero; the basement
storage shed of another apartment on the west side of Chicago, the
setting of his short story "The Basement" and the place pictured at
the front of *Adventures in an American's Literature*, which was written
there. An entertaining (and sobering) inventory of rejection letters (and
three acceptances) is reprinted in *The Second Novel: Becoming a Writer*
(88–97). By 1967 he had written several stories and published some
journalism. "The Hour of the Sunshine Now," a dark story of artistic
self-destruction, was written while visiting Ross LewAllen in Las Vegas,
revised briefly in Berwyn, and accepted on first submission in May
1968. The first novel, *Adventures in an American's Literature*, was complete by October 1968.

The apocalyptic years 1968, 1969, and 1970 (Chicago riots, Altamont,
Woodstock, the trial of the Chicago Eight, Kent State) marked a major
shift of locus in the American counter-culture of the 1960s, a flight from
urban protest and violence to a pastoral retreat. Norbert Blei was part of
that movement. Chicago appeared "unwieldy . . . with the 60's and all the
'revolution' that was taking place . . . more than I could handle" (*Meditations* 84). Blei was also looking for a way to reduce family expenses to
what he could earn as a full-time freelance writer. He moved to rural
Door County, northeast of Green Bay, the thumb in the right hand
mitten which is the state of Wisconsin. Like many Chicagoans, he had
vacationed in Door during the summers of 1966, '67, and '68, experi-
encing "a kind of private peace in place . . . a stillness bordering on the

serenity some men find in religion" (*Door Way* 1). Probably Door brought recollections of his grandparents' farm in Michigan. In 1968 he paid $8,000 for a home and property in the county and moved there permanently in the spring of 1969, quitting his teaching job and committing himself to writing full time, both journalism and fiction.

The move to Wisconsin was not easy. A diary entry reprinted in *The Second Novel* under "Enter Early April" remembers his first night in the Ellison Bay house: "An overwhelming sense of depression set in, and I could think of nothing but the possibility that I had made a tremendous mistake in leaving Chicago. Wisconsin, the Midwest, the county, this whole terrifying sense of nature seemed determined to swallow me up" (110). Blei missed his old connections, especially Rausch, LewAllen, Curt Johnson, and Jay Robert Nash. He seemed cut off from the life of America as well. The frustration of watching America disintegrate from the impotent isolation of rural Door is recorded in some detail as chapter 8 of *The Second Novel*, under the title "The Way We Live, November 14, 1969." Counterpointing news broadcasts (the Chicago Eight trial, the moon mission, Spiro Agnew's attacks on the media, the on-going war in Vietnam) against the placid Door landscape (squirrel and chickadee at the feeder, cold and quiet evenings) and his domestic woes and responsibilities (wife, house, children—"the full catastrophe"), Blei depicts a country, and an individual, broken in two.[5]

Contributing to Blei's depression was an emotional breakdown suffered in Spain by Ross LewAllen, Blei's brother of the spirit, a model for the writer of the artist living always on the edge, pressing himself and his art always further and Furthur. If LewAllen could go down, pulled into his own paintings as he put it, then the writer was in danger as well. "Combined with this," Blei recalled, "was a certainty that I would be dead by age thirty, and the experience of my grandmother's death. I was very attached to her. She had what they used to call dementia—probably Alzheimers—and my grandfather had to put her in an institution. I think. I was very young. I saw her there once, in the institution, this crazy woman. It was frightening, and I formed the impression that there was some kind of madness in my blood line which might one day come for me" (Letter). The scene is reconstructed in his story "The Old Woman's Preserves":

She was gray and thin and chained to a white metal bed. A silky black whisker grew from a mole on her chin. Her mouth was shrunken but moving. Orange soda in a white paper cup lay untouched on a table beside her. (*Hour* 17)

Blei had already seen that dark side and felt it pulling him in and down, in stories like "The Hour of the Sunshine Now" and the apocalyptic conclusion of *Adventures in an American's Literature*. Compounding Blei's problem was guilt over not having rushed to LewAllen's assistance in Spain and keeping his distance after LewAllen returned to the States. He writes darkly about walking "around dead for a year on the outside, afraid of writing, afraid of reading, afraid of explaining or seeking help, fearful of confinement, clinging to a daily life of dull routine as the only salvation" (*Door to Door* 177). A passage in "The Ghost of Sandburg's Phizzog" is possibly autobiographical: "I was hallucinating. I was paranoid. There was no me, nothing whatsoever. . . . I understand Hesse now, and all the business of being reborn. When you're that far down, something must happen" ("The Ghost of Sandburg's Phizzog" 78).

By his own admission, Blei wrote very little during his first year in Door, mostly entries in what would become *The Second Novel*, which is really a book about the process of writing and marketing a book. Finally he returned to journalism, to what he once disparaged as "safe writing" (*Door to Door* 178) and elsewhere termed "Just bread and butter material" (*Second Novel* 156): the people of Chicago and his old neighborhood. This life proved both restorative and lucrative: more than once Blei feature stories appeared in two major Chicago newspapers on the same day. The arrangement, however, required frantic commutes between rural Ellison Bay and urban Cicero, a bipolar life which Blei recounts in "The Chicago Run" (*Door Way* 63–69) and the prologue to *Chi Town*. "In my mind I did not live here at all for at least the first five years," Blei recalls; "Chicago was truly my address. The old neighborhood my home" (*Door Way* 2).

On the other hand, chapter 9 of *The Second Novel* suggests an emerging peace of mind. Under the title "This is December in Wisconsin . . . Click" Blei writes to friend George Taucher, then in Switzerland,

I am gradually being absorbed by   my own setting   *click*
And I'm very much at peace with it   *click*
I miss the city less and less   *click*
I don't think I will ever go back to the city   *click*
When the time comes   that this land is inhabited by   more people
than I care to see   I think I'll move further north   *click*
Perhaps to Canada   perhaps to the northwest   *click*

And there is always New Mexico   *click* . . .
I envy your European setting less and less. . . . (141, 42)

And later in that same chapter, "I think the natural environment is one that we are all going to have to move into if any of us expects to survive" (143). A quote from Gary Snyder justifies his—and the sixties'—retreat to the countryside: "Industrial society indeed appears to be finished. Many of us are, again, hunters and gatherers" (*Second Novel* 114).

A position in the Door County schools was out of the question for the sixties hippie from the city who did not send his children to church, whose greatest message to students was trust your own feelings and question everything (*Door Way* 4). Blei didn't even apply. Besides, he had good reason to believe that a combination of frugal life in rural Wisconsin and freelance work for Chicago publications would indeed support the life of an artist. His last year at Lyons Township he had already cut his teaching, and his income, to half time. ("It was a bad move," he recalled in an interview of July 6, 2000; "I was doing nearly as much work, still had the long commute to school, gained maybe three hours a day, came home with half the pay.") Wisconsin was certainly cheap: Blei claims to have subsisted on less than $2,000 in 1969 (*Second Novel* 110), on $4,000–$6,000 in 1972 (238). His writing career was blossoming. One collection of interconnected short stories, based structurally on Hemingway's *In Our Time*, had been accepted for publication in 1968 by Windfall Press (*Second Novel* 149) under the title *The Restaurant Stories*.[6] A second collection of stories, some unpublished, was ready to go (*Second Novel* 151). For nearly a year a column titled "Himself" appeared in Jay Robert Nash's *Chicagoland Magazine*, first-person journalism of the Norman Mailer, Brendan Behan school: "Fact/Fiction/Me. What could be more 'first person' than writing a Chicago column about who you were, where you were, what you were thinking and feeling?" (*Winter Book* 65). *The Watercolored Word*, a saddle-stapled volume 4 of *Quixote* magazine, printed in four colors, had sold out its print run of three thousand copies after appearing in January 1969. Starting in 1970, both *The Second Novel* and *Adventures in an American's Literature* were being circulated among commercial publishers (including Atheneum, E. P. Dutton, Morrow, Dial, McCall, Atlantic Monthly, Delta, Viking, Fawcett, Doubleday, H. B. & W., and Harper and Row) by a succession of literary agents culminating in Ellen Levine. Blei's journalism appeared regularly in the *Chicago Tribune Sunday Magazine*, *Chicago* magazine, and the Chicago

Sun-Times Midwest Magazine, articles which would become the core of his book *Chi Town*. Blei even taught briefly: winter term 1971 at the College of DuPage (fiction and composition), and, starting in 1967, as writer-in-residence at The Clearing, Jens Jensen's artists' retreat in Ellison Bay, Wisconsin.

Blei's writing place in Wisconsin was first an upstairs bedroom of the house on Europe Bay Road, but by 1976 daughter Bridget was old enough to need a bedroom of her own. Blei renovated an abandoned chicken coop into his now-celebrated writer's den, pouring a fresh concrete floor, adding windows and electricity, replacing studs and shingles, insulating the walls and ceiling, paneling the inside with cedar boards cut by his neighbor Carl Carlson. Blei decorated the coop with pictures, posters, paintings, and objets d'art not particularly in the Wisconsin tradition. "The spirit within the coop speaks mostly Southwest Indian, the Far East, Eastern European, ethnic Chicago, and rituals of old Catholicism," he admits in a long *Door to Door* essay on the coop (26). During the renovation (September 28, 1976–August 8, 1977), Blei wrote almost nothing.

By the late seventies, Blei's freelance markets in Chicago were fast disappearing anyway. "*Himself* could not exist in the Wisconsin countryside where I had settled," Blei recalls; "The voices faded" (*Winter Book* 66). *Midwest Magazine* ceased publication. Old editors retired: John Fink at the *Tribune*, Herman Kogan at the *Daily News* (*Neighborhood* 271). Jay Nash's *Literary Times* and *Chicagoland* magazine gave way to *Chicago* magazine, which, like so many other city magazines, favored "[m]ore visuals, less text. Less literature, more ads" (*Chi Town* 383). Blei turned increasingly to Wisconsin journalism and to short fiction, the journalism again proving more marketable than fiction.[7] Starting in the mid-1970s, he wrote for the Door County *Advocate*, edited by Chan Harris, with whom he carried on a long-term and largely amicable quarrel until Harris sold the newspaper in 1986. The stories earned him $45, compared to the $300–$800 he would have received in Chicago (*Second Novel* 240), but his column "Notes along the Way," a more Zen concept than "Himself," plus his newspaper articles and his books (starting with *Door Way*) established him as the area's premier writer, heir apparent to Glenway Westcott and August Derleth—Door's conscience, if not its official spokesman. They also created enemies, as Blei quickly found out: his *Advocate* column was canceled in 1981, the same year in which Ellis Press published *Door Way*, a book which gathers

many of the profiles Blei had written for that newspaper. In 1988, he began a "BLEI/At Large" column in *The Door Reminder*, a local shopping
guide, which ultimately went the way of his *Advocate* column. *Chronicles
of a Rural Journalist in America* (1990) reprints columns, letters, and
responses to letters, with a preface by Paul Schroeder and a forward by
Blei. Schroeder's observation that Blei's contributions to the *Door Reminder* "as little resemble 'journalism' as his *Second Novel* resembles
'fiction'"(2) is a point well-taken.

After *Chronicles of a Rural Journalist*, Blei published very little
significant fiction, scant journalism, and only one new book: *Winter
Book* (2002). A short story pumped into a fourteen-page "novel" was
published in 1995 by Chris Halla as a Page 5 production, *What I Know
by Heart So Far*, and Northwestern University Press reprinted *Chi Town*.
Blei worked intermittently on a novel and several collections of short
stories, expanded his Clearing classes to spring and fall sessions, appeared frequently on Wisconsin Public Radio, and performed or collab-
orated on performances of or based on his earlier work, mixing words
with sound as he has mixed words with graphics, especially at the Door
Community Auditorium and Warren Wilson's Big Top Chautauqua in
Bayfield, Wisconsin. *Die Mauer*, a series of 42 watercolored collages of
images and words, based on the Berlin Wall, was exhibited at the
LewAllen Gallery in Santa Fe, April 2–30, 1993. Starting in 1994 he devoted considerable time and some money to publishing a series of chapbooks and books on the Crossings+Press imprint, written by friends
and disciples. In 1997 Blei received the Gordon MacQuarrie Award
from the Wisconsin Academy of Arts and Letters for his "deep environmental ethic, and journalistic integrity," and in 1999 he received the
Bradley Major Achievement Award from the Council of Wisconsin
Writers. He is one of sixty-four Wisconsin writers whose work is incorporated into Milwaukee's Midwest Convention Center. Today Norbert
Blei, who has upon occasion complained that "'local' becomes local
anesthesia to a writer's imagination very quickly" (*Chronicles* 9), is famous as a writer of place, of two places really: the Bohemian neighborhood of his Illinois youth, and his adopted home in Wisconsin.

The relationship between place and art has always been troubled for
American writers. The midwesterner especially is tempted to leave
home, like Garrison Keillor's small-town persona in the first chapter of
Lake Wobegon Days. Upon enrolling at the University of Minnesota,

Keillor attempts immediately to redesign himself into a man of the world, practicing various foreign accents and transforming the Keillors into the Keillorinis. "If I could be European," Keillor writes, "I'd be right where I wanted to be as a person" (20). At the chapter's conclusion, however, he abandons the dreary, English-class irony and the clever essays he thinks his composition instructor would appreciate, and returns to Lake Wobegon. "Whatever its faults," he decides, the home place "is not dreary" (22). Out of this collapse, Keillor made a best-selling novel. Explaining a poem titled "Watering the Horse" to Bill Moyers in a television interview, Robert Bly recalled escaping Madison, Minnesota, for Harvard and New York, then collapsing, "a hopeless failure," into his "crummy little place." Traumatic though it might have been, the experience gave Bly the gifts of sight and insight which made him a famous poet.

In ascending, a writer builds connections with the larger world and sharpens his sense of what he is by confronting what he is not; in falling, he discovers his true self and develops those dissonant chords in a minor key which characterize great writing. Both are great gifts not to be disdained. Inevitably, however, splits develop between author and audience, and between two sides of the author's own personality. The process of becoming a writer is alienating, and the process of recovering one's proper voice and material is also alienating. It takes a lot of Grain Belt beer to reconcile the conflicting impulses to break and preserve roots.

The pattern of escape and return is enacted repeatedly in the career and writing of Norbert Blei, with the result that over his career Blei has extended himself to a sequence of places, Cicero and Door most prominent among them.

Urban Chicago and rural Wisconsin would appear to be polar opposites, and Blei often uses them as contrasting philosophical as well as geographical poles, opposite sides of his own personality.[8] This strategy was apparent early: in his afterword to Blei's first collection of short stories, Richard Meade writes,

> The stories in the first part of The Hour of the Sunshine Now might well be called the city stories. Those in the latter part are concerned with the country. To grasp such distinctions is to become aware of the book's subtle organic movement. Blei's geographical regions are also regions of the mind. (Blei, Hour 121)

In "The Chicago Run" (*Door Way*), Blei travels that mental path in reverse, country to city, noting especially the effect of an urban mentality on his driving:

> To bid goodbye with a sunrise to a place of such perfect peace is perhaps only fitting, and the only way to go, to merge into the mainstream of urban landscape which awaits me, where both sunrises and sunsets have all but disappeared from the eyes and hearts of men.
>
> Within a few miles, even I will forget the significance of such natural events and concentrate, instead, on the energies of the city. By the time I hit the Illinois tollway, a sunrise will be the least of my concerns. . . .
>
> So I settle into a different driving pattern as I near Milwaukee, as I begin to fight for survival on the expressways. Not that I reject this. Just that I have grown more aware in the past few years that I am not the same driver in Door County that I am in Chicago. I am more anxious at the wheel on Interstate highways, expressways, city streets. I am more verbal, more physical. I may even be a better driver under such circumstances. I am more aware, though less secure. I lock the doors now, even while driving. Back home, I don't even remove the key from the ignition. (68)

Speed, action, sophistication, and culture are certainly things Blei associates with life in Illinois, and "the sexual energy of a city" as contrasted to "the contemplative aspects of a country life" (*Door Way* 253), but they are probably not the most significant. These are the skyline view of Chicago, which Blei can write, but with which he is least comfortable, about which he has least to say. In *Chi Town*, Blei's attempt to write a comprehensive view of a city which defies all comprehensive views, they are the least interesting vignettes: Art Institute, Kroch's and Brentanno's, Michigan Avenue, the Museum of Science and Industry, Cook County Hospital, Marshall Field's, the Chicago Public Library, Rene's in Westmont, even famous personalities like Dr. Preston Bradley, Burr Tillstrom, and Ben Gingiss. While they show a good eye, Blei's detail rarely rises above the prosaic, and a saccharine sentimentality often mars his tone. Looking back at himself in a preface written twenty years after the *Chi Town*'s contents, Blei observes, "The young man in these small Chicago tales seems obviously enamored of the place, in love with what he is doing, obviously seeking love in return. In a whirl, beside himself at times. Feeling his oats, happy to be alive, on the streets, among people. . ." (17).

Chi Town is more interesting for its depiction of the underside of Big Windy—the small-timers, the lost, the ethnics, the eccentric, the defeated, "the useless, helpless nobodies nobody knows," to reference Blei's own description of Nelson Algren (307). In an early profile of Blei and his work (1970), Henry Shea noted, "Norb specializes in the fleeting look at the little people of the city, the aged newsstand operators, the small restaurant owners, Greek, Bohemian, Slovak, who still provide, in out-of-the-way neighborhoods, national dishes and national atmosphere. And, he is determined to get these glimpses of a disappearing Chicago on paper before they are ploughed under to make way for new high-rise apartments, or succumb to the creeping wave of debris, human and material, so characteristic of most large cities these days" (11). These pieces constitute the best of *Chi Town*: "Nik Klein: The Man Who Made Rocking Horses"; Innocenzo Bonelli, "A Man on a Bench"; Max Marek, the antique dealer who in 1933 beat Joe Louis for the United States Amateur Championship in Boston; Lazos the hot dog vendor; Jim Boer, trash collector; Sam Karnick, the window washer. And Blei's best cityscapes are as broken and battered as his characters:

> It's an old, stained, red-brick building at the corner of Sheffield and Grace, a building highlighted by a cheap white trim around the windows, across the doors and entrances. It's Max Maret's Sat-Sun Antique Shop.
>
> In a cinder parking lot across the street, one derelict car, fallen flat on its wheels, rusts in peace. Horace Greeley School stands like a stage-set on the other corner, with the El throttling close behind. It's a classic Chicago setting of has-beens who battle, flat-footed, to function with some sense of dignity—to stave off the wrecker, the ropes, the canvas, and the final count of ten. (137)

"The writer with a dose of Chicago in his blood inevitably wrote from the wrong side of the tracks," Blei notes elsewhere ("Hearing Chicago Voices" 101); "There was just no other choice."

Blei is also good on artists and writers: Sydney J. Harris, Bill Stipe, James T. Farrell,[9] Mike Royko, Bill Mauldin, Nelson Algren, Paul Romaine, Harry Petrakis, and Studs Terkel. These writers represent a Chicago literary tradition which nourishes Blei, to whose ranks he obviously aspires. The older writers—especially Sandburg and Algren[10]—

both celebrate and represent a tradition of immigrants and outsiders that validates the role Blei claims for himself. In an essay "Paul Romaine: A Writer's Bookseller in Chicago," written especially for *Chi Town*, Blei paints a portrait of himself as a young writer, introduces Ira Adler and Paul Romaine his teacher, and provides a list of models Romaine gave to the aspiring writer back in the 1950s:

> [Romaine] couldn't mention Algren without talking about Sandburg, Farrell, Whitman, Baudelaire, Simone de Beauvoir. And you couldn't talk Farrell without getting into Dreiser, Frank Norris, Upton Sinclair, Anderson, Lewis, Jack Conroy, Hemingway, Bellow, back to Ring Lardner, Ben Hecht, George Ade, Eugene Field, Finley Peter Dunne, into the heartbeat of Chicago's Renaissance, Edgar Lee Masters, Sandburg, Floyd Dell, Margaret Anderson's *Little Review*, Harriet Monroe's *Poetry*, Hecht and Maxwell Bodenheim's *Chicago Literary Times* (to be resurrected after a fashion by the legendary Jay Robert Nash in 1961 as the *Literary Times*) . . . Chicago "the literary capital of the United States," said H. L. Mencken, way back then. (264)

Romaine, Blei notes, taught him not only Chicago writers but Negro writers, Mexican writers, proletarian writers, the Beats, Russian and Soviet writers. "I gleaned from Russian literature a sense of continuity between generations of writers," Blei recalls (*Chi Town* 268), "a sense of place, a sense of history, a sense of common human values, and the writer's responsibilities to make these things known through his art."

Whether he actually made it as "a Chicago writer,"[11] Blei certainly did make the grade as a Chicago ethnic writer, as the voice of the Bohemians in Cicero-Berwyn. Bohemia is Blei's corner of Chicago. After escape to college, to Greenwich Village, to Europe, Blei returned to his ethnic roots, drawn by cultural inheritance, by instruction, and by growing up in a city of many cultures with a respect for individualism. In his Chicago models, Blei valued more than anything a tolerance of eccentricity and individualism which he first learned from Harris ("I could identify with the man's ideas, especially those which championed the individual over the conforming masses"—*Chi Town* 45), and had reinforced by Saroyan and Petrakis. Beginning his chapter on Harry Mark Petrakis, Blei remembers "his first book of short stories, *Pericles on 31st Street*, . . . their sense of place: ethnic Chicago" (333). Ultimately Blei is most valuable not as a writer of Chicago, but as a writer of the Chicago Bohemians, as Petrakis is a writer of Chicago Greeks, Farrell a writer of Chicago Irish, and Gwendolyn Brooks a writer of Chicago Negroes. Blei's ethnic heritage constitutes his own special song and gave him one of his two important places.

Blei's childhood in the Little Village around Pilsen Park and in Cicero is most fully described in the introduction and closing chapters of *Chi Town*, and in Blei's great monument to lost communities everywhere, *Neighborhood*: Pilsen Park, Polonia Grove, the Leader Store, Polacek Brothers butcher shop on Cermak Road, the Hole in the Wall tavern, the Town Theater, the Ritz Theater, the Villas Theater, the Olympic Theater, the Red Arrow jazz joint, St. Francis of Rome School, Mid-America Savings and Loan, Kalavoda's Ice Cream Parlor, Sokol gymnastic school, Old Prague Restaurant. Patiently Blei recounts the history of Libby and Jana's People's Restaurant, its sale somewhere before 1989, its transformation into the L & J Lounge, which, in his description, sounds like "an intellectual cafe in old Prague" (380). He recreates a gypsy camp at 39th and Harlem, and a hobo jungle by the railroad tracks. Carefully he ticks off the names of neighborhood bakeries—Fingerhut, the Manor, Vales, Hruska's, Stetina's, Minarik's, Vesecky's—their present owners, their previous owners and locations, how many years at their present location, how many generations in that location, specialties of the house, daily production, in pounds, of "Babi's rye" bread. In great detail he inventories the stock of M. Pancner's Cards & Gifts, last of the great Czech neighborhood gift shops: glass, ethnic plates, intricately designed and hand-painted Easter eggs from Europe, books and greeting cards in Czech and other Central European tongues, miniatures, porcelain statues, crystal, bells, paperweights, ash trays, music boxes, religious goods, mugs, wood carvings . . . and ornate dolls, a world-class collection, Alexander to Effanbee, Gibson, Bradford, Royal, Steiff, Vogue, Tanzupi. He lists the shops along Central Avenue: "Pavlicek's Drug Store; Ruzicka, Kobzina, Sereka and others for furniture; Sebesta, Shotola, Verner, and many more for meat; . . . and funeral homes like Clasen, Cermak, Chrastka, Marik, and Svec, where Bohemian families expressed certain loyalties and traditions, preferring one funeral home over another . . . Marik, for example, because that's where grandpa was waked and all the family" (*Neighborhood* 5).

The introduction to *Neighborhood* is an especially rich evocation of the ethnic neighborhood, "a neighborhood of senses":

There were silver fish swimming in dark wooden barrels outside the meat markets on Cermak Road in Cicero then. Rabbits, beautiful and dead in their brown fur, hung by their hind legs from under the awnings. Sawdust floors. White enamel meat cases that people leaned into. The sawing, chopping, cleaving of bones. Sharp-pointed knives on wavy, worn butcher-block tables, carving through and around red meat, trimming white fat. Brown eggs, beige eggs, grainy eggs; slabs of bacon, strings of sausage, smoked hams; tubs of lard. The bloody handprints of laughing butchers in once-white aprons. Czech spoken here: praszky, jaternice, debrecinky, buchta, Nazdar! The smell of fresh sausage, dill pickles, garlic, caraway, warm frankfurters. . . .

Wooden streetcars, blue and white, clanked, sparked, wound their way back and forth across the center of Cermak Road (22nd Street) through Cicero and Berwyn, each piloted by a uniformed motorman on the front platform, one hand clutching the wooden-knobbed steel lever which set the car in motion on silver rails, while a conductor made change on the rear platform. . . .

There were two inches of cream in the neck of the glass milk bottles left behind the back door each morning. You could hear the bottles, sprinkled with ice shards, rattling in the crates in the truck, in the hands of the milkman holding the metal basket as he made his way from the street down the gangway.

White sheets, smelling of bleach, flapped in the sunny wind of backyard Monday morning clotheslines weighted down with over-alls, shirts, aprons, house dresses, rag rugs, towels, socks, chenille bedspreads, all propped up with long wooden clothes poles. (1, 3)

Blei recalls village characters known only as Radio Lady, Monster Man, and Mickey Mouse ("because his actions always suggested too much beer"—7). He describes at length neighborhood games and types of soda pop (Kayo, Dr. Pepper, Canfield's Cream, Orange Crush), the butcher shop, the ice cream man, the roller rink, feather comforters and tripe soup, Shorty the locksmith and Joey the peddler, cereal and softball, and sausage and soup. And Frankie Yankovic, the Polka King.

And of course bakery. More than anything, heritage for Blei is bakery. "Bakery is home," he writes in a chapter of *Chi Town* titled "The World's Greatest Czech Bakeries." "It's family, the remembrance of old times, good times, a kitchen afloat in the aroma of fresh bread. Goodness bordering on love" (351). In Blei's writing, bakery carries a sometimes religious, always feminine significance. Food—even when commercially prepared in Vesecky's Bakery—is the province of the female.

The tradition comes more from Blei's maternal grandmother than from his paternal side. The Bleis lived "in a traditional Chicago bunga-low on Avers Avenue"; the Papps, before moving to the Michigan farm, "lived mostly in the basement of their bungalow on Pulaski" (9). As a child Blei shuttled between grandparents, a life predictable and secure at the Bleis, "fraught with fear or sudden love in the basement of the Papps" (11). Grandma Blei spoke English and knew Czech; Grandma Papp spoke only Czech. "Beyond her own neighborhood she was lost, a stranger in a strange land indeed" (11). Grandma Blei cooked well-balanced meals and read health books. Grandma Papp brought home live chickens from the market and butchered them in the basement. "When the family broke bread, they tore it apart with both hands. Knives were everywhere and ever-sharp. Sometimes they flew in the air" (12).

"The region of the early stories" of *The Hour of the Sunshine Now*, Meade notes, "is clearly memory. These stories recall the past, particu-larly the ethnic ways and people upon which many of Chicago's neigh-borhoods are solidly built" (121). It is the spirit of his maternal grand-mother, Babi, who guides Blei's ethnic stories:

> I see only the basement . . . and an Uncle John who came home drunk, fought Grandfather with his fists, and was beaten. An Aunt Stella who entered the kitchen crying because she was diseased and bared her body for us to see the soft, dark marks like spoiled fruit. Grandma screaming and then boiling a solution on the stove. Grandpa, in rage, slapping Stella's face.
>
> There was an old lady Skarda who read cards and spoke only of death, sometimes fortune. A mad uncle who filled the basement with such hard laughter that once, so I recall or have been told, a lady friend of Grandma's was felled and twisted with a mild stroke.
>
> And I see the wine press in a front shed. The barrels of ferment-ing grapes. The bubbles and scum at the top. The stained cheese-cloth. The biting smell.
>
> Finally, the block of wood in the coal shed where Grandma often led me by the hand, laughed, and taught me how a chicken dances. (*Hour* 21, 22)

Babi appears abstractly in the fable which opens *The Hour of the Sunshine Now*, "The Old Woman's Preserves," and more concretely in several other stories: "The Basement," "The Egg Lady," "This Horse of a Body of Mine," *What I Know by Heart So Far*, and "Skarda":

> I was left with Babi in the basement. The blood of freshly killed chickens in the coal bin; the secrets of Grandpa's locks and keys; and the visits of Skarda, her burlap bag of chickens, and her cloth coat trimmed in fox with beautiful glass eyes that I touched and rubbed. Skarda, the card lady, who saw I would be left with all this.
> Babi lived in a long brick bungalow on Pulaski Road in Chicago. (*Ghost* 3)

Blei's ethnic stories and reportages are full of chickens, coal bins and basements, pinochle and tarot cards, knives, keys, women who cook soup and men who drink beer, violent displays of temper and strange language, and ethnic food.[12] In three mythical jars, the wife of "The Old Woman's Preserves" brings from the Old World to the New language, tools, and "the magic of the food you make" (*Hour* 14). Food defines ethnicity and tradition. Food is Slavic soul. "Why don't you eat like the Danes," Barbara Blei asks in chapter 7 of *The Second Novel*. "You fill up on a couple of crackers, and that's it." "Because I'm a Slav," Blei replies; "We're always hungry" (132).

The thematic core of Blei's ethnic neighborhood is loss and the threat of loss, and its markers are institutions and locations gone when Blei described them, or, mostly, lost in the intervening years, which brought the death of his parents and the transformation of an Italian-Czech neighborhood into a Latino enclave:

> All of this was very long ago. All of this seems only yesterday. It was one time on the very edge of another. A time of boyhood in the edge of young manhood. A time of prewar on the edge of postwar. A time of firelight on the edge of electricity—the gateman at the 58th Avenue El station still coming out of his shanty at night to hang red kerosene lanterns on the lowered gates. A time of iceboxes giving way to refrigerators. A time of radio giving way to television. A time of people sitting on front porches talking to neighbors who passed by, yielding to a time of abandoning the porches, locking the doors, drawing the blinds, and sequestering themselves in a TV room. . . . A time of a neighborhood of many voices, intermingled, shared, which

shaped one's humanness, one's spirit for living in ways forever lost as neighborhoods gave way to suburbs, family businesses to franchises, shopping streets to shopping malls where we appear lost in a culture of consumption, self-gratification. (*Neighborhood* 10)

In singing that lost time, Blei suggests, he can fix it in a kind of virtual reality: "Wherever I am in the world, whenever I think of my old neighborhood, I view the setting in miniature the way a child creates imaginary places. . . . All of this is still there" (*Ghost* 165). Blei returns to a lost past with words.

As a high school adolescent, Blei, like Garrison Keillor and so many other writers, had believed he needed to escape his roots: "I was at an age when I was trying to disassociate myself from all things foreign, especially the language of my mother and grandmother. I was an American, not a Bohunk or a Slovak or a greenhorn" (*Ghost* 180). But the neighborhood, not Riccardo's or New York or Paris, provided Blei's true material. As a maturing writer, Blei found his strength not in breaking roots, but in preserving them.[13]

Inevitably Blei realized that in Cicero he was fighting a battle that was probably already lost. He opted out of the neighborhood—and post–World War II America—for rural Door County, where he found a tradition, a community, a way of life similar to what was disappearing in Cicero. The move to Wisconsin was not an ascension, but a falling down; not an escape upward, but a retreat backward. After the initial dislocation, Cicero and Ellison Bay would prove more similar than dissimilar, the road from Bohemian Chicago to rural Door County would become a loop, and Blei would suffer in Door a sense of loss even greater than his lost Bohemian youth.

Things didn't start out that way. In *Door to Door*, Blei writes,

What this place offered initially, essentially, was nothing. Nothing but clean air, fresh water, pristine beaches, cool summer nights, brisk bright autumns, woods, wildlife, acres of silence, nothing to do but find your place in the natural scheme of things and be still. Every road, it seemed, eventually led to water and all its forgiveness, all its mindlessness. (11)

Meditations on a Small Lake, the books of Blei's Door trilogy, and many of his short stories describe the unpaved roads, weathered barns, orchards, farms, woodlands, stone fences, meadows, barns, the birds and birches and wildflowers of Door County (fictionalized as Portal County), as well as the fundamentals: air, earth, space, dark—the quiet, infinite, mysterious, beckoning country dark of Door County, "the vast confessional" (80). And water, which, from the small stream adjacent to his grandparents' Michigan farm to the lake of "Meditations on a Small Lake" to the great gray immensity of Lake Michigan, has always carried religious significance for Blei.[14] The lake of "Meditations on a Small Lake" is Europe Lake, just off the northeast side of the Door peninsula, a little jewel at the end of the road on which Blei lives. The shore on Blei's side is claimed on the south by Carlson's cottages and on the north by private summer homes built within the past two decades. On the eastern shore, between Europe Lake and Lake Michigan, lie the protected woods of Newport State Park. At the end of Europe Lake Road, a small wooden dock, a picnic table, and a public boating ramp. Blei describes the lake, semi-fictional, nearly mystical, as it was in the early seventies. He gives its history, the secrets of fishing there for perch, the lessons of water. A Zen transcendence pervades his collage of meditations and descriptions, which are strikingly similar to Gary Snyder's poem "Rip-Rap." "All a man needs to love is a small lake," he concludes (49).

Blei's Door landscapes, like his Chicago landscapes, are usually beatifically weathered:

> [The screen door] opened quickly as three small children ran out to join the rest of her kids playing in the rusted hull of an old car that lay half buried in weeds and flowers alongside the house. Old farm machinery and piles of wood, broken windowframes and a yellow door lay all around in lazy abandonment. A barn, half red and half weathered, leaned to the south with an open mouth of hanging hay. A broken windmill, ivy spreading across the rusted braces, the vines nearing the top, stood off to the side of the house. The rusted circle of oblique vanes now angled in time with the sky directly above; interlocked and impaled by the center shaft with a crowning gear. (*Hour* 49)
>
> A blue rowboat overturned in a field . . .
>
> A white ceramic doorknob on a weathered shed with no roof, a lilac bush growing through. (*Hour* 73)

Door Steps, a 365-day journal of country life, is Blei's most focused examination of the landscape, a record of "the natural presence of this place" (1), an attempt "to see and feel and know the world as it is" (2).

Here, as in his other celebrations of rural Door, Blei focuses on the northern and eastern side of Door, the less developed area of the county. Here, as elsewhere, Door is a sensual, visceral experience:

February 23   a red gas pump in a distant farmyard, all undulating in gray and white.

March 16   There is a sudden release of odor upon the landscape, a wet woodsiness, a pungency of raw earth.

May 11   Trillium. Bluebirds. Rose-breasted grosbeaks. And those bright orange slices of Baltimore orioles against a blue sky.

October 21   Just gold leaves stuck to a blue sky.

October 28   This was all the color in the world today—one red cardinal.

Still, in Blei's Door landscape it is not difficult to discover echoes of the old neighborhood, of woman and bakery:

January 1   Stolen woman. Herb bread, herb bread love. Ah, the smell of it.

August 19   Ah, the aroma . . . it's dill pickle time.

Also familiar are the ambivalent desires to disappear into the landscape and to escape the landscape, which sends Blei off periodically to Chicago or New Mexico.[15]

As he gave them voice, the people of Door became more important to Blei than the landscape. "What I learned here but I didn't pick up in Chicago was the writer being somebody else's voice . . . all of a sudden people are coming to the door, I felt I was running a social service or something," he recalled (Letter). Blei is less a landscape painter than a portraitist; his real interest is in "the people in the landscape," a subtitle he used for *Door Way*. These prove remarkably similar to the people who had most interested him in Chicago and Cicero: "the old-timers, who pass too quickly from a writer's loving eyes, who made sense of this land—farmers, fishermen, orchardmen, handymen, rural folk—who made little or nothing of their lives, but lived deeply in place, holding the secrets of stones" (*Meditations* 7). "Men like my late neighbor Charley Root[16] whose very name bespoke his entire life: poor farmer, a maker of fish boxes. Chet Elquist, fisherman, cherry grower, all-around handyman who knew more truths to the water, the earth, the good quiet life than every minister in the county could hope to explain in a lifetime of Sunday sermons. Gust Klenke, garage man and beekeeper whose faith was the machinery of man and the mystery of bees" (*Door to Door* 12). Those who, by looking closely and opening their senses, made much of little, like Bill Beckstrom, who after a sixth-grade education taught himself the common name and Latin name of every plant species in Door County, knew where witch hazel grew, and native anemone, and high-bush cranberry, and every kind of mushroom, every kind of tree. Who worked his way out of depression by listening to Dvorak symphonies and Slavonic dances. Who did Europe, alone, at age 66. The strong ethnics, like Ignacio Gonzales, migrant worker, and John Henderson, "The Dark Man of Door," and Louie Smolak, sculptor. The characters "who are so totally and honestly themselves, you can't help but listen and enjoy" (*Door Way* 83): Freddie Kodanko, truck farmer, and Wally Mickelson "The World's Greatest Used Car Salesman." Each has a chapter in *Door Way*, along with Ernie Anderson "Woodworker," Roy Lukes "Naturalist," Sid Telfer "Orchardman," Emery "Dynamite" Oldenburg "Horse Trader," and Tim Weborg "Fisherman." Elquist and Root share, with George and Emily Blei, the dedication of *Door Way*.

In a very real sense Blei did not discover a new self in Door, he recycled his old self. "*Neighborhood* came to be my understanding and search for 'the village,' " he writes in an e-mail (June 30, 2000), "which in turn I found both here in Door—and the old country. Not to mention Santa Fe." It is not difficult to draw direct lines between the village in Cicero and the village in Door, between, for example, drink in the old neighborhood and drink in Door County, between food in Blei's old environment and his new, between Charley the Chicago news vendor and Charley Root, Blei's neighbor in Door. Even the words sound similar:

> When you are seventy-five years old and have been selling newspapers since 1932, mornings like this mean nothing. . . . Today the sharp wind fights from the north. So you build a small barricade of sorts, a barricade of boxes and planks. (*Chi Town* 147)
>
> When you are 88 years old, alone . . . you must barely hear, but you feel the thrust of an autumn wind that hits the house with its own history of seasons. (*Door Way* 13)

Aunt Lorry in Cicero (*Neighborhood* 237) sounds a lot like Dar in Door County (*Door Way* 255–56).[17]

As the eighties became the nineties, Blei—in an irony which he himself perceives, and upon which he has commented many times—did his best to shut the Door behind him. First he found a place in Door for Norbert Blei, writer. Then, through his books and journalism he attracted more outsiders into Door, outsiders whom he celebrated as a useful corrective to the Door County *Main Street* and *Spoon River* mentality, invoking the projected influx of outsiders to validate his own essays on Saroyan and the world beyond Door. Then Blei turned conservationist, preservationist, critic of any change, from paved (and renamed) roads to fire numbers and newspaper mailboxes. Secure in his piece of paradise, Blei seems too eager to deny others theirs. "But have I been good or bad for this place?" he asks in a piece written originally for the *Washington Post* and reprinted in *Meditations*; "Every word seems an invitation. Even to say 'stay away' brings on the hordes" (6).[18]

In one essay Blei laments "The Death of a Country Road" (*Door Way* 156–58), formerly Daubner Road, now widened, paved, trimmed, marked, rebaptized "Isle View." In another essay Blei praises country darkness, which is fast becoming lost in the glare of mercury vapor yard and street lights (*Meditations* 79). In a third he recounts the tale of a farmer who once sold fresh eggs, cherries, apples, and honey to city folks and strangers, then expanded operations to sell old junk from the barn and attic, plots of land, the barn itself (for siding in paneling in a new bar and supper club), his stone fence, and finally his house, only to discover, "I'm a stranger to myself these days. However I got to this place I am now, it ain't home. And I don't know who or what to blame" (*Meditations* 59). In *Winter Book*, he preaches an Ed Abbey Jeremiad against "toxic tourism" (15) and "Boutique Blight": "the erosion of character in our small towns and villages as tourist commerce, unchecked, insidiously works its way up and down Main Street desecrating old stores, eliminating public buildings, churches, and private homes till nothing is left but a cutesy facade of upscale buildings brightly lit, catering to every tourist taste from teddies to teddy bears" (3).

Blei, and the people to whom he gives voice, are sometimes emotional, sometimes dryly analytical in critiquing the situation. Painter James Ingwersen notes, "It's happening all over the U.S. The small farmer is being taxed right out of his land" (*Door Way* 154). Ernie Anderson, English major turned carpenter, explains matter-of-factly, "every craftsman in these parts must pay the same cost of living that the people pay who come up here with their inflated city dollars. Consequently, I can't buy an old rundown farm to live and work like some of these people did 10 years ago" (*Door Way* 59); he continues, "One thing I especially find disturbing—urban people who come up here, buy property, and have this highly developed sense of property rights and privacy . . . they're obsessed with the idea that something's going to be carried away from it, even though it's been standing here untouched for years" (61). "The thing I never saw coming," Blei recalled in a July 7, 2000 letter, "was the influx of wealth. It's turned the whole county around. The locals don't know who they are anymore."

The issue is community, tradition, the integrity of local institutions and individuals. "It's not a case of 'Move back to Chicago if you don't like it here,' " Blei points out in the introduction to *Door to Door*; "It's a case of there eventually being no difference between a city's ugly urban sprawl and Door County. Then we'll all be 'natives'; all our names and houses will be the same. And this place might just as well be called nowhere because it will have lost all those indefinable qualities of a natural landscape that made it unique" (i).

Blei's departure from the *Door Reminder*, like his exodus from the *Door County Advocate*, was triggered in large part by his opposition to commercial development, especially by an essay titled "Shut the Damn Door: Blei's Master Plan for the Future of Door County" (reprinted in *Chronicles* 123–26). The plan is drawn loosely from Ed Abbey's plan for the national parks, outlined in the "Industrial Tourism" chapter of *Desert Solitaire*. Blei suggests that county officials freeze all building, property sales, and residential, commercial, and public planning in the county; turn the entire county over to Nature Conservancy; close the new bridge at Sturgeon Bay and make an outdoor walking mall of it, with artsy-craftsy shops, a Ferris wheel, and Chicago-style food vendors; admit tourists freely across the old bridge May through October, subject to a tax of $50 per vehicle per week and $25 per person per day, but from November through April by visa only; tear up all highways and back roads and return them to their natural state of dirt, gravel, good Door County earth; place a moratorium on new road construction in the county; encourage vandalism of commercial signs while instituting a $3,000 fine for anyone caught erecting new advertisements or newspaper mail boxes; tear up "ugly metal road signs" and either replace them with wooden ones or leave the roads nameless. "Take any dirt road and get lost," Blei concludes. "You may discover the real value of this place. You may discover yourself" (128).

Once again an exploration became preservation bordering on nostalgia, and in moving from Cicero to Ellison Bay, Blei suffered a trauma similar to the loss of his boyhood world. In Door, Blei found a new community that was in many ways like the old community, established new roots which were in many ways like the old roots, only to watch Door in the eighties become Cicero of the sixties. At best he had bought himself twenty years.

Thus a profound feeling of loss permeates all of Blei's work: that set in Cicero, that set in Door County, even that set in New Mexico. Possibly Blei's own sense of himself as an isolated, alienated writer—a consistent self-portrait, through years of economic and literary success and failure, prominence and reduced visibility—derives from his sense of Doomed Place, or, more properly, doomed community in place. For an epigraph to "Wintering Near Death's Door" (*Door to Door*, reprinted from *The Washington Post*), Blei used a quote from Cesare Pavese, which he is fond of citing on other occasions: "What does it all mean then? That you need a village, if only for the pleasure of leaving it. Your own village means that you are not alone, that you know there's something of you in the people and the plants and the soil, that even when you are not there it waits to welcome you. But it isn't easy to stay there quietly" (9). Certainly Blei defines himself as a writer in terms of place and village, and both places with which he chose to identify are, in his view, lost. Whether author imposed his vision on place (others in both Cicero and Door County have found more to cheer about over the past thirty years), or place imposed itself on author, the result is an author celebrating the forgotten, the beaten and defeated: others and himself.

Blei's personal proclivities were reinforced by two other considerations. First, Blei belongs to a counterculture that collectively embraced "the poor, the outcasts, and the good outlaws. They actually preferred losing to winning, outlaws to sheriffs, poverty to wealth, because losing and outlaws and poverty are all somehow more pure. They believed in little people and in big people masquerading as little people" (Pichaske, *Generation* 92). In many respects, including his move from city to country at the end of the 1960s, Blei embodies the values and attitudes of his generation, inheritors of the Beat tradition of Kerouac and Ferlinghetti, and Miller and others before them.

Second, even in his most transcendent Zen moments, Blei is always conscious of himself as a Writer—not only *a* writer, but a particular *kind* of writer, the romantic rebel/outsider/loser in the tradition of Kenneth

Patchen, Henry Miller, and James T. Farrell. Even as a cub reporter, Blei took a position distanced from his subjects; he was the "Man in the Window" of Pixley & Ehler's, reading the newspaper, watching the world go by, finding "it difficult to sit still and concentrate on who he is and what is going on," trying to avoid "walking through the plate glass window himself" (*Chi Town* 22). A recurrent figure in Blei's paintings/drawings is the round, moustached face with the heavy eyebrows—Blei himself—floating above, distanced from, observing the action from the outside. A passage from Francisco Umbral's *A Mortal Spring* which Blei selected as an epigraph for *The Ghost of Sandburg's Phizzog* reads, "the writer is searching for something. I have no idea what, and neither does he. How meaningless, how insane the searching of others is. And what of our own? Does he see me as I see him, lost, anxious, alone? Capturing life in a book, taking time's measurements. That's writing."

The writer in this tradition is lost before he does battle, sings always a dying world in a minor key. He seeks others like himself—the alienated and the outcast, the fallen and the misunderstood—and if he has any proletarian sympathies, he will undoubtedly become a socialist. He will be too disorganized and too in love with the idea of failure to be a successful prol, so the movement will find him more a liability than an asset. Should the movement be successful, the writer will inevitably find reality a sad compromise with image, and break from the movement, to become, again, "lost, anxious, alone."

This self-absorption the modernist borrows from the romantics, and in this respect modernism is a continuation of the romantic tradition. Self-absorption, however, leads the writer away from community, loss of which first precipitated the writer's alienation, so the writer finds himself locked in a self-perpetuating circuit in which alienation produces (defensive) sensitivities, which produce further alienation. The writer's community is reduced to other alienated artists, and his economic support to donations from churchgoers who believe the jeremiad. (Thus this position may—just possibly may—provide some economic stability, or even success in the case of an Allen Ginsberg or Bob Dylan, in a Neo-puritan nation that feels the need for prophet figures and can afford, as a luxury, an occasional Jeremiah.) It is at this point that doctrines of a select audience, the poet as prophet, "the writer's writer," "barbed wire against the Philistine," purity of the small press, and the blessings of oblivion usually enter the picture.

As much as Blei is a hard-nosed realist recording the people and places of Cicero and Door, he is also the writer-prophet, lost in his own world. One measure of his self-absorption is the openings and conclusions of various books, both fiction and the non-fiction books about Door, Chicago, and Cicero:

Tell them how you got up in the dark this morning, here in Wisconsin, went downstairs, broke an egg into the frying pan and nothing came out. (*Adventures in an American's Literature* 4)

"What am I about? Is that the question? Begin again." (*Adventures in an American's Literature* 182)

I came to live in Door in the spring of 1969. (*Door Way* 1)

I began yesterday, or years ago, with winter here in Door. (*Door Way* 304)

I have attempted many journals in the past, and continue to record my observations in a variety of notebooks, but never have I kept a journal so consistently, so religiously, as the daybook that is the heart of *Door Steps*. (1)

I do not think so much of Christmas as *spirit*, alive in all men, in all seasons, in all places, and how it flickers in the darkest recesses imaginable. I think of my gift, my work: to find the people, the place, the time, the words and forms to say these things for all, yet make them mine. (*Door Steps* 230)

There were silver fish swimming in dark wooden barrels outside the meat markets on Cermak Road in Cicero then. (*Neighborhood* 1)

I am sitting at the bar of Old Prague in Cicero on a late autumn night, a stranger in my own neighborhood. (*Neighborhood* 265)

"In my time here I have been many men: City man, country man, outsider, insider, husband, father, son, lover, hater, friend, recluse, traveler, believer, iconoclast, poet, painter, teacher, writer . . . door man." (*Door to Door* 1)

I sit here in the early morning, late winter darkness of the coop, just back from New Mexico. (*Door to Door* 221)

When you settle into the quiet of the country, far removed from a life lived and loved in the big city, you experience a period of withdrawal, a homesickness, which can last for months or years. (*Chi Town* 1)

This is probably my last book of nonfiction set in Chicago. (*Chi Town* 381)

I'm not finished with winter yet. And winter is not finished with
me. (*Winter Book* 1)
I followed the dog, who seemed to know the way back. (*Winter
Book* 184)

The thinly veiled autobiographical nature of much of his fiction, the
frequency with which he introduces—by name, and pseudonymously—
his family and friends into his work, and the frequency with which he
himself intrudes into reportages all reflect Blei's concern for himself as
a writer.

Blei is conscious enough of his self-absorption to use it as material
for his fiction, even to satirize it. In *The Second Novel*, chapter 6, "The
Historical Objects of My Art" (71–113) he inventories Things a Writer
Needs: corduroy jacket, mustache, room, notebooks, beret, pipe, City of
New York, friends, City of Paris, little magazine, mistress, books, con-
tract, photograph, writing circuit. The trench coat:

> The ultimate mark of the American Writer as Myth.
> Hemingway, of course, had one. Read the famous Lillian Ross ac-
> count of Hemingway Buys a Burberry.
> As a writer in search of himself, I began with humbler resources,
> more in tune with my time—the 50's. Salinger. *The Catcher in the
> Rye*. Holden Caulfield.
> I displayed my Holden Caulfield raincoat all through the late 50's.
> It was especially unique on campus. It was unphony. You turned the
> collar up, buried your hands in the pockets, and mumbled to other
> guys in their Holden Caulfield raincoats how depressing everything
> was. We had style. The girls loved us. We were existentially exciting.
> I wanted a working writer's trench coat in Europe. I wanted an
> Original Burberry. I settled for less.
> I threw my ragged Holden Caulfield raincoat overboard on a
> Greek ship crossing from Corfu to Italy. In Rome I bought a very
> fashionable Italian raincoat, imitation trench coat, with a fancy belt,
> buckled sleeves, leather collar, and cut to hang in the latest style, just
> above the knee.
> Goddam it, I was sharp. It immediately attracted a beautiful Ital-
> ian street walker who followed me for block after block in the dark.
> When I finally turned around with my vision of Young American
> Writer astride Beautiful Black-haired Italian Woman in a brass bed

overlooking the fountains, the Spanish Steps, the flowers, the streets of Rome, she was gone. (78)

On the subject of mail, Blei approaches self-satire:

> There are two dramatic incidents in the daily life of the Writer: (1) before the mail; (2) after the mail.
>
> Before the mail, hours of waking and morning, coffee and smoke and working with words. The Writer is confident that the mail will save him. Someone will tell him that his words are necessary. Someone will reward him or make an offer for his words. Someone will promise him fame. . . .
>
> After the mail, the silent afternoon, the night-without-ending-amen, the Writer executes a number of gestures toward dying. No one has sent him anything for survival. Not one friend has found it necessary to answer his words. Not an editor alive is conscious of how quietly he kills a man. (*Second Novel* 159)

In the postmodern tradition, Blei the author can toy with Blei the author-character, creating a humorous dialogue of voices and making the telling of the story the story itself:

> I confess: it worked. Father Kiley, the old man, both of them saved me from a life of crime.
>
> *Hassock, you're a sucker for irony. Who did you steal that from, Chekhov? Well, thank God that's over.*
>
> For a beginning I would forget the past and become a teacher myself.
>
> *Now isn't that a hell of a way to go on with the story? Why should anyone care what happened to a man with an opening like that? Christ, you can do better.*
>
> To tell you the truth, I'm lost for the moment. Looking, as usual, for an opening, a place to begin.
>
> *Hassock, just tell the goddam story, will you? No excuses.*
>
> If there were enough art to my storytelling, I could somehow fade from that criminal past to the virtuous choice of the present and really make you believe that the kind of kid just described could become, quite naturally, a teacher. (*Adventures* 30)

> *the weekend visitors*
>
> The writer needs company. He calls Chicago after midnight and reverses the charges. He calls during the late show when the setting,

character, and plot are too confusing. "Hello, Ralph? Just got back from Tangiers. Who is this? You know, you know, what's-his-name. The Writer. Come on up this weekend. Bring the family. Bring brandy, tobacco, and food. The job doesn't matter, Ralph. So you get snowed in. You get used to snow. I'm hungry, Ralph. Get in that fucking wagon of yours and drive. We'll go sledding. I promise. And someday, some day, Ralph, you're going to hear from me. Someday you're going to feel proud you drove all the way up to this fucking wilderness to feed a friend." (*Second Novel* 153)

The early stories and first novel present probably the most fictionalized versions of his acquaintances. Ralph Rausch is a loose model for Reckelson in *Adventures*, Ross LewAllen is more directly Arroyo, and Jerry Bitts is the novel's Clay. Kirstin, "Princess K" or "the Balloon Lady," was "a combination of two students, one of whom went to Yale, plus a third wild one I never messed with in high school, but spent an evening with until 3:00 A.M. after she graduated" (Letter). In *The Second Novel*, Rausch and family appear as Rausch and family in chapter 12, in which the Rausches visit the Bleis in Door County. In *Door to Door* (1985), Blei is not only recounting his relationship with Rausch, but analyzing it in great, often tedious depth—along with detailed analyses of Ross LewAllen, Arlene LewAllen, Dave Etter, and Chris Spanovich (who had appeared earlier, fictionalized, in "The Hour of the Sunshine Now" and "A Distance of Horses").

In journals (*Door Steps*), and collections of columns, interviews, and letters (*Chronicles, Meditations*) we of course expect the author to take center stage. Conventions of the new journalism, which often encouraged self as subject, and certainly allowed the reporter to introduce himself and his biases into reportage, legitimized Blei's introspective vision and made his personal preferences and history a proper subject even in *Chi Town* essays on Chicago's foreign banks ("Nor do I enjoy being kept waiting in such an atmosphere of ominous silence," 207), trash collectors ("When they approached the ball field like a small army, we knew our work was cut out for us. 'Here come the woodenheads!' we shouted in a false sense of bravado," 217), and a Skid Row evangelist ("But he is a believer, a Christian, a good man. And I am not all of those," 279).

In *The Second Novel: Becoming a Writer*, a book about writing and about the book about writing failing to find a publisher, Blei is of course center stage. The subject might easily have been handled with a persona, and to a very slight degree the unfolding character of this narrator is an Everywriter, growing as the novel unfolds (not unlike Mailer in *The Armies of the Night*) out of his own ego. Despite the ironic distancing evident in "trench coat" and "mail," however, the distance between speaker and author is not great. *The Second Novel* is confessional in the extreme: the notebook entries, the letters of rejection from little magazine editors, the visits to New York and Paris, "The Way We Live, November 14, 1969," "This is December in Wisconsin," "For Years I have Been Waiting for a Letter," the Rausch visit in "What There Is to Tell About," and of course "Anticlimaxes," correspondence surrounding publication of *The Second Novel*, which suggests that other readers found very little fiction in the work. "I'm rewriting in a sense my own life," Blei admits (142); "that's all a writer ever does."

On the last page of *The Watercolored Way*, Blei quotes Miller as saying, "ART is only a lesson—The real art must be one's life."

The presence, and celebration, of the writer's self was less acceptable in the literature of the fifties and early sixties than it is today, and occasioned (or provided an excuse for) strong criticism of Blei's manuscripts. "Henry Miller's statement opening your book cannot be used as a catch-all for all of your work simply because it covers the events of your life," wrote E. P. Dutton editor Hal Scharlatt in rejecting *The Second Novel* (*Second Novel* 223); "Well, maybe it can, but I don't think it works." Agent Knox Burger found the book "so self-indulgent, so solipsistic, so whimsical that its charm, its candor, seem to get rather swamped" (223). Editor Fran McCullough of Harper & Row wrote, "I think it's the most extraordinary example I've ever seen of a writer with nothing to say—a good, obviously talented writer who's more than a little bitter" (227). "Too self-indulgent for my taste," wrote Ted Bent of Atheneum (224).

Even in the eighties and nineties, the obsessively inward vision of some of Blei's books may have been the reason for significantly lower sales for *Door to Door*, in which the chapters are all long, and some are detailed analyses of Blei's relationships with close personal friends, than for *Door Way*, whose people were better known to the Door County public. Sales for *Neighborhood* (presently in its third printing) were larger than for *The Second Novel*.

Blei's proclivity for self-analysis is directly at odds with his need to fix a place. Of the three tasks Blei assigns himself as a writer—to recreate the past and preserve selective elements of a fast-disappearing present, especially the darker or more highly seasoned parts of his environment;

to perpetuate and promote the reputations of writers he considers worthy; and to analyze his own personality and relationships with friends—two are public and found an audience large enough to support a freelance writer (barely). The third, more private vision has always gotten Blei into trouble, and is probably the root of his ambivalence to Door County, where folks naturally harbor the countryman's suspicion of outsiders, city dwellers, book readers, atheists—those who work with their brains more than their hands.

Blei's response to discovering himself again an outsider is usually (a) an attack on rural provincialism or the American cultural monolith, or (b) an appeal to artistic integrity. As good an example as any is the canceling of Blei's column in the *Door County Advocate*. Editor Chan Harris explained the newspaper's position in an editorial of July 21, 1981:

> We wrote to him [Blei] and to several other contributors saying that we were cutting down on the creative and non-Door material. This includes Notes Along the Way, which are personal essays. Norb did a beautiful piece upon the death of William Saroyan. . . . At our editorial conference we had to decide what we were. Does an article on Saroyan belong in the *Door County Advocate*? What are the limitations of our role? How big do we want to try to become? (*Door to Door* 3–4)

The rationale sounds very much like Blei's own arguments against expansion in other areas of Door County, like condominiums, motels, and gift shops. In this case, however, Blei took a position akin to that of the developers he so frequently excoriated, welcoming outsiders as more cosmopolitan than natives, an audience better able to appreciate his columns: "People with summer homes and condos here, but permanent residences in Milwaukee, Madison, Chicago, Florida, and elsewhere. Vacationers from the city who subscribe to the *Advocate* to keep in touch with the country. City people moving here permanently. The audience, as I saw it, would continue to expand and grow more diverse" (*Door to Door* 4).

In *The Second Novel*, Blei attacks the American cultural monolith: "What's wrong is the system in this country which often forces artists to prostitute their talents in order to survive. The artist is to blame only in his moment of weakness. And the quality of his work will suffer for it" (110). In *Chi Town* he invokes artistic integrity to defend the writer: "In the end, it doesn't really matter. He's never home. No writer is. He suffers from a bad case of being out of place. Identity uncertain. Destination unknown. Home is in the writing, the only place he lives" (384). Pressed, Blei reduces his obligations to one: please himself. "I have my own standards," Blei quotes Royko as saying; "What's important is that it satisfies me" (*Chi Town* 104). To which Blei adds, "Pour the wine to that."

Blei's confusion about his role and status as a writer is, of course, a direct result of his wide reading in and outside the company of Chicago writers. Competing twentieth-century literary traditions tug any writer in many conflicting directions, and even such classical modernists as Pound and Eliot attempt paradoxically to preserve an idealized past (or fragments thereof) and to make everything new. Reconciling the claims of tradition and the individual talent was a lifelong work for both.

Blei's range of reading is considerable, and not limited to Chicagoans or twentieth-century authors.[19] *The Second Novel*, completed by 1969, quotes or references Eberhart, Ciardi, Hemingway, Elizabeth Sargent, Saroyan, Colin Wilson (on "The Outsider" 74), Salinger, Kerouac, Lorca, Melville, Wolfe, Dylan Thomas, Steinbeck, Miller, Norman O. Brown, Lawrence, Cyril Connolly, Dostoevsky, Edna O'Brien, Hesse, John Cage, Theodore Roethke, Dylan, McLuhan, Sartre and Camus, the Muromachi Ballads, Konrad Z. Lorenz, Wakayama Bokusui, and Blei's own crowd of Chicago writer friends. As an undergraduate he read the black authors and the Russian writers passed him by Paul Romaine. In a 1970s article on Italians reprinted in *Neighborhood* (1987), Blei mentions the Italian writers Moravia and Silone. As he continued to read, teach, and review through the seventies, eighties, and nineties, Blei's range—and library—expanded exponentially. Wisconsin writers were added to the Chicago writers, especially August Derleth, whose *Walden West* became a model for *Door Way* (people plus village plus landscape). The coop is floor-to-ceiling books; the living room in the house is lined with bookshelves double-stacked and sorted by country: Russians, Czechs, Poles, Latin Americans.

Blei especially recalls three influences on his early writing: Henry Miller, William Saroyan, and Kenneth Patchen. Despite his strong American ties, Miller's real heart was Europe, and Europe was one thing Miller gave Blei. Blei was impressed by the pungent sex of Miller's life in Paris, his experience in Chicago (recounted in *The Air-Conditioned Nightmare*), and his bohemian life abroad and in Big Sur. Blei bought the *Tropic* books on his first trip to Mexico, and was familiar enough with Miller's work to promote him to Ross LewAllen during his second high school teaching stint in the middle sixties. (In *Adventures*, Blei as

Miroslav Blazen recommends Miller's *The Angel Is My Watermark* to LewAllen as Arroyo.) Blei mentions corresponding with Miller "on a number of occasions" (*Chi Town* 265), sending him a watercolor, receiving a thanks in reply (6). Miller taught Blei the use of self as subject, the legitimacy of mixed or impure form, and the art of work that is amateur, unrefined, primitive, and naive. Remembering his early attempts at painting, Blei writes, "[Miller's] own words also helped me to keep going: 'One of the important things I learned in making watercolors was not to worry, not to care too much'" (*Paint* 43; the Miller quote appears on the dedication/copyright page of *The Watercolored Word*). Repeatedly in talking about his painting, Blei credits Miller's *To Paint Is to Love Again*, or just Miller in general:

> Henry Miller helped. Oh, not personally. But in his essays on painting. His books on art. His own watercolors. Coming across his watercolors for the first time was something close to a religious revelation. "Here!" [I believe I screamed out loud] "is a man who can't paint a watercolor! Here are the most joyous watercolors I have ever seen." (*Paint* 43)

This epiphany was transferred directly to the story "A Quiet":

> I laughed and told him: "Nonsense. Just go ahead and paint. Paint anything that really stirs you. Anything you really feel. Just put it on canvas . . . the way you feel. The technique will come later. There will be plenty of time for refinement. First, you must paint." (*Hour* 34)

The "Homage to Henry Miller," reproduced on the cover of *Paint Me a Picture/Make Me a Poem*, features a likeness of Henry Miller, a nude blonde (always) with a face of Norbert Blei above, several postage stamps (including the LOVE U.S. / 8-center, a couple of European nudes, and a Greek Orthodox priest), various pictographs (moon, star, bird, sun), and three lines from Miller: "To Paint Is to Love Again," "Do Something you can't do," and "Paint as you like and die happy!"

Saroyan's gifts to Blei were a moustache, an appreciation for ethnicity, and the magic of madness:

> You're not reading him [son Christopher] that Saroyan book again?
> It's my favorite . . . "And that's how it was when you wanted to say give me the orange, or look at the tree, or listen to the bird, or what is the moon. It was the only word anybody ever heard."

That's crazy . . . Read him something else. He doesn't understand that.

Neither do I . . . that's why I read it. (*Second Novel* 136)

"Saroyan is an adventure," Blei writes in *Adventures* (6); "Sometimes in class, when I really felt dismayed, when perhaps Hester's Scarlet 'A' became too much of a punishment for all of us, I would turn to Saroyan for life. Miller, too. The only writers worth reading are those who lived adventures and are dying to tell about them."

Patchen, he adds, is "another adventure in American Literature" (6). "I can't say I understood the guy at first," Blei recalled (Letter), but Patchen appealed initially to Blei's political side (especially *The Journal of Albion Moonlight*), later as an example of "how one can get buried in this country by being a rebel poet or being an underground poet or being one who just kind of fell between the cracks." Along with the politics, Patchen introduced Blei to "a very personal world, a very intimate world with the love poetry," a world that influenced Blei's early love poems and paintings, especially those in *Paint Me a Picture / Make Me a Poem*. In Patchen Blei found the odd paradox of a political world full of brutality and dark foreboding combined with a private almost mythological world full of gentle optimism and whimsical humor. Patchen reinforced Miller's lessons in concrete poems, mixed form or no form, and the writer's self as subject.[20] Patchen was as much a visual as a literary influence, and Blei painted a series of "Patch Dispatches," adorned with Patchen figures, quotations, and a likeness of Patchen. An early dispatch reproduced in *Paint Me a Picture* (90), reflects Patchen's political activism: "Patchen, / The Killing continues 'round the clock. / War is the national pastime. / AGENT-air-Orange / Water, ash / Branches weep for / the Ghosts / of enchanted Birds / The Business of / Government is Business. / 'What / shall we / do about / us' you / ask? / Heaven's on Fire / Oh / follow the fabulous animals to the kingdom! / Nothing you pictured and poemed / was done in vain. / Creatures smile, the Visionary / King remains!" *Patchen Dispatch #4*, a watercolor which hangs, framed, beside my desk, reads, "There is no hope left in the world / But how drunk I am with LIFE / The Revenge of Albion Moonlight."

Despite his borrowings from literary sources as diverse as Patchen and Miller, Sydney J. Harris and Mike Royko, Ginsberg and Kerouac, Central Europeans (Russian and Bohemian), ethnic realists like Petrakis and Farrell, and the cult of Indian mythology; despite the moustache and pipe and trench coat and other borrowed writerly accessories; despite his absorption into Zen and letting things be; despite his need for the old community and the ethnic society, Blei places great emphasis on originality. The experiments were most extreme early in his career, precisely when his borrowings are most obvious, in *The Watercolored Word*, *Adventures in an American's Literature*, and *The Second Novel*, products of the late 1960s when all America was being renovated.

In "The Hour of the Sunshine Now," Blei shifts point of view from first person to third limited to third omniscient, inside, outside the mind of Mary O'Monahan, the painter from Tawa de La Cruce. Toward the conclusion of that same story he uses one two-sentence, seventy-word paragraph four times to introduce four different movements, as if stuttering or feeling for direction. Into that story he cuts references to paintings by Klee ("I'd love to have that story printed sometime with the paintings, in color") and pictographs, a technique used in other fiction. In "I'm Komher, K-o-m-h-e-r; I'm Moving," Blei brakes a sentence to slowmo by breaking it into sentence fragments: "The first shot. Whistled. And crashed. Through the garage window. Above him. Komher. Kicked. The dog. And dashed. Through the back gate. The second shot. Struck. Him. The dog. In midair" (44). In "In the Secret Places of the Stairs" Blei distinguishes voices in a dialogue by having Pritzker speak in normal typography (without punctuation marks) and Althoff speak in all lower case letters, including the first-person I: "don't say that, pritzker . . . she's a good wife . . . i trust her (*Ghost* 34).

Another level of innovation, which links Blei with other writers of the fifties, is strictly verbal, the story as a performance of itself:

> And then what? And then what? That's the way to begin a story, Hassock! Don't bore the hell out of them. Get down to basics. Get moving. Tell them how you've been trying to write this for many moons. Tell them how this is the 333rd revision of the beginning, and it still isn't true. . . .
>
> Tell them about all the women you've won with your watercolors. . . .
>
> Tell them about the poem you've painted on the ceiling above your head. (*Adventures* 4)
>
> This is enough for TODAY. TOMORROW I will SEE where I am at. TONIGHT I know where I am headed. And YESTERDAY was pretty much the same.

THIS IS THE NEXT DAY: and I try hard not to think too much about what I am doing. It is important for creators to do NOTHING so there is space enough for mistakes to be made. (*Second Novel* 3)

Both *Adventures* and *The Second Novel* contain the de rigueur postmodern false starts, verbal switchbacks, self-assessments, qualifications, and narrative interruptions:

One of the things a writer must finally accept is that he may not be a writer at all.
I accept that now. But I don't accept it.
What else do I want to do?
    nothing   nothing
Then I must be a writer?
    yes   yes
But I am not a Great Russian Writer or a Great French Writer or a Great American Writer.
                 Who says?
I do. I believe this. I have made comparisons. I have letters from editors and publishers and agents to other writers to prove it. And I have all the silence I have been trying to live with for so many years.
But none of this can stop me now. I'm going to write anyway. So fuck everybody. (*Second Novel* 10)

On other levels, Blei moves into mixed forms, following Patchen and Miller. Blei was "pasting down everything that couldn't be nailed down, including, occasionally, nails and rusty bits of other *objets d'art*" (*Paint* 43); later (1967–70) he moved through watercolor painting and paste-pot poems, to "Poem Paintings . . . writing on the finished work, writing slogans, words, thoughts, stories, poems" (43). *The Watercolored Word* (1968) was a saddle-stapled, 88–page 8 1/2 by 11 inch collage of paste-pot poems, text, drawings, photos, watercolor paintings, photocopied coupons (filled out by a Mr. Joseph Brozna, age 17, of 2312 N. Dawagia, Chicago, Illinois), printed in colors variously green, red, blue, and brown, from page to page. Its subject matter varies: Ross LewAllen's home-constructed carousel (celebrated again in the closing chapter of *Adventures*), postcards Blei sends to his son, women, love, teaching, wacky stories culled from the newspaper. The book's real subject, however, is experimentation, in subject, graphic design, and modes of expression.

The graphic experiments continue in *The Second Novel* (on page 234, December Press publisher Curt Johnson expresses some concern over the expense of typesetting), and then largely disappear in the Story Press and Ellis Press books, with the exception, of course, of *Paint Me a Picture/Make Me a Poem*.[21] Possibly Blei's publishers became conservative; possibly the times themselves changed. But Blei's own Cross+Roads Press chapbooks are conservative in matters of design, except for the Emmet Johns and Bill Stipe books. Handsome but not remarkably innovative—text in a single typeface, a few black-and-white illustrations, colored endpaper, maybe a page of holograph manuscript text—they represent a definite retreat from *The Watercolored Word* and *The Second Novel*.

Blei did pursue further experiments in his drawings, paintings, and other word/graphic projects, including the spring, 1990 (12, ii NS) issue of *The Kenyon Review*, devoted to what contributing editor T. R. Hummer called "impure form." These experiments are collected in *Paint Me a Picture / Make Me a Poem* (Ellis Press, 1987). Blei experiments in three major areas of text and graphic form. The first is typography: typeface, point size, leading, placement of text on page, what Charles Olson called field composition, the arrangement of words across a whole page, or field. A second level of text and form is achieved when the shape of the letters of a word take on iconographical significance, which may range from simply being clever to being a part of the painting/poem's meaning. Blei called "Look. Now Love" a written painting. Originally painted and reproduced (*The Watercolored Word*) in brilliant splashes of primary colors, the poem generates its force from the directness of its statement, the simplicity of its style—almost finger painting—and the repetition, twice, of the word *look*. The graceful, open arc of *N* and *W* in *now*, the bold *L* in *love*, the heart-shaped *V* of the same word—these allow the word's shape to underscore its cognitive value. In another moment poem, "Rain on the Tao," Blei's calligraphy heightens similarities between the *T* in *Tao* and the *T* in *lightening*, synthesizing the poem's separate images; the second *i* in *Lightening!* is made to resemble an inverted exclamation mark, the inverse of the exclamation mark which ends the poem, creating a clever visual pun.[22] In "Apartheid," the vertically aligned letters of *heid* form a white wall restraining the disoriented black letters of *apart*, with obvious puns on *heid*/*held* and *apart*.

A third level is the combination of visual and verbal images, in the tradition of medieval manuscripts or the poems of William Blake, sometimes as illustrations, sometimes as expansions, sometimes as counterpoint. Patchen's whimsical combination of words and images reappears in Blei, and some of the figures as well. In the painting-poems, image dominates text. The eye rests first on a primary image, then on a secondary image (drawn or possibly a postage stamp or other icon), and finally on text, which may be very small. Some images re-appear throughout Blei's work; others are painting-specific. Prominent among these is the nude female, which emerged during the 1980s as in-creasingly realistic and festishized. Accompanying the naked woman, floating almost Chagall-like, as a totem, is usually a moustached male figure, Blei himself. Also recurrent in Blei's painting-poems is a series of symbols drawn from Christianity or Native American mythology, dat-ing to *The Hour of the Sunshine Now*: cross, angel, sun, moon, stars, bird, horse, rainbow, spiral, stick figure man, spirit (circle with a dot in-side). The raven carries special significance:

> The painter from a small village in Jugoslavia who prepares the dead for burial . . . and then paints them, to honor their life on earth, he has a pet crow with him in the village mortuary, which serves as his studio as well. And he puts great faith in the survival of that raven. . . . I painted Tisnikar's raven for a friend who has the soul of that raven. Who will survive despite all hardships. And I painted it for whoever happens to see it and identify with it." (Blei, "Painted Word")[23]

When Blei visited Central Europe in the spring of 1990, the Berlin Wall presented him with a fascinating combination of images and words incorporating several sets of balances: professional and native artists, old and new, permanent and ephemeral, artistic and political, the symbol of political oppression converted to a vehicle of free artistic ex-pression for "the words of the people" (Blei referenced Carl Sandburg): "graffiti of anger, nonsense, sarcasm, prophecy, love, hate, joy, despair" ("Echoes" 14). At the end, the art of demolition, as hammers and chis-els reduced words and images to chips of painted cement. Anyone could and did paint the Wall. What particularly interested him, however, was the Wall's constantly changing nature, its randomness,[24] the complete lack of censorship, and the way recent painters incorporated elements of previous painters into their own work.

Starting in 1989, Blei produced a series of watercolors which be-came, collectively, *Die Mauer*. The paintings combine visual icons, real-istic graphic illustrations, postage stamps, slogans, visual references to well-known artists, and just plain graffiti. They sometimes divide and subdivide the field into multiple small boxes, occasionally replicate the color and texture of the graffiti-covered cement wall itself, and sometimes integrate elements into one composed painting. Cultural icons include Ronald McDonald, Karl Marx (wearing a "What Me Worry" button), Marilyn Monroe, Marlene Dietrich, Alice (in Wonderland), Dick Tracy, Charlie Chaplin, and Johann Sebastian Bach (wearing an Orange Alternative button). Recognizable visual references are to Munch, Miró, Fassbinder, Beuys, Grosz, Klee, Picasso, and Raphael's whimsical cherubs. Among the icons, several holdovers from earlier Blei: cross, circle, wolf/coyote, bird/raven, moon, the odd crowned head out of Patchen. Most icons are new, however, the breast/stripper and the skeleton/skull prominent among them. The A enclosed in a circle, symbol of the so-called Orange Alternative (a political graffiti group active throughout Europe on both sides of the Iron Curtain during the Cold War days, and thus a model for what Blei was doing), appears at least three times. Professor Rat, from *The Blue Angel*, appears twice. One painting includes a white cross like those that commemorated people who died trying to escape the East, complete with "Unbekannt 16–4–1963." Slogans are in German and English: "zu spät" (twice), "fight again," "If you love someone, set them free," "Gruppe 47," "Scheisst auf die Mauer" (twice), "Berlin wird Mauer frei," "Nein, man muss nicht alles für wahr halten; man muss es nur für notwendig halten," "Ich will mit den Herrn Kommendanten sprechen," "Keep us informed," "Mehr Fleisch," "Macht's wie die Tauben," "Die Mauer Muss Bleiben," "Solidarnos´c" (from Poland), "Schaut Euch An," "Division/ Bring Sorrow, Tears and Blood," and the German/English pun on *die* (German *the*) and *die* (English *expire*). The result is an unconventional blend of words and pictures that "addresses our fixed notions of what each of these forms of expression mean . . . a visual circus: an amorphous anarchistic pool of symbols and forms, lacking their original context and meaning . . . a living concrete poem chronicling a time period, a nation, and above all else, a division" ("Echoes" 14).

Perhaps the most revealing quotation incorporated into the *Die Mauer* series is, "There are no such things as unshakable principles—everything is alive and in flux."

Provisional art has, in the second half of the twentieth century, received quite as much attention as mixed media, or impure art, and for the same reason: it reflects our twentieth-century sensibility distracted from distraction by distraction to the point at which our attention no longer focuses and we no longer remember. On this subject, Blei sounds like a lecture in postmodern aesthetics at any American university: "Only the hand that erases can write the true thing" (Meister Eckhardt, quoted in *Paint*, 1). "What is art? 'What isn't?'" quoted from Kurt Schwitters (*Paint*, epigraph page). Blei is fascinated with Bill Stipe, "one of the great unknowns in the Chicago art world" (*Chi Town* 77), whose one-man show in New York went nowhere ("Nobody of any importance came to the gallery to see it"), whose Evanston mural "Davis 'L' Bus Stop" was painted over, who never made it beyond associate assistant professor at Northwestern because he was "invisible" (81), who finally disappeared from his Chicago address, phone disconnected, no forwarding address: "The artist is creating his ultimate masterpiece: the invisible Bill Stipe" (84). Nor is Stipe the only portrait in *Chi Town* to end in invisibility or oblivion:

"I don't want nothing from nobody," he smiles, opening his newspaper. "I just say thank you." Then he disappears into the silence of his art. ("A Man on a Bench" 135)

"You asked what comes to mind when I look at these books now? A good question. Ghosts," he sighs. "Ghosts. Haunting in a way . . . haunting." ("The Petrakis Story, 1980" 338)

And though he may be lost or out of place at the moment, somehow I see Sam undoubtedly up there somewhere still making a fast buck, riding for another fall. ("Sam Karnick: Window Washer" 331)

And with those words and a deafening flourish, it's the end. And Dixie dies in Westmont, on the outskirts of town. ("Dixie: On the Outskirts of Town" 240)

Farrell died with less that $10,000 in his estate.
He left a fortune in literature. ("On James T. Farrell: Not Resting in Peace" 228)

"UP KAFKA!" he was heard to yell just before disappearing into a damp corridor of darkness. ("Chicago's Public Library" 157)

Charley sits alone in a room on skid row and waits for morning. ("Chicago's Unforgettable Newsies" 152)

The artist's conscious decision for oblivion is the theme of Blei's story "The Landscaper," in which Portal County watercolorist Sandor Waterman decides "to walk out of his life a failed painter, abandon the Portal County landscape in the dark, and find what there was to ordinary life in the time that remained" (*Ghost* 142). He does, too, leaving Portal County to work in an Oriental import shop on Michigan Avenue and live in an ethnic neighborhood with a nineteen-year-old waitress named Cindy Davinci, a "high school dropout of unknown parentage" (158), who would like to paint. In "Dwelling," a story about the dark period of adjustment to Door, the narrator does his best to disappear, first down a rabbit hole in the neighboring field, then into the darkness of his own basement.

This celebration of oblivion and invisibility is in one sense Blei's excuse for his own failure to be rich and famous, in another sense a mature acceptance of that anonymity which his youthful self feared and resented. It is entirely congruent with the lost and defeated people of his native and adopted native places, Cicero and Door. It is the logical development of the sixties' affection for little, invisible people and the failed, misunderstood artist. It is a reflection of his Zen acceptance of the inevitability, immutability of mutability. It is an invitation, a challenge, possibly a cry: "Come with me. Find me if you can. Find me, please!" It reflects a coy desire to be mysterious. It is the logical consequence of the bankruptcy of late capitalist commercial publishing, and a sixties abhorrence for the commercial, the successful, the slick, the homogenized. Possibly it is a statement that what appears smallest is ultimately the largest; what passes most quickly is, in the mind's eye, most permanent. Analogies in late twentieth-century American culture, high and low, abound. "How strange to think of giving up all ambition," writes Robert Bly.

"She knows there's no success like failure, and that failure's no success at all," sings Bob Dylan.

"Let it go, Indy," advises Professor Jones Sr.

Dylan, Bly, Burroughs, Ginsberg (Whitman, Thoreau) made good literary currency from the small and nearly invisible—Blei is very much in the American grain. Other artists—Patchen comes immediately to mind—have found nothing in this position except poverty and pain. And purity is small consolation for pain and isolation, especially to a young man trying to feed a family, impress a girlfriend, or become a writer. The voices of Miller or Patchen can be comforting and even convincing, but provisionalism and erasure are the precise opposite of reconstructing and preserving in writing everything related to his childhood and self.

If modernism is made of tension and paradox, Blei is a true modernist, committed to exploring endless possibilities and preserving the old neighborhoods, intent on stopping time and transcending the moment, seeking community while exploring his own self, chanting the Latin mass while preaching skepticism, decorating his coop with nude women and crucifixes, practicing commercial journalism and writing/painting whatever spills from typewriter or brush, simultaneously preserving the roots and breaking the roots. Possibly Blei's repeated periods of crisis, self-doubt, and sterility resulted from the exhaustion of trying to reconcile polarities, or from terror, as Blei confronted the truth that he both fears and is drawn toward death and invisibility. What father of two young children could afford the luxury of disappearing down a rabbit hole—especially when he had not yet, like Sandor Waterman, achieved commercial success?

Blei's published short fiction, which is his best work, was produced mostly between 1970 and 1985, when the author was in his late thirties and forties. Much of that fiction, whether it is set in Cicero or Door or the American Southwest, is built around combining contrasting motifs of descent into enclosed space (often sexual, dark, and destructive) and ascent into the open heavens (often religious, light, and redemptive). The wife of "The Old Woman's Preserves" settles first in the ship's hold, then in the dark apartment "underneath this brown building of stone" in the city; her husband speaks of a new land where "rivers and lakes danced in the sun, where mountains shouldered their way above trees and clouds" (*Hour* 11). The terror of "The Basement" ("The coal shed was latched, but something was in there because I could hear feet stepping on coal dust, cracking it to splinters like glass"—*Hour* 28) is balanced against an attic ("but I never climbed that high"—*Hour* 21). In "A Quiet" T. J. Kant works in the warehouse and dreams of Europe and birds, with "their flight through space, their great sweep of the air, their concern with just flying" (*Hour* 33). Murphy, the drunken Irishman, builds a ladder of chairs, disappearing "in the darkness beyond the light" (*Ghost* 114). The Michigan kitchen and Wisconsin chicken coop of the egg ladies in a story of that title contrast to the attic, where its narrator sleeps. In the initiation story "Skarda" Blei's narrator ascends from his grandmother's dark basement full of beheaded chickens, strange languages, and the gypsy fortune-teller to an attic bedroom "so white that I thought the roof had disappeared and snow had fallen in" (*Ghost* 19). In "In the Secret Places of the Stairs," sixty-three-year-old Pritzker enjoys Wilma, his woman of maturity and experience, in the apartment basement; his dreams, however, ascend to nineteen-year-old Ula, just arrived from Vilnius, in a penthouse apartment on the roof. In "Dwelling," Jack hides in the basement, ignoring the voice of Hope in the house above him.

In all of these stories, Blei is attracted as much to the dark as to the light (perhaps more), as much to descent as to ascent. Repeatedly he suggests that descent is a precondition to ascent, or that descent and ascent are both indistinguishable and genderless. Although the male may be identified with intellectual or commercial-practical ascent, and the female with bodily or sexual-sensual descent ("The Old Woman's Preserves," "Skarda"), the roles may be reversed (Jack and Hope, Komher and Mildred, Sandor Waterman and Joan), or a woman of age and experience be paired against a woman of youth and naïveté in the bottom and top of the building respectively . . . with the male opting, finally, for the basement. In "The Hour of the Sunshine Now," given the position of honor at the conclusion of Blei's book by the same title, Blei's artist-alter ego is a woman—Mary O'Monahan, of Boston to New Mexico via St. Louis—who paradoxically descends through mortification of the body's needs for sex and sustenance into oblivion and death, while ascending into fame as an artist. Toward the end, even her paintings become smaller, more minimalist. The story ends with Mary playing the Christ in the annual reenactment of Holy Week by the Penitentes near Los Alamos, New Mexico. Whether Mary dies of starvation before she is actually crucified is a moot point: she has died to be reborn, disappeared to achieve "NOT TOMORROW BUT TODAY" (64).

In "Stars," given the position of honor at the end of *The Ghost of Sandburg's Phizzog*, Blei's protagonist is a Cicero lad caught between his friendships with an adolescent Dutch American sadist named Hookstra, and Davey Nactman ("night man" in German), the Jewish American intellectual/artist who is Hookstra's favorite victim. Davey's mom, "the most beautiful mother I had ever seen" (177), provides an object of sublimated sexual desire, similar to Skarda in an earlier story, to which the narrator would like to ascend. Hints that the narrator's mother is having an affair with a man in a 1941 Plymouth provide further sexual possibilities on a darker, lower plane. Most of the time the narrator plays other ascensionist games: World War II piloting with his friends, riding the El into Chicago ("when the El began to rise from the groundlevel of our neighborhood, over and beyond the prairie and factories of No Man's Land, we would watch everything diminish in size behind us," 167) or, on rainy days, sitting in "the attic alone and [playing] with a toy village that somehow came into our family from some relation in Europe" (169). The view from the attic affords Blei's narrator the privileged although isolated position of the writer, and associates ascension with preservation:

> Wherever I am in the world, whenever I think of my old neighborhood, I view the setting in miniature the way a child creates imaginary places. These are the boundaries, we would say in our hide-and-seek games. Or, these are the sidewalks here, I might say to myself alone. (165)

In the story's climax, Hookstra and his gang, including the narrator, conspire to take Davey "prisoner" in a war game. They lead him blindfolded to a box car in a factory outside the protection of their own neighborhood, abuse him just slightly, then run to beat hell. Returning safely from a terrifying dash through a strange and hostile place, the narrator ascends immediately to his bedroom, "looking up and feeling the roof of the house had been blown off" (196): in his absence his parents have covered the ceiling with glow-in-the-dark paper stars.

In concluding the story, Blei's narrator returns to the present, to a neighborhood altered almost beyond recognition, where nights are light and his key no longer opens his father's front door. He attempts to reclaim through memory the old neighborhood, now invisible—both the dark alleys below and the bright, unattainable stars above:

> In the dead of night in my father's house, we each [narrator and father] retire to our old bedrooms, leaving the doors ajar. "Jesus," I hear him sigh from his bed.
>
> I lay [sic] in the emptiness of my room, putting everything back in place, struggling to find the words . . . *I believe . . . in all things . . . invisible.* (196)

"Stars" contains all the multiple impulses that drive Blei's fiction: the impulse toward light and the gravitational tug of darkness below, the contrasting opportunities of art and life, the opposite pulls of the transcendent and the mundane, the call of the past and the demands of the present, the need to succeed and the compulsion to fail. It reflects Blei's need to preserve and break from his roots. The device of an adult narrator reconstructing his childhood while visiting his father's house creates a dual time frame not unlike that used by Bly, Holm, Keillor, and any number of other midwestern writers of place, and with similar results: Blei's tone is tender without being sentimental, and he remains true to details of place and the writer's special, shaping vision.

In the face of the competing demands of place and art, Blei's writing inevitably fails, but in failing it succeeds as much as art can succeed, as a temporary stay against confusion. And are not most great works of art—and many almost great works of art—thematic or structural shambles? The stories, poems, novels, and essays of Norbert Blei at least offer compelling photos of people in a place and time, and a record of the struggles of one first-rate mind to reconcile the opposites of self and community, idea and landscape, light and dark, local and universal, temporal and eternal. What more can we ask of a writer in the twentieth century?

Linda Hasselstrom

It Is "Like Far"

> *I knew at the end of my next arc, gravity would snatch me*
> *clear, spin me out beyond the stars. Free of the ranch, I*
> *thought, free of my father, but flying out of control into*
> *darkness.*
> —*Linda Hasselstrom*, Feels Like Far

Although Linda M. Hasselstrom, like Dave Etter, was not born in the Midwest, she belongs to the great tradition of Midwest writing described in chapter 1 of this book, a tradition that draws content from "the heart of the heartland" and owes to geography its peculiar style—directness, practicality, close observation, experience as a touchstone of knowledge, and "astuteness about people and the impact of social and economic conditions on their relationships and attitudes" (Mueller, "Midwestern Poetry" 2, 3). A preference for experience over theory and abstraction characterizes all of Hasselstrom's work. A poet and a writer of memoir, she is as likely to speak to a group of environmentalists or the Department of Fisheries and Wildlife as a creative writing class. A feminist by any definition, including her own,[1] Hasselstrom is much more likely to read Ed Abbey, Ernest Hemingway, Wendell Berry, Frederick Manfred, Aldo Leopold, Wes Jackson, Loren Eiseley, and John McPhee than Naomi Wolf or Judith Fetterley.[2] "Broad generalities and shallow theories confuse and anger me," Hasselstrom writes; "Reality hinges on practicality, on knowledge that has daily use" (*Going* 105). Here is Hasselstrom's version of Mueller's argument:

> Those who really become part of the Midwest (either by birth or by immigration) are those who have some sense of the land as central to the region. By "land" I mean not only the actual earth, water, and air, but the attitudes that have come to characterize residents: a certain independence from herd thinking; a willingness—even eagerness— to face hardships that include isolation and physical labor; and pride in our differences from metropolitan sophisticates. ("Questions" 14)

In the preface to *Roadside History of South Dakota*, she not only asserts the primacy of fact over theory, but suggests that some realities never yield to interpretation or re-interpretation: "The important point about the West, the thing that made it different from the East yesterday and today, is that it contains natural elements that are not moved by persuasion. A blizzard can still kill you, as can a bison or a fall from a cliff. The West is still home to wilderness, and wilderness can't be analyzed; it acts" (xiii).

Listing writers who have influenced her style and thought, Hasselstrom identifies contemporary Great Plains writers who extend the arc drawn by Mueller, including Ted Kooser, William Kloefkorn, Bill Holm, John R. Milton, Paul Gruchow, Kathleen Norris, Margaret Hasse, Jim Heynen, and Garrison Keillor.[3] The artistic and philosophical positions that emerge across four decades of poems, memoirs, and essays both formal and personal offer an almost textbook example of an author who tries to preserve her South Dakota roots even while she escapes them. The result is tension and paradox, but always fidelity to place, as she uses her experience with men, women, and nature to escape, transcend, or redefine life on the ranch. On the large scale, we notice the tensions in Hasselstrom's attempts to reconcile the belief systems of a working rancher and an environmental activist, and of a ranch wife and a modern woman-writer. We read the conflicting impulses in page after page describing "the business of packaging grass inside of beef," and almost as many pages analyzing her own need to write poems and stories that ranching friends mostly do not read.[4] The struggle to escape and preserve is reflected in her favorite subject, the intertwined realities of birth (continuity) and death (terminus), and in the two images that dominate Hasselstrom's writing—wind and grass.

In that context—seeking always to develop generalization from fact, and not (despite beginning with Lisel Mueller) fitting data to some preconceived generalization—we can track the thought and art which grow out of Hasselstrom's experiences. In so doing, we note that as her career unfolds, her ideas become increasingly nuanced and the tension between preserving and breaking manifests itself in increasingly complex structures. While the distances from youth to maturity, from grass to sky, from Hermosa to Cheyenne may not seem great, the distance *is*, to quote the title of Hasselstrom's memoir, "like far."

Linda Michele Hasselstrom was born on July 14, 1943, in Houston, Texas, where her mother Mildred Baker Hey was living with her second husband, Paul Bovard.[5] When the couple separated in 1946, Mildred returned to her family in Rapid City, South Dakota, and found secretarial work in a law firm. In 1952 she married rancher John Hasselstrom, because "marriage to him would be a wise investment in her future and mine. She asked a friend in the bank to look up his accounts and came home singing that day" (*Feels* 15). Hasselstrom writes, "I wasn't born on the land; I was reborn here when I moved from a small city to a ranch at the age of nine. I was adopted by the land, and began developing a personal land ethic the first time I looked out on the empty, rolling prairie around my home" (*Land Circle* 240). She grew up to be a hand adept at riding horses, herding cattle, mending fences, mowing and bucking hay. The story of buying her first horse with $80 saved from Christmas and birthday gifts and her 50-cents-a-week allowance is one of the more amusing tales in *Feels Like Far* and constitutes one stanza of the poem "Happy Birthday":

At nine I had visions of horses.
Blaze was fat and slow.
I dreamed her swift. (*Dakota Bones* 18)

In elementary school in Hermosa, "where the school was divided into two rooms, with two teachers, for eight grades" (*Windbreak* ix), Hasselstrom joined the 4-H Club and participated in every activity open to her: dress-making, cooking, garden exhibits. At that time, girls could not participate in the horse or beef cattle projects, and while she complained, it never occurred to her to campaign very hard to change the situation (*Windbreak* 206). She organized a horse club drill team, and learned to fight. Hasselstrom attended high school in Rapid City, where she worked a couple of summers as an intern on the *Rapid City Daily Journal*. The "Happy Birthday" poem continues:

When I was sixteen
I realized my breasts would be smaller,
My hands larger, than I had hoped;
My hair would never be waist-length
Or black. But I still learned to say "No."

At seventeen, I learned boys don't date
girls who live thirty miles from town.
At eighteen, I learned college girls
With cars have friends even when they say "No."

On graduation, Hasselstrom left Hermosa for a new life at the University of South Dakota: student protests,[6] boyfriends,[7] vegetarianism (briefly), William Faulkner and Henry James. "I came back from my freshman year in college filled with my own self-importance and brilliance," she recalls (Roripaugh 10); her father reminded her, "Don't forget how to talk to ordinary people." At the University of South Dakota Hasselstrom edited the school newspaper, won journalism awards, and published as a classroom project a chapbook of poems titled *The Muse Is Blue*.[8] The collection's first poem, "The Moon Is Blue," suggests that the rancher's daughter from West River was not entirely comfortable at the East River university:

> I'm a night-black cat with amber eyes
> And the night is full of a thousand sighs.
> I cry with the trees and
> Walk with the wind
> and sleep when the moon is blue.

After receiving a BA in 1965, she continued with postgraduate classes while working on the night staff of the *Sioux City Journal* and dating Daniel Lusk—seven years her senior, a divorced father of three young children—whom she married in 1966. The couple left South Dakota for the University of Missouri, he to study philosophy, she literature. Hasselstrom taught at Columbia College from 1966 to 1969, and at the University of Missouri-Columbia after receiving her MA, from 1969–71. "I entertained at cocktail parties," she recalls, "with tales of a childhood spent with a rifle in each hand for fighting off grizzly bears, Indians and rustlers" (*Going* 7). "I thought I was doing the right thing," she told Roripaugh; "I felt like a capable, modern career woman. The intellectual challenges were terrific" (16). In retrospect, however, graduate school might have been a false start: "I value the education I received there; I still re-read the American literature that I studied and later taught. But ... I now know those professors wasted a lot of my time" on things like transformational grammar and existential philosophy (*Going* 199, 200). Like Willa Cather before her, she gradually worked her way out of Henry James, with his detached, convoluted style. She told Roripaugh that the simple, colloquial language "I use (and you use) in poetry and essays is a conscious rebellion against the elevated discourse of the university," and one reason she dropped graduate studies was the desire to speak intelligibly as well as intelligently about important issues (9).

Hasselstrom and Lusk moved to Hermosa in 1971, living on the ranch and founding *Sunday Clothes: A Magazine of the Fine Arts* and Lame Johnny Press.[9] When the marriage ended in 1973, Linda Hasselstrom found herself at age thirty pretty much where she had begun: broke, single, living on her father's ranch six miles south of Hermosa, South Dakota. In addition to experience in the great world, her education had given her Thoreau, whom she could quote to explain her retreat: "I love Nature partly *because* she is not man, but a retreat from him" (*Land Circle* 247). Second-guessing herself in *Feels Like Far*, she muses, "When I left the ranch for college, I should have, like the ducks, circled once or twice and kept right on flying" (73). But she could not break the roots, and when an opportunity to edit a magazine in New York presented itself (*Land Circle* 65), Hasselstrom declined, content with a life of ranch chores, running the magazine and press, and teaching at various part-time and artist-in-the-schools assignments. (In a couple of poems—*Dakota Bones* 23 and 26—the speaker poses nude for students in an art class.) Ranching and writing battled for top priority in her life, and not simply because she needed more money than the writer's life generated.[10] The two became inseparable as Hasselstrom converted ranch life and personal disaster into literature, and established her position as a woman rancher-writer. By 1999 she could joke, "When a writer tours to publicize a book, readers often ask odd questions. One of my personal favorites is, 'Did going through infidelity, divorce, death and similar hardships make your writing better?' 'Yes,' I answered; every aspiring Western writer should suffer these unique griefs. And buy a horse" ("Why Do I Write" 50).

Linda Hasselstrom is not unlike several thousand American writers—including Robert Bly, Lawrence Ferlinghetti, James Laughlin, Norbert Blei, Emily Buchwald, Alan Kornblum, the author of this book, and before them Henry Thoreau, Walt Whitman, and Mark Twain—in combining the writing life with the publishing life, including self-publishing. Modern writer-publishers support both expensive habits with teaching and occasional work-for-hire as poets in the schools, Arts Council grants for book publishing and writing projects, and National Endowment for the Arts fellowships. In Hasselstrom's case publishing, writing, teaching, and ranching worked well together: the traveling required for her artists-in-residencies was a form of research for *Roadside History of South Dakota*; in 1983 Lame Johnny Press published a textbook for writers-in-residency gigs: *Horizons: The South Dakota Writers*

Anthology. Hasselstrom's *The Book Book: A Publishing Handbook (for Beginners and Others)*, also published by Lame Johnny Press in 1979, went to two editions.

On one teaching assignment, Hasselstrom met Air Force veteran George Randolph Snell, a student in her class, father of one son, divorced the same year Linda and Dan separated. They married on March 10, 1979, neither sure marriage would work (*Land Circle* 174). This marriage was for both as good as their previous marriages were bad, proving once again that the first time is for practice. On five acres of her parents' land deeded over to her, the couple—and their friends—built a house that Linda designed herself, one that "fit into the landscape" (*Windbreak* 12). George drew Linda into his hobbies, including buckskinning, while Linda drew George into the Hermosa community. Unfortunately, the radiation used by doctors to treat his Hodgkin's disease first rendered George sterile (and thus Hasselstrom childless), then caused or contributed to a tumor on his spine which killed him in 1988, leaving Hasselstrom single once again. Much of *Land Circle* and *Bitter Creek Junction* is devoted to her grief over George's death.

Hasselstrom's literary career developed mostly in the genres of poetry, essays, and memoir.[11] In 1984 she received a National Endowment for the Arts fellowship, and in 1987 came not one, not two, but three books: *Windbreak, Roadkill,* and *Going Over East. Windbreak* was reviewed in the *New York Times Book Review,* then chosen as an alternate for a book club. "[S]oon the mailbox was stuffed with messages from old friends, from people who envied or feared my outdoor life, people who kept diaries, who wanted to move West, people who had lost their land" (*Land Circle* 176). In July, 1989, *Life* magazine published "Journal of a Woman Rancher," with photographs and poems, and a fresh flood of letters began. Also in 1989 she received a South Dakota Arts Council Fellowship and a Governor's Award in Art. The Elkhorn Poetry Prize followed in 1991. Hasselstrom was named South Dakota Hall of Fame Author of the Year in 1989, and South Dakota Council of Teachers of English Author of the Year in 1997. She read regularly at the Cowboy Poetry Gathering in Elko, Nevada, and increasingly published with commercial houses, or was invited to do commercial projects, including *Bison: Monarch of the Plains,* a coffee-table text-plus-photos award-winner, packaged in a specially designed slip-case and produced by Graphic Arts Center Publishing. *Bitter Creek Junction* received the Wrangler Best Poetry Book award in 2000. With Caydell Collier and Nancy Curtis she co-edited three volumes of writing by western women for Houghton Mifflin Company.

The 1990s also brought a series of related crises which threatened again Hasselstrom's connection to Hermosa: problems with aging parents; a move from Hermosa to Cheyenne, where her third significant male partner—Jerry Ellerman—held a job as an engineer for the Wyoming Department of Transportation; and financial arrangements related to the ranch after her father died.

Despite escapes to college, graduate school, places abroad, and now Cheyenne, Hasselstrom grounds most of her writing on the ranch in Hermosa. Hasselstrom fashioned her essays, stories, and poems from material that was, in the judgment of some editors, "boring and brutal" (*Leaning* xiii), drawing the simple, practical lessons which characterize her writing. In a revealing passage of *Feels Like Far*, Hasselstrom writes, "I have come to believe that both my physical life and my spirit are so deeply connected to that particular plot of land, the family ranch, *that I might be a stalk of grass myself, rooted* in arid and meager soil" (2, italics added). And for Hasselstrom, rootedness and wisdom are related: in the title essay of *Land Circle* she writes, "I do not insist that living in the land leads automatically to a more profound wisdom, though I suspect it's often true; anyone who lives in the country and pays attention is often exposed to happenings that are not easily explained, and may take time to think about them" (241). Conversely, breaking connections creates confusion and perhaps unwisdom. Living the writer's life in a house in Cheyenne is difficult for a woman who in 1987 wrote, "I introduce myself as a rancher" (*Windbreak* 10).

Hasselstrom gambled her career on what Meridel Le Sueur called "the little place": "our homes, the garden whose products supplement our own beef to feed our bodies, the wintering and birthing grounds for our cattle, the hayfields that feed them, the boneyard where they slowly return to earth, the junkyard where dead machinery becomes spare parts, and the garbage dump where we get rid of what we cannot use," all within a one-mile radius of the ranch house (*Going* 36). These geographical markers of place will be familiar to anyone who has read her work, and from the map on pages xvi and xvii of *Windbreak*: "a slightly faded red barn; a set of corrals in need of repair; a chicken house left over from a commercial poultry operation, now used for feed storage, as is an old granary; a large garage for my parents' car and the ranch trucks and tractors" (*Windbreak* xiii); boneyard, parents' house, "our house,"

"Harold's Place," the old Lindsay Place with a collapsing two-room homestead cabin, the Lindsay Pasture, "Over East," and the Lester Pasture where Hasselstrom found a brass label from a cream can, marked "Silas Lester" (*Windbreak* 7). Not overly distant are the Hermosa post office, cafe, fair grounds, cemetery, and neighboring ranches described at length in section I of *Land Circle*, "Where Neighbor Is a Verb." Familiar enough with the prairie around her parents' ranch that she could walk it at night, Hasselstrom felt that "the land and its inhabitants knew me, by sight, by scent, by carriage, by light, and by darkness" (*Feels* 7).

Hasselstrom is attuned to grasses and plants, which constitute important geographical and seasonal markers in her writing. In fall,

> The big bluestem seems to become more blue, and a kind of swamp grass becomes a clown green, shading into yellow at the top. After the first frost little bluestem becomes a warm bronze color that seems to shimmer in the sunlight. We have a few fall flowers: aromatic aster, which blooms a vivid shade of blue shading to purple, and white prairie asters. Both look like tiny daisies. A few spiky yellow salsify bloom beside the huge round balls of the mature seedheads. Yellow gumweed, several members of the parsley family, and goldenrod contrast with the deep brown of the seed pods and stems of flowers that bloomed earlier. Pale green stalks of mullein with thick brown seedheads stand like soldiers along the road. The sage looks soft as down and seems to glow silver-blue, and the fences are outlined in brown tumbleweeds. (*Windbreak* 27)

> After lunch . . . we drove home on some obscure little back roads in the hills, enjoying the coolness under the trees. The wildflowers are wonderful: wild iris, blooming strawberries, currants, yellow and white violets, deep purple larkspur, butter and eggs, black-eyed Susans, blue-eyed grass, deep orange tiger lilies, clover, pussytoes, the graceful and poisonous water hemlock. (*Windbreak* 170)

"The prairie is full of stories," she writes (*Going* 94), some "written on the buffalo grass that breaks beneath our tires." And in the trees: outside of the Black Hills proper, trees are rare enough on the Great Plains to be watered and tended when alive, missed when gone, remarked upon individually, especially the great cottonwoods, which give more in shade than they absorb in water. In *Windbreak*, Hasselstrom and a neighbor discuss at length the characteristics and histories of individual trees along the roads they normally travel (79). As an adult, she was serious enough about knowing her environment that on trips around the ranch she carried books to identify flowers and grasses, reverent enough to preserve native species, and generous enough to collaborate with the Great Plains Native Plant Society in creating on her land "a full-scale botanic garden for the Great Plains" (Sutton 78).

Great Plains fauna receive a lot of attention as well. Hasselstrom writes at length about redwing blackbirds, coyotes, raccoons, skunks, foxes, wolves, owls, vultures, golden eagles, bobcats, antelope, mink, rattlesnakes, porcupine, and the two massive turtles ("at least three feet in diameter"—*Going* 72) she saw one afternoon in a pool at the top of the pasture, where she used to fish and skinnydip. Kathleen Danker notes, "She chooses to describe the less conspicuous forms of wildlife on the plains, . . . the bullsnakes, coyotes, nighthawks and other creatures she has come to know by observing their habits all her life" (347). The night hawks which on her first night on the ranch came plummeting "like cannonballs" (*Feels* 188) into her life became for Hasselstrom a symbol of independence and daring; their reappearance in Wyoming, many years later, in large numbers, announced exactly the moment of her father's death (*Feels* 194–95).

Hasselstrom's stories include encounters with elk, badger, and buffalo, which suggest an almost Zen integration of human and animal worlds:

> Sitting before the bison herd, I sensed a holiness I didn't understand. Because I waited patiently, opened my mind, I learned something important from the vigilant herd's silence. Living on the plains for ages, bison have forged deep connections to the grasslands, while humans have survived only briefly on the prairie's surface, doing so much damage in our tenure. From some past reading, I recall a Zen-like line: "Before enlightenment, haul water, chop wood. After enlightenment, haul water, chop wood."
>
> In the presence of the buffalo, I began to understand how I might deepen my own partnership with the plains. Driving dark highways alone or walking down city streets, I often breathe moonlight and remember. (*Feels* 85)

> The aspens hissed again, leaves crunching under a heavy foot. Tiny hairs all over my body swiveled toward the sound. My eyes snapped open.

A bull elk stood just inside the clearing, staring at me, head up. His brown eyes flickered with furious red light. Body heat blasted me. He was ready for mating season, the annual fall rut. His muscles were sheathed in fat, his tawny hair iridescent with health. On his thick neck, the dark brown mane trembled. His antlers spread wider than his chestnut body, wider than my arms could reach. The massive coronet loomed over a broad brow, sweeping over his head, back and up like tree branches. He honed and polished those horns on trees, probably in this private grove. Uninvited, I lay in the dressing room of a dedicated warrior. (*Feels* 158)

The most prominent animal presence in Hasselstrom's writing is of course the cow; her encomium "The Cow Is My Totem" ends in this ringing endorsement: "In many early societies, a mark of respect for vanquished enemies, human or animal, was to eat their hearts. In that way, the victor partook of the courage and strength the other had shown, and honored the loser for putting up such a good fight. Considering that tradition, and the number of beef hearts I've eaten, and all the admirable, underexposed qualities of cows, I hereby record that cows are my passion, as well as my living" (*Between* 186). The second strongest presence is the horse, and Hasselstrom's strongest bonds are formed with horses. Like many girls, she had dreamed of horses since reading *Black Beauty* as a child. Blaze was quickly replaced by Rebel, gift of her Uncle Harold as a yearling filly. Rebel and her owner became "as close to being one organism as is possible" (*Windbreak* 17). "[M]y love affair with her is the most perfect I've ever had," Hasselstrom writes; "The others ended in heartbreak or marriage or both. She never betrayed me. She put up with my idiocies and idiosyncrasies. Every injury I got while riding her was my own fault, and I apologized to her each time" (*Going* 64).

To markers geographical, vegetable, and animal, Hasselstrom would add a fourth: weather. Introducing *Windbreak*, she writes, "Our drama comes with the cycles of nature; with the endless absorption with birth and death; with the lives of our neighbors and friends; with the weather, which is a character in the story of our lives" (xi). Weather is "a separate entity, almost an intelligence" (*Windbreak* 56). In a poem titled "Wind," Hasselstrom writes, "Wind defines the land,/shapes everything outside the window" (*Dakota Bones* 123). Roripaugh notes the presence of wind in Hasselstrom's poems, not simply as an omnipresent fact of life, but as a presence—a muse, a witness, a companion, an adversary (12).

It's hard to be a romantic in South Dakota, and Hasselstrom is pretty much a manure-on-the-boots realist: "I suspect that many folks who love Nature (with a capital N) aren't thinking of manure, any more than they're considering teeth and blood and death," she writes, "but it is another part of life we should not leave out of our calculations for the future" (*Going* 112). The calf born to a mouthful of manure got "a good taste of reality" (*Windbreak* 107), the best possible preparation for life in a world full of wind, hail, blizzards, drought, fire, coyotes, and hawks. Nature—the Land, Place—is a multifaceted character in Hasselstrom's writing. Sometimes the relationship between writer and land is "a covenant . . . less like a battle than a marriage" (*Windbreak* 72–73). Sometimes it is more "a war of nerves, of tactics" (*Windbreak* 54). In *Land Circle* (244) she describes the prairie as "a sister." In *Windbreak* she writes with tongue in cheek, "Sometimes I think Mother Nature has a nasty streak" (19). Sometimes she takes the full naturalist position that Nature is indifferent: in *Windbreak* she writes, "nature simply doesn't care one way or the other" (72). She told Roripaugh, "I think in my writing I have treated the landscape as all of these: friend, lover, spouse, or relative, yet I've never been unaware that the land is none of these, that it is indifferent to human efforts" (10).

Hasselstrom's ideas regarding her place are as complex as Nature herself. Like Norbert Blei, she is a preservationist who tends to believe that whatever is, is best (if not necessarily "right"). Her job as a citizen, writer, and rancher is to protect South Dakota from nuclear waste dumps, accelerated mining or logging, and recreational developments or industrial tourism (see especially *Windbreak* 21, 29, 39). "South Dakota and the Great Plains may look like a chicken neck to the rest of the world," she writes in reference to her husband George getting stuck with the neck at Sunday dinner when a boy, "but we've made it a filling meal, and we'll fight for it" (*Land Circle* xx). On the other hand, as Rena Sanderson points out, "Hasselstrom believes that the survival of the rancher justifies certain measures reflecting the kind of clear-eyed practicality she has been raised to admire," and "some of her practical measures may offend some environmentalists" (174). Hasselstrom defends both grazing and grassland preservation: "the cows don't exist without the grass and vice versa" (Sutton 78). Both she and her father forbid hunting coyotes on their land because "the snakes and the coyotes serve their purposes here, cleaning up mice and other vermin. We give them the same respect we give responsible humans, and don't bother them if they don't bother us" (*Going* 98). But she defends a rancher's right, even need, to reduce an out-of-control native prairie dog population that destroys pastures and endangers cattle and horses by harboring rattlesnakes and creating leg-breaking traps (*Going* 53). "Here I am," she writes, "who marched behind Martin Luther King, / who stood the taunts behind a sign that read 'Silent / Vigil Against the War,' ran like everyone else / when the flying wedge of cops hit the quadrangle, / here I am, shooting prairie dogs" (*Dakota Bones* 25). As opposed as she is to logging in the Black Hills, she notes, "water enthusiasts such as fishermen, hikers and environmentalists have been complaining that streams are drying up and lake levels are being lowered. A little study reveals the problem: the trees are efficiently catching rainfall and holding runoff, and the water isn't getting to streams and ponds. Grass is killed out by the shade, fallen pine needles and lack of water, so wildlife has less forage" (*Going* 139). Hasselstrom's positions on environmental monkeywrenching, hunting, and even doctoring cattle are similarly ambivalent:

A recent issue of *Earth First!* instructed readers on the quickest method for disconnecting a windmill so that water would cease to flow. I can sympathize with the frustration that leads to such direct action—I've taken some pretty direct actions for love of the environment myself—but the author of that article forgot that it is not the rancher who will die of thirst. The rancher may have insurance, and may simply write off the loss, but the cattle—and any wildlife who rely on the water—will suffer the slow agony of dehydration and death.

This type of sloppy thinking angers me most in people who are concerned about the land and its use. (*Going* 167–68)

When the grass looks good and game is plentiful, hunters complain about rich ranchers getting pasture cheaply at public expense. But the land looks good because they're careful with it. And hunters' use of the land may do it even more damage for their own purposes—supporting game—than our grazing does. Prairie grass, once it is cured or dried in fall, is brittle and easily broken. A single hunter in a single pickup who insists on driving everywhere he goes can break off and destroy more grass in a day than fifty cows or seventy antelope would eat in a month. (*Going* 170)

Now we feed cattle special mixtures to aid growth, prevent infections and disease; we call the vet if a steer sneezes or a cow complains of a headache. Some disease prevention is necessary—epidemic diseases could devastate the industry. But why not move toward a more natural cycle in other areas of care? We have turned a useful job—that of veterinarian—into an industry that may ultimately work against us by helping us create a cow that has no natural immunity, but relies on artificial medication to survive. Meanwhile, some older breeds of cattle have disappeared, as market demand has changed from short, fat cattle to tall, lean, bony ones. Reducing bloodlines to only a few, and making those dependent on medication rather than hardiness to survive, is a recipe for disaster; a new disease, resistant to proven methods, could decimate cattle herds. (*Going* 196)

Working from facts always teaches a writer to look both ways: "Both sides of the story are true, even though they may be contradictory," Hasselstrom told Roripaugh (9).

As much as landscape, buildings, fauna and flora, Hasselstrom's place is comprised of the human community, which must be nurtured and protected as much as the biosphere. A broken connection with place is the curse not only of postmodern literature but of postmodern American life: if our early heroes, childhood ideals, and the philosophies on which the country was founded now seem irrelevant, perhaps that is because we have traded a coherent way of living for a "plastic lifestyle"; we "will not be healed until we can find our way back to the center of the circle from which dozens of ancient and Native American cultures tried to speak to us before our single-minded greed, Christian morality, and superior weapons overwhelmed them" (*Land Circle* 267). The remedy for postmodern angst is to reconnect with place and nature—reclaim the roots—and thereby reclaim the old wholeness of life, the old philosophies and ideals, and the reassurance of cyclical death and rebirth (see Sanford, 139). Hasselstrom is herself a case in point, having broken the connection when she went to college in 1961, re-established the connection when she returned to the ranch:

I missed the fairs for ten or fifteen years, when I was living elsewhere. Even when we visited here at the right time, my first husband scorned them, and I was a stranger walking among people who looked familiar but whose names I had forgotten.

When I moved back to the community, the conviction began to grow in me that I *should* participate in the fair in some way. It had been such a struggle of my youth to move it to our little town, and the town had gone so far to support it—building an arena, a grandstand, a women's building, stalls for the horses—expenses the town couldn't afford, all provided through the cash, sweat, labor, and donated materials of the town's men. Somehow I felt I, too, should do my part, even if only exhibiting things so there would be something for visitors to look at.

Because that's what there is to do at a fair: you walk slowly through the aisles, looking at every plate of green beans, every mayonnaise jar filled with marigolds, every calf, every child's drawing, every potholder, no matter how crudely made. You pick up the articles, if you can, and examine the stitching or the finish or the size. You discuss who is showing the item and how their children are. You pause along the way to visit with others who are doing the same thing. Everyone feels an obligation to look at everything. It's a ritual, a way of appreciating other people in the community, though you may not agree with, or like them, at other times. (*Windbreak* 206–7)

Hasselstrom sees the relationship between people and landscape as symbiotic: "The land exists outside of people's memories," she points out in *Going Over East* (8), but "without the men and women who devoted their lives to this land, it wouldn't be the same; they have added a dimension to it by their labor, just as their bodies have added fertility to the poor soil of the little graveyard in Hermosa" (*Going* 8). The connection between land and the spiritual life of people who live on it seems "so clearly logical" (*Feels* 4) that Hasselstrom accepts it a priori. "Where we come from shapes who we are," she quotes an unidentified source as saying (*Leaning* xiv). Sanderson claims that the subtext of Hasselstrom's writings "confirms theories such as those formulated by Hector St. John de Crevecoeur and by Hyppolite Adolphe Taine, that stress a region's formative influences on character" (171), and the stories told and the characters found in Hasselstrom's writings from the 1970s and 1980s exemplify connectedness. One gift from Hasselstrom's stepfather—and neighbors—was stories of the people who worked the land before her arrival, stories often told on a break from work with a sandwich in one hand, a cup of coffee on the dashboard (*Going* 192). This history represents a rich vein that Hasselstrom mines repeatedly for poems, stories, or anecdotes like those sprinkled through *Going Over East*: "In 1949, when John [Lindsay] struggled to the barn after the three-day blizzard and pried the door open, he found it full of snow and live cows. The cows had kept moving around, trampling the snow down, until their backs were against the roof. When he opened the door, they tumbled down into the corral, healthy but a little cramped" (43). Many poems in *Dakota Bones* are either stories of friends, neighbors, and ancestors (the boy who hanged himself in the root cellar, the mail-order bride who didn't work out, the homesteader who managed to shoot his wife but not her lover) or collections of local conversation ("Uncle," "Coffee Cup Cafe," "Ralph Jones: On Borrowing"). Products of their environment, people around Hermosa accept hardship as a condition of life, rarely complain even to each other, and meet adversity with renewed commitment. They are like those "tart little berries on hidden thorny bushes . . ., a little prickly if we've been here long" (*Land Circle* 25). Great Plains women are tough, independent, comfortable with contradiction, proud of their accomplishments, and well-informed about a world that is largely ignorant of them (*Leaning* xx). A rancher who lost his hay and corrals to a fire in August, then rebuilt everything before winter, "was one of us, adhering to a tradition: to rebuild, to recover, no matter how terrible the disaster" (*Feels* 200).

Hermosa stories are, in the main, stories of place and of labor in a place. Thus Hasselstrom's own poems "are in the scars, / and in what I [will] recall of all this, when / my hands are too battered to do it any more" (*Dakota Bones* 50). Most writers these days, suggests rancher-writer Hasselstrom with an eye on what she read in graduate school and products of M.F.A. programs, are not of this fellowship—nor are most people these days. "People who manipulate papers all day long, or tap the keys of a computer, or buy and sell over telephone lines, go home at the end of the day without evidence that they have accomplished anything. Their muscles don't ache from piling up a stack of hay they can walk around with pride" (*Land Circle* 71). Like Carol Bly,[12] Hasselstrom believes the best way to work out abstract ethical problems is in the concrete context of ranch life: "A month on a ranch, especially in spring, exposes one to every conceivable aspect of life and most of the moral dilemmas" (*Windbreak* 128). Even the inherent tension between physical labor and abstract thought is resolved in a manner that both preserves and breaks the roots of midwestern farm and ranch life: "I believe that for a human being to see, literally or figuratively, he or she must look both near and far off; in the same way, labor should be both physical and mental in order to keep all circuits healthy" (*Land Circle* 65). Hasselstrom sees one of her missions as using "the knowledge of people who really live in a place, to educate people who do not, or who are 'newcomers'" (Roripaugh 11). And the newly come like the ancient people, the writer like the rancher, must purchase connection to place not with money, but with physical work:

You earn the land
after your name is on the title.
The sacraments of inheritance
require payment in blood and sweat.
If you only accept, you lose everything. (*Land Circle* 238)

The people Hasselstrom describes most often are those closest to her: mother, father, grandmother, husband, close friends. She judges them, especially in her early writing, by their work ethic and practical wisdom. In light of her life-long interest in gender relationships, it is interesting to note that in Hasselstrom's writing there are good women and bad women, good fathers and bad fathers, good husbands and bad husbands . . . even satisfactory lovers and unsatisfactory lovers. The good ones are the ones who work.

Most Americans these days grow up figuratively or literally without a father (many mothers are now absent most of the day as well), but Hasselstrom's biological father disappeared almost before he could make his daughter feel his absence. She writes little about Paul Bovard: "Only when I have followed an impulse to quit a job in anger, or throw a flowerpot at a wandering husband, have I heard Paul chuckling inside my skull" (*Feels* 12). "I last saw him twenty years ago," she writes in a poem titled "Telegram Announcing the Death of My Father"; "I was five. He was drunk. / I feared his face on every wino, / but how would I have known?" (*Dakota Bones* 42).

John Hasselstrom, his daughter writes, was "the only real father I've known" (*Windbreak* xi). "As a child in the city," Hasselstrom writes in *Feels Like Far*, "I'd been confined by Mother's close attention and strict rules to the narrow limits of the house. On the ranch, I revolved around my new father, following him everywhere. My life began to spin outward in ever larger circles. Mother stayed in the house" (22). Hasselstrom admired her father's skill: "It's a pleasure to watch Father work cattle" (*Windbreak* 141). She admired and emulated his stubbornness when he knew he was right: "Today the propane line runs for miles across private land, but when it reaches our fence line, it jogs into the highway right-of-way" (*Going* 120). She admired his reluctance to drive across good grass (*Windbreak* 9), and the fact that he was still planting trees at age sixty-nine (*Dakota Bones* 12). She admired his courage, which could approach reckless defiance: "My father told stories of neighborhood men killed by lightning on tractors or horses, but he seemed to stay out in the storms longer than necessary for a man so sure of their power to kill" (*Feels* 189). Sanford shrewdly notes (145) that when Hasselstrom speaks of going to church on Easter Sunday as "a yearly gift to my mother" (*Windbreak* 126), she suggests that the other weeks were a gift to the father she preferred.

John Hasselstrom was what Robert Bly in *Iron John* calls "a fifties male" (1), a hard worker, a good provider, somewhat "Saturnian," so protective of his daughter that he would not let the hired men cuss in her presence (the daughter, in turn, never uttered a swear word around the father until she was thirty-five—*Windbreak* 127). The fact that Hasselstrom wore through two marriages the Black Hills gold ring he gave her on the day of her official adoption suggests the strength of their emotional bond. So does an early experience recounted in *Going Over East*:

> Before long, snow began to fall heavily, muffling all sounds and cutting off my view at the tops of the low hills nearby. I could hear nothing but the moaning wind, see nothing but a few brown and white cows, who looked at me, snorted, then turned and ran ahead. Suddenly I felt very small, alone and terrified—until, dimly, I saw the tall, slightly bent figure of my father, almost lost in the blowing snow. He was striding along, looking sure of where he was and where he was going. That may have been the moment when I really began to know him. (4)

Father John is—like the archetypical American father—a wise, reliable, protective, and distant love. Hasselstrom records a dream in which her father "wrapped me in his sinewy arms, saying 'I promise that even though I leave you in the flesh, my spirit will be with you always'" (*Feels* 185). He was the source of many of the ranch stories in *Going Over East* and of much practical ranch wisdom:

> To conserve energy,
> when a pickup is not moving ahead
> shut the motor off.
> Starters and batteries are cheaper
> than gasoline these days.
> Waste not, want not.

Don't keep horses in the corrals.
If there's snow on the ground
a horse can get by in a pasture without water.

Get the calves fed and watered before noon.
John Lindsay used to say
if he didn't get the work done in the morning,
he might as well go fishing the rest of the day.

Don't take chances. Don't get caught in a storm.
A cow can take more weather than you can.

Don't scatter thistles or cheat grass;
stack them in one pile and burn it. (*Dakota Bones* 101)[13]

John Hasselstrom clearly invested enormous psychic energy in the girl
he called "Child," and gave her on her fourteenth birthday "a gift I hadn't
dared to hope for: a .22 rifle" (*Feels* 48). Nevertheless, "when my father
had read the preface of my first book, *Windbreak*," Hasselstrom writes,
"[a]s soon as he saw that I'd referred to him as my 'stepfather,' he stopped
reading, before he got to my explanation that he was the only father I'd
ever known" (*Feels* 196). The distant father disapproved of her writing
and never once told his daughter he loved her (*Feels* 211). Before he was
buried, Hasselstrom placed a complete set of her published works in the
casket beside him.

Linda Hasselstrom's first husband was everything that her father was
not: urban, urbane, literate, abstract, undisciplined, ungrounded . . .
and therefore untrustworthy. Robert Bly would call Daniel Lusk a sixties
man—an ascender, a floater (*Iron John* 2, "Lutheran Boy-God" 209).
Hasselstrom's recollection of a night in Kansas City on their move to
Columbia, Missouri, suggests as much:

"We can live it up one night," you said;
held my hand in the elevator,
reminding me I'd never been higher
than the roof of the barn back home.
You strutted into that saloon
as if already wearing
the silk shirt I'd buy for you
later that year, with money from my night job.

You whispered that the lights below the tower
looked like diamonds just out of reach,
talked the band into letting you sing.
Your honey voice flowed over the room. (*Dakota Bones* 124)

Daniel Lusk was, if not wind, at least stars, and definitely a break with roots. In Missouri, Lusk wrote poems, pursued his career as a singer, and sported the splendid plumage his wife's paycheck provided: Edwardian coats and ruffled shirts (*Between* 85). In Hermosa the "romantic poet who'd never had a callus, who spent his nights consulting with his muse, a scribbler whose idea of work was sitting by a candle sighing while he doodled at his latest masterpiece, a villanelle on spring and love" made an unconvincing cowboy (*Bitter Creek* 8). Having three children by a previous marriage, Lusk did not provide the child for which Hasselstrom longed (*Between* 88), and she suggests that this marriage was merely a conscious or unconsciousness rebellion against her father's strict schedule (*Feels* 157). The sharp break from father, however, taught her the need for rootedness. Like Dorothy, she could best appreciate Kansas from the Emerald City. And like Dorothy, Hasselstrom returned from Lusk and from graduate studies to father John and the ranch with new eyes, a new appreciation of place, a new commitment to ranching . . . and writing.

George Snell—fly-fisher, hunter, weekend trapper—was neither a fifties father or a dandy-intellectual. Hasselstrom's portraits in *Windbreak*, *Land Circle*, and *Feels Like Far* are of a man who is physical, low-key, composed, spiritual, trustworthy, in touch with Nature, and at peace with his inner self. He was protective without being patronizing: "When George wrapped his big arms around me," Hasselstrom writes, "I was enveloped, protected, shielded, and the feeling didn't compromise my independence one bit" (*Land Circle* 135). The passage recalls her dream of her dying father's promise, and her early memory of John riding ahead of the cows in the snow storm. "He helped me up if I fell," she writes, "but he didn't grab my arm / when I strode ahead" (*Land Circle* 133); George was "a windbreak against the cold" (*Land Circle* 164). Elsewhere he is described as "the spring," "the tree," a man tied to the earth's heartbeat (*Dakota Bones* 94). If George represented more security and support than did Daniel, he offered a more spirited existence than her father: "George taught me to enjoy every day on the assumption that it might be the last, but he was one of the happiest people I ever knew" (*Land Circle* 138). When necessary, George could be just as tough as John Hasselstrom:

> As we turned to go back to our own house, I casually asked Father how Rebel is [*sic*] doing; I'd been thinking about her.
> Father said shortly, "She's gone."
> "What do you mean?"
> "I dragged her over the hill."
> I assumed that was his euphemism for having shot her, and walked away without a word, the first time I can recall being literally too stunned to speak. He'd suggested that we shoot her last winter so she wouldn't suffer from the cold, but instead we kept her well supplied with hay, and I felt sure she was still healthy and strong.
> Later, Mother called me, and said he'd spent two of the hot days we were gone burying her, to save me from finding her rotting corpse while riding that pasture. I know he didn't mean to be cruel. I cried after we went to bed. George held me, and told me he pulled the trigger, the day before we went to Denver. (*Windbreak* 22)[14]

After George's death, Geraldine Sanford sees Hasselstrom as consciously absorbing certain elements of his identity into herself (144), as she had absorbed elements of her stepfather.

The male who followed George Snell was the man who had helped Hasselstrom set the tombstone on George's grave, his friend Jerry Ellerman. In Hasselstrom's writing, Jerry is not father, not a demon-lover, not a mountain-man; he appears—insofar as Hasselstrom has defined him—to be a friend. In the final poem in *Land Circle*, she speaks of him as a bridge:

> Your work is linking steel and concrete
> to span wild rivers and dry washes
> on Wyoming prairies;
> mine is fitting words into stories.
> I hadn't known you'd marvel at ancient bridges
> just as I study poems by the masters.
> My eye was tuned to standing stones,
> the shape of poems waiting in the landscape,
> yours to bridges,
> but we began to see each other's dreams. (*Land Circle* 331)

In a later poem, Jerry is a colleague with whom Linda can eat a steak dinner while trading stories, "my meeting / with a Swedish news team in
return / for your bent viaduct of steel / and stories of the crew that
straightens it" (*Bitter Creek* 20).

The women prominent in Hasselstrom's writing offer a similar
range. Hasselstrom's grandmother, more prominent in the poems than
the prose, embodies history, preservation, and earth. She is, like Norbert
Blei's Babi, frequently associated with a root cellar. For Hasselstrom she
provides both a terminus a quo and a terminus ad quem:

Grandmother

I always see her hands first, turning
the handle of the Foley food mill.
The veins are knotted over old bones;
spicy tomato steam rises around
her white hair. A worn gold ring turns on
her finger but never will slide off
over the knuckle. Solid as a
young woman, she grew thin, forgot our
names. Hands that fed four daughters lay still.
She left us little: brown unlabeled pictures,
a dozen crocheted afghans, piles of patched jeans.
In the cellar, crowded shelves bear jars of beans,
peas, corn, meat.
Labels like white silent mouths
open and close in the dark. (*Dakota Bones* 10)

In the poem "Hands" (*Dakota Bones* 50), Hasselstrom writes of her
grandmother's hands, and of her own hands turning into her grandmother's hands (and her father's hands, and her husband George's
hands, but not—significantly—her mother's hands). When grandmother died, Hasselstrom recalls, her "shoes wouldn't fit / anyone but
me" (*Dakota Bones* 13).

Mildred Hasselstrom was what we would call a club woman, stylishly
dressed, attempting at least in the early years to be the perfect ranch
wife (*Feels* 17), providing her daughter with pink birthday cakes, nice
dresses, and practical advice on whom to marry so she wouldn't have to
work. Mildred was obsessed with the pests she was sure lived in the

joints and cracks of the old Hasselstrom house, and "bought big spray cans of every poison available" (*Between* 56).

> [Mother] demanded and got a new house, new furniture and carpeting. My father refused to buy her a set of china, so a Ladies Aid group chipped in and bought it as a welcoming gift. For a while, she plunged into community life, singing in the choir and joining a church sewing and social group, but she quit both groups when they didn't do things her way. She fought ferociously with my father to keep me inside the house learning to clean and cook. She never gave up on trying to civilize me. While I grew to love the land and the cattle we raised, she saw the community and its residents as coarse and ignorant, the animals as a mass of witless creatures valuable only to provide grocery money and enough extra for new carpet every few years. (*Feels* 17)

Mildred Hasselstrom's dislike of mess extended to snakes and apparently to sex, a topic not much discussed between mother and daughter: "My mother's only sexual advice was given the day I married for the first time. . . . 'Men have to have it,' she said, and a woman's role was to 'lie there and put up with it' " (*Between* 74). Noting early influences on her life, Hasselstrom says her father "taught me to work hard at any job I tackled" and her mother "taught me I'd better not rely on good looks to make my life happy" ("Questions" 25). Never a confident driver, an incessant talker, unquestioningly supportive of her husband, Hasselstrom's mother was a typical fifties mother/wife. The complex relationship—a failure to communicate and understand—is best seen in a poem "Showering with a Grapefruit Rind":

> Mother always kept lemon and grapefruit rinds
> tucked beside the sink.
> When she finished the dishes,
> she'd look out the window, rubbing the skins
> over her cracked fingers and elbows
> before going on to the next job.

> When I was nine, I thought discarded citrus rinds
> were her whole beauty secret; that if I
> collected them I'd be beautiful too.
> Sometimes I waited until she'd
> put them in a garbage barrel.

I hid them in my room
among my socks, rubbing them on my face at night
when I remembered. She'd smell them,
feel them scuttle under her hand
when she put clean socks in my drawer,
shriek, and throw them out. (*Dakota Bones* 83)

Although Hasselstrom as an adolescent was what we would call a
tomboy, and as an adult committed herself to her writing career at the
possible expense of other roles, she did not exactly reject the role of
mother. She gives evidence throughout her writing to having thought
long and hard about children and, when having a child was no longer
possible, about being a good stepmother.[15] Married to Daniel, Hasselstrom also tried to be the perfect wife while being the perfect student.
She gave that up, but throughout her diaries and memoirs, Hasselstrom
cooks, cans, sews, puts up buffalo berry jelly, and nurtures husbands,
lovers, and stepchildren. In rejecting her mother's clubwoman model of
a mother, Hasselstrom was clearly not rejecting the idea of wifehood or
motherhood.

Two other women loom nearly as large in her life as George and her
father: Margaret, her nearest ranching neighbor, and Josephine her
aunt. Aunt Josephine presents a kind of Earth Mother alternative to
Mildred: large, earthy, assertive, profane. She *rides horse* better than John
Hasselstrom, who really didn't like horses (see "Sonata for Horses" in
Feels Like Far): "I envied her graceful balance. She'd stand in the stirrups
to bawl at some slowpoke. A moment later she'd flip the lines, her mare
spinning away toward another knot in the parade line. For an hour, Jo
was limber and willowy" (*Feels* 26). She curses, shovels shit in the horse
barn, wipes her face on her T-shirt:

She jerked her shirt off over her head. "God! There's even horse
shit in my bra!" Laughing, she unsnapped it. Her massive breasts
swung free. "Shut your mouth before you get flies in it. Ain't you ever
seen tits before?"
Mother always shut the bedroom door when she dressed. I turned
to scramble through the pile of jeans.
"I guess not. . . ."
"I don't think we're going to cut that little horse colt. He looks like
he's hung well enough to make a stud. . . . Ain't that little stud got the

cutest little do-whopper you ever saw? Guess you haven't seen too many." (*Feels* 42, 43)

Regarding her poem "Clara in the Post Office," Hasselstrom writes, "I always sort of pictured my Aunt Jo speaking this poem, since it is a very strong woman insisting she's not a feminist" (Letter):

> I keep telling you, I'm not a feminist.
> I grew up an only child on a ranch,
> so I drove tractors, learned to ride.
> When the truck wouldn't start, I went to town
> for parts. The man behind the counter
> told me I couldn't rebuild a carburetor.
> I could: every carburetor on the place. That's
> necessity, not feminism.
>   I learned to do the books
> after my husband left me and the debts
> and the children. I shoveled snow and pitched hay
> when the hired man didn't come to work.
> I learned how to pull a calf
> when the vet was too busy. As I thought,
> the cow did most of it herself; they've been
> birthing alone for ten thousand years. Does
> that make them feminists?
> It's not
> that I don't like men; I love them—when I can.
> But I've stopped counting on them
> to change my flats or open my doors.
> That's not feminism; that's just good sense. (*Dakota Bones* 100)

The chapter of *Feels Like Far* titled "Blues for Shoveling Horse Manure" is Hasselstrom's tribute to the woman who taught her things her mother could not, the friend who died of cancer.

Margaret, ten years behind Hasselstrom in high school, also died young. Margaret is something between Earth Mother Josephine and club woman Mildred, a plain-thinking, plain-speaking, hard-working, church-going mother and wife who keeps a copy of Frost's poems by her bed (*Windbreak* 53) and refuses to think of herself as "liberated" (*Windbreak* 34). When it comes to the battle of the sexes, Margaret's opinion is "the ERA would create more problems than it solved. 'Women are better off if they let men think they believe they are inferior,' she said, 'and then work undercover'" (*Feels* 92). She appreciates the concept of monkey wrenching and attends Lutheran church. "Margaret was living my fantasies, creating the life I'd imagined as a child. Merging her roles as wife and mother, she also acted as a responsible rancher and bee-keeper, even when she disagreed with the majority. She never hesitated to challenge a stereotype but could explain her reasoning without fury" (*Feels* 93). "No matter how completely I'd researched and considered an idea, she often voiced a viewpoint that had never occurred to me," Hasselstrom writes (*Feels* 92).

Like the men in her life, these women represent a range of options, each, despite their individuality, representing a particular archetype. To them might be added that of the adolescent American girl, embodied in no one in particular, all polish and shine, lovely and energetic, but a little light on character and understanding. In a female equivalent of Yeats's "Among School Children," Hasselstrom takes a look around the class-room and feels her years, their youth: "I looked at her fresh face and felt old and awkward. None of these children was over seventeen, all were female, their bodies blooming with health" (*Land Circle* 211).

Down the halls of each school
in the land, young girls caracole
and prance. Their long clean hair brushes
shoulders. Faces are open as meadows,
eyes clear as creeks. Fearless, they buy
eye shadow, rouge for false blushes
over fine bones. They ring eyes with color,
force firm breasts higher
into wire cups. (*Dakota Bones* 89)

And by way of contrasting the girl to Mother Earth,

This mat was not woven by the tender white
fingers of virgins, but by the scarred, broken
hands of farm wives. It was created, warp and woof,
of their blood and bones. (*Dakota Bones* 92)

There are other men and women, of course: Mary Ellwein Spencer, who died in a car crash, already "wise at twenty" (*Bitter Creek* 36); the abused wife at the place called Bitter Creek Junction; N'de, a Navajo potter; Calvin the rodeo writer; "Pat, Who Wasn't Home" (*Dakota Bones*

81). Through this forest of males and females, Hasselstrom examines issues of gender, reaching conclusions that reflect her age, and her male and female friends and relations. Always she and her friends think in the context of ranch life practicalities: if the job is shoveling grain out of a pickup, a man can shovel more than a woman, unless perhaps they're high school kids when boys and girls might shovel equally, and even if you could find a woman who can shovel as much as a man, the woman might get pregnant and, even if she's more experienced, "won't be able to lift as much," so are you going to cut her pay because she's not delivering equal work? (*Feels* 92).

As a tomboy child, Linda Hasselstrom was in many respects the son John Hasselstrom did not have. Gender was not an issue, she recalls in the first poem of *Bitter Creek Junction*: her father "didn't care if they were men or women when we needed help. . . . Gender issues didn't surface, not until we got around to branding. Even then he didn't call them that" (8). Growing through the changes of adolescence, she writes, "The blood crooning through my body promised adventure. I loved my tractor, the danger and rhythm of the work. Daydreaming about a wonderful adulthood, I slid my hands over my body and imagined how good I'd be at adult stuff, like sex" (*Feels* 47). As a young, college-educated woman of the seventies and eighties, she explored stereotypes and clichés: men think in terms of rights, females think of responsibilities (*Land Circle* 251); to a calving cow, a woman is "less threatening" than a man (*Windbreak* 208); women love while men "love and kill" (*Dakota Bones* 109); even men like George come with "Damn macho attitudes" (*Windbreak* 202); "Women especially seem to long for the security of a nest, and their husbands often insist, 'We can't afford it'" (*Land Circle* 120). Women are custodians of culture (*Land Circle* 132); men are controlling (*Feels* 214), structured (*Feels* 157), drunken and brutish (*Land Circle* 294, *Bitter Creek* 65). In naming landscape features and towns, they privilege the bawdyhouse madam over the ordinary housewife (*Crazy Woman* xvii).

With the exception of the title poem of *Bitter Creek Junction*, Hasselstrom's position on gender becomes increasingly subtle as she ages. In one poem from her first collection, she renounces romantic love and males in general, mulching both old love letters and "an occasional unsatisfactory lover" (*Dakota Bones* 6). When it comes to haying, John Hasselstrom is described as a typically reckless male: "Impatient, he begins before he's ready, / plunges in" (*Dakota Bones* 36). In *Going Over East*, Hasselstrom sounds like any academic feminist when she complains,

"Steers are always worth more at the sale ring than heifers" (115). Well, as she says elsewhere of western stereotypes, "the myths weren't completely true, but they weren't completely false, either" ("Questions" 19). And Hasselstrom has legitimate complaints: "probably I'm thought of first in this community as a rancher's daughter. . . . I almost had to introduce myself as John Hasselstrom's daughter for people to place me. . . . [W]hen my father dies, the community perception will be that George runs the place while I run around doing other things" (*Windbreak* 10).

In her later writing, Hasselstrom becomes somewhat more tempered. In the essay "Why One Peaceful Woman Carries a Pistol" (*Land Circle* 290–97), encounters with an assortment of sexist and possibly dangerous males convince Hasselstrom to purchase a pistol; it is then George, another male, who teaches her to fire it and gives her the mental preparation to use it. Late poems that look back to earlier situations are nuanced: in "How Women Laugh in the Company of Men" females are almost as culpable as males in creating corporate sexism—"A woman in high heels and slit skirts / who knows when to laugh / can romp right up that corporate ladder" (*Bitter Creek* 62)—and of course most women outlive most of their men. "Perhaps men encourage each other as women do," Hasselstrom told Roripaugh in a 2001 interview; "and certainly some women are as capable of backbiting jealousy as men" (23). "Myth and reality," Hasselstrom notes in the introduction to *Crazy Woman Creek*, "gallop into the same sunset" (xvi).

In later years Hasselstrom came to an understanding of sorts with her mother, and her adoration for John Hasselstrom tempered as a series of strokes turned him into an irrational stranger, driving her finally off of the ranch with his ultimatum "to give up writing and help him, or to get out and not come back" (*Feels* 171). Analyzing his behavior, Hasselstrom considers her grandfather, husbands George and Jerry, her Uncle Harold, Jerry's grandfather Rudolph, and even her mother:

> [My father] has always been "tight as the bark on a tree," a habit he must have learned from his father, along with his practice of keeping a journal. Karl Hasselstrom—who Americanized his name to Charles and forbade his children to learn Swedish—devoted two pages in his journal to each month's income and expenses. On the left page, he noted every penny made, so I know he sold potatoes for fifty cents on April 20, 1904. On the opposite page, he recorded

expenses such as ten cents for stove polish on April 23 of the same year.

A generation later, my father keeps the same kind of records. He has always argued with my mother and me over everything we wanted or bought. He knows our costs, even for necessities, have risen more quickly than our income from cattle sales. He knows the life he has left is shorter than the time he has spent. Every day he grows shorter tempered, confused by the details of modern living— automatic cash machines, recorded voices when he calls the bank. Surely he fears losing control where he has always ruled, here on the ranch. He is failing even to care for his cattle and must realize he can't blame me or modern technology.

Why didn't he plan, as Rudolph did, for the decline that he has always known might come in old age? Is there another cause for his rage? He has never discussed money with me, but he may know that pinching pennies will no longer be enough to pay the expenses of this ranch, or any other. Is he angry because he is afraid he will lose it no matter what he does?

On each return to the ranch, I talk to my mother and other relatives about the stranger my father has become, asking their help. Some shrug and say, "He's just like he always was, except a little meaner." Occasionally, someone nods sagely and says, "You have to make the decision." What decision? I've thought of a dozen possibilities, even talked to my lawyer, and I have no power other than persuasion. When I try to talk to my mother, she tells everyone I am "just exaggerating again." George taught me bad habits, she says, like disobeying my parents. My father tells Harold that writing has muddled my brain. I'm off gadding about when Mother needs me. Good thing, he adds, that George died before he ruined me for life. (*Feels* 143, 144)

Hasselstrom's positions on gender, then, are as complex and sometimes contradictory as her positions on Nature, environmentalism, and preservation. In an essay titled "The Dichotomy Pulse," Geraldine Sanford discusses ambivalence and paradox as features of style as well as thought in Hasselstrom's work. Ambiguity appears early in the form of juxtaposed images of beauty and ugliness, youth and age, comfort and hardship, life and death. One repeated pattern, as Sanford notes (134), is conjoined birth and death, usually a cow struggling to birth a calf, but sometimes a bird of prey killing another animal. Hasselstrom uses the image of a meadowlark caught on a fence several times, possibly as a conscious or unconscious symbol for her own self, a high-flier caught in place:

Staying in Place

Riding fence last summer
I saw a meadowlark caught by one wing.
(My father saw one caught so, once;
in freeing it, taught me compassion.)
                    He'd flown
futile circles around the wire, snapping bones.
Head folded on yellow breast,
he hung by one sinew, dead.

Gathering cattle in the fall
I rode that way again;
his yellow breast was bright as autumn air
or his own song.

I'm snowed in now, only a path
from the house to the cows in the corral.
Miles away he still hangs,
frost in his eyesockets
swinging in the wind.

I lie heavy in my bed alone, turning, turning,
seeing the house layered in drifts of snow
and dust and years and scraps of empty paper.
He should be light, light
bone and snowflake light. (*Dakota Bones* 3)

As Hasselstrom's determination to write from experience bumps into experiences that take her away from the ranch, or into experience that turns her from rancher-participant to writer-observer, or into thought that is at odds with conventional ranch wisdom or experience, the resulting dislocations manifest themselves in patterns of analysis and intricate literary forms (like that of *Feels Like Far*). These forms are far from the straight line of linear narrative, or even the simple juxtaposition of two contrasting realities which characterize most of her earlier writing. Concurrent with the transition from ranch life in Hermosa, South Dakota, to urban life in Cheyenne, Wyoming, comes a shift of style, from something simple, clean, and vaguely rural to a complexity that seems more mature and vaguely urban. Hasselstrom's art becomes as complex as her characters and ideas. The arc of change is best seen in a line from the early fiction "Beauty" (*Dakoka Arts Quarterly*, summer 1981), through the early memoir *Windbreak* (1987), to the later memoirs *Feels Like Far* (1999) and *Between Grass and Sky* (2002). A similar movement can be seen in Hasselstrom's poetry, from the early poems that tell a story, record history, present a character, photograph a moment, or at their most complex juxtapose two images or people (often a younger and older woman), to later poems which move into myth and drift freely through time and space.

"Beauty" is a tight three-part initiation story of a girl, her father, and horses—the father's workhorses and the girl's unbroken filly named Beauty. The story is mostly autobiographical (part of it appears verbatim in *Going Over East: Reflections of a Woman Rancher*, 57–62), and the father's response to the young filly that refuses to be broken is very much in the character of John Hasselstrom: "I was wondering how my daughter would feel if she just disappeared some day" (12). The surface theme is, of course, the oft-reiterated Hasselstrom point about the need for hard-nosed decisions: "how would you feel if somebody else bought her and they got hurt? I'd hate to think that we made money off her, and then she killed somebody" (12). Two small details at the end of the story underscore the truth that this is the way of the West: "There was a shoulder bone, a leg bone—gnawed by coyotes. . . . I turned the skull over with my boot, and saw a little triangular head slip out of an eyehole, then the flicker of a rattlesnake coiled himself where the skull had been" (13). The coyotes and rattlesnake complete the transformation of the narrator who, through harsh experience in ranching and marriage, is changed from a sentimental child sneaking cake to her dad's horses into a woman of the world "testing the air, wondering whether to glide away or strike" (13). The story is told in straight chronology: three sections devoted to girlhood, college years, and return to the ranch. "Beauty" is a lean, unembroidered story without flashbacks, digressions, or shifts in point of view.

Windbreak is a book and not a short story, and therefore it covers a wider range of material. It is also a memoir. But even within the context of a book, it is cleanly designed: each entry beginning with date and weather, each entry a factual record of the quotidian of ranch life, with occasional speculation on the ways of ranchers:

> *February 8 Low, 30, high 46; cloudy, but no snow.*
> George finished feeding early, then went to Harold's to help him vaccinate his cows against diarrhea. I had no idea one could vaccinate against that. Perhaps ranchers aren't immune to "styles" in diseases; maybe they see an ad for something and suddenly have to have it. Certainly they follow styles in cattle. A few years ago (well, twenty) Herefords were the only kind raised here. Now we have Chianina, Beefalo, Limousin, and something called Amerifax, which sounds like a computer company.
> Just as I was going to bed last night a train went by with fire shooting from one stack. I called numbers until I got an annoyed employee who didn't believe it's dry enough for a fire to start. "It's never that dry until June." (88)

Hasselstrom achieves some variety by inserting a poem at the close of each month, but the poems are as closely tied to ranching and ranchers as the journal entries. She adds the standard preface and introduction, a map at the front, a glossary at the end. If there is an aesthetic principle at work, it is the simple one used in her early poems: find a metaphor, tell a story, juxtapose beauty and ugliness, life and death, real and ideal . . . as they are juxtaposed and intermingled in life. This book is all business, and tied closely to place by virtue of its subject. The sequence of dates enforces a rigid linearity through time, "its structure thus reflecting the coherence of the yearly cycle" (Sanderson 171). *Windbreak* contains a great deal of information on ranching; it contains not much ornamentation, and generalizations come as summaries of her stories. A New York editor might call the life therein described "boring and brutal."

The essays in Hasselstrom's first collection, *Going Over East*, follow a similar pattern of generalization illustrated by anecdote, story, or history—the medieval sermon structure of exemplum embedded in argument. But with *Land Circle* (1991), as John Murray noted, Hasselstrom extended the combination of prose and poetry begun in *Windbreak* to create "a narrative counterpoint of poetry and prose" that "calls to mind other modulations: day and night, life and death, hope and despair" (20). Although the architecture of this book is more complex, individual poems remain focused in time and place. Among the essays only "Birth" prefigures the complex web of times and places that will mark Hassel-strom's next book: "My father puts his arm inside the other world again, loops chain over the calf's ankle, and reaches in, searching for the other leg. My father has gone back, retreated into that unknown silence before birth, our shadowy history—narrow and dark as a grave, warm and wet as an ancient sea. From warm oblivion we're squeezed into life; the door to death is narrow and uninviting. Egyptians pulled the brain out through the nostrils. The calf is dead" (*Land Circle* 6, 7).

Compared to *Land Circle*, *Feels Like Far* (1999) is, as folks say in the Midwest, "a whole nother story." Hasselstrom has lost her husband George and her home in Hermosa. The writer finds herself exiled, ab-stracted, to a degree alienated, "flying out of control into darkness" (154). "Without George I'm like a dog, / dangling at the end of a leash / held by someone I hardly know," she observes in a poem written in 1989 ("Walking the Dog," *Dakota Bones* 130). She is uncertain of her roles as rancher, child, wife, and even writer. And structurally *Feels Like Far* is further removed from *Windbreak* than Cheyenne is distant from Her-mosa. Even previously published material (including one chapter pub-lished as a fiction in *Missouri Review*, 1989) is given a new shape by the form Hasselstrom invents for this book: each chapter contains a pro-logue, epilogue, and an introduction, in italics, which begins in the city of Cheyenne, cuts to some memory of the ranch near Hermosa, and wanders—more often than not—among the various males in Hassel-strom's life (biological father, adopting father, Daniel, George, Jerry, and sometimes Uncle Harold) or among women like her mother, her Aunt Josephine, her neighbor and friend Margaret. An epigraph positions it-self between introduction and body of each chapter. The chapter itself may be cut into several sections or, in the case of "Blues for Shoveling Horse Manure" (on the death of Aunt Josephine), may shuttle back and forth between past and present, the last line of one subsection linked to the first of the next by a recurring word or image. In some places, Has-selstrom appears to use deliberate shifts in tenses to blur time distinc-tions; in other places, she moves in a single paragraph across large ex-panses of time and geography:

I wandered through the house, as I walked among the rocks and grasses around my hilltop house, trying to learn my path as thor-oughly. Hidden in darkness, I felt my way along the passages, my fingertips memorizing peculiarities. The house was built about 1911, soon after my father was born. In an architectural style called Prairie Cube, its height and stark symmetry contrasts with my low prairie house and its wide views, making me realize how often I had lived in houses built by people I knew. In eighty years, the city house had housed boarders, been a coroner's home, and sheltered a family with eight foster children. (87, 88)

There is a sense in this book, to quote the author, of "disorientation, more profound than being lost . . . a sensation of drifting, of levitation" (9).

"Looking for the Light: The Elk in the Aspen" is one of the most recently written chapters. It is especially dense, an imagistic collage that begins with a dream of George on the eve of the author's forty-ninth birthday, cuts to Jerry downstairs in the Cheyenne house, moves to Jackson Hole where Hasselstrom is teaching a writing seminar, retreats twenty years to the encounter with the bull elk in the aspen grove, returns to Jackson Hole where Jerry fishes while the spirit of George loiters nearby, and concludes with the author rescuing her dog Frodo from drowning. Hovering over everyone is the presence of her father:

Perched on a warm rock beside the river, below the vast laceration of the slide, I peel the walking stick, thinking how such a staff offers balance, a brace against falls. My father's teaching was my childhood groundwork, offering perspective as I followed Daniel into disaster. Following George, evasive and enigmatic as an elk, guided me to this time and place. Now what? I live with Jerry, but since my father has turned on me like a wounded elk, how can I trust another man? (163–64)

In one sense, Hasselstrom has lost her bearings, physical and psychological, and is no longer grounded. In another sense, Hasselstrom has matured beyond the linear, into Meridel Le Sueur's world of the closed circle (see the title *Land Circle*), or into a mode of perception which seems to come with maturity, the sense of time as a river that we get in the poems of Bill Kloefkorn. Hasselstrom writes, "Now that I'm past forty I feel myself caught in [time] as if in a river of molasses. . . . Yesterday, driving down the entrance road, I noticed the dusty snow blowing across, and thought that I want to be that dust, haunting the places I love after I die" (*Windbreak* 109). The New York editor who suggested that Hasselstrom remove all the women from this book, and narrow the story to the conflict with her father (Roripaugh 8) missed entirely the book's point, and the larger, characteristically midwestern theme of Hasselstrom attempting simultaneously to break and preserve roots.

In the newer essays of her most recent collection, *Between Grass and Sky* (2002), Hasselstrom continues the disjunctures of time and place that mark *Feels Like Far*, most noticeably in the revised story "Running with the Antelope" and the essays "A Mouthful of Mice," "The Owl and the Fence," and "Sleeping with the Grizzly." In *Orion*, spring 2002, Hasselstrom published a revised version of her earlier story "Beauty," which juxtaposed her father's wise and responsible shooting of the filly with her own experience rescuing a runaway saluki in Cheyenne: "Today, on my account with the world, I will enter the joy of rescuing the dog against the loss of Beauty" ("Responsibility" 33). The penultimate story in *Between Grass and Sky*, "Waddling Over the Dam," uses the memory of a beaver-trapping expedition in Cement Ridge, Black Hills, to criss-cross at least five different time frames and two different husbands:

> In later years, when one of us said, "Remember the beaver?" we'd both smile, recalling that long, chilly morning of silent companionship. The last time we remembered the beaver together, George was lying in the hospital bed where he died. He smiled and closed his eyes. I like to believe his breathing slowed as he relived that morning. He'd lost his huge pelts, "blanket beaver," in a tipi fire a few years earlier, too busy rescuing his trapping partner, Jerry, to worry about possessions. He'd left one small pelt at home. It's the only one I have now. Sometimes I open its hiding place and place it on my knees while I write, stroking the fur.
>
> Twenty years later, I went back to Cement Ridge. The view had changed. Gold mining companies have removed entire mountains. (*Between* 193)

A similar increasing complexity can be seen in Hasselstrom's poetry. Hasselstrom's early poems are filled with disasters complete or impending (*Dakota Bones* 3, 11, 23, 46, 76, 139), but her most recent collection of poetry, *Bitter Creek Junction* (2000), is a series of conversations with the dead: father, mother, husbands, friends, and a heap of animal carcasses. It transects time lines and geographies, skips from person to person. Death, time, and loss are not just themes, they're obsessions.[16] It is no coincidence that some of these poems take us to new geographies: Greece, Italy, Crete, and India (42); Wales, England, and Greenland (43). Perhaps Hasselstrom is seeking new landscapes as "a way to go on."

Perhaps the new landscapes cause her dislocations. In either case, the book suggests a writer struggling to put the pieces back together. This is precisely the way she presents her relationship with Jerry in "Jigsaw Dance" (47) and "Loving the Cabinetmaker" (38): "Help me glue these remnants, / Nail these blocks of scrap / Into a graceful cupboard."

The poem "Making Chokecherry Jam" (*Bitter Creek* 16) is mature Hasselstrom, untethered, drifting among Jerry, his grandmother, Hasselstrom's grandmother, an aunt, and a variety of points in time. So too is "Rhubarb Pie" (*Bitter Creek* 40–41), a paradigm of her recent work:

Rhubarb Pie

Fifty finds me
a childless widow
with a new man.
Alone in my city garden
I pull rhubarb, grasping red stalks
down low, snapping them
from the girdle of ruffled leaves
the way grandmother taught me.
(We'd bend over crisp clusters of rhubarb
holding our breath
downwind from the skunk
she killed and buried with her hoe.)
Now I harvest this pie plant
for the bliss of sitting in deep grass,
slicing leaves off stalks
long as my forearm.
Cold water flushes away the dirt,
chills my wrist. Once
I dreamed a daughter
learning through me
the womanly rhythms of such work.

My grandmother married at sixteen,
at twenty-three became a widow with two babies.
Four years later, she married again,
bore her second husband two sons.
She was forty-five the day
he fell beside her on the hay cart,

dead with only time to say,
"I've done too much, Cora."
She raised her family on the canyon ranch,
gave her log house to the only one who stayed,
and moved into the bunkhouse. I always
slept snugly on her lumpy couch
below the screened porch windows.

In my city kitchen, I chop rhubarb stalks
that stain my fingers brown as the faded ink
of her pie recipe. I mix the honey
with orange rind, grated,
roll the flaky dough out thin as parchment.
Tonight, with my new man, I'll eat
this rhubarb pie at grandmother's old oak table,
thinking of the line of mothers, daughters
flowing back through time the way
lemon oil soaks into this dry wood.

Outside the window, dusk will hang
like smoke. Looking up, I'll see a child
reaching up to hold a wrinkled hand.
For the final time, I'll watch my daughter—
never conceived, never born, never named—
walk into the darkness with my grandmother.

This poem contains eight or more points in time, half a dozen geographies, and three different houses. Time is indeed a river, through which flows the line of mothers and daughters, hand to hand, widow to widow. Images of loss—snapped stalks, sliced leaves, dead skunk and dead husbands, cold water, lemon oil absorbed into dry wood, smoke, dusk, that final walk into darkness—overbalance whatever reassurance might be provided by continuities. The biological thread has been broken, as have continuities of place and time and rhubarb pie. Memory and imagination are not enough. The puzzle pieces remain disconnected.

Many writers have survived one significant transplant (Robert Frost to New England, Dave Etter to Illinois, Norbert Blei to Wisconsin), but few survive a second transplant, or a transplant late in life. The work of co-editing three anthologies in seven years has distracted Linda Hasselstrom from finding her own way in her own writing. Aware of this fact, Hasselstrom offers a solution in an essay titled "From Rancher to Nature Writer" . . . a plan which, it seems to me, will not work: "Now that I live in a city all winter, I pay more attention to the interests of the urban population. Freed from much of the physical labor of the ranch, I can concentrate on its future beyond my life" (*Between* 13). In another essay titled, significantly, "The Second Half of Life," Hasselstrom describes her fiftieth birthday celebration, at which she encounters "remnants of past lives drifting through the party" (152) and offers the metaphor of the kaleidoscope (154)—a version of the jigsaw puzzle. Her remark to Jerry's friend Mark suggests that she herself finds the kaleidoscope an unsatisfactory resolution: "This is how it works, Mark. One minute you're thirty, then *pow*! It's *over*! You're *old*!" (152). Or you're anthologizing the works of other writers, asserting again the need for building community: "Why shouldn't the principle apply in families, in city neighborhoods, anywhere? Simply moving our belongings is not joining a community. Being at home requires us to contribute" (*Crazy Woman Creek* xxix).

But we are all of us spinning into space, washing down the river, losing our place, struggling against time to fix what was always in flux, even when we were too young to know the fact. Perhaps the best art requires a sense of that void below our feet, that fore-defeated struggle to hang on. Hasselstrom sensed the void in her twenties; as she grew older, she knew it firsthand. The distance from South Dakota to Wyoming, from ranch to city, from age thirty to age sixty may be only a matter of a few hundred miles, but it turns out to be a long way.

Bill Holm

Holm and Away

In China, I almost never referred to myself as an American: I
was a citizen of a considerably smaller republic: Minneota,
Minnesota.
—Bill Holm, Coming Home Crazy

All of my books are really about Minneota. . . . We travel not
to see something exotic, but to see something inside of us.
—Bill Holm, Holmward Bound

In an essay on midwestern writers, Norbert Blei
quotes Nelson Algren as saying, "Before you earn the right to rap any
sort of joint, you have to love it a little while" (*Winter Book* 38). That observation is true, and it is especially true when applied to Bill Holm,
who alternates between celebrating the austere landscape of his native
southwestern Minnesota, and preaching the jeremiad against the hometown, the university, and the country which drive him at times literally
to drink. Sometimes the sermon is delivered from a transatlantic jet
bound for Iceland or China or Madagascar, where Holm will deliver a
lecture celebrating the cultural and ecological virtues of the austere
landscape of his southwestern Minnesota.

Ambivalence is common among writers closely tied to place, this
love-hate relationship, this pattern of departure and return, this living
with one foot here, the other foot there. And it can be a healthy arrangement. "One must know the world so well," Willa Cather observed, "before one understands the parish." We discover home by exploring the
planet, and we come to know the Self by encountering the Other. In *The
Music of Failure* Bill Holm writes about encountering the Other:

> I close with a poem of mine which I wrote for my students at
> Southwest [Minnesota] State University. It begins with Carl Jung's
> idea that the wild, passionate, sometimes uncivilized inner life of hu-
> man beings is best symbolized by your sexual opposite. The inner life
> of a woman is a young boy; that of a pale Scandinavian like me is a

black haired girl. Either we make friends with this opposite, though it makes us no money, or it turns vicious and poisons our conscious lives. This is not practical; it is necessary. The poem started as advice for my students, but is also advice for you, for stolid Minnesotans, northern Protestants, and most of all, me. Here's the poem:

Advice

Someone dancing inside us
learned only a few steps:
the "Do-Your-Work" in 4/4 time,
the "What-Do-You-Expect" waltz.
He hasn't noticed yet the woman
standing away from the lamp,
the one with black eyes
who knows the rhumba,
and strange steps in jumpy rhythms
from the mountains in Bulgaria.
If they dance together,
something unexpected will happen.
If they don't, the next world
will be a lot like this one. (92–93)[1]

This Self/Other business is scarcely news in a melting pot nation only a few generations removed from the immigrant experience. As Cather shows in *O Pioneers!* and Rolvaag in *Giants in the Earth*, immigrants dancing in the New World discovered, more than the New World Other, an Old World Self they thought they had lost, but had in fact carried in their chests to the wind-swept prairies of South Dakota and Nebraska. What follows immigration is, inevitably, negotiation—Self with Other—and then conjunction, and then amalgamation if not assimilation. Dance is often a polite metaphor for sex . . . and union, which usually produces mixed-litter progeny. Holm himself is a product of cultural negotiation, conjunction, amalgamation. In *Eccentric Islands* he writes of "cognitive dissonance, the mad juxtaposition of contraries, a complete cultural stew pot where the ingredients get to swap flavors and make something new and strange" (306, 307). To some degree we are all culturally diverse hybrids, and the process of cross-pollination has been going on so long—even on the Great Plains—that we are mostly hybrids of hybrids.[2] Holm's pot, left bubbling long enough, yields a stew in which everything tastes *of* everything else, which means that everything tastes *like* everything else, which means everything tastes like nothing really. Gen-Xers are discovering that they know neither their Self nor their Other, and increasingly homogenized dress, language, music, TV, film, religion, gender roles, and even currencies reduce significantly the peculiarities by which we define Self and Other.

Although he is no Gen-Xer, Bill Holm felt at an early age the need to discover his Self. This he did by cultivating his own local Icelandic-American cultural heritage; by exploring the world around Minneota, Minnesota; by traveling away from Minneota, Minnesota; by exercising his imagination; by reading and playing music. While Holm has enjoyed the inestimable blessing of living, working, and retiring in the place of his nativity, and while he is identified in the popular imagination as a writer of southwestern Minnesota place, Holm's Self is ultimately a construction based equally on the linguistic, geographical, cultural, and temperamental peculiarities of what he calls his own "sacred place" and on his extensive travels, reading, and powerful imagination. So powerful is that imagination that the Minneota he describes is sometimes more literary than real, reconstructed or borrowed from writers who are often unrelated to the culture Holm is recovering.

William Jon (Bill) Holm was born on August 23, 1943, to first-generation Icelandic Americans Bill Holm Sr. and Jonina "Jona" Sigurborg Josephson. His mother, Holm recalls (*Faces* 27), had been born on a farm in 1910 to parents who spoke very little English. She herself spoke Icelandic well enough to be mistaken for an emigrant on her one visit to Iceland (*Landscape* 69). Jona attended Minneota High School and clerked in Leland's Drugstore before marrying her childhood sweetheart in 1932. Holm describes her as a woman of energy who longed for adventure which never came her way and, like many women of her generation, compensated for the narrowness of her own world by encouraging her only son to live the life she could not:[3]

Jona used nylon stockings as rope,
made cats out of beer bottles and light bulbs,
Christmas angels from rolled up newspapers,
patched patches on patches on underwear
till they turned into clown suits,
polished shoes with old socks,
and rosemaled coffee cans.

You never know, she said,
when it might come in handy,
and you can always put it in soup
where it'll taste good. (*Boxelder Bug* 17)

Her husband, Bill Holm Sr., was born on a 280-acre farm north of Minneota, less than three miles from the Josephson place: "The Northwest Quarter of Section Thirty-Two in Township One Hundred and Fourteen North of Range Forty-Two West on the Fifth Principal Meridian in Minnesota, United States of America" (*Dead* 26). It sat on the top of a small rise, and from the yard "you could see two or three miles in any direction" (*Coming Home* 217). Great-grandfather Johannes Holm had immigrated to the United States in 1882, while in his early fifties. He had no experience in farming, but he did have four strong young sons. In need of a surname when he bought his land from the Saint Peter and Winona Railroad, he selected "Holm," the Icelandic word for "island." At the turn of the century, two of the Holm sons moved to Bellingham, Washington, where the climate was more temperate than that of Minneota; their parents soon joined them. A third son went to college in Minneapolis and ultimately to New York, a city which he detested (*Music* 35). The farm in Yellow Medicine County, Minnesota, passed to Sveinn who, like his father, fathered children to help with farm chores. But Sveinn died young from pneumonia (*Heart* 189), and his wife moved to town to raise their five children. One of her sons, Bill Sr., reclaimed the farm, which had been "lost in a 1920s land speculation debacle" (*Eccentric* 180), emerging free and clear of debt only in 1943. The history recounted in "A Circle of Pitchforks," though telescoped and embroidered, is personal as well as communal:

My grandfather came out of Iceland
where he took orders from the Danes and starved.
After he died, I found his homestead paper
signed by Teddy Roosevelt,
the red wax still clear and bright.
In the corner, a little drawing of a rising sun
and a farmer plowing his way toward it.
A quarter section, free and clear.
On his farm he found arrowheads
every time he turned the soil.
Free and clear. Out of Iceland.

In the thirties, the farm was eaten by a bank[,]
thrown back up when Olson
disobeyed the law that let them gorge.
In high school they teach
that Hubert Humphrey was a liberal
and Floyd Olson is a highway. (*Dead* 30, 31)

Bill Holm the younger remembers his father as a large, "strong, nervous, profane man [who] loved whiskey, stories and laughter. He had a velvety spirit, but the alligator hide of a blond man who sat on a tractor in the wind and sun too long. . . . He god-damned this, and god-damned that, and god-damned a politician as 'an asshole too dumb to piss with his pants full'" (*Music* 36). Big Bill could bend sixty-penny spikes with his bare hands. His sentences ended in "eh?" He was a Floyd Olson-Franklin Roosevelt Democrat, and "when the Republican uncle poked / fun at F.D.R., my father would bellow: / 'You crooked son of a bitch!'" (*Dead* 14). "I never saw him strike a live creature," Holm recalls, "but he would beat his combine or tractor mercilessly with his cast-iron fists when they had broken down at an inconvenient time" (*Eccentric* 181). William Holm Sr. suffered a massive stroke a week after his son's graduation from high school in 1961, and the farm, livestock, and equipment disappeared in a farm auction. Jona and Bill Holm Sr. moved to a rented cold-water flat in Minneota, and young Bill went off to college. Bill Holm Sr. died in 1966.

Although farm chores shaped very little of his personality, Bill Holm Jr. grew up on that family farm on that remote hill eight miles north of Minneota. A photograph reproduced in *The Heart Can Be Filled Anywhere on Earth* shows an archetypal white, L-shaped, balloon-frame farmhouse, the old portion built in 1885, addition erected in 1900, sheltered by the remnants of a planted grove, most of which disappeared in a tornado in the late thirties. Holm slept in the northwest room of the addition, looking west out of a window covered with ice in the winter. The house was Jona's domain, the barn her husband's. He handled the machinery, she the frying pan. She cooked and he ate. The farm had an outhouse; electricity, running water, and a flush toilet arrived in the late forties and early fifties. Holm remembers bees—to which both father and son were allergic—living in the walls and honey seeping through the white clapboard siding. He remembers the countryside as a vast emptiness, a space looking in at him as he looked out across it, boy growing into space in a manner described by Wallace Stegner:

> It is a country to breed mystical people, egocentric people, perhaps poetic people. But not humble ones. At noon the total sun pours on your single head; at sunrise or sunset you throw a shadow a hundred yards long. It was not prairie dwellers who invented the indifferent universe or impotent man. Puny you may feel there, and vulnerable, but not unnoticed. This is a land to mark the sparrow's fall. (8)

Holm writes also of a cottonwood tree rising from a little island of grass just west of the house. The tree became for him a private place, a place of imagination and going out, a place to dream and fantasize: "I lived in a private mental world, sure that no other human being on the face of the earth had any remote notion of the strange goings-on inside my head, or what singular oddities gave me pleasure. I found my comrades among the dead: Poe, Hawthorne, Shakespeare, Icelandic sagas in literature, the fiercer and stranger books of the Bible" (*Eccentric* 8). "I populated the island with large, plump nerdy boys who, astonishingly, shared my odd tastes" (10).

As a child, Holm attended District 90, Swede Prairie Township, country school eight miles north of Minneota, one of a small group of Norwegian, Swedish, German, Flemish, and Icelandic American children taught by Cora Monseth, a first-generation Norwegian American. In an essay titled "Is Minnesota in America Yet?" Holm points out that "not a single child in that school had a grandfather who spoke English either well or without a heavy brogue, and every parent learned English as a second language. In the fifties, we were the first generation to have only English" (*Imagining* 182). He first encountered what he calls "America" at Minneota High School: "the language of football, a successful high school life, earnest striving and deliberate ignoring, money, false cheerfulness, mumbling about weather" (*Music* 58). He never adjusted to a life at the "nice" school in the "nice" town (*Heart* 126), a school to this day notorious for producing ten-ounce talents with ten-pound egos. As "an oversized, plump, soft, bookish, nearsighted, piano-playing boy with flaming orange hair, a multitude of cowlicks, and conversation decorated with polysyllabic quotations from nineteenth-century poetry" (*Heart* 100), Holm was a perfect target for school bullies. He read books, collected stamps and autographs, sang, debated, and played E-flat alto sax in the band during the school year and at summer concerts in the screened gazebo in Bum Park. Holm describes the teachers as mostly "incompetent, neurotic duds," music teachers who could not carry a tune, English teachers who couldn't read or write, history teachers mired in World War II films . . . but agreeable to doing their drinking out of town, smoking only in private, and—the females—remaining clearly unpregnant (*Heart* 131).

The geographical focus of Holm's adolescence was the town itself, which in the mid-fifties was a prosperous and thriving town of 1,200 or so, not much smaller than its present population. Minneota was half Scandinavian-Lutheran, half Belgian and Irish Catholic. Wednesday afternoon Minneota High School let its students out for an hour of religious instruction at either the Lutheran or Catholic church.

Saturday nights the town was a little more lively than during the week. Like other farmers, Bill Holm Sr. drove in, with his wife and son, finishing his social rounds before disappearing into the Round-Up for "whist, rummy, buck-euchre, beer, Camels, swearing, and male privacy" (*Heart* 112). Jona Holm checked out bargains at O. G. Anderson's Big Store or Johnson's Red Owl and socialized with other women. Young Billy hung out with gangs of kids his own age or disappeared into the Joy Theatre to watch a Hopalong Cassidy movie. Holm remembers the Big Store more than the movie theater or the gang of young boys, for with an opera hall on its top floor and aisles packed with sometimes dated merchandise, it was "so complete and accomplished a time warp that even as a boy I imagined it as a vast museum, the clerks waiting around at their various stations for imminent taxidermy" (*Heart* 90). He also remembers accompanying his mother on social calls to Stena Dalmann and his father on visits to Einar Hallgrimsson, where he passed the time reading while they talked adult talk.[4]

Although Holm declared himself an agnostic somewhere around the age of twelve, the Lutheran Church was a major influence on his character. His parents, no churchgoers themselves, dropped him off each Sunday to sing in the choir and later to play the organ. Jona Holm attended Ladies' Aid meetings—mostly for the socializing—but rarely attended church. Bill Sr. went only on Christmas and Easter. "I went every Sunday until I was fifteen," he purportedly told his son; "Every damn crook in Minneota sits in the front row with a long face and a clean suit. It's no place for an honest man" (*Coming Home* 209). The minister of St. Paul's, Guttormur Guttormsson, brought Holm to the parsonage in

1955, where he could practice piano in warmth and relative comfort, provided a book of music theory, and—at his death—willed to young Bill the piano, which "saved [his] youth" (*Eccentric* 63).

The Lutheran-Catholic animosities on which Garrison Keillor comments so regularly in his Lake Wobegon stories also characterized Minneota of the 1950s. "When north Europe's cast-offs moved to Minnesota," Holm claims, "they brought both their religions with a new ferocity in them further from the sea" (*Music* 51). Western Minnesota was "organized into two pitched, sometimes warring camps—Catholics and Lutherans. . . . In Minneota there was a Catholic Bank and a Lutheran Bank, Catholic and Lutheran groceries, insurance, garages, and you took your business where you preferred the theology" (*Music* 43). For Holm, as for Keillor and Jim Heynen and Robert Bly, the Protestant church involved some repression of animal spirits. "When Lutherans married," Holm recalls, "they read St. Paul, issued warnings, drank coffee in the basement, shook hands, and went to work the next day"; Catholics, he imagines, married in the morning, then "drank whiskey, ate ham, told stories through the afternoon, and finished off by hiring a band, drinking more whiskey, dancing the polka, schottische, and old time waltz all night, ending up at dawn with hugging, lovemaking, well-wishing, and a divine ecstatic hangover" (*Music* 44). For a Lutheran to "turn" and marry a Catholic—or vice versa—was a sin not quickly forgiven by the family elders.

Holm also mentions one "Sister Helen" preaching upstairs at the old Round-Up Saloon, offering more noise than the Lutherans, less liturgy than the Catholics, and "the spirit flopping visibly around a room" (*Music* 45).[5]

Music was what Holm mostly took from St. Paul's Lutheran: "The choir at St. Paul's Lutheran consisted of perhaps ten to fifteen elderly Icelandic ladies . . . [o]nly three men . . . and me, a small, fat boy of 11 or 12 who sang soprano or tenor, depending on his semi-changed voice. I was generally the single member of St. Paul's choir under seventy" (*Music* 68). Holm occasionally played organ and read D. H. Lawrence novels when the sermon got dull. Lutheran liturgy and choral music is in fact a grand tradition[6] which later served Holm well in Madagascar, China, and Iceland, where he encountered Lutherans singing familiar Lutheran hymns; still, Holm recalls, his favorite Christmas carol was not German-Lutheran, but French-Latin: "Angels We Have Heard on High" (*Playing* 23). His writing contains nearly as much music as hometown, beginning with *Boxelder Bug Variations* in 1985 and culminating in *Playing the Black Piano* (2004), which was reviewed in the *Minneapolis Star-Tribune* not by a writer, but by Eric Friesen, network concert host for CBC Radio in Toronto.

Holm preferred the company of adults—those in the choir and others—to that of children his own age. They tended to treat him as an equal or near-equal, even the "old ladies, often born in Iceland, who baked cakes and bread, kept Depression glass bowls well-stocked with peppermints or chocolates, and lived in houses that smelled of moth-balls, powdered sugar, cold cream, and medicine" (*Heart* 102). The po-etry and musical talents derided by his peers brought praise from the older folks. Most importantly, Icelandic community elders outside the church "did not burden [him] with pious moral warnings, whether about sex, tobacco, whiskey, gambling, or blasphemy" (*Heart* 24). Holm writes, "Icelanders who settled in Minneota kept their Old Country habits of bookishness and contrariness in argument. Reading, owning overstuffed shelves of books, spending money on mail-order books, and decorating your conversation with quotations seemed to them normal habits for working-class people. School degrees or social positions had nothing to do with intelligence. The rich and self-important might be more likely stupid or badly read than the neighborhood farmers, car-penters, store clerks, and domestic help" (*Heart* 156). In Holm's Min-neota, every Icelander was second cousin to Sinclair Lewis's Miles Bjornstam, "the Red Swede" of *Main Street*, in whose shack on the wrong side of the railroad tracks Carol Kennicott discovered a better li-brary than Gopher Prairie Public.

Holm writes little of his years at Gustavus Adolphus College (BA, 1965). He was pleased to fulfill his boyhood dream: "At 18, what I wanted most to see in the world was the Minneota city limits sign receding, for the last time, in the rearview mirror of an automobile driving east to New York, Boston, Washington" (*Music* 32), to escape "the farm, the high school, all sports, the constipated timid-hearted small-town culture, American business mania, hypocritical religiosity coupled with smug ignorance" (*Eccentric* 178). He was on his way to his own definition of success: "I would die a famous author, a distinguished and respected professor at an old university, surrounded by beautiful women, witty talk, fine whiskey, Mozart" (*Music* 56). He mentions exploring Ottawa, across the river from St. Peter, and the ruins of an old stone farmhouse he found at the end of an old road through deep woods. Still, all of the first six months and much of the five years after his father's stroke he "got into a canoe and paddled off out to open water . . . exile[d] to the island of forgetfulness for eternity" (*Eccentric* 183).[7]

Holm's graduate years at the University of Kansas are almost as blank, the major event being his acquisition of a single-manual harpsichord and a clavichord, assembled from $150 Zuckerman kits advertised in *The Nation* magazine.[8] Of his marriage, Holm says only, "As a young man I went plumply from the custody of mother to wife, both skilled cooks and devoted attenders on the daily needs of husbands and sons. Then in my thirties, within a year or two, one died and one left, and I found myself standing in a kitchen, alone and hungry" (*Heart* 219, 20). The divorce came in 1974; Jona Josephson Holm died of cancer in May of 1975, one year after the trip to Iceland.

After leaving Kansas ABD, Holm taught at Hampton Institute in Virginia. At a black college, in the middle of the Vietnam War and the civil rights protests, he found "plenty of political interest, but even there, not much sense that books had anything to do with 'real' life" (*Coming Home* 107). He discovered "empty-hearted rootlessness, books used as blunt instruments, a sneering disbelief that hayseed farmers had souls, much less intellects" (*Music* 33). He took to spinning Minnesota stories about fierce winters, treeless wildflower-covered hills in Lincoln County, boxelder bugs, country schools, "and most of all, the rich variety of characters in small towns, whom one could know, tolerate, and forgive in ways not available to the guarded privacy of the big city" (*Music* 33).

Partly in retreat from America in the 1970s (a slum of a decade by any standard, attractive only in comparison with the 1980s), partly in pursuit of something inside himself that he had finally begun to understand, Holm returned to Minneota in 1977, "almost forty, broke, unemployed, divorced, unpublished, my immediate family dead, and most of the people I loved and valued from my childhood ancient, senile, or going fast" (*Heart* 23):

I aged from twenty to forty, found myself for all practical purposes a failure, and settled almost contentedly back into the same rural town which I tried so fiercely to escape. I could not help noticing that personal and professional failure were not my private bailiwick. I knew almost no one still on their first marriage. Friends, too, were short of money and doing work that at twenty they would have thought demeaning or tedious. Children were not such an unpremeditated joy as maiden aunts led us to expect, and for the precocious middle aged, health and physical beauty had begun to fail. It looked, as the old cliché had it, as if we were going to die after all, and the procedure would not be quite so character-building as the *Reader's Digest* and the Lutheran minister implied. (*Music* 57)

Holm purchased for $5,000 a large, square white clapboard house on South Jefferson Street, four rooms downstairs and four rooms up-stairs—plenty of room for books, harpsichord, piano, and clavichord. He began writing affectionate essays and poems about the old folks around Minneota, and publishing in *Minnesota Monthly*, *Crazy Horse*, *Spoon River Quarterly*, and *Milkweed Chronicle*. He published a couple of chapbooks: *Warm Spell* and *Minnesota Lutheran Handbook*. He joined other western Minnesota writers (including Carol Bly and John Rezmer-ski) "traveling from hamlet to hamlet giving readings in churches, nursing homes, libraries, town parks. Since most of the audience had no idea what a poetry reading was, nor had ever been to one, we kept the readings cheerful and light hearted, full of singing and humor" (*Eccentric* 162). The tour is partially recounted in "On Tour in Western Minnesota, the Poetry-Out-Loud Troupe Reads in Four Nursing Homes":

> The poets read. There is a faint stink of excrement, ammonia, scented candles, and sugar cookies. She sits quietly for the first stanza, but then screws up her toothless face. . . .
> "Shit! It's all shit! They're crazy, crazy! Why do we have to sit here and listen to this shit!"
> The dignified Norwegian lady sitting next to her is so used to boredom that she would sit quietly listening to the *Congressional Record* read in Urdu by a computer. She has survived sermons for ninety years, after all. She reaches discreetly for her ear to disconnect her hearing aid.
> The crank goes on: "Shit! Nothing but shit!"
> She will do no such thing as go gentle into that good night. She gets louder and crankier during my poem. I like her even better. I want to kidnap her, first to Minneapolis, then New York, and wheel her into committee meetings, cocktail parties, congressional hearings, celebrations of the mass, and serious cultural occasions. I may even marry her. (*Music* 22)

The circuit brought Holm money, lifelong friends and connections in the literary business, and the beginnings of his audience, which in

Minnesota is large. Most important, it marked the beginning of his serious quest for roots.

Part of that quest was an extended stay in Iceland as a Fulbright lec-
turer in American Literature. Holm applied for and received assignment
to the country his great-grandparents spurned "to find what my relatives
had left behind when they moved to North America" (*Faces* 35). The voyage east he made as the sole passenger on the Icelandic freighter
Bakkafoss, leaving the States on December 22, 1979, taking his clavichord
and his Ford Pinto with him; on the voyage he received an introduction
to the Icelandic tongue and the rules of Icelandic poetry from the ship's
radio operator, Sigurthur Bjorgvinsson (*Eccentric* 89). Iceland seemed to
Holm a chronological warp: "Reykjavík, when I arrived in 1979, felt like
the America of my childhood in the '40s and '50s" (*Eccentric* 188); Iceland was "a time capsule for 1949, or 1939, or 1929, . . . or 1200" (*Eccentric* 127). He met Iceland's President Kristján Eldjárn, hosted visiting
Prairie Home Companion writer Howard Mohr, got roaring drunk at frequent student parties. After a term of promoting "real American voices"
like Henry Miller, James Agee, Edward Abbey, Walt Whitman, William
Carlos Williams, and Carl Sandburg, and subsisting on salt mutton,
peas, rye bread, herring, boiled haddock, and waxy potatoes, Holm
spent a summer—exiled thence by President Eldjárn to improve
Holm's language skills—on a farm in the north of Iceland (*Eccentric*
140ff). Thus "Holm, erstwhile poet, professor of American literature,
and piano thumper, who had spent his first decades trying to escape manure and hay on a farm in western Minnesota" (*Eccentric* 143), fell finally
into the rhythm of farm life, which is much the same the world over. As
the summer wore on, he found his Icelandic improving as his mind dis-
solved into the isolation, the place, his own Self. "If the consequence of
ignorance and laziness is an afternoon in a shit pit," Holm concluded,
"language students might grow smarter faster" (*Eccentric* 146).

After that summer, Holm seriously considered becoming an Icelander. Instead, he returned to the States and to a teaching position at
Southwest Minnesota State University, the baby of the Minnesota State
University System. Located a convenient twelve miles down Route 68
from Minneota, Southwest State was in those days a young, interesting,
and relatively small institution—more a public liberal arts college really—perhaps on its way to becoming. The English Department was
presided over by poet, photographer, and folklorist Alec Bond (for whom
the title poem of *The Dead Get By with Everything* is written); the college

was home to a collection of sixties-type eccentrics, some of whom would later become relatively important writers: Howard Mohr, Philip Dacey, Leo Dangel, Bill Holm, Joseph Amato, Hugh Curtler, and Don Olsen (Ox Head Press). Running the institution during these years were the two best presidents in its history: John Wefald, who later went to Kansas State University, followed by poet-lawyer-English Professor Robert Carothers, who later became Minnesota State University chancellor before moving to Rhode Island. The English Department hosted periodic weeklong writers' festivals, whose list of participants reads like a who's who of Minnesota and rural American writers: Robert and Carol Bly, Wendell Berry, William Stafford, Donald Hall, Linda Hasselstrom, Bill Kloefkorn, Dave Etter, Norbert Blei, Tim O'Brien, Tom McGrath, Meridel Le Sueur, and Frederick Manfred. Students had the virtues and the shortcomings of Minnesotans, which Holm attributes to environment:

> I learned this by teaching school in western Minnesota for many years. This mistrust of genuine questions underlies the general fear of expressing curiosity. Parents cultivate this fear in children, teachers in students, priests and ministers in parishioners, bureaucrats in citizens. This odd fear makes for silent classrooms, silent offices, silent kitchens, silent bedrooms. All statements must be affirmative — or confirmative — thus draining the energy out of conversation well before it shows any sign of quickening. (*Heart* 13)

In 1983 Holm received a Bush Arts Fellowship; in 1985 he published two books from small presses and a one-poem chapbook on Don Olsen's Ox Head Press, and he discovered he had an audience. Then, as the American half of a 1986 – 87 faculty exchange between Southwest Minnesota State University and the University of Xi'an, Bill Holm went to The People's Republic of China. He recounts that experience as best he can in *Coming Home Crazy*, and one chapter of the subsequent book *Eccentric Islands*. Like any East Bloc nation, China was mostly "Dirt, spitting, smelly squat toilets, rude bureaucracy, overcrowding, noise, bad wiring, worse plumbing, nasty store clerks, appalling safety, broken-down machines, cold gray cement buildings, grim apartments, no hot water, no clean air, drab clothes, dust, garlic pickles, greasy meat, surly service, on and on and on, blah, blah, blah, ad infinitum, ad nauseum" (*Coming Home* 103). Although escapes to islands of Western luxury and cleanliness were available, Holm preferred a lifestyle closer to (although not identical with) that of the natives. If he did not exactly ride a bicycle,

Holm at least traveled the people's way, by bus and hard-seat train. He did not shop for foreign luxury items at the Friendship Stores. And while he spent a few nights playing the grand piano at the Golden Flower (westerners-only) restaurant, he mostly declined express seating and service upstairs at the Polite Person's Dumpling Parlor, to queue and dine with the commoners below. He "saw, if not quite from inside, at least a close-range view of what it meant to be truly poor and simultaneously conscious of that poverty" (*Heart* 242) and found himself "simultaneously feared and heroized for being a symbol of something [America] I wasn't even sure I could stomach anymore" (*Coming Home* 89).

In China, Holm carried a load which in America would have had Southwest State faculty up in arms: eight to noon, four days a week, three sections of British and American literature, two sections of composition, and one History of the English Language class. Twenty-five students to a class, every class. He taught in unheated classrooms, with a paucity of books and primitive technologies. About his teaching in Xi'an, however, Holm complains very little. The Chinese students were "a teacher's dream . . . what I went to graduate school to find" (*Coming Home* 200); "they taught me with their humor, intelligence, courage, and failure, more about myself, my own home place of Minneota, Minnesota, and the whole of America than I thought possible" (*Coming Home* 12). For his Chinese friends Holm smuggled into the country editions of Chinese classics not available in The People's Republic—*The Golden Lotus*, the *Dao De Jing*—and English editions of Western writers not approved for communist consumption, notably D. H. Lawrence. He made several excursions to destinations rural and poor, including one long trip, traveling Chinese class, down the Daning River.

The Chinese experience confirmed Holm's distaste for his native land: "I came home to an America that looked to me unwilling to know what our own experience has been, either as a country, as a community, or as individual citizens. The lessons of history had evaporated. . . . This disconnection from history made me ask myself: Am I crazy? Have I missed something?" (*Coming Home* 11). Quickly he recovered the old impatience with American politics that he had almost lost in China. Students at Southwest State were deep into what Robert Hughes aptly calls *The Culture of Complaint*, sunk in "bored passivity" and "whiny resistance to any unreceived idea or language" (*Coming Home* 107). "What insufferable arrogance, I thought to myself, to throw the chance for a real mental life away on people who don't want it. American life doesn't want them to want it, not, at any rate, to want more than the name, surely not the fact" (*Coming Home* 114).

Like every American returning from an extended stay in a third-world country, Holm was suddenly conscious of the sheer blubber of his fellow citizens. Like any such American he was depressed by the public whining of princes and princesses who had slept on peas. Like any such American, he was offended by American arrogance and what passed for politics:

Presidential News Conference

This face is death disguised as Grandpa,
not pitted and terrible, but affable, handsome,
a natty dresser, a good ballroom dancer.
Worst of all, it means well.
When it talks, everything you love—
moose antlers, willow bark, wind
blowing over water—disappears unless
something still animal left inside
your stomach rolls over and growls
when it comes into the room. (*Dead* 24)

The American poor were getting poorer; the business section of any newspaper was five times the size of the arts section; Evangelical Christianity—more repressive even than Minneota Lutheranism—was rich, televised, respectable, and venomous; and Americans debated in public only two issues: smoking and abortion (*Coming Home* 89). In Holm's already jaundiced vision, sharpened by his year in Asia, signs of slippage were everywhere. America did not work the way it once did, and bureaucrats were triumphant. Under the requirements of Section 1324A, Title 8, of the new U.S. Immigration Code, the personnel office at Southwest State required that Holm identify himself by a Social Security card (original only, no photocopies), a birth certificate, or a passport. These were necessary, he was told, before he could be officially registered to receive pay, even though everyone in the office, the college, the community knew him by sight. "If we have to spend a year in an authoritarian country producing papers on demand before we become sensitized to the moral and political dangers of Section 1324A," he fumed in print, "then we are already a nation of slaves, passive and agreeable" (*Coming*

Home 137). Offended by the Big Picture, Holm retreated mentally to an American margin, electing life off the grid in "Minneota, an ugly harsh place far from anywhere, where no sensible American (other than a farmer) would choose to live" (*Coming Home* 97).

In the spring of 1992, lonesome for the (relatively) bright students of the People's Republic, Holm accepted a job teaching literature at a school of technology in Wuhan. Despite a Christmas, 1988, visit which had turned sour when he, Marcy Brekken, and a dozen Chinese students spent December 22 in a police station being interrogated (*Coming Home* 213), Holm boarded the airplane to teach in China once more. This visit was a disaster. His apartment, in a dank cement building all too Chinese, smelled of mildew, rotted wood, and mouse turds. Water was turned off at eight every evening, turned on at six in the morning. Electrical service was intermittent. "[R]aw sewage sometimes bubbled up out of the bathtub drain. From the balcony we looked down on a colony of rats" (*Eccentric* 167). Holm took an immediate dislike to his hostess, whom he nicknamed "Smiley," for her dissimulating smile and her bureaucratic officiousness:

Official Talk in Wuhan: 1992

When nothing has happened there is no need
to mention it, it would only prove
embarrassing if certain policies
were brought up, though of course
everything, as you see, is fully
ordinary, moving forward, though without
any backward to move forward
from, and everyone smiles and is
happy, doing their part, though of what
they are not too sure. (*Playing the Black Piano* 69)

The students were not quite what Holm had expected either: these were "special" students who, although they had failed their entrance exams, were willing to pay for classes.[9] Between 1987 and 1992, it seemed to Holm, China had deteriorated remarkably. One disappointment led to another. Finally he suffered some form of cardiac event and was taken to a Chinese military hospital, where he remained for two weeks "half full of rage and claustrophobia" (*Eccentric* 174) before returning to his smelly apartment and a six-inch centipede for a bedfellow. Holm left Wuhan the next day for Hong Kong, where a cardiologist recommended bypass surgery. Holm checked out of Hong Kong immediately for the States. The romance with China was ended.

The last decade of the twentieth century saw Holm at the height of his literary productivity. He gave frequent public readings; he was the subject of newspaper articles and television documentaries; he narrated a widely distributed PBS video titled *Death of a Dream*; he wrote introductions and blurbs for other people's books, and text for coffee table photo books like *Landscape of Ghosts* and *The Quiet Hours*. He hosted a couple of his former Chinese students who had somehow made the great escape to the United States. He traveled to Panama, Vietnam, and the Island of Madagascar, sponsored by the U.S. State Department and the United States Information Service.

And in 1998, he returned to Iceland where he experienced a worse culture shock than China, 1992. "Was this the Reykjavík I left in 1980? Or, like Rip Van Winkle, had I slept through a generation or two? Four-lane motorways with spaghetti junctions circled the town, there were miles of new concrete office buildings and blocks of flats in the favorite no-nonsense modern rectangle style. . . . Downtown Reykjavík now had both vegetarian smoke-free cafes and little bars on every corner with draft beer, cognac, and tattooed purple-spiked-haired metallic body-ornamented citizens reposing behind black mirror glasses" (*Eccentric* 187). Somewhere beneath the surface Holm found enough of the Old Iceland to rekindle his love for the country. He visited the farm on which Pauline Bardahl's mother had been born; reconnected with Sigurthur Bjorgvinnson, the *Bakkafoss* radio operator; and met a cousin, Cathy Josephson, who had married an Icelander and, after the man died, remained in Iceland, maintaining a small guesthouse on a farmhouse eight miles north of Vopnafjorthur (*Eccentric* 224). In 1999 Holm purchased a cottage on the island's northern perimeter, and now spends a portion of each year in Iceland, reading, talking, and—with friends like Robert and Carol Bly and the Canadian writer David Arnason—running "White Night Summer Workshops in Saga-land" for selected friends and writers. In 2002, William Holm Jr. received an honorary doctorate of humane letters from his alma mater, Gustavus Adolphus College. In 2003, William Holm Jr. began a three-year process of phased retirement from Southwest Minnesota State University, ending his career "a famous author, a distinguished and respected professor" at a relatively new and struggling state college, not fifteen miles from the farm on which he was born.

The sense of place is central to Bill Holm's writing, and to his theory of life. Echoing Linda Hasselstrom, he writes, "for better or worse, you belong in a place, and grow out of its black soil like a cornstalk" (*Music* 33). In *The Heart Can Be Filled Anywhere on Earth* he quotes Flannery O'Connor on a certain breed of younger writers—"You know what's the matter with them? They're not from anywhere" (20)—and asserts the need of all of us, even Americans, to live lives closely tied to *from-ness*: "Some choices in life we don't want to make if we intend to become entire human beings before we die, . . . but *from-ness* is always crucial" (21); Thoreau, Holm points out, was "a stubborn burrower into his *from*" (21). He returns to this idea in *Landscape of Ghosts*, warning against individuals and cultures that fail "to be *from* anywhere at all" (29). But for Holm, *from-ness* is not a given: although in modern America it can be sensed (perhaps more accurately its *absence* is sensed) early in life, integration with place must be recovered, at considerable effort. Nor does formal K–12 schooling assist that recovery. Usually education merely enhances alienation: "Sacredness is unveiled through your own experience, and lives in you to the degree that you accept that experience as your teacher, mother, state, church, even, or perhaps particularly, if it comes into conflict with the abstract received wisdom that power always tries to convince you to live by. One of power's unconscious functions is to rob you of your own experience by saying: we know better, whatever you may have seen or heard, whatever cockeyed story you come up with; we are principle, and if experience contradicts us, why then you must be guilty of something" (*Music* 12).

In *Sex, Economy, Freedom, and Community* Wendell Berry argues that alienation is in fact caused by modern liberal education, with its emphasis on an artificial "cultural diversity" at the expense of functioning, coherent, healthy although monolithic, local communities:

> There is, in fact, a good deal of talk about pluralism these days, but most of it that I have seen is fashionable, superficial, and virtually worthless. It does not foresee or advocate a plurality of settled communities but is only a sort of indifferent charity toward a plurality of aggrieved groups and individuals. It attempts to deal liberally—that is, by the superficial courtesies of tolerance and egalitarianism—with a confusion of claims.

The social and cultural pluralism that some now see as a goal is a public of destroyed communities. Wherever it exists, it is the result of centuries of imperialism. The modern industrial urban centers are "pluralistic" because they are full of refugees from destroyed communities, destroyed community economies, disintegrated local cultures, and ruined local ecosystems. The pluralists who see this state of affairs as some sort of improvement or as the beginning of "global culture" are being historically perverse, as well as politically naïve. They wish to regard liberally and tolerantly the diverse, sometimes competing claims and complaints of a rootless society, and yet they continue to tolerate also the ideals and goals of the industrialism that caused the uprooting. They affirm the pluralism of a society formed by the uprooting of cultures at the same time that they regard the fierce self-defense of still-rooted cultures as "fundamentalism," for which they have no tolerance at all. They look with wistful indulgence and envy at the ruined or damaged American Indian cultures so long as those cultures remain passively a part of our plurality, forgetting that these cultures, too, were once "fundamentalist" in their self-defense. And when these cultures again attempt self-defense—when they again assert the inseparability of culture and place—they are opposed by this pluralistic society as self-righteously as ever. The tolerance of this sort of pluralism extends always to the uprooted and passive, never to the rooted and active. (168–70)

Even without the relatively recent doctrines Berry is critiquing, *education* by definition *leads* students *from* experience in their immediate environment into received wisdom and into analysis, from object to word to abstraction. The process of education, as Holm himself demonstrates, is broadening, healthful, and necessary, but genuine *from-ness*, like genuine community, comes from objects in place. In a late poem for people of a geography slightly distant from Minnesota, Holm informs readers that God is in fact Mt. McKinley ("Looking at God," *Playing* 65).

Bright children who do well in education are thus especially susceptible to a loss of place, and to the sense of alienation which characterizes most twentieth-century intellectuals. And the closer they are to one of Berry's functioning, well-defended, "fundamentalist" cultures, the more likely they are to be led away from their place during the process of education. Rural cultures especially tend to be "fundamentalist" in Berry's sense, and in his book *Wolf Willow*, Wallace Stegner points out that for a rural, regional, or even ethnic writer, education and experience are inevitably at odds:

> I am reminded of Willa Cather, that bright girl from Nebraska, memorizing long passages from the *Aeneid* and spurning the dust of Red Cloud and Lincoln with her culture-bound feet. She tried, and her education encouraged her, to be a good European. Nevertheless she was a first-rate novelist only when she dealt with what she knew from Red Cloud and the things she had "in place of all that." Nebraska was what she was born to write; the rest of it was got up. . . .
>
> Her career is a parable. If there is truth in Lawrence's assertion that America's unconscious wish has always been to destroy Europe, it is also true that from Irving to William Styron, American writers have been tempted toward apostasy and expatriation, toward return and fusion with the parent. It is a painful and sometimes fatal division, and the farther you are from Europe—that is, the farther you are out in the hinterlands of America—the more difficult it is. (25–26)

Bill Holm offers a similar admonition: "I am a moralist," he writes in *Landscape of Ghosts* (9), "a harper on history and the necessity for humans to *grow into* a consciousness of it" (italics added). Recovering history runs not only against formal education, but against the community's own social strictures. In a videotaped interview that went into *My People Are My Home*, Meridel Le Sueur remarks offhandedly, "Of course nobody ever told you the true history of your own place." Bill Holm grew up with a limited history of his place, and probably with no true sense of any place he fitted into. Looking back over the shoulder of his life, he writes, "In my small town secrets disappeared. Retarded children vanished into the upstairs bedrooms of farmhouses, where someone carried food to them. . . . Pregnant, unmarried girls were not mentioned once they had been safely transported to the anonymity of Minneapolis to give birth. . . . When depression or any form of madness visited a house, someone disappeared (often a woman) who was described as resting because of 'nerves.' I spent my boyhood blissfully unaware of how many neighbors had experienced shock treatments . . . I never heard the word tuberculosis, though I even had an aunt dying of it. Suicide? Silence. The gay uncle? More silence. Prison? Nobody we knew" (*Eccentric* 23).

Tradition, like history and voice, is also difficult to recover, because in America, according to Holm, tradition has not yet been properly born: "Tradition grows from the texture of the grass, the shape of the hills, the color of rivers when the snow melts, the swampy pasture where our great-grandfather's horse stumbled and broke his leg. We haven't been long enough in Minneota to earn that kind of tradition" (*Faces* 24).[10] Except for religious intolerances, Old World traditions "seem not to travel well over water; most sickened in mid-Atlantic and expired shortly after they stepped off the horse cart onto the tall grass prairie. This is a country of interrupted traditions, just entering a difficult puberty to start growing real ones" (*Faces* 25). Patriotism, Holm suggests, has nothing to do with foreign policy, burnt flags, or taxation; it has to do with place: "light on a hillside, the fat belly of a local trout, and the smell of new-mown hay" (*Eccentric* 136).

The discovery and recovery of locality is the conscious goal of much of Holm's writings: first *The Music of Failure* (1985), the small collection of "affectionate essays and poems about those people, old Icelandic immigrants with odd accents, aunts, uncles, and baby-sitters who fed and praised me" (*Heart* 23) and *Boxelder Bug Variations* (1985), a book of finger-exercise poems and meditations on the quintessential southwestern Minnesota insect; *The Dead Get By with Everything* (1991),[11] a collection of poems in which the first section is a personal history titled "Geneology," the second section a communal history titled "A Circle of Pitchforks"; *Landscape of Ghosts* (1993), a coffee table book with full-color photographs and plenty of lead between the lines of text, devoted to barns, outhouses, collapsed silos and weathervanes, vacant windows and rusting machines; a revised and expanded *Music*, its title taken from the final line of that seminal essay, mostly family history and photographs, and Minneota stories: *The Heart Can Be Filled Anywhere on Earth: Minneota, Minnesota* (1996); a Christmas book of recollected family traditions (1998).

The essay "Is Minnesota in America Yet?" written for Tammaro and Vinz's *Imagining Home* (1995), is Holm's most extended discussion of the cultural imprint he received as a child. This culture was neither the urban collection of culturally diverse refugees from broken communities which is America these days, nor Old World Iceland. By the 1950s, Holm argues, "The Minnesota immigrant culture [had become] a thing in itself, neither Europe nor America, though with a few toes in both, and a few surprises that neither Europe nor America would have predicted.

This third culture had its own beginning, middle, and end, and its own Götterdämmerung built into its origins and structure, probably within a single century. I call it the 'pickled-in-amber' culture, and my generation is the last gasp of the first wave of it in Minnesota. After me, the deluge— the real America" (182). This culture was out of sync with and often at odds with national American trends like the Cold War, civil rights, and the counterculture of the sixties, but it contained an "amazing intellectual vitality too. Think of the writers who came out of it: Ole Rölvaag, Herbert Krause, Meridel Le Sueur, and Tom McGrath (compare their political energy with a 'real' American like Robert Lowell); Fred Manfred, whose finest work is deeply colored with both the language and culture of Fries-land; and Robert Bly, whose energy comes partly from his role as an old immigrant Norwegian literary circuit rider, filled with passionate Ibsen-esque improving" (186). This tradition is a combination of landscape and human culture, one growing out of the other. Holm writes in part to re-cover and preserve both the landscape and its human component.

In contrast to Paul Gruchow or Kent Meyers, two southwest Min-nesota authors of Holm's generation who are quite as bookish as he and have much to say in *Grass Roots* and *The Witness of Combines* of boy life on the farm, Holm writes little about pigs, barns, corn and beans, trac-tors and combines. And unlike Donald Hall in *String Too Short to Be Saved*, Holm is more intent on salvaging other people's cultural freight than in reclaiming family heirlooms from his own attic. He is espe-cially interested in persons and places. The locations he selects are not much celebrated by others: the Swede Prairie slough, towns like Canby and Dawson and Olivia and Granite Falls, Routes 23 and 68, the Lutheran churches of Minneota and Westerheim and the Catholic church in Wilno, the Icelandic graveyard in Lincoln County and the single tombstone of an Irish soldier a mile outside of Ghent, the Yellow Medicine River, the M & M Cafe, the Comfy Cafe, and cafes in other small towns:

Come into an old cafe
in Ghent, or Fertile, or Holloway.
The air is steamy with cigarette smoke and frozen breath,
collars up under a sea of hats pulled down.
You can hardly see the mouths moving under them.
The talk is low, not much laughing.
Eat some hot dish, some Jello,

and have a little coffee and pie.
These are the men wrecking the ship of state—
the carriers of darkness. ("A Circle of Pitchforks," *Dead* 30)

In one early essay titled "The Grand Tour" (*The Music of Failure*), Holm inventories the things that hallow southwestern Minnesota for him: the local cemetery, the Lincoln County Icelandic Church, one of Rollie Johnson's larger wood carvings, and an unfarmed stretch of land along the Yellow Medicine River which Holm's cousin Daren Gislason appropriated and decorated with discarded furniture, rusting automobiles, discarded Maytag washtubs, and beds of irises, tulips, peonies, mums, lilies, and other flowers. Elsewhere he describes the abandoned round barn built in 1910 by Victor and Elvira Josephson:

> The round barn, since it served no practical purpose, was left to the mercy of weather and decay. The shingles on the vast, steeply curved roof slid off as they rotted randomly, leaving maybe a hundred holes of light forty feet above your head. The effect, like a low sky full of star points, was more romantic and lovely in its dying than it had ever been while still in good repair. The round roof was an acoustical marvel, too. I practiced opera arias there on sunny afternoons. Even a church choir duffer sounded like Caruso after a passionate Italian phrase reverberated around this roof and bounced back onto the bare wood floor, hayless for the first time in its history. A plainsong would have sounded well, too, but somehow seemed culturally misplaced in the barn of Icelandic agnostics.
>
> Not only eyes and ears were charmed by that barn; the nose loved it best of all. Once cattle and horses have eaten and shat and slept, been born and died in a room, the boards smell of them. The smells of old hay, leather, sour milk, dust, cats, petrified manure, cheap pipe tobacco, haunt you forever in old barns. Oddly, almost no one thinks of those smells as decay, sadness or failure. There [sic] are a kind of old quilt pulled over your nose on a blizzardy night. Whoever bottled that smell would earn the gratitude of the human race. One sniff might calm an army or almost make a politician truthful. (*Landscape* 57, 59)

Most haunting, to Holm and a reader, are the vast empty prairies of Lyon, Lincoln, and Yellow Medicine counties ("The Grand Tour" and "Horizontal Grandeur," *Music*), and the hilly Coteau des Prairies which Holm somewhat generously calls, "the spiritual and geological beginning of the Black Hills, the Rocky Mountains, the true west"

(*Music* 27). The landscape Holm presents in his writing is sparse and the climate is harsh:

> Minneota, Minnesota, where I live, sits close to the western border of the state, far from forests, big lakes, or any sizable city. It is a small dot on what geographers describe as the northern temperate tallgrass prairie. Half of Minnesota lies in that zone—the south and the west. As rainfall declines and elevation rises, not far west of Minneota, the tallgrass shrivels to a short-grass prairie of immense size and lonesomeness: the Great Plains. (*Heart* 3, 4)

Holm celebrates tiny scenic details like the kaleidoscope of color in wildflowers and ditch grasses, and he appreciates the occasional lone cottonwood, but for him the prairie surprises in magnitude, not in scenic climaxes. The landscape's true beauty is "in function, rather than form" (*Music* 17): 160 flat acres of rich soil with relatively few rocks and a relatively reliable supply of water. Like other Great Plains writers before him, Holm finds in the amplitudes a certain desolation, threat, and loss. Pioneer wives, he admits, went insane here, and the landscape is as much to blame as religion for the Minnesota repression of spirit. Nevertheless, he is nostalgic about the place and time of his youth.

As an inevitable result of the eclipse of rural America and its needs by urban America with its own very different agenda,[12] Holm's landscape is filled with wreckage of all sorts. "Here is a book full of pictures of stuff nobody wants to look at and of essays on subjects no one wants to read," he writes in opening *Landscape of Ghosts*; "These pictures are for an audience of psychic heroes who are not afraid of decay, collapse, rust, grief, solitude and history" (7). In his essays, Holm meditates on weathered siding, old windows, red barns, abandoned outhouses, rock piles, advertising signs, windmills, silos, and graveyards.

In his overviews of Minneota (most notably the capsule history contained in the first chapter of *The Heart Can Be Filled Anywhere on Earth*), Holm invariably stresses loss: "If you glance quickly, downtown Minneota looks about the same now in 1995 as it did in pictures taken before World War I, an up-and-coming little town that thought highly of itself and its commercial possibilities in the great world. But depressions, bank panics, distance from markets, and aging citizens throttled its rise. Look closely down the street: business blocks are pocked with empty lots, space for wind to blow through and for snowdrifts to pile up in solitude, with dead buildings gone back to scrap lumber, leaving the streets like elderly mouths waiting to be fitted for dentures" (*Heart* 11, 12). The towns in these parts "close by six, the cafes frequently at four. People eat at home, where it doesn't cost money. By ten, silent streets, only the liquor store open, its lonesome Hamm's sign proclaiming a few still up. Nothing but blue, flickering TV's behind drawn blinds, and a random pattern of yard lights stretching off onto the prairies. By midnight, nothing" (*Music* 1).

The people in Holm's Minnesota landscape are likewise full of collapse, rust, grief, and solitude. With the exception of free-spirited John Allen, woodcarver Rollie Johnson, and in later work Dr. Mike Doman, Holm writes little about his contemporaries, "the Minneota friends who have for years sustained, loved, helped, and fed one another" to whom *Boxelder Bug Variations* is dedicated. He writes instead of old Icelanders or eccentric Minneotans: the village bag lady, the village half-wit, the neighborhood drunk eating lilacs in the yard next door, Einar Hallgrimsson, Rannveig and Guttormur Guttormsson, Jona and Bill Holm, great-grandparents Johannes and Soffie, Auntie Clarice, Aunt Olympia, Grandma Rafnson, Stena Dalmann, Pauline Bardal, and her sister Crazy Rose:

Rose, her face pinched toward God,
used to disappear during church picnics.
The men spread out in the field until
they found her preaching in Icelandic
to the cornstalks with a loud voice. (*Dead* 23)

Like the citizenry of *Music of Failure* and *The Heart Can Be Filled Anywhere on Earth*, the people of *Landscape of Ghosts* are mostly ghosts themselves:

The houses I pass on my morning stroll are full of ghosts. Every house is inhabited in my imagination by whoever lived there in say, 1957, the year of the famous Chevy.

There's old Harry, the banker, in dignified brick. There's the chicken magnate, Doc Kerr's house with its hooded awnings. There's the old Josephson house, where Elvira and Victor's father died before I was born, with its grand colonnaded veranda. There's Einar Hallgrimsson's little cottage with its floor-to-ceiling bookshelves. There's Frank and Frida's house where the stamp club met with their perforation gauges and tweezers. There's where Bolga and Sophie made Icelandic pancakes every Sunday morning. There's old Deaf Torgeson's shack. (19)

Holm's portraits are sometimes nostalgic, but from his human and physical environment, he took an attitude and a way of looking at the world which is far from sentimental. Environment, he believes, creates a deep sensitivity to the vanity of human wishes, to time and the passage of time. Both the geographical and social landscapes encourage a rugged individualism—with a large dose of willful contrariness and a general suspicion of received ideas—in the American tradition of Emerson, Thoreau, and Whitman. Holm is often impatient with theory, especially postcolonial literary theory:

In two thousand and one,
if you say in poem or song to your fellow man:
"This is a beautiful bowl," they laugh,
saying: "That is only your view, your denial
that trees have suffered, that one bowl
is necessarily more beautiful than
another bowl." They want an ironic
bowl, not a wooden bowl full of poetry (*Playing* 19)

Holm developed a Luddite distrust of technology which led him to banish television from his home and write his manuscripts longhand on yellow tablet paper, an egalitarianism in which "[t]here was no bowing or scraping" (*Music* 84), a radical populism, and a romantic notion of the blessings of poverty (see "Glad Poverty" in *Heart*) and even failure (see the title essay of *The Music of Failure*). A significant component of the human landscape is the absence of joy and emotion in farm and small-town life (Holm shares this assessment with his close friends Carol and Robert Bly).[13] Life on the Great Plains, Holm suggests, encourages children to "be reasonable, keep our expectations of the world down, not get too excited" (*Music* 91). The Icelandic tradition, Holm believes, values culture more than wealth, and he attributes his verbal skills to old Icelanders who believed "An admirable human spoke admirable speech—precise, witty, without jargon or cliché, with nice distinction in diction and vocabulary. The old idea of a 'word hoard' survived in them; the better stocked the hoard, the more armed the human" ("Is Minnesota" 186–87).

Pauline Bardal—indeed, the entire Bardal family—was an especially important tutor. Pauline "in American terms, was a great failure: always poor, never married, living in a shabby small house when not installed in others' backrooms, worked as a domestic servant, formally uneducated,

English spoken with the odd inflections of those who learn it as a second language, gawky and not physically beautiful, a badly trained musician whose performances would have caused laughter in the cities. She owned nothing valuable, traveled little, and died alone, the last of her family" (*Music* 65). But the Bardals were not culturally poor: after Pauline's funeral, the house yielded "books in three or four languages: Plato, Homer, Bjornsson in Norwegian, Snorri Sturlasson in Icelandic, Whitman, Darwin, Dickens, Ingersoll, Elbert Hubbard, piles of scores by Handel, Bach, Mozart, George Beverly Shea and Bjorgvin Gudmundsson, old cylinders of Caruso, Galla-Curci, Schumann-Heink, John McCormack" (*Music* 72).

Holm developed the characteristic Minnesotan faith in the relative virtue of Minnesotans, including politicians:

> But men like Humphrey, McCarthy, Stassen, Floyd Olson, Elmer Benson, Elmer Anderson, and even Walter Judd—the fierce anti-communist China-lobby man—could be trusted to speak fine direct English in complete sentences (with clauses!), to have their hands in no one's pockets, to keep their discourse to ideas and policies and away from cheap innuendo. They seemed honest, decent men of high intelligence, *public servants* in the old sense of both those words. . . .
>
> This flowering of political decency did indeed arise from some peculiarities of Minnesota as a place—heterogeneous, not long out of the Old Country, and mistrustful of professional politicians. Hubert was raised in a Huron drugstore, Vladimar in the back room of the Minneota newspaper, and if they lost an election, or wearied of public life, they could return happily and ably to filling prescriptions, teaching school, or writing for a newspaper. Their life was not their office, or so we thought, and so we trusted them. No one, on the other hand, could imagine Nixon or Lyndon Johnson with a real job. They were political fish who would dry up out of the water of public life. ("Is Minnesota" 180–81)

More than anything Holm developed a way of looking at things, which he defines as "the prairie eye." He explains it at length in a passage from "Horizontal Grandeur":

> There are two eyes in the human head—the eye of mystery, and the eye of harsh truth—the hidden and the open—the woods eye and the prairie eye. The prairie eye looks for distance, clarity, and light; the

woods eye for closeness, complexity, and darkness. The prairie eye looks for usefulness and plainness in art and architecture; the woods eye for the baroque and ornamental. Dark old brownstones on Summit Avenue were created by a woods eye; the square white farmhouse and red barn are prairie eye's work. Sherwood Anderson wrote his stories with a prairie eye, plain and awkward, told in the voice of a man almost embarrassed to be telling them, but bullheadedly persistent to get at the meaning of the events; Faulkner, whose endless complications of motive and language take the reader miles behind the simple facts of an event, sees the world with a woods eye. One eye is not superior to the other, but they are different. To some degree, like male and female, darkness and light, they exist in all human heads, but one or the other seems dominant. The Manicheans were not entirely wrong.

I have a prairie eye. (*Music* 17–18)

Whether Holm does in fact have the prairie eye, or whether he uses it (and the voice of Anderson) when writing his poems and essays, is an interesting question; however, if the gifts of prairie, as embodied in sky and grass and in long drives in the private solitude of one's own car, are indeed an expanded sense of inner space and a fierce individualism (*Coming Home* 217), Bill Holm certainly has them.

There is, of course, another Bill Holm, the world traveler. The Pacific Northwest, Iceland, China, Madagascar, Molokai—Holm's books give us plenty of Holm away from home. *Coming Home Crazy* (1990) and *Eccentric Islands* (2000) are perhaps best categorized as travel books, or at least as books of adventure in foreign landscapes. They are also encounters with the Other.

The Icelandic adventures are contained mostly in two long chapters of *Eccentric Islands*, and in "Iceland" in *Coming Home Crazy*. Holm incorporates plenty of history and geography and saga literature into his own stories of the voyage east aboard the *Bakkafoss*, adjustment to life in Reykjavík, travel around the island with Howard Mohr, and summer on the farm. He describes in some detail the light of Iceland, and the topography, even more austere than western Minnesota. Clearly this is a trip into legend: "It was all incomparably grand—this myth of the proud unbending farmer intellectual hurling improvised sarcastic poems (in perfect rhyme and meter) into the howling sea wind" (*Eccentric* 85). "The bridges over the gritty glacial rivers were frail one-lane wooden contraptions that didn't look as if they could hold up a respectable semi with a half load" (*Eccentric* 127). Here life is true, language honest ("almost unaltered since settlement"—130), and conversation full of real stories that "grow from paying attention to experience, to cultivating your eye for detail, and to real feeling, for without genuine emotion, you can never have genuine humor in your talk or in your life" (*Eccentric* 124).

The Icelandic Language

In this language, no industrial revolution;
no pasteurized milk; no oxygen, no telephone;
only sheep, fish, horses, water falling.
The middle class can hardly speak it.

In this language, no flush toilets; you stumble
through dark and rain with a handful of rags.
The door groans; the old smell comes
up from under the earth to meet you.

But this language believes in ghosts;
chairs rock by themselves under the lamp; horses
neigh inside an empty gully, nothing
at the bottom but moonlight and black rocks.

The woman with marble hands whispers
this language to you in your sleep; faces
come to the window and sing rhymes; old ladies
wind long hair, hum, tat, fold jam inside pancakes.

In this language, you can't chit-chat
holding a highball in your hand, can't
even be polite. Once the sentence starts its course,
all your grief and failure come clear at last.

Old inflections move from case to case,
gender to gender, softening consonants, darkening
vowels, till they sound like the sea moving
icebergs back and forth in its mouth. (*Dead* 48)

Holm admits to becoming a little lost in culture and time, to losing his moorings just a little, to collapsing into drink and a foreign place and dancing, to having "made a fool of myself" (156) and having liked it. In

Iceland, Holm met the Other, and it was not quite Bill Holm, and it was interesting.

China was another Other, and further mental dislocations. "This is a book about what happened to an American in China, about adventures of daily life and on the road," Holm writes in introducing *Coming Home Crazy* (11). Those adventures include visits to a mosque and a local kindergarten, exploring the rural landscape, giving piano lessons to the son of a friend, celebrating Christmas in a Christless nation, sharing Mickey Mouse and D. H. Lawrence and Emily Dickinson with students to whom these were forbidden culture, living life as "a Barbarian" in the People's Republic. Holm's tales have the charm of the geographically and culturally remote, and of course they are filled with the frustration of East Bloc life:

> The man gives up, the girl disappears to another window, the teller examines the forms, fingers the passport, pours more hot water in his teacup, and tells us to go to another window. The girl stands in front of us, red coat gleaming, glossy black hair cascading over her collar. Falling temporarily out of love, and by now mightily impatient in the classic American manner, I decide to count employees and see why it has taken an hour of my life in an empty bank to do a three-minute errand. I walk back and forth in the big cement room, counting aloud in English.
>
> Fifty-four human beings are on the job behind the glass. Sixteen read newspapers, seven or eight read books, ten or twelve get fresh tea water out of the thermos, nine are gossiping (judging by sound and hand gesture), two quarrel, four play with their abacuses, though in no purposeful way, five or six seem to be fingering piles of forms, three stare off into space or at the clock which now reads 11:52, customer clock, 11:37, thirty-nine are smoking, and one is sound asleep.
>
> These fifty-four employees make an average of seventy cents American per day, and are worth every penny. They have managed in one hour of working time to service three small and routine transactions. (*Coming Home* 41)

China and Iceland, Holm claims, "are *nether* images of each other," although like all opposites they "share some amazing resemblances" (*Coming Home* 93) in all things important. The differences are those of population, cleanliness, population density, workmanship, governance, government, justice, and general efficiency. The significant similarities,

Holm argues, are poverty and "the grandeur of their own literature" (*Coming Home* 95). In both similarities and differences, Holm finds significant cultural deviations from life in the States, and it is more than a little amusing to watch the preacher of the American Jeremiad develop that grudging appreciation for the Available Plenty which comes so quickly to expats in third-world countries.

The reader gradually realizes, however, that in encountering an Other, Holm is often recovering a part of his own personal Self (Iceland) or psychic history (China), or using America and the distant geography to measure each other. "Humans travel to see their own home clearly," he writes in *The Music of Failure* (44), and again, "The prairies become a richer place by being observed by people with one eye pointed at each world. So does Minnesota" ("Is Minnesota" 190). Holm sometimes appears to measure the foreign geography with an American yardstick, as when he observes, "It struck me while I lived there, and must equally strike many American tourists, that Iceland *is* what America *says* it is and is, in fact, not" (*Music* 83). The Minnesota "repression of erotic life" (*Coming Home* 112) provides a context for measuring the cynical manipulation of human feeling in China (*Coming Home* 112); Holm's grandfather's 160 acres of Great Plains prairie are a measuring stick for cramped Chinese cities and villages (*Coming Home* 164). Sometimes Holm draws parallels: Chinese tourists, like his mother, arrange their photos for people, not for landscape (*Heart* 67); American arrogance at finding the country on top of the global heap replicates "the Chinese mistake—to assume that you are the center because you are where and who you are" (*Coming Home* 242); the lemurs of Madagascar sound just like Big Bill Holm's Swede Prairie pigs (*Eccentric* 300). In "The Ghost of Wang Wei Looks at Skagafjord," both China and Iceland are measured with the prairie eye Holm describes in *The Music of Failure*:

How the old Chinese poets would have admired Iceland!
Everything appears one at a time, at great distance:
one yellow wildflower, one brown bird, one white horse,
one old ramshackle farm, looking small and far away. (*Playing* 5)

Sometimes geographies merge, bridged by idea, and it's the same deal both sides of the Atlantic: "Icelanders resemble Minneotans (at least of the last generation) in this regard: if nature has condemned you to life in a continuously foul climate, you have no choice but to ignore it and proceed with your plans" (*Eccentric* 133).

And occasionally the home place is measured by a foreign tape measure or seen with a foreign eye: "I saw this muskrat house before," Holm
writes in "Spring Walk around a Swede Prairie Slough"; "on a cliff a thousand feet / above the sea in Iceland. / A saint lived in it there" (*Dead* 34).
Upon his return from China, Minneota assumes the mantel of margin-
ality that belonged to China: "Two years later, I am back in America, still
trying to live on the margins. Most of the old Icelanders I grew up with
are dead, and I've had to invent new kinds of margins in order to detach
part of myself from the rage and disappointment I still feel in America.
The new margin might be Minneota" (*Coming Home* 97). Holm's various
excursions abroad are not so much escapes into an Other from southwestern Minnesota—Minnesota, America—as attempts to gain perspective on the Self.[14] Toward the end of *Coming Home Crazy*, Holm remembers his return to Minneota:

> I stopped in front of my house and looked at it for a minute. Five
> bedrooms empty for a year, all the pianos, furniture, appliances un-
> used. Twenty Chinese could have lived there, grown all their vege-
> tables in the half acre of ground behind the house. My yard was big-
> ger and more fertile than a great many Chinese farms. They would
> have raised a pig and a handful of chickens and fished the Yellow Med-
> icine River clean of bullheads. The books would have been dog-eared
> and the pianos in need of tuning. They would have eaten the burdock
> that I poison year after year, and beaten the birds' time to get the mul-
> berries for themselves. My hand-carved wooden chess set would be
> finger-marked from game after game. Yellow Medicine County, that I
> had just driven through to get here, would be populated not by a few
> thousand farmers going broke and sinking into despair but by a mil-
> lion thriving inhabitants, all eating better than they ever had before.
> I blinked my eyes.
>   I went into the empty house, flipped on the air conditioner, made
> coffee fresh from beans, and listened to the end of the Schubert quin-
> tet. No policeman or bureaucrat had any idea where I was. No one fol-
> lowed me. No one watched me. I sat in silence for a long time, think-
> ing how things would never look the same again. (*Coming Home* 243)

On the other hand, while Iceland and China—and Holm's other foreign places as well—provide an Other against which Holm can define a
Self rooted in Minnesota, Holm's real alternative to Minneota is not so
much a distant geography as words and—even more abstractly—music.

It is a mistake to underestimate the importance of *logos* in the writing of Bill Holm Jr. Data, facts, experience, and things are primary, but they convert easily into abstraction: "whoever owns facts," Holm writes, "owns the bricks to build imagination. To see and feel boxelder bugs, imagine three roads, the three ideas that run through this book: the poetry of experience (observation, memory); the poetry of fact (learning, science); the poetry of the invisible (music, the soul). All three roads arrive at the same place, and you can travel them in any sequence. If you start on any of them and are persistent, you will arrive at the end of all of them" (*Boxelder Bug* 24). Holm confesses elsewhere, "[B]ooks [not place] changed my life and, God forbid, even my opinions" (*Coming Home* 106). The primary virtue of Icelandic and Chinese cultures are not their landscapes, farms, or even people, but their literatures, their words.

"God is the imagination," writes Holm in "Playing Haydn for the Angel of Death" (*Playing* 33). Often, like a good Lutheran, he begins with abstraction (word or music) rather than with experience: much of *Boxelder Bug Variations* is filled with parodies of Dickinson, Moore, Williams, Sandburg, Frost, and Jeffers. Holm's first essay in *Boxelder Bug Variations* ends not with bugs but with Emerson and Whitman. *The Heart Can Be Filled Anywhere on Earth* opens with two pages of climate and weather, but moves quickly to a dozen pages of books: botanist David Costello, then nineteenth-century tourist Galiot François Edmond, Baron de Mandat-Grancey, then Rolvaag, then Whitman, then the Internet. In *Landscape of Ghosts* (41) Holm writes, "any trip into the world of spirit starts, as Emerson reminded us, with the world of fact," but the sentence undercuts itself in that Holm begins it not with fact, but with a quote from Emerson. And as for conclusions, "There is always one more idea" (*Heart* 156). Holm is as likely to use Emerson, Thoreau, Whitman, or Lawrence to define his sacred place as he is to use a landscape feature of Iceland, China, Madagascar, or Rainey Lake. Sometimes Holm defines a place in terms of literature quite unrelated to the place: the stone farmhouse in the woods near St. Peter, Minnesota, is "a house straight from Brontë country" (*Landscape* 47). Often Holm focuses so much on ideas that his place becomes a geography of the mind, as much an abstraction as a reality.

A word is, if Aristotle is correct, an abstract representation of a thing or things; music, while it can convey emotion, is entirely an abstract structure. Holm works with music as much as with place and idea, as early as his first books: in *The Music of Failure*, sound conveys the sense of failure which is not Holm's place, Minnesota, and the prairie is described in terms of a Bruckner or Mahler symphony (18). *Boxelder Bug Variations*, subtitled *A Meditation on an Idea in Language and Music*, is in fact a musical, not a literary form, a "variations on a theme" filled with long lectures on Bach, Beethoven, Busoni, Bruckner, and Liszt. Music or a musician is often the subject of a poem or essay—most prominently section 2 of *Playing the Black Piano* (where music seems to provide the grace or affection we might expect to derive from human or geographical landscape). At the reading which celebrated publication of that book in Marshall, Minnesota, Holm had plenty to say about music—and Iceland—but not a word about Minneota, Minnesota. He closed his reading with the book's final poem, "Letting Go of What Cannot Be Held Back," which he described as "the theme of the book": "So quiet down. / Let them [the dead] go. Practice / your own song. Now" (*Playing* 128). He did not mention recovering one's own place.

The voice of Holm's own song is usually not noticeably Minnesotan, although he can use the language of Minneota when recording the speech of his father (*Music* 36), Ronald (*Music* 41), farmers in the M & M Cafe (*Heart* 248), and a cemetery marker salesman in Echo (*Playing* 125). In speaking, Holm uses the Minnesota [fUrgIt] and the short, undipthongized [šUr]. In writing he drops occasionally into the Minnesota voice with words like "clunk" (*The Weavers*), "chunk" (*Music* 4), "batch" (*Boxelder Bug* 98), and "rickety" (*Boxelder Bug* 99), and sentences like "Get your butt in here—if we don't get there by noon, the special will be gone" (*Heart* 248). But for the most part, Bill Holm's written style is as far from the language of everyday Minnesotans as Chinese or Icelandic. It is educated, in the T. S. Eliot manner, filled with polysyllabic words borrowed from nineteenth-century British authors, foreign phrases, cultural references, literary allusions. As much as Holm admires Williams, Frost, and Twain, and contemporaries like Leo Dangel, Howard Mohr, and Dave Etter, who get the true sound of spoken midwestern or American English into their writing, Holm's own speech is, in what he takes to be the Icelandic tradition, an educated grammar and syntax and vocabulary generously sprinkled with literary references.

Sometimes the facts of place and history seem more a construct of memory or imagination than a photograph of actuality. On this we have Holm's own word: forty years ago, when young Bill lived in a world apart—his own imagined island—he did not live "in America"; possibly he did not live in Minneota. In *Coming Home Crazy*, he admits,

"I described empty prairies, cranky immigrant farmers, cornfields, hay-barns, disagreeable relatives, graveyards of Belgians, Norwegians, Icelanders. Probably I described Minneota in 1947 rather than today" (89). As a youth, Holm admits in *Eccentric Islands*, he sometimes just "made it up" (10). This is perhaps the reason Holm had to recover his sense of *"from-ness"* at middle age. But recovered place is always something of an abstraction, including Holm's first, and in many ways his most important construction of Minneota, the title essay of his first book, *The Music of Failure*. It is a long essay—thirty-two pages, including four of Tom Guttormsson's photos—divided into thirteen sections: "Prelude: the Theme for the variations; 1, Another idea from Walt Whitman that no one wants to hear; 2, The music of experience; the noise of failure; 3, Pauline Bardal at the piano; 4, The history of a failed immigrant; 5, The further history of three children, all failed; 6, Music for an old pump organ; 7, Pack rat houses, and what they tell; 8, The idea of failure noted in literature, both old and new; 9, A fortissimo blast from Walt Whitman, swelled by the author's imagination; 10, The poor and the drunk: two more kinds of failure; 11, Failure in national life: a little history of Iceland; 12, A reprise of Walt Whitman: real and transcendental failure. This list of subsection headings suggests not only Holm's geographical range from Minneota into Iceland, but also his use of "literature, both old and new." In his opening lines Holm tells us that the true subject of this essay is his own life, and ours, and "how they flow together to make the life of a community, and then a country, and then a world" (55), but as the "prelude" and sections 2, 9, and 12 suggest, Holm will begin and end not with his life, or our lives, but with Walt Whitman. In opening the essay, Holm detours quickly away from his life in small-town Minneota to—revealingly—his desire to "rise up out of a mean life . . . die a famous author" (56), and thence to Whitman writing "marches for conquer'd and slain persons," and what Holm perceives as the national collapse of the sixties and seventies, and to collapse in his own life and his friends'.

Finally Holm turns his attention to the Minneota of his youth, especially to the Bardal clan: Pauline who played piano badly but with emotion and devotion; Frithgeir Bardal, who died after being tossed from the seat of his mowing machine and dragged a distance by his own horses; Guthlag Bardal, who lost the farm in the Great Depression; Gunnar Bardal, "gaunt, melancholy, silent"; and Rose Bardal, "not quite right in the head" (67). The wealth of literature contained in their house takes

Holm quickly to the subject of literature as wealth, and thence to *Gilgamesh* (on the virtues of failure), Forster's *A Passage to India* (one learns goodwill by becoming conscious of the death in things), back to Whitman's *Democratic Vistas* (an extended passage on American hypocrisy, especially in the official and business classes), to Agee's *Now Let Us Praise Famous Men*, to *The Sturlunga Saga, The Prose Edda, Njal's Saga, Laxdaela Saga, Madame Bovary, Anna Karenina, Moby Dick*, and finally back to Whitman. Holm's conclusion is that "our false language of power and success, and its consequent notion of sweeping genuine failure harmful to other humans and ourselves under the rug, has left us no true language (except perhaps poetry or song) to describe or think about their lives and thus absorb their history into our own" (81).

Literature may have given Holm a slightly jaundiced eye on Minneota and America. The country is indeed full of false rhetoric, but, as Holm himself suggests elsewhere (*Landscape* 137), not all who came to the States came as failures: some came as comfortable, middle-class citizens intent on making themselves even more middle class, an enterprise in which they succeeded admirably. In the Midwest Village, especially in the period from 1860–1960, there seemed to be real substance to the American Dream. And even today, Minneota, southwest Minnesota, and America in general are filled with people who, measuring their lives by criteria different from Bill Holm's, find themselves not failures but glowing successes.[15]

A less extreme example of Holm's penchant for constructing place in terms of literature can be found in his telling of a Minneota tale of teacher-student romance in *The Heart Can Be Filled Anywhere*, under the title "The Garden of Love." Holm takes the title of his chapter from a Blake poem; the girl is pseudonamed "Hester." The details of this romance (and pregnancy) in 1950s Minnesota you can easily imagine, but the telling would surprise you. Holm turns his essay literary beyond expectations or needs, and beyond Hawthorne: "I thought of Hester and Art again in high school when I discovered William Blake. How well Blake understood Minneota, though he died a half-century before any settler ever set foot there" (147). Two pages of Blake ("binding with briars my joys and desires"; "The lineaments of Gratified Desire") lead past token nods to Don Juan and D. H. Lawrence, to closure in Carl Sandburg: "Everybody loved Chick Lorimer. / Nobody knows where she's gone." Despite the "clear, starry night, the milky way vast and diaphanous, a three-quarters moon, the gully under them," the bur oak and cottonwood leaves, the frogs and crickets and owls, the tiny lights of town flickering in the dark (146), the story of Art and Hester is rooted as much in American literature as in Minneota, Minnesota. This is not the way Rolvaag, Cather, or Bly would have handled the scene.

Other examples fill Holm's work. In "Lawrence in China" (*Coming Home* 106–14), D. H. Lawrence becomes a measure of China; in "Iceland, 1999" (*Eccentric* 185–246), W. H. Auden becomes the measure of Iceland. Auden wrote a book titled *Letters from Iceland* which, Holm tells us, "is more than anything else a book about books, mostly a poem about poems" (*Eccentric* 189); Holm's "Iceland 1999" is likewise an essay about essays written in or about that country (notably Auden's travel piece and the sagas), and occasionally about literary criticism. The bridge, again, is *logos*, the word:

Auden and MacNiece meet Grettir's ghost on Arnarvatn Heath just south of his old farm Bjarg. Grettir asks MacNiece:

> Memory is words; we remember what others
> Say and record of ourselves—stones with the runes.
> Too many people—sandstorm over the words.
> Is your land also an island?
> There is only hope for people who live upon islands
> Where the Lowest Common labels will not stick
> And the unpolluted hills will hold your echo. (*Eccentric* 202)

Holm has been led into a trap here, of course. He opened his essay with the admission that what brought him back to the States in 1979 was love of language "as it is spoken by ordinary people, even the phlegmatic Minnesota farmers. Not the English spoken in the academy, the government, the church, the striving suburbs, but the true music of everyday speech in tavern coffee shop, hog yard, old folk's home" (185, 186). But Holm's language becomes literary and even hyperliterary, and we get Iceland through the prism of literature about Iceland, just as we got Minneota through the prisms of Whitman in one case, of Blake and Sandburg in another. Significantly, two of the islands in *Eccentric Islands* are not geographies at all: "The Island of Pain" and "The Necessary Island: The Imagination." A third island is William Holm himself: "Call Me Island." Thus the essays of place become essays of ideas, which is quite possibly where they began.[16]

Even in *Landscape of Ghosts*, an apparent exception to this general rule, Holm often works from idea to landscape, and from literature to life. In

this book, many of the poems and short prose passages Holm incorpo-
rates into his narrative are written by locals—Tom Hennen, Robert Bly,
Carol Bly, Leo Dangel, Jim Heynen, Phebe Hanson, Phil Dacey, John
Rezmerski, Fred Manfred, David Bengtson, Gail Rixen, Will Weaver,
Howard Mohr, Nancy Paddock—yet he also references or quotes
David Ignatow, Mary Wilkins Freeman, Whitman (of course), Henry
Adams, Goethe (translated by Bly), Wang Wei, Cervantes, Dr. Johnson,
W. B. Yeats, Robinson Jeffers, Chopin, Schumann, Bach, Van Gogh,
Jung, D. H. Lawrence, Walker Evans, and James Agee. Holm's walk
through Minneota begins with Emily Dickinson who, "though not a
Minnesotan, would have understood" (17). Holm ends where you'd ex-
pect: "it's pleasant to think, as Walt Whitman did, of all this sweet earth
being continually fed by all those sour dead. Just another miracle in a
long string" (141).

Holm values language at least as much as he values place, and—as
he suggests in his comments on Iceland and China as countries who
value their languages—language carries place and acts as an almost
permanent stay against chaos and the change and assimilation which—
while Holm acknowledges them—obviously bother him as a thinker
and writer. "While the rest of Europe sacked ancient libraries and
burned manuscripts," he writes, "the Icelanders busily turned out poetry, novels, short stories, histories, the only books with real information
about the old destroyed religions, codes of law, genealogical tables,
translations out of Latin and other languages, manuals of seamanship,
and much, much more poetry. When the culture began sinking under
the weight of its poverty, those magnificent books buoyed it up, along
with the Icelanders' fierce attachment to their archaic, impractical old
inflected language" (*Coming Home* 94); the Chinese point out that the
characters of their archaic language "were all right for the Tang poets
and *The Dream of the Red Chamber* and that a billion Chinese seem capable of using them without complaint," nod their heads to linguistic
improvement, and continue to "adore the grandeur of their own literature" (*Coming Home* 95). In a poem Holm certainly knows, although I
have never heard him quote it, W. H. Auden writes, "Time . . . [w]orships
language, and forgives / everyone by whom it lives." So did the old Icelanders, and the Icelandic Americans of Holm's youth. While the physical landscape of southwestern Minnesota may have given Holm an eye
for scope and grandeur, the Icelandic American cultural landscape of
his own boyhood made him also a word man.

So Holm is a writer of place and a writer of ideas, and in his opinion God may be either Mt. McKinley or one's own imagination.

In *Mapping the Invisible Landscape*, Kent C. Ryden offers one of those observations which are so commonsensical you never really thought them before, but once they're articulated they illuminate the entire universe:

> Since places are fusions of experience, landscape, and location, they are necessarily bound up with time and memory as well. The experiences which create and establish places recede inevitably into the past, so that one important quality of places is that they are "the present expressions of past experiences and events" [Edward Relph, *Place and Placelessness*, 33]—contemplation of place quickly brings to mind earlier stages in one's life, episodes in the history of a community, formative and notable events and experiences. The landscape of a place is an objectification of the past, a catalyst for memory. (39)

Later in that book, Ryden notes that Thoreau—Holm's model in so many things—"was not . . . primarily an essayist of *place*, despite his extensive, intense personal and imaginative engagement with the natural landscapes" (223); his method is "to look *through* the landscape over which he rambled and penetrate to the lessons and higher truths of nature" (224). Thoreau "frequently allows literary associations to get between himself and the landscape, so that he appreciates scenes not for their particular physical and cultural qualities but for the works of literature that they remind him of or for the literary patterns and paradigms into which they seem to fit" (227). "As Thoreau walks, thinks, and writes, he presses place into service as the protean raw material of literature, passing it through the filters of philosophy and accumulated reading, transcending any significance inhering in the scene itself and achieving whatever literary end of effect or meaning that he, as a writer, desires" (230).

Like Hasselstrom, Kloefkorn, and Blei, Holm is at his best as a writer when he combines place and idea . . . as in the concluding essay of *The Heart Can Be Filled Anywhere on Earth*, "The Art of Brown Bread and Vinarterta." Holm opens his fifty-page essay with a quotation from Wallace Stevens's poem "Bantams in Pine-Woods": "Fat! Fat! Fat! Fat! I am the personal. / Your world is your world. I am my world." These lines he applies to himself, his love of food, and the product of that love of food: "fat boy, blubber-belly, lard-ass, tub-of-guts, piled-high-and-deep. He's just big for his age. He's so tall, he carries it well. He'll trim down when he gets older. No, he won't" (203). In a trice, Holm is into family history: mother in the kitchen, father in the barn (cooking pork and beans during those months when Jona was tending her sister during the late stages of a pregnancy), Auntie Clarice's recipes. With excursions into Minnesota foods from lutefisk to hotdish, banquets in China, lunch at the M & M Cafe, a story from the Minneota *Mascot*, a pinch of Roman legend, and a dash of Sherwood Anderson, Holm tracks the homogenization of American culinary culture from Aunt Clarice to Betty Crocker to Julia Childs:

> As much of a town's history lies buried in its cookbooks as in its tax records, or even its roll call of war dead. I own two of the three cookbooks published by the "Young Ladies Union" of Saint Paul's Icelandic Lutheran Church. The 1905 edition has disappeared from the planet so far as I can tell, like Shakespeare's thirty-eighth play, Beethoven's tenth symphony, Venus de Milo's arms. That first cookbook may have been in Icelandic, though I doubt it. The Icelanders had been here twenty-five years, sent children off to war and college, anglicized their citizenship names, and in general—Americanized. They would never quite get to California, but they would never go home either. There was no more for them to eat in northeast Iceland than there had been when they left. Like so many American immigrant groups, they left the old country not so much for freedom as for dinner. They preferred a more regular arrival of food on the table than was ever possible in Vopnafjörður. (*Heart* 213)

This observation launches Holm on a close reading of the two extant editions of the cookbook published in 1913 and 1926. "When I was a boy in the forties and fifties, the Y. L. U. still met and functioned," Holm recalls (215); the average age of the young ladies was about sixty. But the Y. L. U. and the cookbooks both have disappeared by the time Holm writes his essay, enacting in the culinary realm the cultural homogenization which produces that confused and partly unsatisfactory species of human: the American. "Progress has marched inexorably onward, a grim, steely cast to its mouth and an ice-cold eye. It has just eaten Chop Suey made with two cans of soup, finished off with a couple of Coconut Macaroon Cup Cakes, wiped crumbs from its thin lips, and decreed the end of the New World Icelanders. This will be the last of 'those' books from 'those' people, thank-you very much" (219). The pickled-in-amber culture is history, although a vestige remains in Holm's own writing: particulars of Minneota, Iceland, and China; pronouncements on America; eight different recipes; and references to or quotations from Stevens, Whitman, Twain, M. F. K. Fisher, Shakespeare, Sherwood Anderson, David Arnason, Mozart, Bach, Schubert, Liszt, Czerny, Hummel, Elgar, and Venus de Milo.

The result is a well-spiced stew of many places and ideas, a literary performance with substance and sustenance: Holm at home and away from home, a Holm—to conclude with Henry Thoreau—everywhere at home.

Jim Heynen

Parables of Innocence and Experience

*Any time you feel the well is dry, write about your first
thirteen years—they are your only inexhaustible source.*
—Jim Heynen, "Fifty Hints for Fiction Writers" #25

On the cover of his 1976 book *Notes from Custer* Jim
Heynen is identified as "a brilliant young poet of the West." This poet of
the West later wrote a delightful satiric vignette of suburban middle-class
ennui titled "Sad Hour." But Jim Heynen is best known for his one- and
two-page stories of archetypal Iowa farm boys: *The Man Who Kept Cigars
in His Cap* (1979), *You Know What Is Right* (1985), *The One-Room Schoolhouse* (1993), and *The Boys' House* (2001). He has also written two young
adult novels set in northwestern Iowa: *Cosmos Coyote and William the
Nice* and *Being Youngest*. Across a wide range of hometown addresses,[1]
Heynen preserved memories of growing up on a farm in Sioux County,
Iowa, which he made the signature material of his writing. "In my
hands," Heynen writes, "there still lives a farmer" (*Suitable* 9).

Born in 1940, Heynen spent his first eight grades in one of those
one-room schoolhouses pictured on the obverse of the Iowa state quarter.[2] He attended Calvin College and the University of Iowa, pursued
graduate studies in Chaucer and Renaissance literature, then took an
MFA at the University of Oregon. He lived briefly in Great Britain on a
U.S. State Department fellowship in 1977, and won National Endowment for the Arts fellowships in poetry and fiction. Heynen has served
time in academia: University of Michigan, Calvin College, University of
Washington, St. Olaf College in Minnesota, University of Alaska, University of Oregon, University of Idaho, Lewis and Clark College, Santa
Clara University, and Gustavus Adolphus University.

Despite his many mailing addresses and academic connections,
Heynen is a typical writer of place in that for him setting determines
other elements of literature. A reviewer of *You Know What Is Right* notes
that for Heynen conscience is formed "inevitably" by physical con-
frontations with the world around us (*Review* 905), in his case the world
of the Iowa farm. In his first book of poems, he speaks of things being

"redeemed to their places" (*Notes* 30); in his most recent book of poems, he writes, "I know what I know: / how the seasons forgive and / restore the dormant and listless" (*Standing* 28).

Heynen further suggests the debilitation of dissociation from place. In the poem "Miniature Golf," suburbanites disappear into huge malls, shrink into their own TVs:

> Look at them now.
> These tiny people drive about
> in compact cars no bigger
> than what is left of their lives.
> Arriving here, they smile
> through mouths grown small
> as cordial glasses. (*Standing* 22)

Customers in a suburban bar look "more like hats and coats draped over counters and tables than they do like people," decide that a good "Sad Hour" (free peanuts disappear, the price of drinks jumps from one dollar to nine, organ preludes replace rock-and-roll) is exactly what they need ("Sad Hour" 58).

Looking over his shoulder in the introduction to his 2001 anthology *Fishing for Chickens: Short Stories about Rural Youth,* Heynen himself gives perhaps the best analysis of his own boyhood, and a defense of bioregionalism that echoes the arguments of Hasselstrom, Holm, and Blei:

> It's true that, just like urban kids, we worried about doing well in school, we worried about who was and who wasn't our best friend, and we had spats with brothers and sisters and parents—but we still knew there were some basic differences. Most of us were poorer, or at least had far fewer conveniences. We probably spent more time with our families—usually helping them with the work that needed doing—and we also spent more time alone, often making friends with trees and meadows, or with animals—most of which were being raised for food.
>
> Living close to nature and its creatures may be the most essential difference. In fact, for rural young people the land and its animals can be as much a part of daily life as family members. And like dealing with family members, dealing with the land and animals can bring both pleasure and pain. The weather can be treacherous, living

conditions can be tough, and the work can often be exhausting and dangerous. Learning to love both wild and domestic animals requires openness to nature's wonders, as well as an awareness of pragmatic necessity. Rural kids often see the births and deaths of all kinds of creatures at a very early age. Sometimes they take in an orphaned lamb or chick and lovingly care for it, only to have to sacrifice it to dinner one day. They marvel at the beautiful pheasant or graceful deer glimpsed from afar, but they and their parents probably hunt for some of their food or know people who do. Chances are they've seen another pheasant or deer being brought home for a holiday meal. As common as these experiences are, it is still not easy for young people who can so easily identify with creatures who seem as vulnerable as they are themselves. (vii, viii)

"I am interested in developing a distinctively rural American esthetic," Heynen told *Contemporary Authors*, "one which I would not call a sentimental ruralism, but rather a clear and even harsh acceptance of the earth and animal presence in our historical and contemporary lives." Heynen's stories are a combination of the innocence and experience of late twentieth-century life in rural northwestern Iowa, a magical-realistic mix of pain and pleasure, bane and blessing, what out-of-state visitor Cosmos Coyote calls "a battleground of contradictions" (107).

This vision and these experiences are not necessarily restricted to kids who grew up on farms. As Bill Holm points out in his introduction to *The Boys' House*, the larger dimensions of Heynen's stories are universally applicable: stories which describe "the enormous claims made on human beings . . . by Nature with a capital N" also reflect "our own frail, sometimes mean-spirited human nature" (xii). Holm notes that "Iowa is never named; nor are the characters. . . . Considered from one angle, 'the boys' may not even be a gang, but only the prisms of light that travel through a single consciousness, acquiring the world and having arguments with itself. 'The men' may not be multiple either, but only the voice of country middle-aged prudence trying to protect itself from any more surprises" (xiii, xiv). In her blurb for *The One-Room Schoolhouse*, Teresa Jordan reads "the secret life of boys and of the land" as "our own memories, whether we be male or female, urban or rural." In his blurb for that book, Robert Bly speaks of "half-conscious minds" brought forward "without judgment or condescension." Heynen's stories are songs of innocence and songs of experience familiar to us all.

They are, however, firmly located in place through markers of speech and geography. Certainly Heynen's Iowa place will be familiar to anyone who has spent time in the Midwest: flat corn and alfalfa country where mile roads run straight and you can always see the weather coming at you. From a treehouse, a kid could see "miles and miles, out across the alfalfa and cornfields and pastures and all the different farm buildings and silos looking like little toys in the distance . . . telephone wires running along the road a half mile away, and a mile beyond that the telephone wires along the road, and a mile farther a shining glint that must have been a cupola or something on top of one of the barns" (*Youngest* 42). Cosmos Coyote describes this as a landscape of clean cars, clean-cut students, and straight rows of corn (*Cosmos* 107).

Heynen's details are northwestern Iowa: boxelder bug, barn swallow, zucchini, horse flies, milkweed, cream separator, stock tank, binder, sandpit, farmer tan, mourning doves, a dog dead in the ditch after being hit by a gravel truck. Heynen's names, when he uses them, are recognizably northwestern Iowa: Jake, Josh, Gretchen, Henry, Dutch Center, Hilda Vander Camp, William De Haag, Cherlyn Van Dyke. Heynen's voice is northwest Iowa because he understands the relationship between place and speech. "Some communities have terms and expressions only insiders understand," Heynen points out in a West Coast guide for community history projects titled *Writing about Home*; "We might say, 'The mountain is leaning the wrong way today,' as a way of saying what the weather is going to do" (44). In his own writing, this means attention to local Iowa idiom: "short end of the stick," "tipped the scales in more ways than one," "if you have any wits about you," "the way he saw it," "swat you a good one," "wasn't everything it was cracked up to be," "no picnic," "keep out of any really bad scrapes," "a little bit of the bear in him," "spilled the beans," "licking the wounds," "blowing them sky-high," "one for the record book, least ways in the kitchen," "wasn't all that deep," "all she wrote," "what made him tick," "one way or the other," "too big for his britches," "we're skunked," "off an old tractor," or even "plum crazy."

Heynen's vocabulary, perhaps because of the region's inherent conservatism, does not seem as dated as Etter's: "critter," "swat," "flush," "cow-pie," "spitfire," "git," "sucker," "sploosh," "swayback," "clunker," "pail," "dump rake," "two-bottom plow," "contraption," "grove," "sore bottom," "fatso," "whopper," "clodhopper," "doily," "globs," "stuff," "lickety-split," and "mess with." "Dinner," in Heynen's stories, is the noon meal.

Heynen's metaphors are current rural Iowa metaphors: "like a stone from a slingshot," "like dog turds," "as the stripe on a skunk's back," "like a steer that's about to have its horns sawed off," "like a hawk attacking a rabbit," "like stray cats to a bowl of fresh milk," "faster than a cat covering its business in the dirt," and perhaps the most telling rural Iowa metaphor, "loud as an auctioneer."

Also idiomatic, although not narrowly so, are spellings that reflect midwestern pronunciations like "ya," "kinda," "gettin," "outta," "lookit," "betcha," "dunno," "a-pointin and a-yellin." And Heynen's use of *their* and *they* with *someone*, his frequent use of *would* in the past tense, his use of *them* for *those*, his omission of *of* from the expression *a couple of* (in dialog; as a narrator, Heynen includes the *of*), his use of double and even triple negatives ("don't got no other pets"—*Youngest* 98; or "ain't never been afraid of no goose before"—*Youngest* 83), and his use of the generalized *you*: "Here's where you get your art and finesse" (*Boys'* 21), also reveal his midwestern background. In dialog, Heynen uses many regionally popular non-standard verb forms: *give* for *gave*, *seen* for *saw*, *brung* for *brought*, *tore* for *torn*, and *come* for *came*. In dialog Heynen also uses the regionally popular tags *so* and *then*, and questions that are statements:

"Having a pretty good summer then?" his father asked as they walked across the yard. His father breathed loud through his nose. Always. It was embarrassing in church.

"Pretty good," said Henry.

"Been getting around quite a bit on your bike then?"

"Quite a bit," said Henry.

"That North Dakota girl likes to ride her bike pretty good too then?"

His Iowans are persons of few words, and often echo each other:

"So," the old man said, and rocked his head and shoulders. "North Dakota."

"Yep," said Gretchen. "North Dakota."

"So," the old man said again. "North Dakota. That's quite a ways."

"Yep," said Gretchen. "That's quite a ways."

"That's an awful long ways for a little girl like you to be going. You come over here in a car then?"

"Yep," said Gretchen. "We come over in a car." (*Youngest* 65, 66)

Heynen's old men talk like old Iowa farmers:

"Sort of like your jack-hammer kicker was your pogo-stick kicker. She liked to bounce on her rear legs and could just as easy break your jaw with her hip as smash your foot with her hoofs. Main difference between your jack-hammer and your pogo-stick was that the jack-hammer kicker tried to give you a knock-out punch and the pogo-stick kicker tried to get you with quick jabs." (*Boys'* 21)

Talking about Iowa farm boys, Heynen sounds like an Iowa farm boy:

The boys didn't like buttermilk pop, and it didn't help matters to watch how it was made. It wasn't even real buttermilk. It was regular milk with some vinegar in it. Then some flour was stirred in there, along with an old egg and a couple handfuls of raisins. The whole mess was cooked until it was thick as leftover oatmeal. By this time it was slimy too, and looked like it would make better wallpaper paste than food. (*Boys'* 118)

Heynen's younger adolescents talk like younger Iowa adolescents:

Some growing up anybody could do with the likes of Granny around. When she did manage to get up and walk, she looked like she was carrying two ten-gallon water balloons on her backside. And she wasn't much better from the front. (*Youngest* 4)

Heynen's older Iowa adolescents sound like older adolescents: twenty years past their parents and eight years behind the rest of the country:

A few surprises catch [Cosmos's] eye: a couple of boys with earring studs, and more than a few in cowboy boots and tight jeans. Little slices of speech catch his ear too: "Rad, man," "Awesome, dude," "Chill, man," "That's mass trouble," "Bummer, man," "To the max, dude," "Gross, man"—a whole list of phrases he hasn't heard since grade school. (*Cosmos* 77)

More to the point, Heynen's characters behave like Iowans, exhibiting restraint in their speech and action, and low-to-modest expectations for their lives. They are leery of excess, skeptical about innovation, suspicious of differences. They are introspective people who take few risks and keep their secrets. The young may be slightly more open to wonder and exploration, but acorns do not fall far from the oak. Having crunched a boxelder bug to a pulp to see how it tastes, the youngest boy elects to remain Midwest mute about his experience:

> This was one of those moments he decided to keep to himself. Nothing to brag about. Nothing worth telling to the older boys. The only good he thought could come of this would be if someday he saw a twitch on someone's face at the sight of box-elder bugs, that little signal that says, I know, I've been there too. Only then would he say anything. (*One-Room* 67)

A farmer who, in a year of bad crops, converts one of his empty grain bins into a gigantic seesaw that lifts him higher than the Ferris wheel at the county fair decides at the end of one day to tear the thing down: "it started to creak and someone said they thought some nails were pulling out. I didn't stop farming while I was ahead, said the man who had made the seesaw. But I think we should stop this while we are. And so they did" (*One-Room* 137).[3]

Heynen's place does have a time dimension, especially his stories of the boys which, Marian Blue notes, "connect, through style, setting, and characters, to build a complete vision *of the time* and people" (326 italics added). Heynen has his boys picking lice and nits out of each other's hair, and butchering chickens with a hatchet and butcher block. He remembers radios with tubes, and the circus coming to town with a hootchie kootchie dancer who could puff on a cigarette with her private parts fore and aft. He remembers cookstoves and oil burners, scissors, grinders, pet squirrels and pet rats, and pet cats that would eat rats (except for the tails), and rats which—oldtimers claimed—might run in panic up the dark tunnel pant leg of an unsuspecting corn husker and sink their teeth into his calf or thigh. He remembers milking cows by hand. He spins one story of the boys using the chamber pot as a foot warmer in their unheated bedroom on a cold winter night[4] and another tale of a throw-up pan tied to a string and passed from bed to bed while the sick boys remained snug under their covers in an unheated bedroom.

Heynen remembers the days of outhouses and "so many tricks that privy owners and boys played on each other that a book could be written about it" (*Boys'* 40).[5] Even after indoor plumbing has been introduced (the late 1940s, early 1950s) some of Heynen's farmers believe there is no sense using all that water for flushing and "no sense tracking up the house when the weather is nice enough to use the outhouse" (*One-Room* 70). Peach tissues make good toilet paper, but corncobs are rough on tender skin. Both tissues and corncobs teach a lesson or two in life: (1) "even though having things bad after having them good is worse than not knowing how good things can be, it's still better to have some good with the bad than not to have any good at all," and (2) "there are more corncobs than peach tissues in the world, that's for sure" (71). One of Heynen's farmers wants nothing to do with indoor plumbing, and explains his convictions in words that still make a certain amount of sense: "Now you people with your indoor toilets, what have you done to your houses? You put a place for people to shit in them. . . . A house is almost a holy place. Now you tell me what kind of person would build a room for shitting in a place like that! Not even a dog shits in his own house" (*You Know* 87, 88).

Heynen remembers gypsies camping on the school yard, mysterious migrant workers who followed the harvest by the hundreds, traveling in old army trucks packed with wives and children. The happy noise of their singing, giggling, and laughing was a marked contrast to the Protestant decorum of the town, although nobody ever complained to or about the mysterious strangers. Heynen remembers Saturday night in town, a social extravaganza which ended, as Richard Davies points out, with the arrival of television in the early 1950s (146–52). He recalls the 1950s battles between Protestants and Catholics, the missing fingers of farmers who had come too close to corn-pickers, and the fecundity of small-town gardens, especially in cucumbers, tomatoes, and zucchini:

> The oldest boy had a plan. Over supper, as they all swallowed the soggy chunks of zucchini, he said, We have so many zucchini, we should give some to the poor people who don't have anything to eat.
>
> The oldest boy had never in his life suggested giving anything to anybody, not even to his friends. And now he was thinking of poor people he didn't even know?
>
> The grown-ups thought it was a wonderful idea and even brought it up in their family devotions: *That the abundance of the earth should be given to all*, they prayed. *Yea, even to the neediest of our number*. (*Boys'* 11)

Despite the omnipresent odor of manure—which locals claim "smells like money" (*Cosmos* 48)—Heynen's Iowa is not such a bad place to be. The land is healthy and health-restoring, beneficial to locals and to all those jittery animals who grow up in a city and have to deal with whatever it is—"what building, what noise, what stink in the air"—that makes city folk turn out the way they do (*One-Room* 129): jittery, insecure, pretentious, disconnected. The place offers several absolute blessings, including tranquility, family, community, necessary work and thus a work ethic, a regular diet, and abundant opportunities to observe the intertwined realities of sex, birth, death, and animal life. Old folks teach young folks community history, local legends, and stories. Grandfathers show grandsons the magic of a flashlight made of a fruit jar full of fireflies . . . and the joy of letting the fireflies free. The electorate models community by settling "a pretty stupid fellow" into a job as county road supervisor (*You Know* 159). Church members seal their noses to a minister who has a bad habit of passing gas at the wrong time, bite their tongues when a new minister, fresh from the Old Country, pronounces *Nigeria* "Nigger-ia" (*You Know* 162). If a kid gets in trouble, his probation officer is likely to be a cousin. Because the town policeman knows the boys, and the boys know the policeman, when the hormonal youth plaster passing automobiles with tomatoes lobbed from behind the church steeple ramparts, the officer merely shines his patrol car spotlight on the cross above their heads. This is all the discipline that's necessary for him . . . and for the boys. The whole God-fearing community acts as the police and courts.

Independent of Sunday School instruction, boys who have spent their lives growing up "dominated by sensory input unburdened with symbols and morals" (*Review* 905) exhibit considerable innocence, and moments of great kindness, generosity, and forthrightness. Hired by a neighbor lady to kill garter snakes, Heynen's boys sometimes fake the kill, nurse an injured snake back to health on vegetables and milk, and release it in a distant pasture. Anxious to save the life of a stray dog they have decided is not the killer their fathers think it is, they rub its hind end with corncobs until it bleeds, then splash turpentine on the tender spot, sending the animal "howling and running to who knows where," maybe home, maybe the river bottom with all its bushes to hide behind and field mice for dinner (*You Know* 35). When a storm coats fields, trees, and live pheasants with ice, and adults "harvest" them with clubs, the boys act to protect the vulnerable birds:

The boys went out into the freezing rain to find pheasants, too. They saw dark spots along a fence. Pheasants, all right. Five or six of them. The boys slid their feet along slowly, trying not to break the ice that covered the snow. They slid up close to the pheasants. The pheasants pulled their heads down between their wings. They couldn't tell how easy it was to see them huddled there.

The boys stood still in the icy rain. Their breath came out in slow puffs of steam. The pheasants' breath came out in quick little white puffs. One lifted its head and turned it from side to side, but the pheasant was blind-folded with ice and didn't flush.

The boys had not brought clubs, or sacks, or anything but themselves. They stood over the pheasants, turning their own heads, looking at each other, each expecting the other to do something. To pounce on a pheasant, or yell Bang! Things around them were shining and dripping with icy rain. The barbed-wire fence. The fence posts. The broken stems of grass. Even the grass seeds. The grass seeds looked like little yolks inside gelatin whites. And the pheasants looked like unborn birds glazed in egg white. Ice was hardening on the boys' caps and coats. Soon they would be covered with ice too.

Then one of the boys said, Shh. He was taking off his coat, the thin layer of ice splintering in flakes as he pulled his arms from the sleeves. But the inside of the coat was dry and warm. He covered two of the crouching pheasants with his coat, rounding the back of it over them like a shell. The other boys did the same. They covered all the helpless pheasants. The small gray hens and the larger brown cocks. Now the boys felt the rain soaking through their shirts and freezing. They ran across the slippery fields, unsure of their footing, the ice clinging to their skins as they made their way toward the blurry lights of the house. (*One-Room* 3, 4)

The words "unsure" and "blurry" in Heynen's last sentence connect boys and pheasants, emphasizing their shared vulnerability and innocence, which is further underscored by Heynen's metaphor—"like little yolks inside gelatin whites"—and by adjectives like "helpless." The same wide-eyed innocence is captured in the opening story of *You Know What Is Right*, the tale of the youngest boy who liked to lower his face right over the end of the birth canal of a brood sow, to greet the piglet eye to eye, only an inch away. "What the boy liked to see was the expression on the pig's face. It was a look of surprise" (3).

The farm boys are also imaginative, especially the youngest. They do not depend on technology—television, machines, games, toys, or even books—for their fun: they make their own, and in making their own they're inventive. They ice-board with their sleds and coats, the oldest and youngest competing for the lead by virtue of having the largest coat and the lightest weight respectively. When the minister's wife breast-feeds her baby, the boys develop ingenious plans to get a look at that breast. They bring a bloated cow back to life by jumping up and down on its belly until "the cow exploded, belching and farting and coming back to life in gusts of hot alfalfa fumes" (*The Man* 41). When the men mistakenly hoist Big Bull into the haymow and decide to butcher him there to avoid public humiliation, the boys invent a clever story to save their overweight pet: "Why don't we just tell people that Big Bull climbed up the haymow?" (*You Know* 53). They improvise lightning protection from the rubber tires rotting in the grove, and suggest fly-fishing for bats in the summer twilight. The scheme works, too, because as the youngest boy theorizes (and scientists later discover), bats catch their food with their wings before stuffing it in their mouths.

Like rural people from Henry Thoreau to Robert Frost to Norbert Blei, Heynen's characters are skeptical of progress. You buy an oil furnace, and the thing breaks, and you have to burn the chopping block in the old woodstove, and then where is the chopping block when you need a chopping block? The one-room schoolhouse is torn down, and the land sold cheap to the owner of an adjacent farm for cropland; where will the gypsies camp in the fall? Where will a young boy take his first date for a picnic? Even good things, like rural free electrification and drainage tile, have their drawbacks. Fluorescent lights spray light everywhere, including behind the barn, where you don't want it. Drainage tiles dry up the duck pond along with bottomlands, and sometimes cause spring flooding when water runs too quickly off the fields and into ponds and rivers. On the Fourth of July, even those farmers who tiled their wetlands into bean fields appreciate the one old-timer who refused to tile because "People have got to have a pasture with trees and a curvy creek in it for big picnics" (*Youngest* 101).

Even the Old Folks—for whom rural progress brought absolute positive advances like d-CON for rats, poison for gophers, DDT for thistles, and shampoo for head lice—believe "Something is going too fast nowadays" (*One-Room* 222). In the title and capstone story of *The Boys' House*, the gang of young boys, weary of the smell of feedlots and weed killers and the constant sounds of diesel tractors and electric feed augers, decide to build a hideout "away from all this noise and stink and light." With two-by-fours and shingles, plywood and tar paper, sheet metal and disk blades, bricks and blocks salvaged from the grove, they build a fort down by the pond, "thick as an army tank with cement blocks and bricks at the bottom, [bristling with] sharp-edged metal blades and axles as it rose up" (184). It is certainly the kind of place no outsiders would want to mess with. When they are done, they crawl inside and the oldest boy invites the others to sniff the air:

> They didn't smell anything but the oily and rusty dirt on their own hands.
> Listen, said the oldest boy.
> They didn't hear anything but the pond water lapping against the old tires.
> Look around, said the oldest boy.
> Little chinks of light came through some of the cracks and through the front opening, but it was still dark enough that they could feel like they were well hidden.
> Perfect, they agreed, hoping no one in the world would notice where they were or what they had been up to. (185, 186)

Wendell Berry has remarked that what is wrong with us contributes much more to a money economy than what is right with us, and what is wrong with a place and a person certainly contributes more to literature than what is right. Heynen's "distinctively rural American esthetic," with its "clear and even harsh acceptance of the earth and animal presence in our historical and contemporary lives," opens the door to darker aspects of rural Iowa life, which tend to overshadow the light side. One less than pleasant feature is the ongoing decline of rural America, and Heynen's Midwest has diminished significantly from the Iowa of his youth. Although Heynen is not as obsessed with loss as Norbert Blei — change in Sioux County, Iowa, is less drastic than change in Door County, Wisconsin — in *Being Youngest* Heynen offers an all-too-familiar picture of an aging population fighting a losing battle to maintain their place:

> The old people's place was a run-down little acreage, with the garden and several apple trees closest to the road. The house was a peeling white two-story building with a lean-to porch on the front. To the right was a red barn that had seen its better days, and straight ahead was a small red chicken coop, and next to it a corncrib with a wagon and a faded old Farmall tractor in its alley. There was a big doghouse that didn't have a dog in it, and right on the edge of the grove was an

outhouse with a half-moon cut out above the door. Beyond the out-house and in the grove you could see several pieces of old machinery parked—a two-bottom plow, a disk, a harrow, a grain binder, and an old manure-spreader. The grove kept on going beyond the machin-ery, leafy branches on top and tangled-up bushes and weeds on the bottom. The whole place looked run down and beat up except for the garden. (64, 65)

Weather is another drawback to life in Iowa. Heynen does not begin with weather, as do Rolvaag and Cather, but it's on his mind, and on the minds of townsfolk and farmers alike:

When a dark cloud hung low in the southwest in the summer and the air grew still and heavy, people looked at each other as if to ask, Is your soul ready for the hereafter? Or when the spring thaw came too quickly and the creeks rose with large tables of ice turning and over-turning in the current, people looked around for the highest ground as if closeness to the sky, not the earth, might save them. And hail-storms, or wind gusts that took with them more than their fair share of leaves—these scared people. (*One-Room* 51)

The enormous white emptiness of a blizzard, the dark purple-black of a tornado sky, even the sound of ice breaking up in the spring: these are all fundamental and not especially comforting components of rural midwestern life. The boys know only too well about the tongue on frozen metal, "the jaws of a growling boar . . . [t]he bull that crushed a man against a gate. The woman who drowned trying to save her child from rushing spring floods, . . . the lightning that splintered a huge box-elder tree right after they decided to run out from under that very tree and play in the rain" (*Boys'* 5, 6). Older men remember the close calls of their own youth: "The tree that fell the wrong way, the rope they almost didn't get loose from a friend's neck, the ice that was just as thin as they were told it was" (*One-Room* 193).

Then there are the abstract dangers, including tedium and habit, the things "you do over and over again so you don't have to think about what you're doing every time before you do it" (*One-Room* 95). Con-ventional wisdom encourages the cultivation of "good habits"—like brushing teeth and washing hands and not slurping soup—through hours and days of practice. Habit, however, quickly becomes a mental-ity of not thinking, of missing the magic in the ordinary, of mindless repetition that is something between contentment and complacency. This mentality helps in the daily drudgery of field work, as Willa Cather points out in her portrait of Oscar Bergson in *O Pioneers!*,[6] and helps "control impulses" one might want to reign in (*Cosmos* 60), but has its drawbacks:

> One by one the boys drifted off into daydreams. In the middle of the knee-high bean field, giving in to their three-hour duty of "walking beans" for sunflowers, for volunteer corn, for milkweed, for cockleburs. For whatever wasn't beans and needed pulling. . . . Shuffling steadily, they drifted off, moved past duty or work, past praise or blame, without word or effort, crossed that line into the blur of trying and not trying, of doing and not doing, where tedium could be leisure and boredom contentment. (*One-Room* 38)

This state of mind produces other spiritual dangers: limited aspirations, an exaggerated sense of privacy, introversion, suspicion of differences and of outsiders, and the tendency to be judgmental. The midwestern restraint (in grief, in joy, in expression) is often mentioned by Carol Bly, and is a cornerstone of Garrison Keillor's Lake Wobegon humor.[7] Old-timers consider it a significant accomplishment to have maintained a car in mint condition, spending their lives driving slowly up and down Main Street between home and store. Or just tracking down laundry that has blown off the clothesline. Or hunting deer or pheasant instead of going after that albino fox that everyone in the neighborhood has been talking about. And when somebody exceeds community expectations by actually shooting and mounting that fox, locals turn petty and critical:

> That sure was easy, said one farmer who was watching.
> Ever try shooting the broad side of a barn from the inside? teased another.
> I'd bet you'd have good luck hunting sheep with those dogs, said another farmer. (*Man* 56)

Heynen's people value their privacy perhaps a little too much, a reflection, he suggests, of the landscape which puts them too much in the open. "Land there in Iowa lay so flat / we never dared run naked through the fields," he recalls, "and only joked of swimming nude / in the creek so close to the railroad" (*Standing* 40). Only at night can a fellow pee outdoors, and on Sunday morning the family sits in church rigid and tight-lipped:

> father,
> brother, and I in our black suits and starched collars;
> mother, tightened in her corset, black hat and veil;
> sister, too fully developed, draped in her loose
> brassiere and the dress that kept everything private.
> We liked things this way: the inside, the out. (*Standing* 40)

Strangers, eccentrics, and the merely different encounter a combination of suspicion and shunning: the girl with six toes; the itinerant saw sharpener who hands out International Workers of the World pamphlets, accepts only a dollar for his work and must therefore be a communist; Roman Catholics, who drink, swear, gamble, have too many kids, eat too much fish, dance dances other than square dances, and have "no clear sense of honoring the Sabbath" (*One-Room* 108); visitors from Nigeria who are black, whose singing sets the parishioners to swaying, and must therefore be "dangerous all right" (*One-Room* 106); a man with a beard who is "out of kilter" and "must be up to something" (*One-Room* 160); the goose lady who is most certainly crazy; a kind of new-age farmer who specializes in raising "happy turkeys" and must be "as stupid as the turkeys" (*Boys' House* 44); a farmer who plants Pioneer seed corn instead of Dekalb and owns an Oliver tractor instead of a John Deere (*Boys' House* 32); and, most prominently, the man who kept cigars in his cap, who, everyone agreed, "had been asking for trouble right from the start when he put cigars in his cap" (*Church* 16).[8] The old couple in *Being Youngest* is shunned, Henry's father explains, because the husband "had married this wild girl from the next county who had no religion at all." And "nobody was surprised," the father adds, "that their son was a troublemaker too, and that he had ended up in a mental hospital" (*Youngest* 180).[9]

The roots of this judgmentalism lie not only in the homogeneity of the cultural landscape, but in the unexamined piety of the region's inhabitants. In most of his work, Heynen depicts the strict Dutch Calvinism of this place as more a bane than a blessing. Church elders terrorize the young with threats of punishment, including fictional bears living in the church steeple: "If the boys didn't sit still during the service, they would have to go up in the steeple" (*One-Room* 97). The minister's annual visit to the home of each parishioner is "like the IRS coming to

check out the bottom line of everybody's hidden lives" (*One-Room* 101).
Then there is the minister who farts, and the minister's wife who sweet-
ens the coffee cups of visiting parishioners with drops of breast milk.
The strict church "taught that people are evil, and that if they were left
to themselves the whole world would turn the world into a cesspool. If
left to themselves, they would eat each other like dogs. Or worse" (99).
Everything is either good or bad; usually what's bad is what feels good,
and what's good makes you feel bad, and how can you blame someone
for doing what feels good, when "[h]e was just being his naturally bad
self" (100)? Besides, church folk are hypocrites: the very older members
who won't let the boys go to movies use them as lookouts when they are
illegally night hunting (*One-Room* 113). The superintendent is as eager
to skip Sunday School as the students:

> During the hymn sing the Superintendent checked the seating chart,
> and anyone who was not present had to memorize Psalm 23, Isaiah
> 53, or I Corinthians 13. . . . Later the church got modern, but the rules
> stayed strict. Now all the seats for Sunday School had big numbers
> painted on them and a camera on the ceiling took pictures automat-
> ically. Empty seats showed up as numbers in the picture. . . .
>
> The boys decided to fool the camera. They took balloons to Sun-
> day School, blew them up, and tied them to their seats. This way the
> numbers didn't show up in the picture. Pretty soon more and more
> children started tying balloons to their seats instead of going to Sun-
> day school.
>
> After many weeks an Elder of the church decided to visit Sunday
> School to tell the children how wonderful they were for their good at-
> tendance.
>
> When he walked in the back, he saw a sanctuary full of balloons
> swaying back and forth in the seats, and behind the podium where
> the Superintendent was supposed to be was the biggest balloon of all
> swaying slowly on a thick piece of twine. (*Man* 34)

Fundamentalist Christianity is oppressive and repressive and
depressive—especially the meals that begin and end in devotions used
to warn or punish family members:

> He didn't look up, but all the boys, and Granny, sat up straight and
> folded their hands on their laps. "'*A soft answer turneth away wrath,*'"
> he read, "'*but grievous words stir up anger.*'"

He stopped and took a deep breath. He was letting that sink in. Henry knew those "grievous words" had to be bad. They had to be about him. (*Youngest* 33)

A lifelong obsession with doing the right thing, being square with God, keeping to the straight and narrow, walking in the light, and knowing the truth may do more harm than good. At the end of "The Book of the Grotesque," which prefaces the stories of *Winesburg, Ohio*, Sherwood Anderson writes about "truth"—or more properly, "truths":

> The old man had listed hundreds of the truths in his book. I will not try to tell you all of them. There was the truth of virginity and the truth of passion, the truth of wealth and of poverty, of thrift and profligacy, of carelessness and abandon. Hundreds and hundreds were the truths and they were all beautiful.
>
> And then the people came along. Each as he appeared snatched up one of the truths and some who were quite strong snatched up a dozen of them.
>
> It was the truths that made the people grotesques. The old man had quite an elaborate theory concerning the matter. It was his notion that the moment one of the people took one of the truths to himself, called it his truth, and tried to live his life by it, he became a grotesque and the truth he embraced became a falsehood. (24)

Anderson's theory may explain the most outstanding trait of Heynen's people: they are weird. It's not just girls with six toes, boys with bowed penises, ministers who fart, or ministers' wives who breast-feed. Everyone in northwest Iowa seems "off-key," Cosmos Coyote decides (87). One reviewer of *You Know What Is Right* called these characters "an unfortunate breech of the collection's integrity" (*Review* 906): the fat old man with a cane, who was "like one of those broken limbs you think is going to break off the tree but just goes on hanging there with most of its leaves dead—but not all of them" (*One-Room* 158); the old woman who flosses her teeth in public. One old farmer prays to his animals; another talks to his bees. Another is obsessed with building sheds, including one very spiffy shed which contains nothing but another spiffy shed, which contains yet another shed. . . . One family sets the chamber pot beside the front door on a cold winter night, and when it freezes solid they continue to use it until "a big mound had grown up on top" (*Man* 24). One housewife uses her false teeth to shape waves around the edges of her pie crusts; another pays boys ten cents apiece to kill garter snakes while she watches; another plays hide-and-seek games with her husband, leaving him little clues along the route. A third runs around with her hair in pink curlers all the time to deflect attention from her remarkable beauty. An elderly couple shares the same set of false teeth and keeps a flock of geese in the second story of their home (the Goose Lady in *The Man Who Kept Cigars in His Cap* keeps them on the first floor). A prosperous jeweler closes his business and moves to another county to set up shop creating "Hand-Made Miniature Christmas Tree Decorations" which, of course, nobody buys. Fearful of losing her loose diamonds in a tornado, a woman swallows them . . . and spends the next day picking them out of her shit with tweezers. A girl who flunked third grade three times sets herself up as a target for town boys to throw stones at, and spits at farm boys who try to rescue her.

Gradually Heynen's boys develop a dark side of their own, although by balancing light side and dark side they manage to avoid the grotesqueness of people who seize a single truth and make it their own. Whereas Kloefkorn tends to dichotomize light and dark into, for example, narrator and Carlos, or narrator and loony, Heynen usually synthesizes: the same boys that shelter the pheasants tip the toilet of the local librarian who complains in a letter to the local newspaper editor of "the scatological obsession of our youth" (*You Know* 17). They smoke corn silk in corncob pipes. They invent dares that involve hanging by heels from the top of the windmill and drinking milk fresh from a cow's tit, no hands allowed. They play rude and crude games like lighting farts or "let's jerk off."

They learn to deceive, to conceal with half truths: "They knew that to keep a secret you had to hide it down a blind alley of stories that are only part of what happened. . . . Too much silence was like honey to a hungry bear, and grown-ups were bound to start pawing around in it. It was best to throw them a few scraps of the truth to keep them away from the real honey of what you did" (*Youngest* 73).

And the boys are more than acquainted with the harsh realities of death and the facts of animal sexuality. Like Linda Hasselstrom, Heynen considers an early confrontation with the intertwined realities of birth and death to be one benefit of growing up rural. His poem "Butchering" recalls both Leo Dangel's poem "The Art of Hog Butchering" and Linda

Hasselstrom's poem "Butchering the Crippled Heifer" in painting a graphic picture of this aspect of farm life:

> For kids, it starts with a dead pig.
> You may spend a few days wondering
> about the red mark on the one chosen,
> wondering why he's best, and, puzzled,
> you may ask about the sharpened knives
> in the porch, the sledge hammer against the fence.
> And you may awaken one day to the squealing
> near-miss. You may see the bleeding ear.
> Usually, though, it starts with a dead pig
> and a steaming barrel of water.
>
> You stand ready. The throat cut,
> the blood drained, you hold your nose
> because you know next they will slice the
> belly for the first smell and your first job:
> the bucket, the shovel. You move quickly,
> carrying what there is to the other pigs.
> They're hungry, you get it over with. (*How the Sow* 20)

Experience brings knowledge, but it comes with a price. At the low end that price is a butchered pet pig, a drowned possum floating in the drinking tank with an apple in its mouth, a blind pony, a few chickens pecking each other to death. At the high end, the price of knowledge is a four-year-old cousin who drowns in the silage pit or a pet run over by the gravel truck:

> Days later, when he wasn't crying, when the shocks in his chest didn't come at him anymore when he least expected, when he no longer got sullen to keep from crying in front of everybody, he thought about the driver. He hadn't even seen the driver, only the back of the gravel truck speeding on even faster than ever down the road. The boy hated gravel trucks after that, the sight and sound of them. (*One-Room* 87, 88)

The boys watch orphaned piglets trying to nurse on the "useless little teats" of an old boar who has adopted them, watch the next day when "[t]he old boar sniffed the dead pigs for a moment and then ate one" (*Man* 47). They happen accidentally upon their missing pet terrier, dead in a virtual "animal cemetery" concealed in the neighbors' grove, bullet holes in his rib cage. They watch their lucky piglets, the ones who survived an early blizzard, grow up and head off to the stockyard to be killed, butchered, and eaten.

As a result, the boys develop a callous side. When an injured fawn they have nursed through a summer with black horse salve and a wooden splint develops gangrene and dies, the boys do not mourn. "Did anybody cry?" Heynen asks. "Nobody cried. The boys buried the fawn in the orchard and kept the wooden leg to show people later how it had gotten worn smooth from that fawn's being so happy" (*Man* 58). The turtle in the pasture creek will, they decide, "probably be dead pretty soon. . . . Cut worm or gopher poison would get in its water—or some new weed spray that hadn't been tested on turtles" (*Man* 53). Death is "natural," the boys decide in the last story of *The Man Who Kept Cigars in His Cap*: "There's only one thing to be done about all this death, said the smallest boy. Clothespins. So they put clothespins on their noses and ran off to play" (61).

The boys learn birth as well as death . . . and sex. "The thick air's full of lust," a Kansas farmer observes in a Heynen line that echoes Dave Etter's "Stubby Payne: Stocking Tops"; "The dry air / smells so clean you sniff yourself / remembering the scent of semen / in sweetclover after rain" (*Suitable* 24, 25). The boys watch pigs and cows being made and birthed, speculate on how chickens mate:

> They had watched horses mate, and what happened there was no secret to them. The boar mounting the sow left little to be imagined. Dogs, cats, rabbits, sheep, and cattle had very open mating habits. There were no secrets with these animals. The boys could see what was happening.
>
> But try as they did, crawling up behind roosters and hens, peering through knotholes and from behind wagons—from only a few feet away!—they could not figure out how [chickens] mated. (*Man* 43)

The boys castrate sheep and pigs, toss the testicles to their pets, and later hunt the boar with the hidden testicle who went on breeding even after he had been castrated. The boys help the older men disinfect and replace a ruptured uterus, then retreat into their imagination: "Boys have dreams and cows have dreams. Think about that for a while," writes Heynen in ending the story (*Man* 50). One boy with a boomerang of a penis takes care of business in the fatty folds of his own stomach.

In *Being Youngest* both Henry and Gretchen aid in the birth of piglets by reaching their arm up the sow's birth canal to pinch off a ruptured blood vessel (213).[10]

All this the boys learn by growing up rural.

The boys not only grow callous and crude; they develop a streak of gratuitous meanness, which goes well beyond boys being boys or boys knowing life's harsh truths.[11] They taunt the dog with three legs, reaching to shake a paw that is not there. "The boys liked to hold out hay toward the steers across the electric fence wire and pull it back when the steers tried to eat it. They kept pulling it back until the steers leaned too far and got a terrible shock" (*The Man* 42). They tease Maggie, the girl with six toes: "What are you hiding in your shoe?" They harass girls, and each other, and themselves:

> Instead, one of the boys ran by and jerked the blanket so that one end of the girls' house came off the ground. And there they were where everybody could see them, sitting in a circle with their dolls and mud pies and dress-up clothes, laughing and having a wonderful time.
>
> Stop it! one of the girls yelled, and then a grown-up came by and told the boys to go play ball and get ready for the tug-of-war.
>
> They did, sulking away to where they were told to go, rubbing the softball in dog droppings and spitting on the tug-of-war rope where the next person would have to hold it. (*One-Room* 180, 181)

> What they liked best was to stand in a circle, especially in a quiet close place, then take turns hurling the explosive [rotten] eggs down in the center of themselves so they could gag and reel together in hilarious misery and, later, have something wonderful to tell friends who were not lucky enough to have been there with them. (*One-Room* 21)

> Everybody knew how stupid it would be to put your tongue on freezing metal. So the boy waited until he was alone to try it. (*One-Room* 218)

For a twenty-cent bounty, the boys will kill pocket gophers; for a forty-cent bounty, they will trap barn pigeons; for a fifty-cent bounty they will drown ground squirrels. They drown puppies for kicks, burn a trapped rat on a fire made of corncobs, stuff a firecracker up a chicken, tie another to the leg of a sparrow or the back of a gopher.

In the final story of *The One-Room Schoolhouse* the boys' dying grandfather becomes irrationally upset by a mourning dove that has built its nest outside of his bedroom window. The book ends with a gratuitous execution, which counterbalances the rescue of frozen pheasants:

> On their next visit the boys brought their BB gun. One climbed the tree where the mourning dove nested on her eggs. The beak stuck over the edge of the nest. He shot the mourning dove in the throat, and it flapped wildly to the ground. He threw the eggs down for the other boys to smash while the mourning dove fluttered and bled on the grass.
>
> The boys brought the dead bird inside and held it up for their grandfather. They extended their arms toward him, each of them holding part of the bird's wings between his fingers, so he could see that this gift was from all of them. (224)

Here and elsewhere, Heynen suggests that his farm boys have an attraction not only to scatology, but to the world of darkness itself. Like Kloefkorn and Blei, Heynen has a habit of going down into darkness, into forts built to shut out the light, or into dark tunnels in the barn. "But what could you do at a time like this?" Heynen asks when the shadow of autumn lies long across the land. Make deep, dark tunnels out of hay bales, Heynen answers. "And you could seal off all the light with handfuls of hay wedged between bales, and you could hide the cave entrance with another bale . . . Then you could slide in and take the world of darkness with you. . . . And that is just what the boys did" (*One-Room* 39–40). In an early poem titled "The Clean People," Heynen suggests his own attraction to the dark knowledge of experience:

> The clean people worry me.
> Wherever I go, I face the glare
> of their immaculate smiles,
> their polished demeanor
> declaring the good life of order.
> Where is the smudged
> message of grief,
> the scuff-marks of pain?
> With all the dirt in the world,
> who got theirs?
>
> I think I am one
> and take my place with the soiled.
> We are *the others*. (*Suitable* 69)

The farm boys and the farm men are thus closer than the genial battle between them would suggest. Of course a double standard obtains: an adult who steals things ("Little things. Cookies. A doily from the coffee table. A bathroom towel. An egg or two") can discipline the boys (with a stolen paddle, no less) when he catches them stealing shingle nails from his tool shed (*You Know* 14). And the men always have the last word, even when they've been shown up. "Go to the house and wash," they remind the boys who have resurrected the bloated cow. But men and boys are usually co-conspirators, and in a way the boys bring out the child still living inside the men. When the boys try to pass off a twin calf as one which the men had butchered *in utero* to save the mother, and claim they decided to put the pieces back together (*Man* 49), the men buy into the joke, just as they buy into the story of Big Bull climbing into the haymow. The men learn flyfishing for bats from the young boys, and the boys learn to hoax early morning hog calls from the men. Both men and boys are thorough-going materialists: "There was more than pride at stake. There was money," writes Heynen in the story "Ground Squirrels" (*You Know* 98). Both are suspicious of the stranger who charges only a dollar for sharpening saws, and the man who keeps cigars in his cap. The boys ultimately betray a coyote they befriended to men who they know will set cyanide traps for it. Watching one of the older men stuff a mean tomcat head first into his dusty boot, they do not protest. "Like drowning a gopher," says one, shrugging his shoulder (*One-Room* 163).

Both men and boys dislike city folk. "You want to learn something, boy?" asks one of the older men when the insurance adjustor arrives after the hail storm; "You just come with me to see how these slickers operate" (*One-Room* 77). City folk put on airs, let the farm kids know who's who. Town boys harass a farm kid, whom they easily recognize by "the big steps he took and by the way he looked around when there was nothing to look at" (*One-Room* 83). Farm boys know that town kids are gullible, diminished, somehow enfeebled.[12] They can't sit still, they talk too fast, they call dinner "lunch" and supper "dinner," they say "tell me" instead of "show me," they smile when there is nothing to smile about (*One-Room* 129). When one boy spins a tall tale about a flock of ducks strung together on a rope, one of the older men suggests, "That would make a good story to tell some city slickers" (*Man* 45).

In the title story of *You Know What Is Right* the exchange is verbal. The town boys give the farm boys the finger and yell, "Hey, Stinkeroos, / You got cowshit on your shoes!" The farm boys respond in kind: "Oh yeah, city fellow? / Your underpants is yellow!" (72). Tensions sometimes break out into fights. In "Spitting Sally," farm boys throw stones at their city cousins; in "Specs" the town boy and the country boy duke it out. When a cow simultaneously coughs and shits just as one of the farm boys is passing behind it with a full pail of milk, he intentionally passes the mess along to the dairy and its urban customers:

> What do you think happened to that green milk?
> One guessed that an old man was putting it in his tea. Another guessed that it had been made into green cheese. But the guess that they liked the most was that it was made into ice cream and shipped to the city. (*Man* 36)

Girls are a different story. Unlike the protagonists of his novels *Being Youngest* and *Cosmos Coyote*, the boys of Heynen's poems and short fictions are mystified by girls. This is especially true of the older boys, whose muscles attract town girls "in tight pink jeans and smiles / too radiant to be pure" but who lack the social graces to approach them:

> . . . our legs were thick:
> we couldn't dance or sway
> or stand on wheels.
> Our hands
> we couldn't trust
> with strum or touch.
> We didn't have a chance. (*Suitable* 21)

It's the town boys, "loose and slouchy," who win the prizes, who gather all that beauty into their slender hands.

Girls seem inaccessibly lovely, even Marta who at age fifteen sports a beard so thick she has to shave: "Her voice was soft, her arms and body were thin, and when she walked she was like a feather carried by a gentle breeze. When a strange boy came to the neighborhood, he seemed always to be drawn toward Marta" (*You Know* 77). The girl at the swimming pool is especially inaccessible, tan, and graceful, with a "smile as if nothing bad could ever happen to her" (*One-Room* 72). Then there are the giggling girls at the county fair: "Those girls looked so pretty to him that he knew if they [the boys] kept watching he would cry right there in front of a whole midway full of people out looking for laughs" (*You Know* 94). Girls are also smarter: Maggie, the girl with six toes, who gets all A's in school and "probably knew what she was saying" (*Man* 23); the woman at the bank who spots the mismatched feet of two pocket gophers who gnawed off one leg each to escape a trap. In the story "Yellow Girl," the boys transform a dress washed into the farm slough by a spring flood into a mysterious totem:

> As a joke one of the boys drew a head over the dress. The other boys joined in, scratching legs and arms in the soft dirt. There, one of them said. There is our yellow girl.
>
> The boys left her lying there, knowing there was little chance that such a flood as the last one would come and wash her away. They went down to the pond often that summer, always saying they were going fishing. And they did catch a few small bullheads. The yellow girl stayed in place through the summer, and when the weather changed her at all the boys fixed her up again by retracing her head, arms, and legs in the dirt. They came to think of her as their sleeping beauty, though none of them stooped to kiss her. (*You Know* 6)

Boy meets girl and experience meets innocence in Heynen's novel *Cosmos Coyote and William the Nice*, a book that deserves more attention than it received. Experience in this case is high school senior William De Haag (alias Cosmos Coyote), from Port Swan, Washington; innocence is high school senior Cherlyn Van Dyke, from Dutch Center, Iowa. Facing six months in a juvenile detention home for being a "habitual offender," Cosmos cops a plea: he will spend his senior year rehabilitating himself in Iowa, "the land of our people, the heritage of our people. And it's the most religious community left on the face of the earth" (13). After a month or two of adjusting to farm work, to Sunday church services, and to his aunt and uncle, Cosmos enrolls in the Dutch Center Christian Academy. Inevitably he meets Cherlyn: class president, newspaper editor, and musical director for daily chapel services. Inevitably they fall in love. This improbable romance allows Heynen to explore the light side of dark-side people, and the dark side of the children of light.

Admittedly Cosmos is not a particularly bad egg. His criminal offenses seem almost trivial: painting a peace sign on the rump of the bronze pig at the Pike Place Market in Seattle, pointing a water pistol at a couple of drunk sailors. He is the son of the "experienced" half of a pair of farm brothers, the one who got into trouble, the one who got divorced, the one who left Iowa for Washington. In Cosmos's defense, his father admits, "The cops are going nuts these days. . . . When I was a kid on the farm in Iowa, we stole watermelons out of farmers' fields, tipped outhouses on Halloween, stuck corncobs in people's mufflers, hid behind trees and threw tomatoes at cars when we went into town on Saturday nights, drank sloe gin mixed in with our Cokes right in front of the cops, went tearing through farmers' fields at night with spotlights hunting jackrabbits, spray-painted our names on every rock and overpass in Iowa, drove eighty miles an hour down gravel roads. And that's just for starters. . . . The country is trying to criminalize its youth" (3, 4). But Cosmos does smoke pot, play in a band, dress like a Goth, quote Bob Dylan, and have sex with a dark-haired siren named Salal, five years his senior. Salal is "Cosmos's dark angel who came down from alternative-rock heaven over a year ago and volunteered to be the manager of the OughtaBs" (10). She has so much soul, Cosmos writes in one of the band's songs, he "can't tell where [her] pretty body's gone" (35). As Cosmos heads off for Iowa, Salal reveals that she's in a lesbian relationship with Bridgette—a waitress at the local coffee shop—begs him not to be her "gender barrier," and asks him to leave her free to find her true self without "some stupid barrier that society has built up" (39). Cosmos has definitely been through some experiences.

Cherlyn's life has been church and school. She is Iowa blonde, she has the fully developed body of a farm girl, and she looks "wholesome" and dresses "modestly." She has a cheerful Christian smile. She became class president because at a Bible Study Group retreat, the Lord told her she was to become a leader (148). "Cherlyn is like a hospitality hostess who shows no desire but the comfort of the person she is talking with," Cosmos decides (67). Cherlyn also gets good grades and is popular with both teachers and classmates. She is like the community which discourages hugging (133); she is like the schedule of dusty, sweaty, tedious farm work which, Cosmos has to admit, provides "rescue from misery by work" (140). In one sense she is Cosmos's "Ought to Be."

The discovery of a "dark side" in the most ethereal of creatures has been a staple of literature and film forever, but lately we have seen the postmodern phenomenon of thugs reclaiming their lost "light sides." Not long after Kevin Costner as Eliot Ness in *The Untouchables* found himself becoming everything he had sworn to oppose, Samuel L. Jackson as Jules in *Pulp Fiction* found himself quoting scripture and jumping noble. Cosmos Coyote can be seen as a dark-side character who discovers his light side, while innocent Cherlyn develops an appreciation for "experience." When the two kiss at the Tastee-Freez Truck Stop, "a solid kiss on the lips" (122), experience weds innocence.

Cosmos Coyote finds salvation not only in Cherlyn but in the community values she represents. These include honesty, work, integrity, and not ratting out your friends. They also include playing almost-Christian rock songs and attending Sunday church services. Cherlyn's Dutch Calvinism is both refreshing and redemptive. Fundamentalist Christianity is not all oppression, repression, and depression. If we miss that point, we miss the entire point of Heynen's novel with its frequent discussions of morality, ethics, and faith:

> "What do I believe?" He pauses again, letting her continue the head massage. "I'll tell you what I believe. I don't believe in bullshit."
>
> Her hands stop rubbing. "Translation?" she says.
>
> "I can't pretend to know something I don't know, and I can't pretend to be somebody that I'm not."
>
> "That makes sense," says Cherlyn. "Do you believe in God?"
>
> Cosmos hesitates. It sounds like a trick question—but Cherlyn doesn't ask trick questions. "Sure," he says.
>
> "And do you think God can be known?"
>
> It sounds like another trick question. "Are you going evangelical?" he says.
>
> "I'm trying to understand you," she says.
>
> "I don't want to pretend to know what I don't know. The universe is filled with mystery. To me, believing in God means accepting the mystery of everything." (152, 153)

Cosmos Coyote and William the Nice is full of this kind of talk—including an extended discussion of the Calvinist doctrine of total depravity. The talk was controversial and worked the book some harm with reviewers and teachers. *Publishers Weekly* found it "refreshing to see Christian faith presented without dogma or piety" (73), while *School Library Journal* thought the religious message was "too strong" (104).

However, neither the community nor Cherlyn proves to be as lily white as they first appear. The school shelters a liberal sociology teacher,[13] marijuana smokers, covered-up suicides, and petty thieves and drug dealers. Halfway through the novel, Cherlyn begins to dress in tight jeans and form-fitting sweaters. She expresses her admiration for Bill Clinton's charisma (while faulting Lewinsky for her misuse of female power), argues that she and Cosmos are not dating because they're not kissing, and when she can no longer hold to that technicality, decides that they really didn't "do it" because they keep their clothes on during the steamy make-out sessions:

> She laughs at his comment, then looks toward him, and her eyes rest on his erection, upon which the tiny ignition light shines.
>
> "If I were a man, I'd look exactly the way you do," she says. "Oh, Cosmos, aren't bodies beautiful?" . . .
>
> "Nothing that I have is as beautiful as everything that you have," he says. He slides closer toward her. He takes her hand and places it on himself. "Is that all right?" he says.
>
> "Yes," she says, and her hand tightens over his zipper. "Bodies are beautiful. I think God wants us to enjoy them. There's nothing in the Bible says we can't touch each other in a loving way." (222)

It isn't just the pressure of his erection that is giving her pleasure but also the hard ridge of denim, the double-folded fabric on the zipper of his jeans, which, like a long narrow finger, comes down on the most sensitive source of her pleasure. She moves against the denim ridge, rocks against it, then makes small circular movements which he can tell are taking her along the edge of ecstasy and pain. He lets her take control, following her hips and pelvis. As her breathing becomes panting and her movements grow faster and more intense, it occurs to Cosmos that it just might happen. Not in his most fact-defying fantasies has he imagined that a religious girl from a farm in Iowa could reach an orgasm under these circumstances. (287)

When Cosmos asks if she loves his Cosmos Coyote side or his William the Nice side, she answers, "I don't much get along with the William the Nice types either. I don't fit in with the regular church-folks" (310).

The message of *Cosmos Coyote and William the Nice* is that while we all need "structure and fucking discipline" (to reference *American Beauty*), we do not need the cloistered and sequestered virtue of untested rules and regulations. Early in the book Cosmos assumed the persona of William the Nice as a Raven/Coyote device to survive Iowa. Later in the novel, Cherlyn admits to being "the biggest pretender of all" (156). The novel also examines candidly the difficulty of identifying roots and finding values in a postmodern world. Heynen's conclusion seems to be that we go away to come home and we discover ourselves by meeting our other. Cosmos's dad left Iowa to break his roots, then sent Cosmos back to Iowa to reclaim his roots. Cosmos thought he was rooted in Washington, but by the conclusion of the book he inclines toward Iowa. Certainly he favors Cherlyn over Salal. Cherlyn, on the other hand, talks enthusiastically about escaping Iowa for a three-week summer mission program at the suggestively named Redemption University in Seattle . . . where she can be with Cosmos in his world. Innocence needs experience and experience needs innocence. "If you live where winter comes / you'll get to know your soul," Cosmos writes in an Iowa-inspired song which counterbalances his earlier song about Salal. Before boarding the airplane to head home, he gives Cherlyn the raven totem his father carved for him just before sending him to Iowa. "Raven is the Trickster of the Northwest," he explains, "just as Coyote is the Trickster of the Plains" (342).

Oddly, Cosmos Coyote is not a trickster figure—he is one of Heynen's most level-headed, credible creations, more realistic than many of his boys or men, and certainly more realistic than most Jim Harrison characters. Elsewhere, however, Heynen creates characters and scenarios that sound like something out of *Carnivale* or *Deadwood*. They are not exactly grotesques; they are more figures out of the world of surrealism, or at least magical realism. In these stories, Heynen's aesthetic moves beyond realism or psychological archetypes and into a mode of pure art. Surrealism is, after all, more art than psychology. What can we say about a family of nudists moving to town? When the women of the neighborhood pluck up the courage to visit and complain, they are met at the door by a nude husband who hands them blindfolds:

> Here, he said. Put these over your faces. It will make you feel more comfortable.
> The women did not dare to refuse the naked man. They put the black scarves over their faces so that they could not see him.
> There is a problem in the neighborhood, said one of the women from beneath her black scarf.
> Really, said the naked man. Where is it?
> We can't see it right now, said the woman. (*You Know* 177)

In his early work—"The Falcon/Her Dreams" in *Notes from Custer*, "Building a Cradle" in *A Suitable Church*, and the title poem of *How the Sow Became a Goddess*—Heynen seems to borrow his surrealism from the French symbolists or Sioux mythologies. Later he works within the tradition of Italo Calvino and Dave Etter, using local characterization "to give the flavor of truth to a depiction in which the whole wide world was to be recognized" (Calvino viii). Heynen's magical realism also has roots in the Midwest tall tale spun one spin too far. The boys' dance with chickens and the celebration over pigs saved from a barn fire (with apples, coffee, popcorn, and a rainbow made by water from the fire hoses and light from the burning barn) have the feel of weird but true farm moments. Swallowing a snake while drinking from a puddle of rainwater has the feel of a farm superstition stretched by the writer's imagination or the boy's: "As they walked home, the boy felt the snake curl up in his stomach and go to sleep. This will be easy, he thought. For supper, he said he wasn't hungry. He drank one glass of warm milk. The snake woke up and drank the warm milk, then fell asleep again" (*One-Room* 28). The story of the boys who save a mixed-breed litter of pups by cutting their tails off (so that the men can't tell one from the other) and then celebrate their success by stringing the tail tips together into "a good luck necklace" (*You Know* 110) feels like a farm story gone grotesquely awry, perhaps with the help of Tim O'Brien's story "Sweetheart of Song Tra Bong." Cosmos Coyote's vision of his punker girlfriend Salal becoming "like a Salvador Dali painting, her hands getting longer and drooping like the hands on a Dali clock, her neck elongating like a stretched piece of taffy" (98) is probably a dope dream. The Iowa cloud that transforms itself into a big white lamb similar to the six-legged lamb the children tried to save might, Heynen hints, be a bit of indigestion:

It floated along in the air without moving its legs, cruising along as if there was nothing to it. One eye of the lamb was hidden, but the other one looked straight at Henry and Gretchen, almost as if it were asking them a question. Then they saw the extras hanging on the front of this lamb. The lamb slowly turned toward them, its hind quarters moving in the sky while its head stayed in one place. It was Sixer, and she was turning in the sky to look straight down on them. Now both of the cloudy sheep's eyes were trained right on Henry and Gretchen, where they sat on their grass cushions. (*Being Youngest* 162)

On the other hand, this vision in the sky may be something more—surrealism on a grand scale, something akin to the tornado that transformed a woman, and the sow which is transformed into a goddess in *How the Sow Became a Goddess* (1977). Heynen's first treatment of the yellow girl story in *A Suitable Church* (1981) is this kind of archetypal surrealism:

a delicate and torn yellow dress
the flood had brought from somewhere.

He watches it move on waves,
wanting to reach and take it
but sees it live for water,
moving with the form
of a lovely girl swimming.

He has never learned to swim,
but he leaves his clothes
floating with hers on the water
where their sleeves reach to touch
like friendly fish or ducks.

He returns to his fields,
through the briars,
steps naked into the pasture
where he cannot find the yellow girl
nor imagine the fields where she lives. (12, 13)

Heynen's 1985 treatment of the same story in *You Know What Is Right* is something of a retreat into magical realism, inventing drainage tiling, spring floods, and the marvelous little detail of the boys checking the dress pockets for money ("They were empty"—6) while transforming the dress into a totemic "sleeping beauty."

Much of Heynen's magical realism is contained in a true Raven/Coyote trickster figure named Uncle Jack. Uncle Jack is different—"silly," "unpredictable," "stupid," "probably crazy"—and therefore not trusted by anyone with a good grasp on truth. He talks in rhymes and riddles: "Well, when I wish to sell a wishing well, I wish you well my wells to wish" (*Boys' House* 52). When the boys try to pass ducks off as pigs, Uncle Jack turns their scheme on its head before turning himself into a barking duck and "fluttering off down the road, bits of down wafting up from his shaggy coat" (*You Know* 125). When Uncle Jack takes an interest in the floral underwear of an old woman at the laundromat, she herself begins blossoming into flowered panties and bras, some falling from under her arms, some from under her dress (*You Know* 131). The shadow-puppet encounter between Uncle Jack and the beautiful school teacher moves quickly from the merely improbable to the surreal:

> After a few moments of this admiration, she held up her right hand in such a way that the shadow of a rose appeared on the shining white side of the trailer house.
>
> Ah, yes, what a wonderful projection screen, said Uncle Jack. The petals of the shadow-rose quivered as if responding to the same breeze which was bringing color to their cheeks where they stood side by side. Then across the screen came the shadow of Uncle Jack's right hand in the form of a butterfly which lit pulsing on the rose. Then like a second movie being projected on the same screen, her left hand formed in such a way that its shadow became a rabbit. As quickly, Uncle Jack's left hand made the shadow of a carrot which dangled over the rabbit's nose and which the rabbit, in what seemed to be a natural and instinctive move, set up to nibble. (*You Know* 133)

The beauty of imagination envelops the small reality of Iowa farm life, transforming natural objects like rose, butterfly, rabbit, carrot into a dialog of love . . . but we understand that Uncle Jack is no more likely than Shoeless Joe walking out of the Iowa cornfields.

The eleventh of Heynen's fifty Axioms for Writers reads, "At any point in a story anything can happen." This approach to fiction, so very different from that of Henry James and other nineteenth-century writers who saw a well-crafted story as narrowing continuously to its one logical conclusion, is pure magical realism, and exemplified in any number of stories and yarns. A haysling, when we think about it, would probably not hoist Big Bull into the haymow floor. A boy would probably not be able to hit a tin can with his slingshot from thirty yards, nor would a farmer be able to conceal a tame skunk under his engineer's cap, as did the man and boy of "The Man Who Kept Cigars in His Cap." The first boy to tie a balloon to his seat in Sunday School and skip out the back door would be betrayed immediately to the church elders. These stories are not life—they are little parables on epistemology and place, in which old women may turn into geese, old men turn into dogs.

The title story of *You Know What Is Right* is in this regard Heynen's most characteristic work. The key line comes from the grown-ups' parting words every time the boys head to town on a Saturday night: "You know what is right." It reminds us again of the tremendous weight of

Calvinism carried by Iowans young and old, the necessity to work hard and speak truth and stay square with God. The boys, Heynen writes, have been schooled so long they "figured they really must know what is right. But when they were on the downtown streets, it was not always so easy" (72). The town boys taunt them; the farm kids taunt right back, giving them the finger and shouting, "Your underpants is yellow."

"Was that the right thing to do?" the youngest boy wants to know. The group is not sure and walks away from this commonplace experience into the tale's second adventure: after a car salesman reprimands them for leaning against the new car show window, the boys slip into a new car just ahead of a well-dressed couple looking at autos, do "a stinkeroo," and slip out before the couple slips in. Of course the man and wife blame each other for the odor, and the boys are revenged. This less-than-likely adventure also leaves them wondering—was that the right thing to do? Laughing so hard they're afraid of peeing their pants—and would *that* be right? one of the boys wants to know—they head for the gas station john, and episode number three, an adventure in symbolic surrealism:

> Inside the urinal was a handful of change. It was the kind of urinal that has a few inches of water in the bottom, like a cup. Someone had dropped the change into the urinal and then urinated on it. If anyone flushed the urinal, the change would go too. But for anyone to get the change he would have to stick his hand into someone else's urine. (74)

Suddenly the boys know what to do. One after the other, the boys add their coins and urine "until the mound of coins glowed like a collection plate" (74), deciding that was definitely the right thing to do.

Although coins in the urinal are the last thing we would expect at the end of this little tale of town boys versus country boys, the surprise proves thematically correct in a fable that begins in religion and yellow underpants and contrasts the country boys' contempt for possessions with the materialism of up-scale urbanites. On the surface "anything" has happened, and the three episodes are not really connected except by happy accident. Nor is the action of this parable entirely credible. Surely the boys would have been noticed sneaking into and out of the car; probably they could have leaked a little water through the urinal and salvaged the coins without putting their hands in somebody else's urine. The story is not realistic, but symbolic. It coheres imagistically and thematically to give us an accurate depiction of late twentieth-century Iowa farm life. The psychology is correct: certainty and confusion and certainty again. The curious mixture of sacred and profane in that final metaphor, suggestive of several such combinations in Sherwood Anderson's *Winesburg, Ohio* stories, is a stroke of genius. It embodies in a single, memorable image the light and dark sides of Heynen's boys, and of small-town Iowa in all of Heynen's writing.

And it might provide a directive for all of us no matter where we live or how old we are: you fight a little, but only verbally; you pull a few pranks, but only on the pompous and the proud. Sooner or later, you happen upon some money (usually just small change) . . . and then you pee upon it, and walk away.

Jim Harrison

Reluctant Postmodernist

*What in God's name was I doing in this particular time
and place? My sense of dislocation was becoming
absolute.*
—*Jim Harrison*, True North

*Turning to the French is a form of suicide for the American
who loves literature—or, as the joke might go, it is at least a
cry for help. Now, when I was sixteen, I had turned to the
French.*
—*Annie Dillard*, An American Childhood

Wallace Stegner, whom Jim Harrison often mentions
and clearly admires, observes in his 1980 memoir *Wolf Willow* that any
writer of place confronts dislocations of language.

Contradictory voices tell you who you are. You grow up speaking one
dialect and reading and writing another. During twenty-odd years of
education and another thirty of literary practice you may learn to be
nimble in the King's English; yet in moments of relaxation, crisis, or
surprise you fall back into the corrupted lingo that is your native
tongue. Nevertheless all the forces of culture and snobbery are
against your *writing* by ear and making contact with your own natural audience. Your natural audience, for one thing, doesn't read—it
isn't an audience. You grow out of touch with your dialect because
learning and literature lead you another way unless you consciously
resist. It is only the occasional Mark Twain or Robert Frost who man-
ages to get the authentic American tone of voice into his work. For
most of us, the language of literature is to some extent unreal, because school has always been separate from life. (25, 26)

Bill Holm, whom Jim Harrison has met, offers a similar admonition:
"[L]isten carefully to any consciously remade voice you hear. Always the
ghost of the old voice lives under it, waiting like some body buried behind

a parlor wall in a Poe story, to fall through the weakened plaster at a tea party, revealing you for who you really are—the murderer of your own voice. What kind of truth can you tell in that false voice?" (*Heart* 21–22).

The difference between voices may be greater for rural midwestern writers than for writers whose "place" is academia or suburbia or New York City, but it's always there. And for most writers the problem is more than linguistic. I have noted earlier the ways Norbert Blei, Linda Hasselstrom, Bill Holm, and William Kloefkorn confront and work to resolve, however tentatively, dislocations of time and place. Nor are writers alone: dissociation from place (both the natural environment and its human component, including our own history) is the root of postmodern anxiety, and reconstructing a sense of communal place—which would not necessarily have to be rural in the traditional meaning of that word—is our only real hope of regaining sanity.

In the decades since Stegner wrote, centrifugal forces have increased in both American education and popular culture, most prominently in the cultural diversity agenda of American education, the expansion of television channels and programming, and the worldwide Internet. As I noted at the close of my first chapter, most modern Americans live so insulated by condominium walls from their immediate surroundings and so plugged into "elsewhere" via books, take-out food, radio, television, and computers that "Midwest literature," and even "Midwest sensibility," may be memories of the past. In twenty-first-century America, there is less *there* there than ever.[1] And Americans, always a mobile lot, are more mobile than ever: most of us these days, in Woody Harrelson's memorable line from *The Cowboy Way*, "ain't from around here." Or there. Or anywhere.

And yet, as I have also argued consistently throughout this book, the process of recovery appears to be ongoing. Since Twain and Garland, the initial impulse of ambitious and intelligent midwesterners has always been up and out—in Bill Holm's words to rise out of a mean life, to make yourself new; in Robert Bly's words to get away from your crummy little place, to get published in the *New Yorker*; in the words of Bob Dylan's "Not Dark Yet," to get to London and to gay Parie. It is also true, however, that for over a century of midwestern literature the rule has been to return home, or to as much of home as you can find, to the place where your language and your thought patterns may still fit comfortably. Departure and return—the two great themes of midwestern literature, encapsulated in a brief poem I myself extemporized many

years ago toward the end of a long day of fishing with my friend Ed
Kaizer near Ludington, Michigan:

And the boats go out
And the boats come in
On the shores of old
Lake Michigan.

Jim Harrison, a fisherman and hunter who grew up not far from
Ludington, departed early from his place, and returns frequently. The
central question in his fiction is whether he ever managed a successful
return geographically, philosophically, and stylistically. It seems to me
that the rural-realist in him, which detests literary fiction's addiction to
dread and irony, came close; the postmodernist aesthete in him did not,
but wishes that it had. "Indeed, one would do well," Patrick Smith observes, "to include Harrison himself in the group of writers who
struggle mightily (and with varying degrees of success) against 'dread
and irony' in their works" (50).

In Harrison's 1998 novel *The Road Home*, Nelse Northridge discusses
the process of going out and coming in, and the forces which shape language and thought, with a friend from Omaha named Derek. Derek is
an art dealer, and the core of his thinking is art and the art world; Nelse
is a naturalist, more tied to nature and the close observation of the natural world. Nelse speaks for the importance of place in shaping thought
and language: "People are limited by their central obsessions, from
which the nature of their language emerges, whether it is sports, raising
cattle, the stock market, anthropology, art history or whatever. I added location." Derek objects, having "assumed that television had leveled the
differences" among places, but Nelse insists this is true only in the
minds of television people (222). After further discussion, Nelse con-
vinces Derek that he might be wrong in disregarding place-based differences, because he has limited himself to "a specific class of art buyers
in Omaha, and to memories of New Hampshire, New York City, and
Europe" (222); he has dealt only with people, including himself, who
lack any sense of place. In the novel, Nelse wins the argument: location
shapes enthusiasms and "obsessions," and thus language and thought.

Jim Harrison is both Nelse and Derek, having discovered shortly after marriage "the primary dichotomy of my life, a nearly schizoid pulling
at the soul. Simply put, it is inside and outside" (*Off* 69). Harrison was
presented with more opportunities to see the world than any of the

writers I have been discussing, and in his fear of missing out he explored most of them. There has been a lot of inside and outside, a lot of going out and coming back, a lot of place and absence of place.

Harrison spent his childhood in rural Michigan fishing, hunting, playing doctor and football, working in the library, reading books and *The Nation*, diving headlong into Youth for Christ, escaping Youth for Christ, working on farms, escaping farm work for a summer job as a busboy in Estes Park, Colorado—all the while dreaming of being a painter or a writer. Whereas his dad read mostly historical novels—Hemingway, Garland, Caldwell, and Dreiser—Harrison saw the world with what Bill Holm would call a woods eye and read what Holm calls woods-eye writers: Faulkner, Dostoyevsky, Rimbaud, Henry Miller, and James Joyce. Hemingway seemed to Harrison "a woodstove that didn't give off much heat" (*Off* 37).[2] Then Harrison, like Norbert Blei, left home for the obligatory writer's stint in Greenwich Village, New York. "I was at the age," he told Kathy Stocking in 1977, "when you think all your problems are geographical and if you can only get to the right setting, you'll begin writing. Of course, you never do" (qtd. in Reilly 1). In the "false memoir" *Wolf*, Harrison's narrator takes with him to New York his "Scholfield Reference Bible, Rimbaud, Dostoevsky's *The Possessed*, *The Portable Faulkner*, Mann's *Death in Venice*, and *Ulysses*" (210).

But despite the pleasures of frequent casual (and possibly fictional) sex, Harrison's narrator has only negative memories of New York, which proved to be "impenetrably immense, incomprehensible" (*Off* 60). Harrison lived in a windowless apartment on Grove Street with photos of Rimbaud and Dostoyevsky taped to the wall, worked at Marlboro Books and Brentano's ($40 a week), played the beatnik and leftist civil rights worker, and found a girlfriend who read Apollinaire and Valéry to him in French. "[T]he average dumpster ate better than I did," he recalls in *Just Before Dark* (7). Assessing New York in *Wolf*, Harrison writes, "I would be happy to see her leveled by a giant tidal wave caused by a comet plunging into the Atlantic a few miles off shore, the harbor clogged with dead squid" (156). Assessing media types in *Just Before Dark*, he writes, "The New York group, particularly, bites like Dobermans on quaaludes" (159). Even the books that drew Harrison to New York are reconsidered, as is literature in general: reading a thousand books had brought "no wisdom at all" (*Wolf* 138). "Books can be so utterly powerful to some-one quite vulnerable in their teens," Harrison muses looking back (*Off* 39). "I had no defense against the world and my own preposterous oafishness than language, my own written word and what I read, which I used as armor. . . . I read *Finnegans Wake* over and over as a college freshman trusting that its music was a substitute for wisdom. I was a peacock, an aesthete, an asshole" (55).

Harrison returned to Michigan, drifted in and out of Michigan State, got married, and became a father in 1960. Finally finishing his BA, he started graduate school on an assistantship that involved teaching ESL students whom he "could barely understand" (*Off* 177), flunked out, worked at or applied for a series of jobs including one at the Chrysler Tank Arsenal and another that "involved traveling around and visiting farmers and giving speeches to farm organizations on what to do to protect farm animals in case of atomic attack" (*Off* 181), returned to the school, then dropped out again. The death of his father and sister in a car crash in 1962 precipitated one of Harrison's many episodes of near-clinical depression and then another departure, this time to Boston to join his older brother John and attempt to reassemble his life. Having heard Boston called "the St. Petersburg of the United States" (DeMott 95) made him imagine Boston a more benign environment for a writer than Michigan or New York City. Having found employment with a book wholesaler, Harrison brought his wife and daughter to Boston. Again like Norbert Blei, he joined the local literary scene and began writing—poems, not journalism or fiction. He met with Charles Olson on many occasions, although his tastes tended to Robert Bly, James Wright, Robert Duncan, and Gary Snyder. And he came to a startling realization: "Steinbeck like Mark Twain might have been generally denied a higher place [in the academic canon] because he was insufficiently puzzling to produce a goodly number of professional jobs like Eliot and Joyce" (*Off* 197).[3] In 1965 Harrison published three poems in the *Nation* and five poems in *Poetry*. In one of those happy accidents of fortune that seem to happen more to folks living in New York City than to folks living in the Upper Peninsula (UP), Harrison dialed what he thought was Galway Kinnell's phone number and got Denise Levertov instead. Harrison had read Levertov's work, and the two chatted. Levertov had just become poetry consultant for W. W. Norton, and was actually looking for poetry manuscripts. After reading Harrison's only ten completed poems, she arranged a contract with Norton.

Before the book appeared, however, Harrison tired of urban life and returned again to Michigan, where he rented a $35-a-month house and worked for $2.50 an hour laying concrete blocks. His old comparative literature professor Herbert Weisinger used the Norton contract to leverage an MFA for Harrison out of Michigan State; Harrison used the degree to leverage a teaching appointment at Northern Michigan University and, after Weisinger moved to New York, another appointment at New York–Stony Brook. Patrick Smith describes Harrison's career at SUNY–Stony Brook as "eminently short and unfulfilling" (12). The department there, Harrison recalls, "had all the charm of a streetfight where no one ever actually landed a punch" (*Off* 215). A string of visiting writers culminating in an International Poetry Festival allowed Harrison to expand his network of nodding literary connections to include the likes of Auden, Dickey, Lowell, and Wright. He spent a lot of time in New York City, eating at ethnic restaurants, writing "haughty reviews for the *New York Times Book Review*, so pompous that they embarrass me to this day" (*Off* 221), and connecting with the Coordinating Council of Literary Magazines and the Academy of American Poets. Harrison claims to have brought up the tail end of the Washington, DC protest march described in Norman Mailer's *The Armies of the Night*, where he, J. D. Reed, and Robert Bly thrashed a contingent of American Nazis (*Off* 223).

The poetry (and the connections) got Harrison a string of National Endowment for the Arts grants and a Guggenheim fellowship. "I'm not absolutely sure that when I eventually had lunch with [Alfred] Kazin at his club in New York and we had a drink with Gordon Ray who was president of the Guggenheim Foundation that it had anything to do with me getting a grant," Harrison writes, "but I don't discount it" (*Off* 213). The family returned to Michigan in 1967 and rented a nine-acre farm (cherry orchard and alfalfa) in Leelanau County, which in the middle sixties was the Michigan equivalent of Norbert Blei's Door County.

Eventually with writer, friend, and Buddhist priest-teacher Dan Gerber, Harrison founded the little magazine *Sumac*, which published nine issues and twenty-one books, including poets like Robert Duncan, Charles Simic, Hayden Carruth, Gary Snyder, Richard Hugo, Diane Wakoski, and Jim Welch. At the suggestion of his old writing crony and Michigan State alumnus Tom McGuane, Harrison turned from poetry to fiction with *Wolf: A False Memoir*, "hopelessly autobiographical" (*Off* 235), published in 1971. This he followed in 1973 with *A Good Day to Die* ("a thoroughly 'noir' novel in an American setting"—*Off* 245), and in 1976 with *Farmer*. Long years of scraping along on $10,000 a year writing poetry, occasional fiction, and freelance pieces for magazines like

Sports Illustrated ended with another stroke of good luck in 1978 when *Esquire* published "Revenge" and "Legends of the Fall" (a novella written in nine days and based on a journal kept by Harrison's great-grandfather-in-law) and Hollywood shoveled about a million dollars in options and contracts at the man who for many years had not even bothered to file an income tax.

The Hollywood experience, Harrison recalls, was like "being on the high board, mostly at night, and possibly the pool below you was empty" (*Off* 253). Key West, where Harrison hung out on R & R with his old friend Tom McGuane, was even worse.[4] Even San Francisco was a nightmare: "Six hundred and ninety-three people have jumped off that goddamned bridge," Harrison notes. "There's something sort of haunted in the air there. Nobody would do that in Missouri, and they don't do it in Northern Michigan. But in New Orleans, and San Francisco, these apparently perfect places where everybody's so happy . . ." (DeMott 40, 41). While few of the fifteen film scripts with which Harrison was involved ever ripened into films, the experiences in California and Key West brought him a group of friends outside the literary world, including Sean Connery, Jack Nicholson, Jimmy Buffett, and French count Guy de la Valdéne. Nicholson underwrote a year of writing with a personal check to Harrison and after the money "fairly rolled in" would accept in repayment only his original loan of $30,000 (*Off* 249). "Many people can afford to behave this way," Harrison observes wryly, "but very few actually do." The rolling money allowed Harrison to indulge his taste for travel, gourmet dinners, and French wines: "Despite my humble background I found I enjoyed saddle of wild boar, or a 1928 Anjou with fresh pâté de foie gras in slabs, trout laced with truffles, *côtelettes* of loin from a small forest deer, called a *chevreuil*, pheasant baked under clay with wild mushrooms" (*Just* 149).

Harrison found a lot of time for Valium and cocaine as well, and for writing a coked-up postmodernist macho (or macho-wannabe) male fiction[5] which made him many enemies (especially academic feminists) but also won him many readers (especially in France). One book followed another, and one depression followed another, to the number seven. "There is the obvious conclusion that in each case I was behaving in a way I shouldn't preceding the depression," Harrison muses, "living an outward life my inward being couldn't accept. . . . The most consistent feeling is suffocation, lack of oxygen, an atrophication of the strange breathing apparatus of the soul life. . . . There was the persistent visual image that I had become dead meat wrapped in plastic in a supermarket" (*Off* 33, 34).

Later he observes, "The solution to this crushing sense of claustrophobia turned out to be ridiculously easy. I simply drove north one June day into Michigan's Upper Peninsula, the scene of my first novel, *Wolf,* and looked for a cabin, a retreat" (*Off* 265). Harrison bought the cabin, settled into a pattern of alternately writing (fiction and screen projects), traveling (New York and Paris), and fishing (Key West, Montana, Michigan, Mexico, Ecuador, Costa Rica). The cabin "tended to detoxify me from other pressures. I could go in twenty-four hours from Los Angeles to my cabin where there are only ravens and bobcats and coyotes around" (DeMott 50). He also bought a house in Lake Leelanau. Harrison's work in Hollywood diminished, undermined, he claimed in *Off to the Side,* by "Keats, Christopher Smart, John Clare, and William Blake" (260). Harrison began to write novels with female protagonists (less fishing and fighting, still a lot of casual fucking, and increasing amounts of exotic travel, food, and wine), and epic histories in the Louise Erdrich mode, rooted in both history and place (usually Michigan and western Nebraska). By degrees Harrison became a famous American author: his work translated into several foreign languages, subject of a volume in the Twayne's U.S. Writers Series and of doctoral dissertations, serious articles, and scholarly books. In 1990 he received the Mark Twain Award from the Society for the Study of Midwestern Literature, headquartered at Michigan State University (MSU); in 1993 he was honored by Institute Lumière in Lyon, France. In 2000 Jim Harrison, who rarely misses an opportunity to take a shot at MSU archrival the University of Michigan, received Michigan State University's Distinguished Alumni Award.

More than most writers, then, Harrison struck various writer's pacts with diverse devils of late twentieth-century dislocation: at the low end, academia, commercial book publishing, and slick magazines; at the high end, Hollywood film and television.[6] His early literary (and artistic) influences were voices more popular with the International Fellowship of Poets and Writers than with his Michigan neighbors, not exactly the prairie voices we associate with the Midwest. Any high school teacher who passes *The Nation, Harper's,* and *Atlantic Monthly* to a word-struck student is probably at war with the village and the pupils themselves, in the tradition of Sinclair Lewis's Carol Kennicott or Sherwood Anderson's Kate Swift. So too, probably, was Harrison's college mentor,

a familiar type of displaced Easterner who slums it in the Midwest because he can't get a job in an Ivy League school, subscribes to the *New
Yorker*, listens to public radio, imports visiting poets exclusively from
The Fabled East in an effort to politic himself into a job back home, and
spends his days making himself—and everyone else—miserable because East Lansing is not Manhattan. While these mentors made
Harrison a writer, they may have worked him more harm than good:
"Only much later in life did I come to understand that there was a bridge
between my early life in the natural world and the arena of literature,
music, and painting. It was the moral and aesthetic equivalent of the
'suburbs' in between that goaded my intolerance," he writes looking
back over his own work (*Off* 44). Harrison never quite managed the synthesis of foreign surrealists with midwestern voice and subject that
marks the work of a John Knoepfle, James Wright, or Robert Bly. Later,
making his way as a successful writer of commercial journalism, fiction,
and film scripts, Harrison made the inevitable compromises with his
audience which took him further from the tradition of Midwest realism
and from his own voice. It is no surprise that *Farmer*, the early novel
closest to the Midwest in place and style, was a complete failure on its
initial release. As a result, much of the voice and many of the motifs
common in Harrison's work do not reflect the author's background,
his personality, or, for that matter, his unusually stable marriage and
family life.[7]

Many features of Harrison's stories may in fact be dismissed as
quirks which the inquisitive boy from Michigan picked up—like a cocaine habit—from his reading or his residencies in Key West, New York,
California, or France and passed along to his characters: the narrator-
as-Christ-figure and postmodern wordplay of *Wolf*; an obsession everywhere with elegant meals and haute cuisine;[8] the cellar full of French
wines purchased with part of his Hollywood booty which he gives to
Ludlow's wife in "Legends of the Fall," and to Ted and Ruth Northridge
in *Dalva* and to the Burkett clan in *The Road Home*;[9] perhaps even the
Lolita Complex, which characterizes many of his older men and several
of his adolescent girls.[10] The many lanky women in bra and panties and
the casual sex, the violence, and the violent sex[11] may be attributed to the
tastes of his *Esquire/Sports Illustrated* readership, just as the portrait of a
slightly loopy middle-class woman in search of herself (*The Woman Lit
by Fireflies*) may be attributed to the tastes of readers of *The New Yorker*,[12]
and at least some of Harrison's obsession with Native Americans may

reflect the late twentieth-century enthusiasm for Indians as a group onto which Anglo intellectuals can project their Other.

The result, as many reviewers have noted, is a menagerie of quirky characters who strain the limits of credibility.[13] Midwesterners traveled, even in the nineteenth century, but the global gallivanting of Tristan Ludlow in *Legends of the Fall* defies all likelihood and pushed Harrison's narrative upward toward myth. Occasional casual sex has been a fact of most of our lives, but in Harrison the casual sex is not only casual but stunningly frequent and often stunningly implausible (17-year-old Catherine's attraction to 43-year-old Joseph Lundgren, Sylvia's attachment to Tim, Dalva's affection for a man she admits is an asshole and a bad lover). Some of the sex in Harrison's novels seems a parody of *Playboy* fantasies at their worst, or even technically impossible: "'Ten . . . nine . . . eight . . .' came Charles's voice, muffled under the pillow. She arranged herself, hovering over him, aiming his dick with a hand. When he reached one, she thrust down, screaming 'Bingo!' and rotating her bottom as if she were working a pepper grinder" (*Julip* 72). One game the reader of a Harrison novel can play is guessing the number of pages it will take a newly introduced couple to get it on, even if the visiting scholar from Stanford University has been warned that this particular high school student is under eighteen and off limits (*Dalva*), or the babe in question belongs to a jealous Mexican drug lord ("Revenge").

The motivation for Harrison's characters is questionable beyond their sexual shenanigans. In contrast to Ed Abbey in *The Monkey Wrench Gang*, in *A Good Day to Die* Harrison is never able to establish credible motives for his eco-saboteurs to attack a dam that doesn't even exist. How likely is it that Isabela Ludlow would set up in Boston around the turn of the century, far from her husband and sons, to take there a new lover each year, including John Reed (*Legends of the Fall*) . . . or that her husband would "not greatly care" (201)? Why would Eulia take any interest at all in the pretentious narrator of *Sundog*? If David Burkett IV recognizes Vernice as a dingdong Francophile poet, why does he select her to edit his life's work (*True North*)? Why would anybody return from Mexico to work for the man who had raped his twelve-year-old daughter (*True North*)? And why can't David Burkett III make a conscious decision to lay off the twelve-year-old girls? And if Cochran is stupid enough to persist in his affair with Tibey's wife after receiving several perfectly explicit warnings from the drug lord, how does he become savvy enough to shank Tibey's huge bodyguard and outwit the drug lord at the novella's conclusion? And why, at the moment of their confrontation, do vengeful Tibey and the even more vengeful Cochran toss their guns away, ask each other's forgiveness, and drink a beer together (*Legends* 94)? And speaking of that old enemies-turned-sudden-friends scenario, why, after Nordstrom pitches Slats's hired assassin through a motel window, do the two of them sit down to a friendly dinner? Other than the fact that these twists make for great reading to an audience accustomed to television and movies where, Harrison admits, "nothing is true to the life you have experienced, or true to a life you could conceivably comprehend" (*Sundog* 87).

The range of books read by Harrison's characters, and their familiarity with fine art, often strains the limits of credibility. Most of their enthusiasms reflect the tastes of Harrison during his high school and college years, and Harrison was not your typical midwesterner. Julip Durham, a twenty-one-year-old dog-trainer who bangs lawyers, psychiatrists, and a string of older boy-males in an effort to free from prison the brother who shot her lovers for "defiling" her, reads a dog-eared copy of Emily Dickinson before bed each night. Her psycho brother reads Nietzsche, Ayn Rand, Hesse, Hemingway, and "a Tibetan by the name of Trungpa" (*Julip* 43). Robert Corvus Strang builds dams in a string of foreign countries and discourses on Saul Bellow, Thomas Wolfe, and Tennessee Williams. At age eleven Dalva Northridge was reading Dickens and the Brontë sisters (*Road* 5). At age fourteen Cynthia Burkett reads Jane Austin and the Brontës (when not smoking dope and doing sex), books passed along by her gay teacher in the Upper Peninsula of the 1960s (*True North* 21); in college she's reading *Lady Chatterley's Lover*, *The Brothers Karamazov*, and Henry Miller (*Road* 319). Brown Dog— one of the Upper Peninsula's poor and uneducated—according to Harrison a "kind of American that never gets into fiction" (Reilly 135)—reads *Popular Mechanics*, *Outdoor Life*, girlie magazines . . . and *One Hundred Years of Solitude* (*Julip* 109). At the suggestion of his high school English teacher, David Burkett reads "Stendhal, Hamsun, Céline, Gogol, Dostoyevsky, and Alain-Fournier" (*True North* 64), then Camus and Salinger (79), Huxley (81), and later on Mann, Joyce, Marcuse, Paul Goodman, Oscar Handlin, Schopenhauer, Nietzsche, and Niebuhr (98). ("I never cared for Hemingway," he adds on page 281, which figures, because his own writing is so stilted and falsely academic that he hires Vernice to clean it up.) Tibey's wife Miryea courts Cochran with a parcel of leather-bound books from her library: "some Barója novels, also *The Family of Pascual Duarte* by Camilo J. Cela, *Nina Huanca* by Faustino Gonzalez-

Aller, and books of poems by Machado, Guillén, Octavio Paz, Neruda and Nicanor Parra" (*Legends* 23).

Because Harrison (like Holm) often follows his reading rather than his ear, the language of Harrison's characters also sounds precious and sometimes precocious, a shade too close to Harrison the college prof for their own credibility.[14] The literary voices which lured Harrison away from his native Michigan are many, and they began speaking early. In Harrison's first novel *Wolf* they are very much on the surface: Dostoyevsky, Faulkner, Dylan Thomas, Rimbaud, Henry Miller, Jack Kerouac, James Joyce. The years of reviewing books and editing *Sumac* drew Harrison further from the voice of Michigan . . . or even Hannibal, Missouri, or Clyde, Ohio. As a result, Harrison is in love with diacritical marks and with the word "banal."[15] His language is suited to a college professor from Michigan ("The Beige Dolorosa"), a graduate of Michigan State who went on to graduate studies at Seabury Western Seminary in Chicago (*True North*), or a Stanford University professor (*Dalva*), although in *Dalva* Michael mixes colloquialisms like "kick in the balls" (117) and "wiener" (135) with "pule," "repertoire," "willy-nilly," and "umbrage" (67). Harrison's vocabulary may even suit the effete yuppie narrator of *Sundog*,[16] who, being familiar with Magritte and Dali, might well use words like "tosspot" (34), "abstruse" (31), "fleering" (20), "emetic" (18), "android parrots" (18), "redoubtable" (14), "fer-de-lance" (12), "ubiquitous" (15), "prattled" (14), "petulance" (15), "nominal" (13), "aplomb" (42), "honeyed somnolence" (43), "banal" (45), and "abbatoir" (174). Robert Corvus Strang speaks for all of us when he says, "I don't get what you're talking about" (xii), and the pretentious language is one way Harrison manipulates readers' sympathies against his narrator.

But such language does not ring true when Harrison is not satirizing academics or yuppies: "Even now the challenge of having risked a pomposity and perhaps won its opprobrium is a signal that a new shower of lint and sulphur should fall to further laminate the human condition in its habitual shield of filth" (*Wolf* 11); "Margaret was a virago, and even her silences were tortuous" (*Julip* 4); "my captious nostrum for Copperfield and Cratchit was to shoot their tormentors" (*Road* 24).[17] Elsewhere the writing is clichéd in a manner untied to place ("Julip . . . filled out her life to its limits"—*Julip* 39; "losing her meant everything to him"—*Legends* 46), grammatically incorrect or inconsistent ("for Cynthia and myself . . . for Cynthia and I"—*True North* 126), idiomatically stilted ("facilitate her ambition"—*True North* 238), or pretentiously French (*bete noire*, 83; *en passant*, 39; *cinéma-vérité*, 101; *salade niçoise*, 127 in *Dalva*). Harrison remarks in *Sundog*, "there is a wonderful fraudulence to literacy" (89), but we are not always conned. Neither, apparently, is an older Jim Harrison, who in 1986 told interviewer Jim Fergus, "I'm not interested in showing off anymore. I think what's important in style, which is of course someone's voice finally, is that you have a firm sense of the appropriate. There's a temptation to enter into rhetorical sections because they're fun to write. That's probably a problem William Styron has, particularly as he's so good at it. It was very difficult for me in 'Legends of the Fall,' the title story, to subdue that impulse" (DeMott 80).

Oddly, in a hundred other places Harrison's midwestern language shows through: give a shit, tough shit, worth a shit, oh pig shit, right on the money, up in years, killed dead, "you're a mess" (*Farmer* 23), "words dropped like turds in an outhouse" (*True North* 238), "a fer piece" (*Wolf* 107), "hotter than a two-peckered goat, as my dad used to say" (*Wolf* 185), "What do you want, hey?" (*Sundog* 16), "shitstorm of an argument" (*Woman* 20), "isn't a big item here" (*Sundog* 74), "jacklighted a doe" (*Sundog* 112), "skidding logs" (*Farmer* 105), "none of your beeswax" (*Dalva* 167), "killed dead" (*Just* 99), "funny money" (*Just* 84), "a couple tours" (*Off* 186), "a sure-thing bed and a guaranteed supper" (*Off* 187), "pony up some money" (*Julip* 36). It is interesting that rural expressions like "DNR" (*Woman Lit* 57), BLM (*Julip* 236), "popple" (*Sundog* 77), and "down below" (*Woman* 5) get parenthetical explanations not deemed necessary to French phrases.

Harrison is capable of dialogue and monologue that approaches Hemingway in capturing the terse Midwest style:

I had some good fishing this month, then I had to tell those parents their little daughter had leukemia, and you know I couldn't fish then worth a shit, though in all these years I've told hundreds they were going to die. Children are different. They die like beautiful dogs who don't know what's happening to them except it hurts. Over in the Ardennes there was this boy in the grass who looked like he was sleeping. Our messenger. I said wake up wake up we got to get out of here but then I couldn't see in this wheat field that his leg was blown off and he was dead. And just an hour before we had found some wine in this French farmhouse and drunk it. It was good wine. But even that was easier than those parents and the child because she wouldn't live until eighteen like my friend the messenger. She will die at seven and when her parents die in who knows how many years their hearts will still be busted by it. (*Farmer* 100)

With the character Brown Dog, created in 1990, Harrison achieved a language that sounds recognizably working-class midwestern: "the lady's got beautiful tits" (6), "running on at the mouth a bit here" (16), "made a big deal of the fact that" (18), "a tad criminal" (21), "this old burial mound I found way back in the forest" (20), "you stupid bitch" (24), "as luck would have it" (34), "gone goofy on me" (34), "flat-out hysterical" (34), "shaking the living shit out of her" (35), "ran smack-dab into" (35), "settled their hash" (53), "take a powder" (53), "hightailed it for my van" (54), "dingbat" (57), "tore off a quick one" (61), "went for it" (67). Unfortunately Harrison loses his voice in *Brown Dog* just about the time he hits the subject of food, and the novella ends with Brown Dog absurdly playing Mozart on the piano at the House of Ludington Hotel in Escanaba. In the 1994 sequel "The Seven-Ounce Man," Harrison's omniscient narrator mixes "eventuated" (87), "palliative" (86), "circuitry" (87), "commodious" (91), "burgeoning" (93), "sodden" (84), "mongrel anchorite" (94), "in a trice" (111), "the proffered pint" (113), "incohate" (145), "petulantly" (145), and "albeit" (164) with "don't got a pot to piss in" (90) and "like it or lump it" (101) and "I hoofed it back" (127).

The self-consciously literary style is especially odd in light of Harrison's ambivalence, if not actual distaste, for the sources of this language: the East Coast, the West Coast, Europe (including France), and academia.[18] In *The Road Home*, John Wesley Northridge II writes, "The prairie and the forest on a moonlit night are not threatening to me but Chicago and New York are, with Paris a little less so. In these cities, even among polite company, my skull tightens, and I sweat nervously from the degree of attention required to keep oneself out of a thousand varieties of trouble" (107). On the subject of France, one of Harrison's "real people," who has the author's sympathy, tells the narrator of *Sundog* (who does not have the author's sympathy), "We've become like the French. Everything must be *incroyable* or *bizarre*. If the information is sufficiently novel, it's a twenty-minute buzz while the bath is being drawn, sort of a three-dollar round-trip ticket before bedtime. Your type is drunk on novelty, not reality" (3, 4). In the early *Wolf*, Harrison muses that America was "becoming Europe in my own lifetime and I felt desperate" (44), by which he means that America is becoming materialistic, overly refined and overly populated, self-consciously verbal, and pretentious.

In the much later *Off to the Side*, Harrison admits that New York and Paris are made tolerable only by his habit of walking several hours a day (274).

In *True North* David Burkett IV, a young writer-anthropologist-environmentalist who wishes in odd moments that he was "Jewish, black, or Indian so [he] would have something valid to complain about" (129), meets Sharon, a waitress-poet wannabe who writes under the name "Vernice" because it's more dashing. "She was from far southern Indiana," Harrison tells us, "but wanted to be a 'city poet' so she moved to Chicago" (130) and studied up on city poets and on Cesare Pavese, Valéry, Ponge, Corbière, and the *Tao te Ching* . . . as well as Yeats, Kavanaugh, William Carlos Williams, Pound, Olson, and Duncan. Vernice uses words like "epistemology," "phrenology," and "otiose," and informs David that poetry is not an obsession, but a calling. The two have a brief affair, but inevitably Vernice gets the French wine, the fancy food, her own published book of poems, and a "prominent" poet for a lover.[19] When the lover receives a Guggenheim, the "Queen of Poetry" (197) gets Paris . . . and then Aix-en-Provence, and then Chicago again when the couple splits up, having decided that poets shouldn't live with poets. Of course both are poor as family farmers, and when David sends Vernice money, she gives half to her poet. In exchange for tepid sex and help editing his journal, David finally buys Vernice an airplane ticket home, so she can work on a sex novel that, one editor claims, is "elegant but not very erotic, too literary" (334). This is the sort of American, Harrison suggests, who loves living in France, and this is what happens to the sort of American who loves living in France.

Academics, being pretty much disconnected from place, take it pretty much on the chin from Harrison . . . and not just the Queens of Poetry and their tall, tortured poet-lovers. His satire of academics begins with his first novel, *Wolf*:

I called an acquaintance in Vermont, a teacher at one of those small colleges in New England that turn out a distinctive brand of adult by the cultivation of a certain style of inclusive discipline. The point is not like the Marines, to make "a man out of you," but to make a gentleman with isolatable characteristics. Later, after they graduate, these young men recognize each other, without previously meeting, as "Tulipberg Men." They avert their eyes and blush, then slam together in an arcane embrace yelling secret words and exchanging earlicks. Harvard, Yale, Princeton, Dartmouth are less obvious about such things. The superiority is assumed. (71)

A dozen or more addled professors appear in the books that follow, and Harrison's other characters who have attended schools like Macalester, Brown, and Yale are pretentious and self-conscious. The only academic with any guts at all is Nelse Northridge, who threatens his senior professor with "racism, ethnic slurs, academic fascism and whatever" when the man calls him a romantic humanist and a mixed-blood Lakota (171). Michael, Dalva's teacher from Stanford, is a smooth-talking yuppie con man—Russell Chatham calls him "a dipshit" (Reilly 119)—who loses what grace and common sense he ever had the moment he steps out of the classroom. As a grad student Michael stole books from the library and faked the interviews on which he based his dissertation. Since graduating he has bought snappy clothes and a BMW, lost a wife, banged at least one student, developed Harrison's own obsession with gourmet dining and fine wines (he and Harrison also have similar tastes in writers and musicians), and used a one-hour quick read of a Fodor guide to scam a student committee into choosing him—not the lumpy woman from the Russian department or the black linguist who actually speaks Russian—as mentor-guide for a trip to Russia. Michael binges on drugs and alcohol, and obsesses over a private school education for a daughter who does not really want a private school education. He is using Dalva and her family—and she knows it—to access family papers that will give him the book upon which his tenure depends:

> The center of the difficulty was that a professor from the University of Wisconsin on the grants committee had previously been denied access to our papers and had demanded proof of Michael's access as a contingency to the grant. He had to deliver this permission in a week's time to his own chairman at Stanford. At this point, if he couldn't do so, he would lose his grant, sabbatical, and very probably his job due to "moral turpitude"—i.e., lying—no matter that the students had voted him teacher of the year for his lecturing techniques, his wonderfully amusing oratory. If he lost his job his daughter would have to be withdrawn from private school which would break her heart. (63).[20]

Unable to manage any real connection with the landscape, history, and social structures contained in those papers, Michael is at a loss to understand them, and Dalva's comments on Michael's obtuse interpretation constitute satire on the level of Swift. "I have never met a man less in touch with the 'dailiness of life,' so relentlessly blind to his immediate surroundings," muses Dalva's mother Naomi (*Road* 306). As an outlander in Nebraska, "Michael's bumblings are indeed comical," Reilly observes (121), as he loses successive encounters with geese, horses, black snakes, pheasants . . . and the father of Karen Olafson, the high school girl he partners up with.

In "Brown Dog" Harrison creates a more attractive predator-academic, an anthropology grad student named Shelley, who drives a Land Rover, snorts cocaine, dresses in Patagonia clothes, and pals around with a new-age yuppie colleague named Tarah and two male anthropologists whom Brown Dog identifies only as Jerk and Jerkoff. Shelley is using Brown Dog to locate some Indian burial mounds she and her friends hope to (and finally do) excavate, thereby securing her position in the academic world. Both Shelley and Tarah are as neurotic as Michael; Shelley has been "probed from eight to eighteen at who knows what cost" (*Woman* 9) by a string of psychiatrists, therapists, and psychologists because her father was distant and her uncle used her sexually on camping trips.[21] Tarah believes that a Taos "empowerment ceremony" has made her one with nature, yet loses her marbles at the sound of a bear cub crying after its mother. Brown Dog strings them along for the sex, feeling guilty over the plundering of a heritage he'd promised to protect, but enjoying the laughs as he feeds them Indian malarkey in the tradition of Coyote, the trickster:

She was sitting in what she called a "full locust" and you couldn't help but wonder what was possible with a woman with that much stretch in her limbs. She fixed her green eyes on me.

"What did you become? I could see your trance state was very deep."

"I became a big condor from olden times. I was feeding on a dead buffalo I scared off a cliff." I fibbed, remembering a trip to the Field Museum when I was on the bum in Chicago. If you're in Chicago you should go see these ancient stuffed animals.

"That's truly wonderful, B. D. It means your spirit wishes to soar far above your current problems. Your spirit wishes to use your condor being and blood to help you. In order to do this you must not deny the proud heritage of your people. You must let us help you rediscover your heritage." (*Woman* 27)

In "The Seven-Ounce Man," Harrison continues the adventures of Brown Dog, introducing Lone Martin, the outside agitator-artiste-former AIM member, who creates The Wild Wild Midwest Show as a tourist attraction and assists Brown Dog in his attack on Shelley's camp before whisking him off to California for a colloquium at UCLA on the subject "Will Whitey Ever See Red?"

Harrison's ultimate academic is Phillip Caulkins, fifty-year-old prof at an unnamed Michigan college, a private school which, like so many other small midwestern private schools, calls itself, "The Swarthmore of the Midwest." Like other Harrison academics, he is divorced (his former wife had a fling with his dean) and a former *wunderkind* (his analysis of Christopher Smart and John Clare, titled *The Economics of Madness in English Poetry*, brought him tenure at age thirty). Unlike Michael from Stanford, Phillip has behaved himself—not that behaving one's self matters much in post-1980 academia, when sexual (and even non-sexual) harassment can mean anything it is politically useful for anyone to want it to mean. Phillip's problems begin in April, when the dress of coeds has changed with the season; he greets a group of girls in his Milton class with "Good morning, you ladies are looking lovely today." Naturally, he is charged with sexism. The problems continue when he uses an umbrella to shield himself from a runaway hoard of Earth Day demonstrators and accidentally pokes one of the mimes with its point, when his car bumps the basketball coach's auto and he nearly fails a Breathalyzer test, when he accidentally locks himself out of his apartment wearing only his underpants, and when he quotes from Ezra Pound, a known anti-Semite, in a course on English poetics. Because "ounces eventually added up to pounds" (*Julip* 207), Caulkins is vulnerable to the dean's blackmail: if Caulkins will supervise Elizabeth's senior thesis, then the dean will purge his record. Elizabeth is the fourth generation in her family to attend the college. Elizabeth is not particularly bright and definitely dislocated, having spent one year pretending to be Jewish after spending the previous year pretending to be Indian. She is apparently having a relationship with a younger creative writing teacher whose low-grade arts magazine Caulkins helped to torpedo. Elizabeth, who coincidentally filed the anti-Semitism charge, wants to write on "Sexism in Yeats":

> "I guess what I want to say is that Yeats's creepy values are repulsive to today's women," she said, offering a tentative smile.

It was at this point I began to develop a sense of suffocation, as if I were in a dentist's chair to get wisdom teeth pulled, the gas mask strapped to my face but nothing in the tank, nothing at all that could be drawn by the breath. The problem had nothing to do with feminism (I had lived with two brilliant and shrewd examples in my wife and daughter) but with simple stupidity, also the profoundest sense that I was betraying a code of values, a tradition. (*Julip* 210)

One day two sorority sisters drop Elizabeth at Caulkins's apartment to work on her paper. Wearing a deep V-neck T-shirt, a short skirt, and sandals, she corners him in the kitchen, gives him a kiss, an embrace, and a fondle, then hikes up her skirt and fumbles at his fly. The sorority sisters are waiting in the next room when she begins to screech and sob, chirping as if on cue: "What have you done to her?" "[I]t didn't take any prescience on my part to realize my goose was cooked," Caulkins muses (213).

This story is in part Harrison's revenge on feminist ideologues who could never tolerate the sex in his books, and any college prof would understand that a co-ed could dispense with the embrace and the fondle and just file a charge, but any male who taught in American colleges during the 1980s and '90s will also understand that Harrison's scenario is not over the top in depicting what passes for life in academia these days. "Beware of the deep manipulativeness of rich students who were neglected by their parents," writes Camille Paglia; "They love to turn the campus into hysterical psychodramas of sexual transgression, followed by assertions of parental authority and concern" (53). As we will see shortly, Caulkins gets an extreme make-over in the desert Southwest (the lone Harrison academic to achieve redemption in place) and ends up happier outside of academia than inside. In this regard he thinks much like Harrison himself, who in *Just Before Dark* wrote, "I am not going to spend my increasingly precious days stuffing leaks in an educational system as perverse and sodden as the mercantile society for which it supplies faithful and ignorant fodder" (294).[22]

In one incarnation, of course, Harrison himself was the postmodernist prof of *Wolf* (69), the highly regarded Francophile poet on a Guggenheim, who, while he likes to believe that the number one disease in postmodern literature is subjectivity (*Just* 297), can be just as subjective as anyone else and can write just as pretentious an essay about writing as anyone else. Harrison, like Swanson in *Wolf*, "wanders the wilderness in an attempt to transcend the banality of a society at odds with itself, all the while recalling and reconstituting his reality in terms of the books he has read" (Smith 5, 6). Harrison is as full as anybody of new-age psychologies of the Hillman-Laing-Horney-Adler-Jung-Bly school and has spent his share of time and money on psychoanalysts (see DeMott 159).[23] Harrison's novels are often betrayed into postmodernist disorganization by literary models,[24] and Harrison himself is betrayed into the world of postmodernist dislocation by his obsession to do, see, and be it all . . . and especially by the seductions of language and literature which are not his own. He understands this fact even while performing it. He is a reluctant postmodernist who embodies the multivocalities and ironies he himself considers the curse of modern fiction or "showing off."

A conversation in the suggestively titled *The Road Home* implies that when it comes to postmodern alienation, the writer (and the reader) chooses his own poison by creating the conditions which cause his alienation. Grandfather John Wesley Northridge II has been able to reconcile his Depression-era faith in progress with memories of the simple, utterly basic life. His grandson Nelse argues that "everything we deem natural" has disappeared or would soon disappear, citing as evidence his father's own house with its carpeted bathrooms and taboo on the mere mention of sex. Grandfather Northridge points out that "the old life is still everywhere," although now the garden is "only flowers a black man comes in once a week to tend" (234). He even suggests that he's ready to return to the Lutheran Church he left when Nelse was a young boy. Grandfather Northridge has gone out and come back; Nelse has not. "I also said our civilization is its own religion and that's why we're in such a total mess. But we're not a mess, he [dad] said, it's the fact that you think it's a mess that makes your life so problematical" (235). Had Nelse been a character in a different novel, he might have responded with, "Maybe so, but then the television doesn't portray the outside world as an attractive place" (*Sundog* xi). Ultimately it's a matter of faith, and Jim Harrison seems both to believe and disbelieve. He is, as I pointed out earlier, both John Wesley and Nelse.

Jim Harrison is most comfortable—and convincing—when writing about home. Given the dichotomies of French cuisine and the UP favorite of french fries with a ladle of gravy, of rare wines and a cold beer, of thing and idea, of academic discourse and the language of the people, of the landscape of New York or Paris and rural Michigan, when it is time to find *The Road Home* or *True North*, Harrison comes down mostly, ambivalently, on the side of the place where he began:

You could travel west out of Reed City, a small county seat in an unfertile valley with a small yellow brick courthouse and a plugged cannon on its lawn next to a marble slab with the names of the World War One and Two dead inscribed in gold and the not dead plainly inscribed with the suspicious neatness of cemetery script, *those who served*, farther west through fifty miles of pine barrens dotted with small farm settlements often of less than thirty people, or merely a grocery store and gas station adjoined by a shabby aluminum trailer or a basement house with the first and perhaps second stories awaiting more prosperous times, the stores themselves with little and aged stock—lunch meat, bologna pickled in a jar, Polish sausage, tinned foods covered with dust, plaquettes of fish lures, mosquito repellent in aerosol cans, live bait and a pop cooler outside the door—but not many of these—a narrow road through mixed conifers, cedar and jack pine, some stunted scrub oak, birch, and the short-lived poplar, a pulp tree usually living less than twenty years and clotting the woods floor with its rotting trunks and branches. (*Wolf* 17)

From one perspective, Harrison admits in *Off to the Side*, his periodic returns to Michigan are a romantic desire to retreat to the past, an example of that "most extreme and improbable yearning, no matter that it is a homesickness for a home that never quite existed, a longing for a pre-lapsarian, Adamic existence that the mind creates out of filaments of idealized memories, as if by finding a similar landscape I could return myself to a state before everyone started dying" (205). You can't go home again, because there never was any home in the first place, or it's been transformed by developers as John Lundgren discovers in *Warlock*, or the towns and schools built on small family farms are lost in an age of corporate farming as Joseph Lundgren discovers in *Farmer*. Return is only "a literary urging" (*Good Day* 92). Smith sees *Wolf* as "a literary recreation of place" (29); Harrison saw *Farmer* as homage "to a way of life that was almost totally vanished" (Reilly 60), and was as disappointed when it failed almost as badly as the family farm.

From a different perspective, the home place is simply a fact of biography, neither romanticized nor debunked, "merely the given" (*Off* 9). In looking back, Harrison finds not sentimentality but "something closer to the Portuguese notion of *saudade*, a person or place or sense of life irretrievably lost; a shadow of your own making that follows you, and though often forgotten can at any moment give rise to heartache, an obtuse sentimentality, a sharp anger that you are not located where you wish to be" (*Off* 23). One of Harrison's most complex figures, his female alter-ego, Dalva, finds enough place, family, and history back in Nebraska to restore a soul wasted by seven years of Santa Monica. There are always remnants, Harrison suggests, usually contained in some dark subterranean or subaqueous cave: the hollow stump of a white pine (*True North*), the burial mounds of ancestors ("The Seven-Ounce Man"), the preserved corpse of a drowned Indian chief ("Brown Dog"), the family journals locked in the bank vault (*Dalva*), the museum of relics in the sub-basement (*The Road Home*). Harrison repeatedly finds restoration in returning from the world of high culture and abstract ideas to rural place and to simple manual labor (laying concrete blocks, hunting, fishing, and just plain walking): "Trout fishing and grouse hunting maintained my often slumping spirits when nothing else would work except possibly my daughter Jamie and an English point puppy" (*Off* 207).

As a writer, Harrison is at his surest on the home turf. His preference is for . . . not "regional literature" but "literature with a pronounced regional flavor" (DeMott 70). In 1981 Harrison told *Contemporary Authors* that northern Michigan, "where I was born and raised," is "the only place I've ever been able to write" (DeMott 23). Except for Key West, the Sandhills region of western Nebraska, Montana, and the Patagonia region of Arizona—places in which Harrison has lived and spent a great deal of time—his descriptions tend to fade or fail outside of Michigan. *Legends of the Fall* offers no sense at all of Europe, or of Dar es Salaam, Singapore, Manila, Panama, Cape Horn, Rio, Dakar, Havana—these are mere names on a map. The Laramie of *Wolf* seems borrowed from Kerouac, the New York and Boston from Salinger, the Salt Lake City from Steinbeck. The private college in southern Michigan ("The Beige Dolorosa"), Stanford University (*Dalva*), San Francisco and Oakland in the sixties (*Sunset Limited* in *Woman Lit*), and Ohio University (*True North*) have a vague wasn't-there-for-long feel.[25]

In Michigan and Nebraska, however, Harrison has the local fauna and flora down cold, including the smell of the town ("depending on the wind: fresh-cut pine and creosote"—*Just* 139) and the image of ground ivy, which triggered the idea of *Farmer* and opens the novel: "Ground ivy, *glecoma hederaceae*, or called gill-over-the-ground: it spread from the pump shed attached to the kitchen out to the barnyard where it disappeared under cow and horse hooves and the frenetic scratching of chickens. . . . It was a fact of life" (3). He knows other facts of life as well: when a pinched finger brings blood under the nail, drill a hole into the nail with a pocket knife. When cutting pulp, watch out for widow-makers. "Fools drank water from a stream going through a cedar swamp and often were violently ill far from help. Unless the stream is big, has a strong current, is far from civilization, you should boil all water. . . . I once drew water fifty yards downstream from a deer carcass half in the stream and stinking" (*Wolf* 47). "[I]f a chicken fed on wintergreen, chokecherries, wild grape it would taste as good as a grouse" (*Farmer* 19). "Trout don't care for water much above sixty, and they'll travel up and downstream to seek the cooler waters of swamps or locales where there are feeder creeks, seeps or springs" (*Sundog* 103). "An owl hitting a rabbit makes the rabbit scream like a woman which will startle you when you're in the woods at night. The yelping a bunch of coyotes make chasing a deer or rabbit will tend to make you light-hearted while a wolf's howl makes your mind lose its balance" (*Woman* 39). "Lift your dick slightly to avoid peeing on your pant leg" (*True North* 240).

Much of this is a culture the rest of the country, like Michael the Stanford professor, considers "an America I supposed to be vanished" (*Dalva* 121), but it's still around, a little bit in life and a lot in memory. Although he does not use it much in his early novels, Harrison remembers a Swedish American "pickled in amber" farm culture—"what now seems the nineteenth century" (*Just* 98)—not much different from Bill Holm's pickled-in-amber Icelandic American world around Minneota, or, for that matter, Norbert Blei's Little Bohemia:

I can return at will to a summer dawn in an upstairs room where I was confined: in a corner were three old trunks from Sweden with stickers in that foreign language, and lined with pasted newspaper I think from Göteborg (Gothenburg). I hear the screen door of the pump shed slam and in the dim light I can see my grandfather heading to the barn with two pails of milk skimmed for the calves. The rooster won't stop crowing. There has been a little rain in the night and I can smell the damp garden, the strong winey smell of the grape arbor, the bacon grease from the kitchen below. My older brother, John, runs out the pump-shed door followed by my maiden great-aunt Anna carrying a pail of slop for the hogs. Both John and I loved to watch pigs feeding at their trough. . . . Anna turns now to the gathering chickens and John has retrieved ground-shell corn [sic] from the granary and he and Anna broadcast it out to the frantic chickens with Anna pausing to scratch her arms which are covered with psoriasis. Grandpa has finished milking and turned the cows and the two big draft horses out to pasture. . . . He carries the milk to the house and soon I hear the cream separator whirring. Sometimes I'm allowed to turn the crank and this whirling machine divides the cream and the skim milk fed to the calves and pigs. We eat the heavy thick cream on our cereal. In bad weather I'm allowed to fork down hay from the mow to the horses and cows. Across from the granary is an outside toilet called a privy. (*Off* 10)

The midwestern character, which Harrison understands so well, has not changed much. The modest lifestyle and hurried meals: "The prescient ones in the restaurant who have eaten much more slowly than the couple have made up their minds. It is a farmer and his wife. And likely from the midwest, as the farmers from the west, ranchers, tend to dress more extravagantly, and those from the east with enough money to travel wear more fashionable clothing" (*Farmer* 2). The understated humor and emotional restraint: "Joseph had found himself in a rare public act of affection: he lifted her hand and kissed it. She was taken aback" (*Farmer* 8). The way everyone in the community (especially a mother) knows everyone's business and history and family dimensions, and speaks frankly about it to them and others, with no real malice or judgment:

> "Just out this way hunting and thought I'd stop by." He refused a drink.
> "No you weren't," Joseph said. "Your boots are dry and I heard you got a buck the second day of the season." Joseph poured himself a drink. "You're out here trying to get me to apologize to those pompous assholes." He laughed. "How much did your deer dress at?" (*Farmer* 27)

The candid speech: " 'Here's what I mean and right on the money.' The doctor lit his pipe and stared at the steamy window" (*Farmer* 96). The value placed on tools . . . and in a grudging manner, on education. The winter games of cribbage and pinochle.

Harrison is not entirely kind to the midwestern mentality. In *The Road Home* he calls it, at least in part, "a bumpkin idiocy that would die quickly elsewhere under intelligent scrutiny, the exception being the Deep South" (68). The bestiality jokes and crude bar talk. The drinking and fighting. The brittleness of temper in the waning months of winter. The lesson of nature: kill or be killed. Midwestern Protestantism can give a kid the "naive New Testament brain" (*Wolf* 59), especially on the matter of sex, of which Bill Holm, Garrison Keillor, and Jim Heynen all complain: "Sexually, the U. P. was a sensory deprivation tank. That's why they sedated themselves with booze, my own special poison" (*Sundog* 137). In *True North*, David Burkett writes, "[I]f I actually thought I was looking into the heart of evil in my family I ought to include their sense of Christianity which they viewed as a further entitlement for their conquests" (156). Patrick Smith points out that the very restlessness which allows Joseph in *Farmer* to dream of other places is out of place in his culture (61).

Then there is the weather: "In this age where every niche on earth has been discovered and rediscovered countless times, there is an open secret why the upper Midwest is generally ignored: it is relatively charmless, and it competes with Siberia for the least hospitable climate on earth" (*Sundog* 6).

Oddly, religion provides a solid foundation on which to build, or, in the case of the Burketts and Northridges, a coherent doctrine against which to rebel and return to . . . or, like Joseph Lundgren's mother's conservative Swedish piety, a set of values to balance Catherine's brassy new-age sexuality and Robert's new-age homosexuality. And inside the austere Protestantism linger vestiges of the Grange and the People's Party and the Socialist Party, a prairie populism which is oddly tied to religion (*Wolf* 131), a populism which inspired Blaine, Debs, and Sandburg and which infuses the thought and writing of Bill Holm and Dave Etter, as well as the protests of the sixties. "My ancestors, inasmuch as they were literate, were Populists," announces the narrator of *Wolf* (115); "Up the road in the schoolhouse there were Communist Party meetings during the Depression" (219). Not too far back in Joseph Lundgren's family tree in *Farmer* is a great-aunt who left home at a young age and "wrote she had become a Communist. Even that wasn't so terrible as her father was basically a Populist who read Herbert Croly and Lincoln Steffens and whose hero had been Eugene Debs" (126). When Brown Dog was a student at the Moody Bible Institute, he got tangled up in a student protest, led the charge against police, and got kicked out of school (*Woman* 6). Harrison himself once organized a strike of restaurant busboys in Estes

Park (*Wolf* 136). His Populist background, Harrison writes in the MA thesis reprinted in *Just Before Dark*, made it impossible for him to become comfortably absorbed in the modernists' concerns (198). Of others in the Upper Peninsula he writes, "many people up here strike me as more populist than conservative, and there is the kind of generalized suspicion of Big Government that one finds in non-urban Arizona" (*Just* 73).

A firm base in Calvinism may also serve to keep a kid—or a writer—more or less between the fences ("My own specious Calvinist breeding made me unable to cheat," remarks the narrator of *A Good Day to Die* on page 40, and later on page 131, "All lapsed Calvinists continue to crave that simple monism by which everything is excusable because it is inevitable. 'God willed it' when one still believed, and after that, 'At least I'm honest' "). Most of all, midwesterners believe in sticking things out, complaining little if at all, grinding ahead, being solid and reliable and self-possessed (this is Nordstrom's main virtue in "The Man Who Gave Up His Name," and Strang's in *Sundog*). Perhaps this is the reason that both humor and sex fade slightly in Harrison's later writings: they were borrowed traits, with which he was never entirely comfortable.

The populism, the tough guy self-image, and the Protestantism[26] combine to produce a work ethic for which the Midwest is justifiably famous, even though Harrison—like Garrison Keillor and Bill Holm—finds it something of a nuisance at times. In his memoir *Off to the Side*, Harrison mentions with some ambivalence the "Midwest backdrop where all good things come from hard work and grit" (188). However, neither Harrison's characters nor the writer himself can escape the work ethic. "My work was my play in that it always gave me tremendous pleasure," says Robert Strang in *Sundog* (35), and even when epilepsy and a couple of near-fatal accidents have reduced him to a regimen of painful physical therapy for his legs, Strang tells us, "I do the crawling because it's the only work at hand and I'm a worker and it's my only chance to get back to my real work" (63). In an interview with Gregory Skwira, Harrison linked Strang to himself: "My pleasure in life is just work itself, not the reward. Just like Strang and his dams" (Reilly 113). "Oddly the grace note of my own early life," he mentions in *Off to the Side*, "was manual labor" (59); thus the "ideal MFA writing program would require one year of manual labor in the country; one year of life in the city; one year spent along [sic] reading; and only then would anyone return and begin writing" (DeMott 162).

In *True North*, narrator David Burkett turns an overnight visit into a "fine week" by helping his sister and brother-in-law retile their septic system and dig footings and hand-mix cement for new porch steps. "It was tough going but the exhaustion was wonderful," he remarks (148).[27] Brown Dog and his grandfather developed a philosophy which he calls "don't Doggett" after second cousin Lester Doggett; the philosophy is "what Grandpa said to me when I whined, complained or expressed any self-pity. It still means to stand up and take your medicine, though it doesn't mean you can't get even" (*Woman* 25). Having lost his college teaching job, Phillip Caulkins moves to the desert Southwest and finds unfamiliar satisfaction in working as a cowboy—not exactly a hand, but a respectable helper: "My bones ache and my body is bruised. We trucked the last of the cattle to Tucson three days ago, barely making it across the creek. I have been paid five hundred dollars for the over three weeks of work and the amount, though absurdly small, has thrilled me to no end" (*Julip* 234). Offered a return to the college, Caulkins decides he "wouldn't return to the college at gunpoint" (*Julip* 248); instead he has sex with a Mexican chiquita and outwits a gang of dope peddlers. "All of us work," Dalva tells readers; "My mother has an involved theory of work that she claims comes from my father, uncles, grandparents, and on into the past: people have an instinct to be useful and can't handle the relentless *everydayness* of life unless they work hard" (*Dalva* 12).

Harrison understands the premium midwesterners place on "thingness." For an epigraph to *Just Before Dark*, Harrison selected a Wallace Stevens quotation: "The worst of all things is not to live in a physical world." This preference for a physical world is reinforced by William Carlos Williams ("no ideas but in things") and Zen philosophy, and it underlies his articles on hunting, fishing, travel, and food. Among Harrison's fictional creations, Brown Dog is perhaps closest to unrefined experience and data, and therefore the most savvy, resilient, content, and open to his surroundings. "You have to know a great deal about food and shelter and the stalking of game and many of the aspects of this knowledge come only through astute, almost instinctive openness to your surroundings," Harrison writes in *Wolf* (173). Looking over his journals, and his life, in *The Road Home*, John Wesley Northridge II finds this attention to detail the one redemptive quality in his youthful romantic self: "I simply had no gift for abstract thought at the time and what saved me were the countless afternoons of sketching which was a visceral act" (54). "I checked my journals for that European trip and was amazed at their banality, as if a literate chimpanzee had been taken on its first trip to the zoo. None of the emotions, the feelings, the moods, as it were, had any interest, while descriptions of buildings, crowds, meals, and paintings still held a tinge of fascination. The latter were textural concretia while the former were romantic filagree" (67).

The natural world becomes a base from which we press upward into abstraction and metaphysics, but the distancing can cause trouble and always needs correction. "It has become apparent to many that the ultimate disease, the abyss of postmodernism in art and literature, is subjectivity, and that the disease is both sociopathic and terminal" (*Just* 297). The problem seems to be that we make the leap from concrete to abstract too early in life, and have to backtrack, reconstruct, or recover. Harrison himself recalls his experience of losing reality and recovering reality in the final essay of *Just Before Dark*: "I had begun to swim in waters that sensible folks would readily drown in, mostly in the area of consensual reality. The therapy began to take effect and my outward life gradually became more and more absorbed in hunting and fishing, and walks in the undifferentiated wilderness of the U.P." (312). Dalva, whom Harrison has often identified as his female Other, also understands the primacy of things and advances a "theory that we can only go so far with thinking, and then our minds have to be refilled by the 'thingness' of life — landscapes, creatures, any sort of travel, people we could not imagine not having existed" (*Road* 390–91). One remembers Bill Holm, another bookworm, with his sense of "from-ness."

In relating character to place, Harrison advances several bioregionalist arguments. Certainly he realizes that in writing "you tell the story that emerges from the locale" (Reilly 17), and "character so often arises out of location" (DeMott 172). In *Dalva* especially, Reilly notes, the characters' lives are "shaped, defined, and identified by the landscapes" (130). Weather in Harrison's fiction often determines mood and thus behavior. "In the upper Midwest, no doubt due to the weather, many things are considered chores — including funerals, weddings, baptisms — that need to be accomplished with a certain dispatch," Dalva muses, explaining the midwestern work ethic (29). Trying in *A Good Day to Die* to explain a gang of sixties activists, Harrison's narrator recalls his childhood in Michigan and speculates, "Maybe the cold makes us more economically resourceful" (53). It is the midwestern emptiness which over generations produces "a certain lonely farmboy type" who "wants to know everything" from Spanish to how to disassemble a Ford V-8 engine

(*Legends* 19). Conversely, in *The Road Home* Paul Northridge speculates that women of the Southwest are more interested in astrology than those of the East because the stars are more visible there (350). And certainly nature creates the opportunity for hunting, and hunting in turn creates character.

In *Wolf* Harrison suggests a Darwinian process of natural selection as Finns were imported to the Upper Peninsula "as coolie labor and stuck to the area because of the snow and cold and short summers. It reminded them of another uninhabitable planet, their homeland" (69). Naturalist Nelse Northridge points out, "The periodic recurrence of natural phenomena such as bird nesting and migrating as related to time, also mammals screwing and having their young, also tree budding and leafing, plants coming to flower" are "all related to local climate and precise time of year" (*Road* 374). After environment selects and shapes the human population, and the human population self-selects to the environment, place becomes part of genetic inheritance. In *Just Before Dark*, Harrison writes, "A girl in New York City once told me I talked like Herb Shriner. It takes many generations of rural indigence to make a Herb Shriner voice, long evenings of pinochle around a kerosene stove trying to pick up Chicago on a ten-dollar radio" (55).

Although he is in love with Keats's idea of "negative capability," and with new-age psychological notions of "Other," birth twins, and soul-building, Harrison repeatedly suggests that in shaping character, the nurture of nature is inescapable. Because the narrator of *Wolf* grew up in Michigan, he can't adjust to the city: "when I am in New York seven or fifteen floors above the ground I get vertigo. I simply can't adjust to layers and layers of people below and above me. I suffer excruciatingly on airplanes" (70). Dalva cannot escape the midwestern notion, promoted by the landscape, that "anything too tall tips over. Stick your head out and you might get it cut off. Only the grain elevators are allowed to emerge" (31). Regional patterns of thought and behavior persist outside of the region, an inescapable lifelong take on life evident in Harrison's own life and theories. "Not to push it too far," Harrison writes in *Off to the Side*, "but there's certainly an element of stalking in a New York or Los Angeles meeting, and when you enter a saloon you are prone to study which of the couple of dozen human animals there might present a problem" (106).

Although Harrison sometimes suggests—in the manner of William Kloefkorn—that the losses of place and time may be healed by place fixed in memory and writing,[28] redemption usually requires a physical turn to place. Proximity to nature and Indians, Harrison suggests, can provide a counterweight to alienation . . . besides, "Eastern college girls especially like the part Indian bit" (*Wolf* 106). Redemption in nature—through fishing, farming, ranch work, walking, botanical study, even travel, or (in the case of redemption through human nature) through sex—is Harrison's primary theme, as the destruction worked on nature by civilization is his secondary theme. That is because restoration in place is his primary experience: healing from the experiences in New York City, Boston, and Los Angeles came in returning to Michigan. Writes Harrison, "If you hunt or fish a couple of weeks in a row without reading newspapers or watching television news a certain not altogether deserved grace can reenter your life" (*Off* 104).

Many novels replicate their author's experience. William Barillas describes *Wolf, Sundog,* "Brown Dog," and "Seven-Ounce Man" as "pastorals in the Cooper/Hemingway tradition, featuring male characters escaping from civilization into wilderness, sex, and occasionally violence" (244). In *A Good Day to Die* Harrison's narrator says, "[T]here was no sense of balance left . . . I needed a few days of fishing to sort my feelings out" (77). Likewise *The Road Home,* John Wesley Northridge II recalls, "I got off the horse to let her water, inhaling deeply from a handful of crushed flowers I had grabbed from a bush. Holy God, I thought aloud, where am I and do I care? I am simply at this creek at this moment, kneeling and drinking, rinsing my face in the moonlight, my senses as fully alive as any ancient animal's" (105). The Northridge land in Nebraska, like Strang's cabin in the Upper Peninsula and Harrison's own home, is "idyllic, a haven to which Dalva returns to heal her personal world-hurts—as do, by extension, Naomi, Ruth, Dalva's son Nelse, and Michael" (Reilly 129, 130). Brown Dog admits that his favorite life choice is just walking in the woods, which, like Harrison, he can do for days on end. "Nature has erased my occasional urge toward suicide," Caulkins confesses in Arizona (*Julip* 246). The fact that Caulkins, who was not born to rural living, can reclaim his life suggests that even those of us who were raised in the city and the suburbs carry some memory and feel some sense of displacement from nature which needs answering, and will respond to a season in the wilderness. Even Michael, the Stanford prof, finds temporarily "that rare feeling of being more than myself, that my human failings were being absorbed by the leaves in the trees above us, and perhaps the darkening sky above the trees was helping out" (*Dalva* 155). Cochran, a fighter pilot turned yuppie tennis player who is so far from his place that "he realized he had no home" (89) recovers from a nearly fatal beating at a peasant's hacienda, "a green world, a huge vegetable garden with the rows raised between small trenches for irrigation, and beyond that, some sheds and corrals holding a big Percheron and three sorry-looking quarter horses, a few sheep, a large pen of pigs and some milking goats" (*Legends* 38). He finds a "new life that made the old seem a light-year away, flat and stale as a bad magazine article" (43). Clare, the fifty-something wife of an unconvincingly loutish businessman, climbs the fence at a welcome center on I-80 and walks away from him and a marriage of thirty years to reclaim herself in an Iowa cornfield.[29] In the novel *Farmer*, Joseph drifts into an affair with Catherine, which takes him socially, if not physically, for all practical purposes out of place and community, into what Patrick Smith aptly calls "the unreality of the books through which he has educated himself and through which he has gained most of his knowledge of the outside world" (67). Joseph's "renewed clarity of purpose upon his spiritual return home from a year-long crisis" and recognition of "the advantages of living in a place where people look out for each other" (71) mark salvation in place for one who never physically left. This is Harrison's "triumphant avowal of the power of place—not the place that forces its appeal on us through its novelty, but the familiar place that renews itself and heals us through its simply stated everydayness, the dichotomy of life and death that delves deep into our existence and, finally, so readily affirms life" (72). What happy endings there are in Harrison's work all involve integration or reintegration into place.

Then there are the other novels. Renewal in place is often only temporary, and for Harrison personal renewal in place is one of at least two options, perhaps three. In a 1997 interview with Terry Phipps, Harrison spoke of another kind of renewal: long trips in his car, pointed nowhere, enclosed in a small moving space far from Michigan or Patagonia or western Nebraska. In his fondness for car trips, Harrison resembles his neighbor across the lake, Norbert Blei. He finds this kind of disconnectedness as beneficial as rootedness, especially for a writer:

Many artists are permanently dislocated. In this world, it probably makes them more functional.

Place anonymity—that's why I like interminable car trips. I think my longest one ever was eleven or twelve thousand miles around the United States. I like complete freedom, and you're not a target because you're moving and nobody can get to you except by your permission; so it's like "Brown Dog" in a sense; he's free. He has no papers. His only mail is every four years; he gets a notice to renew his driver's license—that's all. But sometimes what they get in the bad sense is that old sense of army brats where they never had any home really to even long for. . . .

I've always been a Steinbeck fan. There was a Steinbeck scholar up here for a couple of days talking to me this year, and I had brought up that point that he had met many people in *Travels with Charley* and enjoyed this freedom of the road and freedom of movement. When somebody says, in the Thoreau sense, does he own the farm, or does the farm own him? Like a teacher-writer sometimes is, once he makes the down payment on the house and has a kid or two, then his mobility is permanently atrophied, and consequently it becomes easier to kiss ass because it's the only thing there is to do. (DeMott 168–69)

The moving car is a countersymbol for the cave, the hollow stump, the thicket, the dark sub-basement, in which Harrison's characters sometimes store their psychic history.

In places like *The Theory and Practice of Rivers*, Harrison finds his renewal in river, the same sense of freedom and escape that Twain offers in *The Adventures of Huckleberry Finn* or Kloefkorn offers in *Loup River Psalter*: "In four days of work I would develop stress-related eczema, and then in two days of fishing this skin disease would retreat back into its venomous lair," Harrison writes in a *Field and Stream* article titled "Fifty Days on the Water: The Only Answer to an Insane World Is an Insane Amount of Trout Fishing." In 1986 Harrison told Jim Fergus, "In a life properly lived, you're a river. You touch things lightly or deeply; you move along because life herself moves, and you can't stop it; you can't figure out a banal game plan applicable to all situations; you just have to [g]o with the 'beingness' of life, as Rilke would have it. In *Sundog*, Strang says a dam doesn't stop a river, it just controls the flow. Technically speaking, you can't stop one at all" (DeMott 65). Talking with Eleanor Wachtel in 1998 Harrison suggested, "If you're willing to say try it sometime, sit down on a stone or a cushion or just on the bank of a river for two solid hours. And you find, if you're willing to give up everything, or open up a bit, the river does absorb rather nonchalantly your poisons" (DeMott 180).[30] Patrick Smith suggests that for Harrison water carries its baptismal significance: it "gradually washes away the psychic offal accreted through years of experience and the subsequent bittersweet memories" (28), and Harrison himself writes in *A Good Day to Die*, "For a few hours though all problems—money, sex, alcohol, generalized craziness—disappeared in concentrating on the flow of water" (121).[31]

Elsewhere, following Jean François Lyotard, he uses the dream to embody this fluidity, this disjunction, this lack of focus; he is a great believer in dreams and finds his material in dreams. Harrison concludes an essay published in *Psychoanalytic Review* titled "Dream as Metaphor for Survival" with "I continue to dream myself back to what I lost, and continue to lose and regain, to an earth where I am a fellow creature and to a landscape I can call home" (*Just* 317). Clare's adventure "over the fence" is in one sense a renewing contact with nature, but it is in another sense an off-interstate adventure. In her case, Harrison has, in a typically postmodern manner, created the ultimate clever paradox: driving 70 miles per hour down the interstate is stultifying while hunkering in a thicket in some Iowa cornfield is liberating. What is reality, what is dream? In any event, neither nature nor trip will endure: Clare will inevitably find her way to some farmhouse, to civilization, and if not back to her husband, at least to upper middle class urban life. In *Wolf*, as Edward C. Reilly points out, "Unlike Fenimore Cooper's Natty Bumppo, who finds solace and God's plenty in the forests and on the prairies and casts off the accoutrements of civilization to retreat to the wilderness, Swanson needs civilization and so casts off his wilderness accoutrements— specifically, his 20-pound pup tent—and escapes to civilization. He admits that he 'wants tobacco. And a porterhouse and a bottle of Chateaux Margaux . . . and [a] car driven straight through to New York City to the Algonquin or the Plaza'" (32–33). The only permanent release comes from the ultimate *Thelma and Louise* roadtrip over a cliff or into the Gulf of Mexico. This is also the choice of Harrison's male alter-ego Strang. This is the fate of Orin in *Farmer*, who "said night after night *Joseph you got to get out of here, you're not really going to farm and there's a whole world out there*" (124), only to lose his own life when his plane crashes in the China Sea, far far far from Michigan and far far far above the safety of land. This is the choice of Harrison's female alter-ego Dalva, who concludes her reclamation of self and son and family history by passing the Northridge journals on to an academic who will neither understand them fully nor use them well, emptying out the sub-basement in which her grandfather attempted to preserve the artifacts of his life, leaving her place, and drowning herself off of the Florida Keys:

> The ocean would feel much better in the brilliantly hot noonday sun. I've quickly packed my beach bag with my Niobrara stone, the piece of hammock, and the belt I will take with me on my long voyage downward. Nothing else but my body and the fresh pull I had just taken. I send a kiss and a good-bye to those I love so much. Naomi, Paul, Lundquist, Nelse and J. M. I hope I am going to join my lover. (*Road* 446)

In a similar conclusion to *True North*, David Burkett pushes his father—at his father's request—off the back of a rowboat to drown in the Gulf of Mexico, then pours the ashes and bone fragments of his mother into the sand along Lake Superior, where they are quickly washed away by water from the lake.

And there it all goes.

"The bottom line, as they like to say nowadays, is that we no longer feel at home either within, or without, our skins," Harrison writes toward the end of *Just Before Dark* (309). He is finally and reluctantly a postmodernist in a postmodernist world, and place, like poetry, is but a temporary stay against confusion.

NOTES

1. MIDWESTERN LITERATURE

1. Frederick C. Stern cites a passage from Merle Curti's 1943 *The Growth of American Thought*, "a volume of massive importance for its day," to support his argument that before independence, exaggerated regional differences were one thing which set the American colonies apart from Europe, and that "the notion of 'region' as a category by means of which one can understand the experience of the United States is deeply ingrained in our intellectual history" (11).

2. Lucien Stryk, in selecting poems for his *Heartland* anthology, thought it would be "foolish" to insist that all his selections be set in the Midwest; he sought biographical ties, markers of language, and a way of looking at things.

3. Also, "Americans have no urban history. They live in one of the world's most urbanized countries as if it were a wilderness in both time and space"— Sam Bass Warner (4). James Kunstler writes, "When Americans, depressed by the scary places where they work and dwell, contemplate some antidote, they often conjure up the image of the American small town. However muddled and generalized the image is, it exerts a powerful allure. For the idea of a small town represents a whole menu of human values that the gigantism of corporate enterprise has either obliterated or mocked: an agreeable scale of human enterprise, tranquility, public safety, proximity of neighbors and markets, nearness to authentic countryside, and permanence" (185).

4. Holm might have added Dreiser, the reporter unable or unwilling to draw moralistic lessons, or Mark Twain's narrator/persona Huck Finn. He might have been quoting John T. Flanagan: "The literature of the Middle West . . . has been an honest, a forthright literature, a literature notable for vigor and individuality and originality" (232). In *Lake Wobegon Days*, Garrison Keillor writes, "When Lucy of composition class, who let me have half her sandwich one day, asked me if I had a job and I told her I was a dishwasher, she made a face as if I said I worked in the sewer. She said it must be awful, and of course when I told her it was terrific, she thought I was being ironic. Composition class was local headquarters of irony, we supplied the five-county area. The more plainly I tried to say I liked dishwashing, the more ironic she thought I was, until I flipped a gob of mayo at her as a rhetorical device to show *un*subtlety and sincerity and then she thought I was a jerk" (23).

5. On the decline of the Midwest village, see Davies, *Main Street Blues*, and Amato, Amato, Pichaske, and Davies, *A Place Called Home*. Many of the details included by William Gass in *In the Heart of the Heart of the Country* to emphasize rural decline in mid-century seem rather upscale by today's standards.

6. Note also "[Cyrus] COLTER: Are most Chicago writers historically and presently realists in their writing? Is that a benchmark? I've wondered about that, because generally people say that Chicago writers are realistic" (Gibbons 346).

7. Peirce F. Lewis argues, "We often boast that we have 'conquered geography,' meaning that contemporary technology is so powerful that we can build anything, wherever we like, and effectively ignore climate, landforms, soils, and the like. . . . But 'conquering geography' is often very expensive business. . . . Thus, the South differed culturally from the North largely because it differed physically. Southern cities stopped looking Southern about the time that cheap air conditioning made it possible to ignore the debilitating heat of a super-tropical summer, which lasted sometimes for five months, a season in which nobody who could help it did any work between noon and 7 P.M. The 'Southern way of life' was renamed 'the Atlanta spirit' and began to take on Yankee ways, largely because of air conditioning. Then the Arabs tripled the price of oil, and suddenly air conditioning became 'uneconomical.' Sitting on verandahs came back into style" (25–26). In a rather remarkable letter-editorial in the July–August, 2004, *Utne Reader*, founding editor Eric Utne admits, "I'm completely clueless about nature, and figure that there must be people like me who could use an updated, twenty-first century, urban almanac" in the Benjamin Franklin tradition.

2. DAVE ETTER

1. The Carl Sandburg Award came in 1981–82 for *West of Chicago* (the winner in fiction that year was Saul Bellow for *The Dean's December*). Carver's endorsement came in the lead ad (August 1983) of a series of National Endowment for the Arts–sponsored Pushcart Press "Writer's Choice" advertisements of select small press titles. The NEA then exhibited *Alliance, Illinois* (1983), with other books selected for the series at the Frankfurt Book Fair. All citations to *Alliance, Illinois* are to the 1983 edition.

2. One must be careful here, however, because *Alliance* poems mention also west-central Illinois towns like Pittsfield, Beardstown, and south-central towns like Sparta and Prairie du Rocher; Chicago locations like State Street and Marshall Fields; and fictional villages like Pioneer Grove (formerly Bible Grove, probably a reconfigured Sugar Grove, Illinois), Noon Prairie, and Goodenowville. ("Goodenow," a family name, appears in "Schoolhouse" in *Go Read the River*, in "Country Graveyard" in *Central Standard Time*, in "Crepuscle with Nellie" in *Well You Needn't*, in "Light in August" in *Boondocks*, in "Will Goodenow: The Red Depot" in *Alliance* . . . and in the dedications of *Go Read the River* and the 1978 *Alliance*.) Etter also mentions Yellow Medicine County, Minnesota ("Peggy Daniels: Moonlight Yodel," *Alliance* 63).

3. Also "a corker," "peachy," "keen," "zigzag," "nincompoop," "copacetic," "vamoose," "heist," "slouch," "chitchat," "shindig," "loonies," "lingo," "nuts," "this doll," "screwball," "highjinks," "swankiest," "standoffish," "whippersnapper,"

"hooligans," "hunker," "doohickey," "loony," "erstwhile," "cutup," "whooping," "davenport," "old coot," "grouch," "kaput," "scoot," "busted," "ruckus," "oodles," "ba-zooms," "yokel," "haul-assing all over hell," "naked as a jailbird," "it's no picnic," "no need to sweat blood," "in a tizzy," "a hot number," "a real creep," "good riddance," "cracking up," "off my nut," "a thin dime," "putting us on," "hightailing it out of," "never had a beggar's chance," "she's a punkin," "big thundering trouble," "liquored up like a payday coal miner," "hung my hat," "good grief," "too bad, so sad," "gaudiest glad rags," "go for a spin," "a big pain in the ass," "give a hoot," "damned Dutch stubborn," "great balls of fire," "knock her on her can," "bum a cigarette," "belly up," and "oh, dry up!"

4. Others include comic strip characters such as Joe Palooka, Dick Tracy, Blondie, Moon Mullins, Donald Duck, and Foghorn Leghorn; the musician Tommy Dorsey; the television character Clark Kent; and writers Zane Grey, George Ade, William Inge, and Ring Lardner. The games people play: Monopoly, dominoes, hearts, and bingo. The poets studied by teenager Pearl Ingersoll: Masters, Robinson, Sandburg, Lindsay, Pound, Moore, and Eliot. The baseball player cards collected by Mickey Conway: Smokey Burgess, Ewell Blackwell, Wally Post, Solly Hemus, Curt Flood, Roy Face, Mickey Vernon, Elmer Valo, Eddie Joost, Larry Jackson, Johnny Logan, Whitey Lockman, and Richie Ashburn.

5. Also Kool-Aid and Ovaltine; Benzedrine; Maybelline eye shadow; Farmall tractors; Maytag washers; Rainbo bread; Peter Pan peanut butter; Elgin watches; Nunn-Bush shoes; Lucky Strike cigarettes; Eveready batteries; Fuller brushes; Ace pocket combs; Kodak cameras; Pabst, Grain Belt, and Potosi Beer; Burma Shave; Hallmark; Doublemint; Country Time lemonade; Bon Ami; Spic and Span; Quaker Oats; Mayflower; Ritz; Popsicles; Trailways and Greyhound buses; Sinclair Oil; Marsh Wheeling, White Owl, and El Producto cigars. The various pipe and chewing tobaccos: Days Work, Skoal, Bull Durham, Carter Hall, Red Man, Union Leader, Beech Nut, Levi Garrett, and Union Station. Etter's railroads are the Chicago and Northwestern, Erie Lackawanna, Santa Fe, Illinois Central, Cadiz Railroad, Burlington, Soo Line, and Union Pacific. The pinball games played by Anthony Fasano: Flying Chariots, Buckaroo, King of Diamonds, and Abra Ca Dabra. The candies in "Diane Gubicza": Squirmy Worms, Atomic Fireballs, Gummi Bears, Root Beer Barrels, Pixy Stix, and Licorice Bites. The hybrid seed companies of "Amos Blackburn" are Pioneer, Northrup King, Stewart, Dairyland, Pride, Lynks, DeKalb, Cargill, O's Gold, Acco, Funk's G-Hybrid, Hughes, Jacques, P-A-G, McNair, Trojan, Big D, Super Crost, Hulting, and Bo-Jac. The implement dealers of "Flora Rutherford": New Holland, Masey Ferguson, and John Deere.

6. "Nostalgia" antedates *Alliance, Illinois* by several years. It appeared in the "new poems" section of *Central Standard Time* (1978), was not used for the Kylix Press edition of *Alliance* (1978), reappearing in the Spoon River *Alliance* in 1983. See also "Gary Shackhammer: Remembering the Thirties," "Ernie

Keepnews: Then and Now," "Elwood Collins: Summer of 1932," "Murray Harris: Fall of 1956," "Lloyd Kellogg: The Man Who Played Clarinet in the High School Band Back in 1936, But Then Never Amounted to Anything Much After That, Is Here Again Today."

7. Alliance was originally Whistlecross and passed through several permutations before becoming Alliance. Etter liked the fact that both "Alliance" and "Illinois" contain eight letters, with three of the first four being identical.

8. Linking *Alliance, Illinois* with Edgar Lee Masters's *Spoon River Anthology*, John E. Hallwas writes, "Likewise, the people of Dave Etter's *Alliance, Illinois* (1978) suffer from a loss of community and pervasive spiritual poverty. Many are lonely and frustrated. There is an apparent lack of shared experience. A few have memories of more meaningful days, but the present is bleak" ("Introduction" 3–4).

9. The unit includes Etter's poem, Gina Berriault's story "The Stone Boy," and Harley Elliott's poem "Brothers Together in Winter."

10. For a detailed analysis of this poem, see David Pichaske, "Stubby Payne: Stocking Tops," *Indiana Review* 8.3 (1985): 71–81.

11. Etter also alludes to this passage in the poem "Twisted Apples" in *Go Read the River* (1966).

12. For the epigraph to "Chicago" (*HS* #10) Etter selected a line from Nelson Algren: "You have to love a town a little before you earn the right to knock it."

13. When the Chicago suburban sprawl reached the borders of his Elburn, Illinois, rejuvenating the sleepy country village, transforming cornfields into new developments of condos and country estates, and sending land values high as a sunflower, Etter escaped expanding Chicago for Lanark, another little village, lost in the dusty roads of western Illinois . . . where Chicago will never in five hundred years reach, where you slam the car door, step out on the street, and wonder if maybe you haven't walked onto a set for the film version of *Alliance*.

14. In her unsuccessful run for the 1986 Republican senatorial nomination, State Representative Judy Koehler attempted to make political capital out of this passage, and others criticizing Thompson, which appeared in a book whose writing and publication were funded in part by the Illinois Arts Council. The attack, with its implicit threat of government censorship, worked Ms. Koehler little good to begin with; the revelation that the book, like all other Spoon River Poetry Press books, had been printed in her home district, helped end her campaign. She subsequently lost her House seat and went to law school.

15. "Doreen Mitchell is (was?) a girl I really liked in the 7th grade and even more in the 8th grade. But I liked other girls too and never got around to Doreen as I should have. Then she moved away the summer before 9th grade. I didn't know she was going to move. It didn't really hit me hard until I was out of high school; then it devastated me. I was mature enough to KNOW SHE WAS THE ONE. Although I tried, I could never find out where she went. I think my childhood

was very sad, and I try not to think about it," Etter wrote in a letter of March 27, 1999. In the Follstad interview, Etter claimed Doreen was "a certain person from the past, but she's more of a person from the present, although I don't know her all that well." Doreen Mitchell appears in the poem "Why I Don't Go to Parties Anymore," in *Open to the Wind*, the dedication to which reads, "To Doreen Mitchell, wherever you are."

16. For the record, Etter's favorite artists, at least in 1985, are George Ade, Sherwood Anderson, Thomas Hart Benton, Richard Bissell, John Steuart Curry, Miles Davis, William Faulkner, Robert Frost, Dizzy Gillespie, Thomas Hardy, Stan Kenton, Thelonious Monk, Carl Sandburg, Dylan Thomas, Mark Twain, Walt Whitman, William Carlos Williams, Grant Wood, and Andrew Wyeth. Favorite books are George Ade's *Fables in Slang* and *In Babel*; Sherwood Anderson's *A Story Teller's Story* and *Winesburg, Ohio*; Steven Vincent Benet's *John Brown's Body*; Richard Bissell's *Good Bye, Ava, How Many Miles to Galena?*, *High Water*, and *A Stretch on the River*; Norbert Blei's *The Second Novel*; Ray Bradbury's *Dandelion Wine*; Earnest Elmo Calkins's *They Broke the Prairie*; Davis Grubb's *Fools' Paradise*; Weldon Hill's *The Long Summer of George Adams*; Ross Lockridge Jr.'s *Raintree County*; William Maxwell's *Ancestors*; H. L. Mencken's *The American Language*; Carl Sandburg's *Abraham Lincoln: The Prairie Years, Always the Young Strangers*, and *Complete Poems*; Jean Shepherd's *In God We Trust, All Others Pay Cash*; Mark Twain's *Life on the Mississippi*; Walt Whitman's *Leaves of Grass*; and William Carlos Williams's *Paterson*.

17. The distinctions between modernism and postmodernism are not always clear. In *Living by Fiction*, Annie Dillard meditates, "In fact, on a very gloomy day one could say this: that contemporary modernism accurately puts its finger upon, and claims, every quality of Modernist fiction that is not essential. It throws out the baby and proclaims the bath. Joyce wrote parodies and made puns and allusions on his way to elaborating a full and deep fictional world called Dublin. Now people write little parodies full of puns and allusions. Kafka wrote fiction rooted in profound cultural criticism and in metaphysical and theological longing; along the way he had a character turn into a cockroach. Some contemporary writing has jettisoned the rest and kept the cockroach for a laugh. Joyce and Woolf bade their characters think on the page to deepen the characters, not to flatten the world solipsistically. Proust and Faulkner fiddled with time to create an artful simulacrum of our experience of time and also our knowledge of the world; now some contemporary writing may fiddle with time to keep us awake, the way television commercials splice scenes to keep us awake, or they may fiddle with time to distract us from the absence of narration, or even just to fiddle. The wit that was perhaps incidental in Joyce has become an end in itself. In short, Modernist writers expanded fictional techniques in the service of traditional ends—one could say on this putative very gloomy day— and those ends have been lost" (*Living* 63–64). Even on a sunny day we can

agree that the qualities of modernism espoused by postmodernist writers are those listed by Dillard.

18. Paul Hoover, *Postmodern American Poetry: A Norton Anthology*, xxv–xxxix.

19. James Joyce ("Eagles," *How High* 90), Kafka ("Maynard Lewis: Kafka," *Electric* 43; "Czechoslovakia," *Carnival* 78), Apollinaire (epigraph, "Reception," *Carnival* 16), Villon ("Derek Vreeland: The Apple Trees of Pioneer Grove," *Sunflower* 241), Mallarmé (epigraph, "Reception," *Carnival* 16), Lorca ("Ribs," *Carnival* 50), Pasternak, Neruda (epigraph, "Words for a Friend. . . ." *Go Read* 4), Rilke (epigraph to "Nearing Death," *Central* 81), Heinrich Böll (epigraph *Midlanders*), Alberto Moravia (epigraph *Midlanders*), Francisco Umbral (epigraph, *Midlanders*), D. H. Lawrence (epigraph, *Midlanders*), Henry Miller ("Jubal Montgomery: Oddball," *Sunflower* 138), Dylan Thomas (epigraph, *Electric Avenue*), William Faulkner ("Emmett Beasley: Man Talking to Himself," *Sunflower* 147), e. e. cummings ("Shindig," *Carnival* 75), Theodore Roethke (epigraph to *Electric Avenue*, epigraph to *Home State* and *HS* #50), William H. Gass (epigraph to "An American Holiday," *Last Train* 34), Gottfried Benn (epigraph to *Home State*), Antonio Machado ("Spanish," *Carnival* 67), William Carlos Williams (epigraph to *Home State* and *HS* #175), Chagall, Miro, and Matisse ("Ozzie Navarro: Just the Facts," *Sunflower* 366), Van Gogh ("For Miles and Miles," *How High* 49), Toulouse-Lautrec ("Where I Am," *Go Read* 15), Picasso ("The Red Nude," *Last Train* 85), Andrew Wyeth ("Notes on Regionalism," *HS* #58), Jackson Pollock ("Culture," *Carnival* 68), Edward Hopper ("Ernie Keepnews: What's Missing Now" *Midlanders* 11), Modigliani ("Neighborhood," *Wind* 28), and Grant Wood ("After Showing Grant Wood's 'American Gothic' to My Children," *Central* 83).

20. This technique is to be found in "After Showing Grant Wood's 'American Gothic' to My Children" (*Central* 83); "Tallgrass Prairie Plot" (*HS* #4); *Alliance, Illinois* poems "Jerome Holtsapple: Flower Thief" (118), "Gretchen Naylor: Nowhere" (134), "Lance Boomsma: Wedding Reception" (160), "Russell Hayes: Federal Highway" (206), "Kermit Olmsted: Roots" (207), and *Midlanders* poems "Craig Barnet: Tune Box" (12), "Herman Fox: Happy Hour" (36), and "Duane Ford: Buffalo Nickel" (41).

21. Not surprisingly, pure "talk poems" are most prominent in *Alliance, Illinois*: "Roger Powell: The Talk at Rukenbrod's" (14), "Ralph C. Kramer: Gossip" (144), "Hamilton Rivers: Noon at Carl's Mainline Cafe" (232).

22. Although catalogs and lists appear in many Etter poems, pure "catalog poems" are poems like "A House by the Tracks" (*Read* 79), "Amos Blackburn: War of the Hybrids" (*Alliance* 30), "Pearl Ingersoll: Homework" (*Alliance* 93), "The Man Who Invented Swimming" and "Pipe Tobacco" (*Looking* 23), poems "carried" by a list of *things*. The catalog of pipe tobaccos is followed by the lines, " 'Is this a poem?' she said. / 'Yes, I think so,' I said."

23. Apostrophes are absent in *West of Chicago* (1981), but replaced in those *West of Chicago* poems reprinted in *Alliance, Illinois* (1983). "At the time when

I was dropping the apostrophes in words like 'can't' 'won't,' etc., I was reading all of Faulkner, every book. He spelled *wont* and *cant* and *dont* this way, so I did too, until I grew quickly to dislike it" (Letter).

24. To take but a single example, "Molly Dunaway: Rainbow" and "Zachary Grant: Guilt" face each other on opposite pages of *Sunflower County*, the one about a woman so angry with her man she removes her wedding ring and wraps it in a Rainbo bread wrapper, the other about a father whose unloved daughter has just left home for New Hampshire. Grant sums up both broken relationships in a single line: "I was always right. Now I'm wrong." The poems comment nicely on each other.

25. The opening poem of *Alliance, Illinois*, for example, brings George Maxwell into bruised and broken Alliance in a semi-trailer, half mindful of old friends and old relationships, knowing that nothing probably changed since he left. The closing poem, "Kirby Quackenbush: September Moon," sends its speaker on a late-night walk through the same bruised and broken town, toward "the depot of many fierce goodbyes," mindful of Luanne, the lost and lonely love of his life. On page 100, halfway through *Alliance*, Booth Schofield records his own "Dream of Old."

26. See especially Jones, 88–90.

27. See Michael Lind, "Where Have You Gone, Louis Sullivan: Will America Recover from Its Fifty-Year Bout of Europhilia?" *Harper's*, February 1998, 53–59.

28. For the complete story, see Amato, *When Father and Son Conspire*.

3. WILLIAM KLOEFKORN

1. "Over the course of four uncolored seasons / I'll throw the javelin ten thousand times, / salvage one bronze medal" (*Sunrise* 23). Also, "Athletics in many small towns in America is a catechism not easily or quickly shucked. . . . But athletics do not limit themselves to the games or the events themselves; they provide a context from which innumerable possibilities emerge" (Letter 2).

2. In *Burning the Hymnal* (27), editor Ted Genoways quotes Kloefkorn as having at one time projected a series of six "long Frost-ian narratives" that would portray the most critical points in Alvin Turner's life. Only one of the six was written ("The Color of Dusk," *Burning* 29–35), but it is, to paraphrase Pound, "vury Frostian." In his letter of July 21, 2001, Kloefkorn admits, "If he [Alvin Turner] sounds a trifle Frostian, it is because many of Frost's lines are, like my brother's blood, touchstones. Then, too, both Frost and my grandfather wrestled with rocks" (8).

3. Thucydides and Aristotle (*Loup* 74), Homer (*Death* 32), Virgil (*Drinking* 44), Sophocles (*Death* 9), Dante (*Honeymoon* 40), Chaucer (*Living* 26, *Uncertain* 44, *Restoring* 9, 121), Cervantes (*Carlos* 66), Shakespeare (*Honeymoon* 14, *Not Such* 13, *ludi* 66, *Welcome* 31, *Loup* 24, 79), Marlowe (*Going* 81), Christopher Morley (*Restoring*, epigraph), Milton (*This Death* 6), Vaughan (*Drowning* 17), Herrick

(*Shadowboxing* 64), Swift (*Not Such* 15, *This Death* 49), Shelley (*Cottonwood* 19, *This Death* 29), Keats (*Welcome* 19, 24), Arnold (*This Death* 6), Joyce (*Loup* 52), Yeats (*Voyages* 35, *Loup* 82, *Welcome* 76), Hopkins (*Cottonwood* 1), Thoreau (*Loup* 79, *This Death* 9, 90), Whitman (*Cottonwood* 1, *Loup* 29, *Houses* 72), Cooper (*Loup* 98), Melville (*Life* 52), Twain (*This Death* 26, 79, *Loup* 95, *Restoring* 118), O'Neill (*Loup* 77), Hemingway (*Loup* 26), Lindsay (*Sunrise* 16), Frost (*Alvin Turner* #12 and #14, *Burning* 19 and 29, *Carlos* 8), Tennessee Williams (*Shadowboxing* 66), Eliot (*Alvin Turner* #27, *ludi* 7, *Cottonwood* 21, *Honeymoon* 8), cummings (*Where* 55), and Steinbeck (*loony* epigraph).

4. Kloefkorn has frequently acknowledged the influence of Dave Etter in dedications ("Jack Daniel," *Burning* 68; "Argyles," *Visible* 54; "County Fair," *Not Such* 71; and "Walking the Route," *Life Like* 5). Persona collections like *Stocker*, *ludi jr, loony, Honeymoon,* and *Welcome to Carlos,* and individual character poems in collections like *Uncertain, A Life Like Mine,* and *Collecting for the Wichita Beacon* reflect Etter's *Alliance, Illinois* poems; Doris of *Honeymoon* bears more than an alliterative resemblance to Doreen from Etter's *Home State* (Doreen actually appears in Kloefkorn's "County Fair," *Not Such* 71); and lines like "so I give her a wet Mississippi River kiss / smack on her wet Mississippi River mouth" ("Hannibal," *Going Out* 83) and "Sunset is a mellow Picasso dream, / purple to aqua, crimson to pink" ("Argyles," *Visible* 54) may be traced to specific Etter poems: "Wade Hollenbach: Hard Cider" (*Alliance, Illinois* 11) and "Picasso" (*Live at the Silver Dollar* 17). Kloefkorn himself offers "these lines from a little poem I published not long after having immersed myself in an Etter book: 'My purple Monarch bicycle / sits flat in the purple shade / of a purple October afternoon'" (Letter 3).

In *Burning the Hymnal*, Ted Genoways writes of what he calls Kloefkorn's persona poems, "Still not quite comfortable with his own voice directly appearing in the poems, he simply 'superimposed my insights into a persona. . . . This technique was used by Faulkner and Twain, both heavy influences on Kloefkorn. Yet they were perhaps as influenced by the Illinois poet Dave Etter. Etter's diverse voices and ability to 'become' his subject held great appeal for Kloefkorn and eventually became a technique he adapted into his own style" (37). Genoways cites "Frank Fairchild: Young and a Bachelor and a Farmer"—with its name, colon, subtitle, and the voice of its persona—as especially strong "evidence of the influence of Dave Etter's writings on Kloefkorn's work" (*Burning* 55). I would add the dialogue poems of *Honeymoon* (for example 6, 8, 9, 22) and the rare instances of form in Kloefkorn's poetry. When Kloefkorn does shape his poetry, the forms he selects are often those favored by Etter and occasionally in a poem dedicated to Etter: a simple 2-, 3-, or 4-line stanza (*Where* 65, *Platte Valley* numbers 6, 28, 41, 43, 48, 65, 69, 70; "Benediction," *Cottonwood* 34), a three-line stanza with each line indented successively ("In the Cemetery at Cedar Vale, Late September," "Definitions," "At Maggie's Pond," and "Late Evening, and My

Mother Calling Me In," *Dragging* 22, 44, 59, 73), and a rough syllable count ("Late to Work," "Summer 1946," or "Greasing the Tracks," *Where* 50, 58, 60).

5. In "An Open Letter," Kloefkorn writes (concerning *Alvin Turner* #45), "I'm a sucker for sound, so the repetition of the 's's' and the 'd's' and the 'o's' in this poem gives me some delight—more, probably, than it should" (35).

6. That particular phrase (also, coincidentally, used by Tom Joad in concluding his conversation with a truck driver at the end of chapter 2 of Steinbeck's *Grapes of Wrath*) appears in an early Kloefkorn poem called "Fairport":

from Maine to Medicine Lodge,
from time to Timbuktu,
from hell to breakfast (*Uncertain* 3)

It crops up again in "Aunt Flora":

Well, it's a long journey from hell to breakfast,
Aunt Flora says (*Collecting* 17)

And yet again in the title poem of *Welcome to Carlos*:

[Carlos] could rhyme anything from hell to breakfast,
from Kansas to Timbuktu. (1)

7. See especially Mark Sanders, "Rocks, Water, and Fire: Kloefkorn's Use of Symbol."

8. The fact that the towns of this book—Spivey, Cunningham, Sharon—are actual south-central Kansas towns suggests that the characters, although fictionalized, may also have had true-life models.

4. NORBERT BLEI

1. The Bleis followed a paradigm established long before the Bohemians, and followed by most ethnic groups that arrived in America after the rise of large cities, in which groups of friends or relatives from the same country—and frequently from the same town in the old country—buy homes in an ethnic urban neighborhood on the deteriorating edge of downtown; then, as they establish themselves economically, buy homes in another more up-scale neighborhood closer to the suburbs; then, often, upon retiring or achieving still more wealth, move, again collectively, a third and even a fourth time, always further from the downtown area. Sometimes, claims ethnic historian Ted Radzialowski, you can track their increasing economic stability by their street addresses: 5th and 6th streets, 30th and 34th streets, 65th street.

2. "On the outside you can start right in the teacher's parking lot, filling gas tanks with sand, stealing hub caps, filling them with stones, or just denting them with your foot. Slashing tires. Breaking hood ornaments. . . . Stealing cars

for the hell of it. Taking the babes for joyrides. . . . Shoplifting we did almost everyday after school. Almost anything a guy could need could be lifted from dime stores, hardware stores, drugstores and groceries" (16). An old photo shows Blei in his middle teens, in black leather motorcycle jacket and greased-back hair, with his motor bike, hanging out with his gang of punks, also with greased hair and motorcycle jackets. But in *The Second Novel*, Blei writes, "He [friend Ross LewAllen] lives what I only write about" (83).

3. This relationship was troubled from the start. The list of mysterious women in Blei's work is long even for a writer (Astrid in Denmark, a prostitute in Paris, a lover in New Mexico, Kirsten and Green Eyes in *Adventures*, Kirstin from Duluth and the mistress of the mails in *The Second Novel*, the dedication to *The Second Novel*, a list of women on page iii of that book), and in discussing writers and their mistresses in *The Second Novel* Blei declares, "a mistress re-mains the most vital object in a writer's life. A writer's wife must learn to live with that or there is no living with the writer. The writer who is not aware of this will never write a word worth a good fuck" (98). Elsewhere in that book Blei lists Sixteen Things I Learned from My Wife: "We can't live like this[.] Where are you going now? We don't have any money[.] Everyone thinks you're lazy[.] Nobody understands you[.] What do you mean you don't know what you want to do? I'm not living in this apartment for the rest of my life[.] I want children[.] How can we live on a cub reporter's salary of $35 a week? What's wrong with teaching? Why did you quit graduate school? You tell the folks you want to become a writer[.] Why didn't you tell me that before I married you? What will you do when we come back from Europe? You can't afford to freelance for a living[.] Do you think I am dying?" (13). In his short story "Dwelling," clearly based on the first years in Door County, Blei writes of his protagonist's wife, "For Hope to come down the stairs and join him for breakfast would make his day irretriev-able" (*Ghost* 88). However, also in *The Second Novel*, Blei writes, "I am over-blessed with a wife who is childlike and therefore beautiful. We have truly be-come more married during the past year." However, Blei follows that 1963 observation with a 1978 note: "Bullshit. This is the voice of a writer trying to ex-plain away his failure to become what he needs to be, after another fall into dark-ness. . . . He might just as well become a Born Again Christian" (88).

4. In view of the similarities with *Dead Poets Society*, it should be noted that Blei's book antedates the film by over a decade. Compare also Blei's "This is an exceptional high school, Hassock. We have a high number of National Merit stu-dents. The parents expect their kids to go on to the Big 10 colleges and even the Ivy League. They want these kids to be ready. They expect the teachers to work the kids hard, and what's more, the kids themselves expect to be worked hard! . . . I talked to one of your kids, and he told me you weren't doing much in class, just a lot of talking. A lot of ideas. Now some of that's all right. But it's basics,

Hassock. Basics!" (123). And Blazen's lessons on the individual versus the collective (pages 146–47) and on poetry (150–51, 158–61).

5. The same dichotomy can be found in that other great Chicago writer whom Blei so admired, Carl Sandburg, and perhaps in another major midwestern poet, T. S. Eliot. In an essay titled "Eliot's Contrasts: From the Regional to the Universal," Bernard F. Engel observes that Eliot's double regional identity (Midwest and New England) contributed to his habit of seeing polarities, and perhaps to his uncertainty about geographical roots and thus to "his feeling that people of the modern era, including himself, are hollow men" and further "to his frequent feeling that . . . he himself was more the observer than the participant" (143). Engel further speculates that Eliot himself sensed that the transplantation from one geography to another "put him in isolation" (143), that "The alternation in regional identities may have given rise to Eliot's observation that one needs a strong sense of place" (145), and that it contributed significantly to a willingness "to entertain ideas of the self as flowing, as lacking in permanence" (147). He does not raise this pattern into a paradigm for either midwesterners or bilocated writers, and it is not a pattern I will apply to Blei in this essay, although Engel's points regarding Eliot might illuminate Blei.

6. Windfall Press reneged on the contract and ended up finally under indictment; the book became *The Hour of the Sunshine Now*.

7. From July 1976 to January 1978, Blei logged sixty-seven fiction submissions—and one acceptance—but gradually his luck (or talent, or connections) improved. Chris Newman at *Chicago Magazine* was helpful; the *New Yorker* took "The Chair Trick" and almost took "This Horse of a Body of Mine." By the mid-1980s, Blei's fiction was appearing in prestigious small and literary magazines like *StoryQuarterly* and *TriQuarterly*. He was twice cited (although not reprinted) in Martha Foley's *Best American Short Stories*.

8. As an epigraph for his short story "The Ghost of Sandburg's Phizzog," which counterpoints modern versions of the Chicago and prairie poets, Blei selected an epigraph from Borges: "Now of course there are two Sandburgs" (*Ghost* 65).

9. Describing James T. Farrell in *Chi Town*, Blei writes, "His mission was clear-cut: to become America's Balzac, to get down every aspect of life at that time in telling detail" (227). The 384-page *Chi Town* itself—both the essays it contains and the immense list of essays Blei regrets never having found the time to write (17–18), "much he witnessed but never got down, much he wishes he could some day return to"—suggests that Blei saw himself as a latter-day James T. Farrell.

10. Sandburg, a writer "like God himself" (*Chi Town* 3) also appears in the title story of *The Ghost of Sandburg's Phizzog*. Algren is "an extension of Sandburg, and the city's legitimate poetic heir" (*Chi Town* 305). Also, "The measure of any man's work is clear: Would Algren approve?" (*Chi Town* 384).

11. Blei's story "Stars" appeared in the *TriQuarterly 60*, "Chicago Writers," among work by Harry Mark Petrakis, Angela Jackson, and Dave Etter, sandwiched between interviews with Saul Bellow and Gwendolyn Brooks. But Blei was not part of the October 29, 1983, radio round-table on "The Writer in Chicago" recorded at WFMT-FM and transcribed for *TriQuarterly*. "At one time back there I felt briefly that I belonged to a community of writers who hung out in Riccardo's and O'Rourke's," Blei recalls in the 1990 epilogue to *Chi Town* (383); they were "trying to find the words to show the way. Some found them. Some didn't. Most disappeared in what today I might describe as Kafka's Castle of thinking-they-were-writers" (*Winter Book* 64).

12. Chickens: "Remember Grandma's farm in Three Oaks? How she killed the chickens for supper?" ("This Horse of a Body of Mine," *Ghost* 128). Basements: "If there's one thing Bohemians have in their blood, it's basements" ("Chicago's Basements: The Best Bargains in Town," *Chi Town* 23). " What other culture but the Bohemians bought their first house (perhaps a beautiful brick bungalow) and 'saved' it by living in the basement? My own grandparents first did this in Chicago. All the chaos of living, all the entering and leaving, eating, drinking, cooking, baking, visiting, washing, fighting, pinochle playing, loving and hating was done in the basement. The upstairs was a dustfree museum of unused furniture, clean white curtains, hand-worked doilies, Czechoslovakian crystal, thick soft carpets that you seldom walked upon without being ordered to 'take your shoes off'" (*Neighborhood* 38). "Though a vague childhood memory remained, an image of his grandmother's basement, cellar-like with foods and smells, where harsh sounds of the old tongue could be heard, where people of the same blood gathered, where the family once dwelled" ("Dwelling," *Ghost* 94). Pinochle: "In my own Bohemian neighborhood, the Card Players—a scene out of Cezanne" ("Europe in Chicago," *Chi Town* 60). "Years later I would come back to visit them in the bungalow in Chicago, and we would play pinochle throughout the night" (*Adventures* 32). "Fun? Play cards. Lots of pinochle" (*Adventures* 172). "Old Gramps . . . wait for his soup to be served / then deal out two hands of pinochle" (*Second Novel* 43). "*the pinochle game that lasted till 2:00 in the morning*" (*Second Novel* 157). "*the second night of pinochle*" (*Second Novel* 160). Knives: "When he was full, he would chase / Grandma through the basement / with the knife / and kill her as much as he liked" (*Second Novel* 35). Women/soup, men/beer: "Five quarts [of beer] a day . . . that's not much . . . for a baker, five quarts a day" (*Neighborhood* 22).

13. In this sense Blei is a realist, writing from his own, not a borrowed experience, in his own, not a borrowed voice. Something deeper is at also work: a philosophical or aesthetic preference for the old, the highly flavored, the weathered and textured, the poor over the new, the bland, the shiny and smooth, the affluent. Certain aspects of Blei's youth interest him not at all—his father's business at the bank, for example. The bank certainly, by 1974, represented a family

tradition as old as much of the rest of *Neighborhood* or *Chi Town*, and George Blei was even a preservationist of sorts . . . when it came to the family's "1965 Oldsmobile four-door sedan with 35,000 miles on it, original tires, spotless interior, and two coats of Simonize he hand-rubbed the day before we left" (*Ghost* 119). But the preservation of Detroit gas-guzzlers appealed to Blei as little as Elvis Presley, cars with fins, and sock hops—1950s icons which, fifty years later, have become objects of much nostalgia.

After his death in 1999, of course, Blei's father—and the family Buick— became a tradition worth preserving. "I made one tape with him . . . I should have made ten," Blei observed in July 2000, pointing to a file on his computer labeled "In My Father's House," before heading to lunch at Gils Rock in his father's old Buick.

14. "When the creek suddenly appeared deep in the woods he approached it with the same reverence and awe he approached the holy communion rail Sundays in church back in Chicago. Everything about the creek and the woods was something like that. Like church, without the altar, without the candles, the priest" (*What* 3).

15. One story that bridges Cicero and Door is "The Egg Lady" which, as Richard Meade points out, forms the transition between city and country in *The Hour of the Sunshine Now*. Blei describes three egg ladies: a grandmother, who talks to herself in a language John Lifka never understood, and provides an ethnic experience (transplanted from Cicero, Illinois, to Michigan City, Indiana) replete with soup, chickens, bakery, and eggs; a second egg lady, who delivers fresh farm eggs to his parents back in the city; and a farmer's wife in what is obviously Door County.

16. Charley Root attracted Blei's attention almost immediately, as well he might, living right next door. *The Second Novel* reprints a journal entry from May 1969: "A Midwestern Robert Frost of sorts. A gentle, kind old man whose life has been pioneering in a sense. I must learn all the doing and reason of his years. There must be all kinds of answers locked up in this old man" (111). Charley reappears in that book in a chapter recounting the visit of Ralph Rausch (162–63), and in *Neighborhood* in Blei's chapter on soup (235). *The Second Novel* entries, expanded, became the newspaper profile reprinted as the second chapter of *Door Way*.

17. My art student Nick Schlief, however, pointed out in a paper that *Door Way* and *Chi Town* also represent contrasting visions, something along the lines of Holm's "prairie eye" and "woods eye." Although all of Blei's characters are natural story-tellers, the Chicago restaurateurs are big operators in contrast to Uncle Tom and even Al Johnson; the symbolic Clearing in Ellison Bay is agrarian peace and quiet in contrast to the whirlwind tour of the symbolic Museum of Science and Industry given Cousin Woodrow on fifteen minutes squeezed into his pre-departure schedule; Door painters grow healthy and wealthy painting

traditional landscapes in traditional media, while in Chicago Bill Stipe grows poor and invisible creating experimental art on a Xerox copier. "Everything Blei writes about in each book was chosen for a very specific reason," Schlief theorized; "However, the reason is most often found in the other book."

18. "The center of Portal County retained an innocence, a privacy and purity of place that was off-the-beaten-track for tourists, and very special to Sandor Waterman. Portal County was slipping into sameness, a resort community that in time would be no different than any other resort area or suburban development. And how much was he, the artist, responsible? Was the sale of his art any different than the greed of developers subdividing large tracts of land into one-acre parcels for gentleman farmers? The greed of the gift shop people, motel people, condominium investors? Sandor Waterman no longer painted the center because he wanted to preserve it from the hands of the real estate people" (*Ghost* 146).

19. The "Required Reading" for Blei's June 2000 Writing Workshop was *The Tao Te Ching* according to Lao Tzu (read it again); *Mexico City Blues* by Jack Kerouac (also *On the Road*, if you never read it); *Howl* by Allen Ginsberg; *Earth Household* by Gary Snyder; *Coney Island of the Mind* by Lawrence Ferlinghetti. Supplemental materials, which "advanced writing students are advised to read into and around," were *One Continuous Mistake (Four Noble Truths for Writing)* by Gail Sher; and *The Spirit of Zen* by Alan Watts. The writings of Michael McClure, Philip Whalen, Lew Welch, Ed Sanders, Frank O'Hara, Anne Waldman, Tuli Kupferberg, Bob Kaufman, LeRoi Jones, Diane DiPrima, Ken Kesey, Bob Dylan, and Richard Brautigan. *The Hero and the Blues, The Blue Devils of Nada, Stomping the Blues* (essays) by Albert Murray; *The Bear Comes Home* (a novel) by Rafi Zabor; *But Beautiful* (creative nonfiction) by Geoff Dyer; *The Jazz Poetry Anthology* by Feinstein and Komunyakaa; *Moment's Notice* (jazz poetry and prose) by Lange and Mackey; *Bluer than This* (poetry) by John Harvey; *A Jazz Passacaglia* (essay) by Henry Miller; and *I Want to Talk about You* (poetry) by Dave Etter.

20. In the late nineties, Blei invested a great deal of energy and some money in publishing and promoting the Bottom Dog Press biography of Ken Patchen. After being rejected by commercial and academic presses, the book was published by a "consortium" of small presses, including the author's Bottom Dog Press, Blei's Cross+Roads Press, and Blei's publisher's Ellis Press. Members of the consortium supported Bottom Dog with money toward the print and bind bill, and assistance in distribution. Blei is credited in the book for editorial contributions, and writes in a letter that he put a lot of effort into selling the book once it appeared.

21. Later books were not without innovation, however. Fifty copies of *Door Way*, signed and numbered and with an original hand-painted Blei painting on the half-title page, sold at the pre-publication price of $50. One hundred covers to *Adventures in an American's Literature* were printed on watercolor paper, then

overpainted by Blei, varnished, and bound onto one hundred specially signed and numbered copies of the book. Special editions of *Door Steps* contained block prints. These books are now collector's items.

22. In a *Chi Town* essay on Northwestern University artist Bill Stipe, Blei mentioned the visual pun in viewing/printing the German word *und* upside down (it reads *pun* in English).

23. This painting appeared on the cover of Iveta Melnika's *Tale of the White Crow* (Ellis Press, 2003). Blei painted another crow for the cover of Leo Dangel's book *The Crow on the Golden Arches* (Spoon River Poetry Press and Cross+Roads Press, 2004).

24. In a letter of July 7, 2000, Blei commented on working his way into "*The New Yorker* mold" of carefully crafted fiction, with its endless revisions and polished style, then consciously opting out of that style as too crafted, too professional.

5. LINDA HASSELSTROM

1. "The editor requires me to use nonsexist language; I am not sexist, so I have complied wherever possible. This manuscript written in the twentieth century will not offend twentieth-century ideas of right and wrong. But the requirement strikes me as an ironic commentary on the differences between modern times and the times that are the subject of this history. The men and women who made history in Dakota in the seventeenth and eighteenth centuries were doing the best they could to survive in their own time. . . . Only by pretending to be men could [rebel women] have a man's freedom. Faced with that fact that in their society, they didn't make up a new term, or find a therapist, or pass a law (mainly because they couldn't vote)—they acted. When they started coming to the West in record numbers, they modified society in record time. Even women who were content to wear skirts demanded the vote; female suffrage was ratified in western states first. Women roped and branded their own cattle, used weapons when necessary, and swore if they felt like it; still do" (*Roadside* xii). About her poem "Clara in the Post Office," Hasselstrom writes, "It was published in *High Country News* and I was fiercely attacked by a feminist for not being liberated, which I thought was ironic" (Letter 2).

2. "Mike dozed for the first part of our drive, I read *The Monkey Wrench Gang*, for the sixth or seventh time . . ." (*Windbreak* 178). On Hasselstrom and Hemingway, see Sanderson, 173. "Addicted to Work" and "Land Circle: Lessons" (*Land Circle* 63–79, 240–59) are very much in the stylistic and intellectual tradition of Wendell Berry, who is quoted several times in those essays and elsewhere. For Hasselstrom on Manfred, see *Land Circle* 91–95. On Leopold, see *Land Circle* 305. On Jackson, see *Land Circle* 253.

Hasselstrom is a long-time admirer of Le Sueur, whose presence she increasingly comes to assume: "I move through my own workshops revitalized by

Meridel's presence, and eager to finish so I can listen to her. I have never felt more vital, more alive, more aware of my womanhood—and all because of this aged goddess" (*Windbreak* 161). The influence of Le Sueur can be seen in Hasselstrom's opinions on gender and—supplemented with Indian teachings—on life and nature as a circle (see especially *Land Circle* 244ff.) and in poems like "Drought Year" (*Land Circle* 298), "Tapestry" (*Dakota Bones* 92), and "Alice Johnson: Matriarch" (*Dakota Bones* 106).

In *Land Circle*, Hasselstrom writes, "This generation's heroes are people who work to save our environment: the dead Saint Ed Abbey, Wendell Berry, Wes Jackson, Annie Dillard, Ann Zwinger, Gary Snyder, Barry Lopez, Gretel Ehrlich, Bil Gilbert, Kim Stafford . . ." (325–26). Elsewhere she writes, "when I really became interested in modern essays through my reading, I began to read Loren Eiseley, John McPhee, Wendell Berry, Annie Dillard, Edward Abbey. I have read every book those five have written. . . . Lately I've been reading writers who began as scientists, like Gary Nabhan, David Quammen. I enjoy Tom Cahill. The more of that kind of reality I read, the less I enjoy most modern fiction writers" ("Questions" 14).

On the other hand, Hasselstrom disdains academic feminists, probably for good reason. Delivering a keynote address at Marshall Fest IV (Southwest State University, Marshall, Minnesota, October 9, 1995), Judith Fetterley confounded half of her audience with her opening remark, "As a child I noticed that animals of indeterminate gender, including cows, were usually given male names. . . ." Academics in the audience nodded solemnly; writers who had grown up on farms, ranches, and small towns scratched their heads, then tuned out.

3. One complete list reads, "Robert King, Kevin Woster, Mark Vinz, Thom Tammaro, Ted Kooser, Cary Waterman, William Kloefkorn, Larry Holland, Kathleen Norris, Joe Paddock, David Allan Evans, Leo Dangel, Phil Dacey, Kent Meyers, Bart Sutter, David Dwyer, David Bengtson, Elizabeth Cook-Lynn, Tom Hennen, Kathleene West, Gary David, Don Welch, Bill Holm, John R. Milton, John Calvin Rezmerski, Thomas McGrath, Carol Bly, Susan Strayer Deal, Diane Glancey, Paul Gruchow, Patricia Hampl, Twyla Hansen, Margaret Hasse, Jon Hassler, Jim Heynen, Lois Phillips Hudson, Garrison Keillor, Meridel Le Sueur, Jay Meek, Dan O'Brien, William Stafford, Gerald Vizenor, Sylvia Griffith Wheeler, Roberta Hill Whiteman, Maxine Kumin, Verlyn Klinkenborg, Wendell Berry, Ann Zwinger—and having hit a Z, I'll stop, knowing the list is incomplete and changing every day" ("Questions" 16).

4. In a biographical statement at the end of *Dakota Bones*, Hasselstrom writes, "The work that occupies most of my time—writing and ranching—is complementary; physical and mental labor blend smoothly into a whole. I see my life as a circle: writing about, and laboring on the land of the Great Plains. As I've grown older, keeping my roots in this arid soil has helped me to develop as a writer and as a human being, and to be a responsible rancher" (164).

5. Hasselstrom herself was often puzzled by details of her early childhood: "The photos in her album don't always match Mother's stories. Several pictures show her staring deadpan at the camera from a street lined with towering buildings, holding a lipstick-stained cigarette and wearing a broad hat tilted over her upswept hair. Several other photos show her with a cocktail glass, yet she taught me that ladies don't smoke or drink. . . . When was she smoking cigarettes and drinking martinis in a city? I asked her once. 'I married my high school sweetheart and moved to Pittsburgh,' she said without looking at me. 'I shouldn't have done it, because I never loved him.' She divorced her first husband to marry my father, Paul, a short man with dark eyes under a tilted hat brim, who appeared in her album a few pages later. . . . Though he was my biological father, I've never seen any physical resemblance between us" (*Feels* 11, 12). Later Hasselstrom writes, "I know now that my mother ran away from my father because she caught him in bed with her best friend" (*Feels* 14).

6. "When we Quakers and other war protestors stood in front of the World War II memorial in silent protest against the Viet Nam war, I studied the faces of the young people who screamed epithets at us, and realized that most of them would call themselves Christians. Farm boys with fresh, familiar faces sicced their dogs on us when we sat on the grass on Gentle Thursday. The highway patrolmen who charged out through the front door of the administration building swinging batons and clubbing us to the ground—after the students were killed at Kent State—were good, clean-cut family men . . ." (*Land Circle* 245).

7. The breakup with one boyfriend is described in the poem "Ironing My Husband's Shirts":

Each Saturday I ironed his shirts,
laughing with the other women.
One day I set down my iron and thought.
My father fed cows alone so I could study;
I worked at night to join a sorority.
I needed to study, but I was ironing shirts.
I wanted to write, to wait for children
until my first or tenth novel was successful.
But I was ironing shirts. . . .

I was too young to wear his ring,
but I ironed his shirts.
It meant the same thing.
It meant we would be married
when he graduated.
It meant

I would iron his shirts
for thirty or forty
years.

I set the iron's face
in the center back
of his favorite shirt, turned it on high. (*Land Circle* 227–28)

8. "Everything signed 'Michele Michaels' is me" (E-mail).

9. The press was named after a horse thief who had lived in the Black Hills in the late 1800s; Lame Johnny Creek runs not far south and west of the ranch, and one of Linda Hasselstrom's published articles is "On the Trail of Lame Johnny" (*Black Hills Monthly*, June 1981, 16–17). The press and the magazine operated from the Hasselstrom bunkhouse, formerly the kitchen of the Lindsay house (the rest of which had been torn down for lumber), hauled closer to the Hasselstrom house and provided with a fourth wall (*Going* 42). Its address was Star Route 3 Box 9A, Hermosa, South Dakota. Between 1971 and 1984 Hasselstrom published twenty-three books, including *The Book Book: A Publishing Handbook (for Beginners and Others)*, in which Hasselstrom distilled "what I've learned in 15 years of publishing" (ii). Other Lame Johnny Press titles include E. R. Zietlow, *A Country for Old Men and Other Stories*; Robert Schuler, *Where Is Dancers' Hill*; Margaret Condon, *Topographics*; Carolyn Bell, *Delivery*; Craig Volk, *Mato Come Heal Me*; Alma Philip, *Next-Year Country: One Woman's View*; E. R. Zietlow, *The Indian Maiden's Captivity/The Heart of the Country*; and Linda Hasselstrom, editor, *A Bird Begins to Sing: Northwest Poetry and Prose* (from five South Dakota schools). A complete set of Lame Johnny Press books and issues of *Sunday Clothes* is housed in the special collections room of the University of South Dakota library, an MA thesis waiting to be written.

Lame Johnny Press ceased operations in 1984, and the bulk of the magazines disappeared on October 22, 1985:

> In the afternoon I loaded up the pickup with assorted junk including paper cake sacks left from last winter, huge tangled masses of baling wire from the hay we fed, and boxes of the magazine I once published and took it all to the city dump. It was heartbreaking to load all those magazines—inadvertently seeing layouts I'd been proud of, articles I was sure would gain enough subscribers to make the magazine pay—but I couldn't stand walking past them in the basement, the bunkhouse and the chicken house any longer. When it actually came to throwing them off the truck, however, I felt exhilarated, as though I'd been carrying them on my back. Perhaps this is a sign it's time to stop thinking of publishing for others and concentrate more on my own work. (*Windbreak* 33)

10. In an unpublished forty-two-page database titled "Questions about Linda Hasselstrom," she speaks candidly about her income from writing: 1988, "an exceptionally good year," almost $2,000; 1990, expenses almost $2,000 above income, which was $10,000; 1996, gross income from writing and teaching, $11,251; not one cent from writing between June and December 1997 (but plenty of expenses while promoting *Leaning into the Wind*).

11. Throughout *Windbreak* (1985–86) Hasselstrom talks about working on short stories, and the entry for November 26 reads, "I got my Crazy Horse novel back from the agent" (45). For *Horizons: The South Dakota Writers' Anthology*, published in 1983 by Lame Johnny Press, she wrote the introduction to the fiction section and represented herself with the story "Beauty." Elsewhere she mentions "four novels" lying in her drawers and more than a book's worth of stories, but in 2001 she admitted to Lee Ann Roripaugh, "I failed miserably at fiction" (17).

12. "The moment, for example, that someone finally decides not to take the promising job offered by Reserve Mining, for example, or the moment someone decides not to pad a travel-expense account at the Ramada is a moment in which ice and snow and bare trunks look better, less happenstance, less pointless," writes Carol Bly (44).

13. This list also appears, slightly expanded, in *Windbreak* (61); elsewhere appear other John Hasselstrom aphorisms: "Never count the dead ones" (*Going* 136); "It's a dry country" (*Land Circle* 303); "Take care of little things, and the big things will take care of themselves" (*Windbreak* 9); "It helps to be smarter than the cow" (*Land Circle* 10).

14. "I think it is fascinating that the two men worked together in this instance; my father was not willing to shoot my horse, even though he believed it needed to be done, and he also respected George's greater skill with the rifle, and asked George to help him" (Letter).

15. The following selections are representative:

I have not borne a child,
I refused that sacrifice
of blood and gaping pain. ("Helicopter Crash," *Dakota Bones* 61)

I dreamed last night I was having a baby. (*Windbreak* 25)

I did, when deciding to marry George, consciously note the fact that he is sterile, and that I would thus not have to decide—again—not to have children. Since then, when we've talked of adoption I've resisted my motherly urges because I know I would find it difficult to write, and I must write—and that's a conscious decision. (*Windbreak* 147)

Carolyn has hot cocoa;
I put a shot of whiskey in mine,
wonder if I should have had a child. (*Land Circle* 14)

At thirty-six I understood
I'd never have children. (*Dakota Bones* 69)

    I'm 41,
hair going gray,
divorced,
childless. (*Dakota Bones* 115)

It is possible that Hasselstrom's attention to birth (and death) on the ranch reflects and perhaps compensates for the absence of birth in her own life.

16. "It's been six years or better since we closed the box" (8), "the son he never had" (9), "Ten years next moonrise since I buried you" (10), "he'd been working on that ranch / nearly sixty years" (14), "They all / sat with her on the porch recalling / Tom" (15), "Two grandmothers—Jerry's / and my own—join me in our kitchen / this November night, although they both / died years ago and never met" (16), "The room congeals / with memories" (18), "lives gone by / too soon" (24), "tired of waiting for my dead husband / to come back" (26), "that bright December / thirty years ago. / The day you died beside your husband" (35), "Your death was just the first / in a list too long to contemplate today" (37), "Eight years ago today I watched your coffin / lowered into gumbo on a prairie hill" (42), "I sink into a padded booth / opposite my husband, dead / now but always waiting" (60).

6. BILL HOLM

1. This poem, as a framed broadside, hangs on the wall of Holm's house in Minneota, beside his piano. In the same book, Holm writes, "How do you fill an ego, make a self strong? The ego requires first the power to sympathetically imagine something outside itself: the lives of other human beings, perhaps enormously different from your own; second, the capacity to love something outside the self in the world of nature, art, or human beings" (85).

2. Tombstones in the small country graveyards tell this story most intriguingly: a young man with the resoundingly Icelandic name of Olaf married to a young woman named Marie in the cemetery south of Minneota, west of Ghent; a wife named simply "Anne Poland" buried among the Lutherans west of Granite Falls.

3. Holm traveled little as a child, but his imagination kicked in at an early age. "I discovered the imagination early," he writes (*Eccentric* 8), "then fed it with books, music, and daydreaming till it grew to the usual monstrous human size." Beneath Holm's picture in his high school senior class album are written the words, "This is my philosophy. I made it."

4. Einar Hallgrimsson, Holm recalls, offered Carlyle, Anatole France, Goethe, Longfellow, Pope, Gray, Dante, Poe, Whitman, Homer, Wordsworth, Browning, Scott, Emerson, Whittier, Heine, Villon, Schiller, Shakespeare, Mrs. Hemens,

Hannah More, the *Eddas*, Halldór Laxness, Snori Sturluson, Hallgrimur, Milton, Dante, Dunbar, Eugene Field, Robert Service (*Heart* 175). Nor was Einar the only source of a literary education outside of school. Stena Dalmann gave Holm Goethe's *Faust*, *The Stones of Venice*, *Fanchon the Cricket* by George Sand, Herbert Spencer's *First Principles*, Emanuel Swedenborg's *Heaven and Hell and the World of Spirits and Things Heard and Seen*, Tom Paine's *The Rights of Man* and *The Age of Reason*, Henry George's *Progress and Poverty*, *The Complete Lectures of Colonel Robert W. Ingersoll* . . . and, yes, *The Communist Manifesto* (*Heart* 165).

5. Holm provides no date for Sister Helen's ministry, but it was common in early western Minnesota towns for itinerant ministers to hold church services in saloons. Photographs exist, although written records are scant. Holm's remark about "pool-shooters, rummy-players, snoose-chewers, and beer-drinkers barely looked up from their games" (*Music* 45) alludes to another lost element in the culture, which Holm obviously knew, and that is pool, originally billiards imported by the Belgians, which was apparently a strong although unrecorded tradition in western Minnesota up through the early seventies. In *Landscape of Ghosts* (19) Holm specifically identifies the Round-Up as a pool hall.

6. But see *The Heart Can Be Filled Anywhere on Earth*, page 155: "The only sin for which I've never forgiven Lutherans is the attempted willful destruction of their tradition of ancient language and choral singing. Each revised hymnal grows steadily stupider in its efforts to be fashionable and to remodel the prose and voice leading of its betters." Elsewhere, Holm mentions "a watery liturgy out of the watery new green hymnal, signs about caring and sharing, a watery handshake followed by watery coffee" (*Coming Home* 102).

7. Holm's friendship with Elmer Suderman dates to his Gustavus years. He read the *Dao De Jing* and edited the school literary magazine, *Prospects*, his senior year, contributing four poems of his own, including "Traverse Cemetery on a May Night or Meditation on the Grave of Amos Huggins, Killed in 1864 by the Indians at Lac-Qui-Parle at the Age of 29. . . . or Three Questions I Would Like to Ask a Corpse."

8. Actually, Holm writes little about either the sixties or the seventies. In *Eccentric Islands*, he blows by them as quickly as he did in *Heart* and *Music*: "By the age of forty, I had survived the deaths of parents, the failure of a marriage, financial ruin, a collapsed career, a few disastrous love affairs, the usual stuff" (158).

9. This two-tier system of education is becoming common in communist and formerly communist countries, including, that I know of, Poland and Latvia. While the brightest and best still receive tuition-free education, others pay for either special courses at state institutions or degree programs at private schools. During his year in Xi'an, Holm had met the brightest and best of China's 1.3 billion people, the kind of students who in the States would have attended Harvard, Northwestern, Stanford, or Duke on full scholarships; in Wuhan, Holm encountered the equivalent of his Southwest State students: those who could not

make the cut and had to pay for a degree from a second- (although not third-) rate institution and figured that their money bought certain entitlements, including the right to receive good grades while being bored and boring.

10. Compare Kent C. Ryden in *Mapping the Invisible Landscape*: "Since places are fusions of experience, landscape, and location, they are necessarily bound up with time and memory as well. The experiences which create and establish places recede inevitably into the past, so that one important quality of places is that they are 'the present expressions of past experiences and events' [Edward Relph, *Place and Placelessness*, 33]—contemplation of place quickly brings to mind earlier stages in one's life, episodes in the history of a community, formative and notable events and experiences. The landscape of a place is an objectification of the past, a catalyst for memory" (39).

11. The aphorism "the dead get by with everything," not to my knowledge a midwestern commonplace, appears in Kloefkorn's *Welcome to Carlos*, where it is attributed to Carlos (79).

12. Richard O. Davies points out in *Main Street Blues: The Decline of Small-Town America*, "One of the overlooked tragedies of modern American history has been the trashing of its small communities by federal policies [especially the highway lobby]. . . . The condition of the cities became one of the highest priorities of domestic policy, and the nation's villages were overlooked" (186, 187). The fact that, according to the 2000 census, over half of all Americans now live in places they call "suburbs," may mean tough sledding for the agendas of both the towns and the cities.

13. The influence of both Robert and Carol Bly on Bill Holm's thinking is enormous. From Carol Bly, Holm took the phrase "Minnesota nice" and his habit of moralizing the landscape, as in "I am a moralist" (*Landscape* 9). Robert Bly shows up in Holm's affection for the dark and his insistence that we drop down into failure, grief, and death before ascending to success, joy, and everlasting life. Robert, Carol, and Bill are all pulpit orators against the sin of cheerfulness which masks unconsciousness. Behind Holm's assertion that advice like " 'Concentrate on the present joyfully' will land you in more wars, depressions, and catastrophes, both personal and public, than you can well imagine" (*Landscape* 25) lies the analysis of Robert Bly; reading Holm's poem "Bach in Brimnes" (*Playing* 14) one cannot help hearing Bly's brief poem—which Holm quotes in at least two essays—"Six Winter Privacy Poems !" (*Selected* 56); behind Holm's poem "Sparrows" (*Dead* 58) lies Bly's "I can't tell whether this joy comes from the body, or the soul, or a third place" (*Selected* 56) and Bly's whole concept of Nature. Bly's remarks about Lutheran boy-gods ("Being a Lutheran Boy-God" 209–12) and his analysis of the son-mother relationship (*Iron John* 7ff.) are reflected in Holm's "I was a classic spoiled boy, the creation of my mother's thwarted ambition to escape her farm life. My relation to my father—any eighteen-year-old boy's relation to his father—was, to make an understatement, awkward" (*Eccentric* 180). For a

footnote on Holm's "joyful weeping" at "something female [which] softens the prairies" (*Music* 53), see Robert Bly, "A Busy Man Speaks."

14. Holm's work contains at least two early examples of seeing the world to see home. In *Boxelder Bug Variations*, a bug who likes to travel glides down the Yellow Medicine River to the Minnesota River, and thence to the Mississippi, to New Orleans, to the great world beyond, catching the Gulf Stream north to Norway, where he is picked up by a Canada goose migrating to Lac qui Parle, Minnesota. When the goose is shot by a hunter and dressed by his wife, the bug finds himself back home, where the cycle begins anew. Holm titled the poem, "The Afterlife, or the Great Mandala (Take Your Choice) Illustrated by a Boxelder Bug Who Gets It into His Wings to Travel." In *The Music of Failure* a "Lucky Stone" from the Acropolis travels with a Minneota Chevy dealer from Greece to southwestern Minnesota, and is passed along to Bill Holm, who returns it to the Parthenon. The stone sings, "I've traveled now, / seen corn and beans, / felt mad winter, / heard new speech, / wind in fall grass. . . . But time to go home; / I need that history / no one wanted though / it was their own, / need heat and sea, / moon on white hills" (*Music* 97). Holm understood early on that one goes away for the privilege of coming home.

15. I offer a small piece of second-hand anecdotal evidence. One my former Polish students, Kacper Barczak, won a Fulbright research scholarship to the States, which he spent at Stanford University in the spring of 2001. More than once he has told the story of being at a small gathering hosted by a recent Polish immigrant to the States, a man who had married, bought a house, settled into a job in the service industry, trucking or chauffeuring or some such like that. His guests included Kacper, a Hollander, and a German. The Hollander and the German began the usual cocktail discourse on American crudity, vulgarity, materialism, you can't get this here, the food stinks, the television is pointless, this is the worst country in the world. The Polish host looked puzzled, then agitated, then angry. Finally he broke into the conversation. "What are you talking about?" he wanted to know. "What you are saying is just stupid. America is the greatest country in the world. In Poland, I am one of those drunks who beat their women, live on the street, and amount to nothing ever in his life. In America I have a beautiful wife, I have fine children, I have house, new car, plenty to eat. I have two jobs, I make a little extra money on the side. I am happy."

16. While Holm occasionally bends place to fit literature, he sometimes bends literature to fit place. His affection for Thoreau matches his affection for Whitman, Lawrence, Bly, and the Icelandic sagas, and in the name of friendship, Thoreau is led into some strange places. In *Eccentric Islands*, Thoreau, a shore man if ever there was one, is made an island man in the name of necessity: "Our great American conscience nagger, Henry Thoreau, was not, in the geographical sense, an island man, but in the spiritual sense, he was never anything else" (7). In *The Music of Failure*, Thoreau, a woodsman, is given prairie

vision: "Trust a prairie eye to find beauty and understate it truthfully, no matter how violent the apparent exaggeration. Thoreau, though a woodsman, said it right: 'I can never exaggerate enough'" (19).

7. JIM HEYNEN

1. Ann Arbor and Grand Rapids, Michigan; Iowa City, Iowa; Lewiston, Idaho; Eugene, Portland, and Port Townsend, Oregon; Santa Clara, California; St. Peter, Northfield, and St. Paul, Minnesota. "Jim Heynen is an Iowan turned Oregonian turned Idahoan turned Washingtonian," reads the biography in his 1977 chapbook *How the Sow Became a Goddess*.

2. The school is mentioned in *The Man Who Kept Cigars in His Cap*: "The Boys said, He can't do that to us! We're boys from Welcome #3! Which was their township and schoolhouse number" (4).

3. Heynen's sense of humor is wry, in the tradition of the Midwest rather than Vaudeville, the gradually escalating absurdity told with the straight face of a Mark Twain tall tale. In one story, the fact that dogs and geese eat dog shit and goose shit is spun into a tale of geese eating a bacon rind shat out by another goose, which is spun into the story of a flock of birds strung together with a bacon rind tied to a string. In another story, a hay sling deposits Big Bull in the haymow floor, but the boys invent a tale of him climbing up the ladder. Then they embellish: "The boys pulled out some of Big Bull's hair and stuck it to the boards at the top of one of the ladders going up the haymow to make it look as if that was the opening Big Bull squeezed through. And they loosened a couple of the ladder rungs to make it look as if the ladder almost gave way on him as he climbed up" (*You Know* 53). The problem of limited space in a rural graveyard is pumped into a political battle between the town and the farmer who owns all the land surrounding the cemetery. Zoning battles loom, cartoons show triple-decker burials and high-rise tombs, and someone invents a pre-death starvation diet to make people thinner so they take up less space. In an election year the farmer accuses the mayor of running on a "graveyard ticket," and having a heart attack as a campaign gimmick; when the farmer finally sells some land at a very inflated price, people accuse him of cashing in on "Death Futures" (*You Know* 188).

4. In a 2001 version (*Boys'*) of this 1985 story, it is the boys' grandfather, not the boys themselves, who discovers this unusual use for the chamber pot.

5. The trick of moving the outhouse six feet ahead, so that pranksters who came to tip it over on Halloween night fall into the pit, is the basis of the poem "Old Man Brunner on Halloween Night," by Heynen's friend Leo Dangel (*Home* 50). Heynen's story was published in 1985, Dangel's poem in 1987.

6. "Oscar . . . was a man of powerful body and unusual endurance; the sort of man you could attach to a corn-sheller as you would an engine. He would turn it all day, without hurrying, without slowing down. But he was as indolent of mind as he was unsparing of his body. His love of routine amounted to a vice.

He worked like an insect, always doing the same thing over in the same way, regardless of whether it was best or no. He felt that there was a sovereign virtue in mere bodily toil, and he rather liked to do things in the hardest way" (Cather, *O Pioneers!* 55).

7. "There is restraint against enthusiasm ('real nice' is the adjective—not 'marvelous'); there is restraint in grief ('real sober' instead of 'heartbroken'); and always, always, restraint in showing your feelings, lest someone be drawn closer to you," writes Carol Bly; "This restraint was there with the first pioneers; the strong-minded Swiss-American writer Mari Sandoz, in describing her family's settling in Nebraska, called the newer, Scandinavian influx 'mealy-mouthed'" (*Letters* 2). In the footnotes to the "News" chapter of *Lake Wobegon Days*, Garrison Keillor reprints *95 Theses 95*, "a neatly typed manifesto . . . brought home in late October 1980" by Terpsichore Terrace (251): "9. You taught me to be nice, so that now I am so full of niceness, I have no sense of right and wrong, no outrage, no passion. 'If you can't say something nice, don't say anything at all,' you said, so I am very quiet, which most people think is politeness. I call it repression" (254, 255).

8. This character, based on a man Heynen knew as a boy, also appears in *The Man Who Kept Cigars in His Cap* (5) and *Being Youngest* (68).

9. Heynen can satirize this kind of hypocrisy in a character like the woman whose greatest talent was in seeing what other people were doing wrong (*You Know* 156), or in local commentary on the man who suddenly inherits his father's three farms: "He should give the farms to charity for a memorial, someone said. That would be the decent thing to do. People said that being rich was making the man too big for his britches. He had more stars than tears in his eyes, that's for sure, they said" (*Boys'* 54).

10. The story is first told in *A Suitable Church* (41).

11. The older the boys grow, Heynen suggests, the meaner they become, and only the youngest retain enough innocence to be embarrassed or outraged: "Henry looked at Gretchen. He thought he saw an almost-throw-up look on her face. He didn't just feel angry with his brothers. For the first time in his life, he felt ashamed of them. Maybe Gretchen's sister was a creep, but she didn't go blowing up little gophers for fun" (*Youngest* 108).

12. "How we pitied these creatures," Robert Bly writes of the bank clerk sent out to his father's farm in the thirties. "Getting out of the car with a white shirt and a necktie, stepping over the stubble like a cat so as not to get too much chaff on his black oxfords, how weak and feeble! What a poor model of a human being! It was clear the teller was incapable of any boisterous joy, and was nothing but a small zoo animal of some sort that locked the doors on itself, pale from the reflected light off the zoo walls, light as salt in a shaker, clearly obsessed with money—you could see greed all over him. How ignoble! How sordid and ignoble! What ignobility!" ("Being" 213).

13. His favorite authors, whom he recommends to Cosmos Coyote, are Gary Snyder, Terry Tempest Williams, Paul Gruchow, Scott Sanders, Rachel Carson, Barry Lopez, Edward Abbey, Annie Dillard, and Gretel Ehrlich (193).

8. JIM HARRISON

1. Harrison offered his own version of Gertrude Stein's witty aphorism, which he often quotes, in his first novel *Wolf*: "—All you have to do is tell it like it is. —But nothing is like anything" (69).

2. Harrison, and many critics, consistently underplay comparisons between his work and Hemingway's: "It's annoying, in the end, this way journalists who are in a hurry always compare him to Hemingway, whereas Faulkner is his real brother, Faulkner is the true writer" (Levy 85). There are similarities, and there are differences. Meridel Le Sueur may have provided the best gloss in a remark she made in a lecture at Southwest Minnesota State: "When I was young, people used to tell me, 'You should write more like Hemingway.' I can't write like Hemingway—fishing, fucking, fighting . . . that's not what my life is all about."

3. This notion—which is the mature Harrison's appraisal of the younger Harrison—reappears in the novel *Farmer*, where country-school teacher Joseph recalls a summer course in short fiction at the University of Michigan: "Joseph had liked 'The Bear' the best but was troubled deeply by the Dostoevski book. . . . He liked Sherwood Anderson least because he wrote only about what everyone knows, but the professor insisted that that was precisely why he was good, a point of view that flew over Joseph's head like a migrating teal" (113).

4. Harrison describes it as "an island totally devoid of rules of behavior, a tropical island fueled by sunlight, dope, and booze, as far from Kansas as you could get in America. Later I noted that the movie business never quite equaled Key West for questionable behavior" (*Off* 242).

5. See Prescott; by way of rebuttal, see Lorenz; for Harrison's own opinion, see DeMott, 75.

6. Writes Harrison in *Just Before Dark*, "I despise the word 'vibration' but the media always extrudes [*sic*] a sourness, a negative energy. They live and work in a voyeuristic space where they're always outside jacking off while watching life taking place on the other side of the window" (159). In *Off to the Side*, he notes, "people who watch a great deal of TV never again seem able to adjust to the actual pace of life" (15). In *Conversations with Jim Harrison*, he says, "Hollywood's always making movies about making movies. Or the movie business. Well, that doesn't play in Kansas. Who gives a shit? It's like making movies about dope. They think everybody does dope. Well, very few people do dope. Why do people in Topeka want to see a movie about cocaine? They don't know shit from cocaine" (DeMott 38).

7. "John Harrison has said that, 'if you read *Dalva* and *The Woman Lit by Fireflies*, you can see that' Jim's wife, daughters, and family are 'central to his

existence.' Indeed, like Jim Harrison himself, the son, brother, husband, father and now grandfather, Harrison's characters often find purpose, meaning, and stability within the circle of family love and solidarity" (Reilly 11). "In marriage I found something to tie me to earth," Harrison observes in *Off to the Side* (66).

8. Harrison wrote four food columns for the literary magazine *Smoke Signals* in 1981, a series of sporting food columns (many reprinted in *Just Before Dark*) for the mass-circulation magazine *Smart* around 1990, and a series of columns for *Esquire* in 1990. He is famous (or infamous) for having shared with friends a thirty-seven-course lunch that cost approximately the price of a new Volvo station wagon on November 17, 2003, an exercise in gluttony reported in the *New Yorker* of September 6, 2004. In Harrison's fiction, the obsession with fine foods does not really appear until "Revenge" and "The Man Who Gave Up His Name" in *Legends of the Fall* (1978), but thereafter it becomes almost a running joke: "Duck feet looked funny to some but to the Chinese they were a delicacy" (*Legends* 129), "filet of sole Bercy aux champignons" (*Legends* 135), "Pet, a Cree noted for her beauty whom Ludlow's wife had taught to cook well over the past few years from an antique French cookbook known as the Ali Bab" (*Legends* 202), "a simple gumbo made from dark roux, a duck stock where the meat is reserved for the final dish, garlic, hot peppers, a mirepoix, a little okra, andouille sausage, then within ten minutes of completion you add the shrimp, oysters and crabmeat" (*Sundog* 93), "poached Maine lobsters . . . and finally a rough-cut filet covered with garlic and pepper" (*Dalva* 18), and John Wesley Northridge II's description of a down-home meal prepared on the plains of western Nebraska in 1952: "I chop an onion and put it in a pan with butter, then pluck a few leaves of fresh sage from Frieda's herb pots in the window. She also churns butter, the likes of which you can't get in Chicago or New York, but must travel to far-off Normandy. I mince the bird's gizzard in the pan with the onion, then tear some bread in pieces. Dalva likes the dressing roasted, not 'gummy' from inside the bird. She will only eat rutabaga if it's mashed with the potatoes, and brussels sprouts are out of the question unless halved and fried in butter rather than boiled" (*Road* 14).

9. Consider the case of Dom Perignon in "Revenge" (*Legends* 17), the three magnums of Ruffino Barolo and the "bottle of Sire de Gouberville calvados with its 'autumnal flavors'" in *Julip* (78); the "bottle of La Begorce in my snack container" in *Sundog* (5); the "Grands Echezeaux and her last bottle of Romanée-Conti" in *Dalva* (18); the '49 Latour Boordeaux, "an outstanding wine, the gift of which moistened my unworthy eyes" in *Dalva* (181); the cases of Meursault or Chambertin in *The Woman Lit by Fireflies* (181); and the "Ducru-Beaucaillou, bought in Chicago because I liked the sound of the name though it was more than palatable" in *The Road Home* (17).

10. Joseph in *Farmer*; Nordstrom in *Legends of the Fall*; Jim Crabb, Charles, Arthur, Ted, and Marcia's various male partners in *Julip*; the fifty-year-old Phillip Caulkins in "The Beige Dolorosa" (*Julip*); even Emmeline, who in *Sundog* se-

duces her uncle Earl (122), and "a red-haired busgirl" in *True North* who, after suggesting she and David Burkett could "get together after she finished work" (324) admits that she's too young to have a driver's license.

11. Reilly records the following conversation between Harrison's mother and her son the writer: "Don't your people ever have normal sex?" "What the fuck is that? Give me a break. I don't allow it—normal sex" (9). Joseph, the forty-three-year-old country school teacher in *Farmer* who is having an affair with his seventeen-year-old student who "flat out screws like a lunatic" (36) admits he "had never until Catherine experienced anything remotely similar except in his imagination" (12).

12. Harrison told Hank Nuwer in 1985, "I couldn't write for *The New Yorker*, although I read it occasionally when it has McPhee or Matthiessen or Ed Hoagland. *The New Yorker* doesn't publish stuff that has food and sex in it, which leaves me out" (DeMott 56); in an interview with Patrick Smith he expressed considerable satisfaction that when *The Woman Lit by Fireflies* was published in *The New Yorker*, it produced "something like 120 favorable letters, which is an awful lot" (DeMott 214).

13. "I'd like to talk about your characters," said Eleanor Wachtel to Harrison in an interview; "Sometimes they're not only a little off course, it's as if they've dropped through a hole in their own lives" (DeMott 184). Writes Harrison, "Kazin was offended and I never heard from him again except for a tersely negative note on my second novel, *A Good Day to Die*, suggesting that such characters couldn't exist" (*Off* 233). *The New Yorker* reviewer of *Farmer* thought that Harrison is "at his worst when he is describing relations between the sexes" (Reilly 51). The *Atlantic Monthly* review of *Legends of the Fall* thought "These stories skim dangerously near the category of thrillers," while W. H. Roberson found the characterizations "shallow and underdeveloped" (Reilly 63). A. C. Greene found the main weakness of *Sundog* to be Harrison's weak characterization of both the narrator and Strang (Reilly 102), although both Strang and the book's narrator share many traits with Harrison himself, including the narrator's remark, "I might have been born up here [in Michigan], but I didn't belong" (13). John Clute found *Dalva*'s characterization "at times rather difficult to swallow" (Reilly 114). Michiko Kakutani found Strang "not a character capable of supporting an entire novel" (quoted in Smith 46). Patrick Smith finds Harrison's characters "linked by their essential inability to function within the constraints of a society that has become alien to them, either through their own machinations, or at the hands of someone who represents that society and wishes to keep them in abeyance to society's mores" (137–38).

14. Harrison caught himself later in his career: speaking of old man Nordstrom in *The Road Home*, he told Patrick Smith, "I knew I had to enter honestly into his individual voice and I couldn't betray it by showing off, by making it too consciously an act of literature, which would prevent being carried long

[*sic*]" (DeMott 206). Harrison's intention was for Northridge's voice to "become mangled and intolerable, a prairie Lear" (*Just* 288).

15. Another game readers can play is guessing how many pages it will take for Harrison to use the word "banal": *Legends of the Fall*, 2; *Sundog*, 45; *Dalva*, 15; *The Woman Lit by Fireflies*, 3; *The Road Home*, 52 (see also pages 67, 208, 328, and 409); *Off to the Side*, 27; *True North*, 3.

16. The narrator sounds very much like the author: "In *Sundog* a fictional Jim Harrison is a depressed novelist whose work has deteriorated to writing a book about game cookery and who has found that 'gluttony, alcohol, painkillers . . . didn't work anymore' (xii; while discussing *Sundog* I will refer to the fictional character as 'Jim Harrison' and the author as 'Harrison')" (McClintock 196). The author-narrator who satirizes himself is one way in which Harrison embodies the postmodernism of which he complains; the often-noted disjointed organization of his novels is another, adapted from Joyce, Faulkner, or even Vernice's favorite, Lawrence Durrell's *Alexandria Quartet* (*True North* 359).

17. One anonymous reviewer quoted by Patrick Smith expresses a minority opinion: "It is appropriate that Harrison, a man who can choose a learned word like 'fetor' over its synonym 'stench,' should also enrich his rustic hero's thoughts with some basic details of rural life: oiling an old harness, butchering hogs. Moreover, Harrison's dialogue is true to its setting—flat, almost toneless, yet still expressive" (6).

18. Harrison suggests in *Sundog*, they are all the same: "The younger man said that in the past year he had been in Beverly Hills, Palm Springs, Aspen, Deauville, plus a month at the Carlyle in New York City. 'Those are all the same places,' quipped the older man" (xi).

19. The fictional poet's book, titled *Études*, contains "a long poem about how much he missed his young daughter Lila in California. It was a lovely poem but raised the question of why he didn't go visit her. 'Destiny has swept me away from you,' he wrote" (285).

20. Although much of the rubbish in Michael's brain is the rubbish that infected Harrison at Stony Brook (see especially page 175), Harrison doesn't quite understand 1980s academia: Michael would be in far more trouble for sleeping with a student than for coming up one book short.

21. "What's the point, then," Brown Dog wonders; "She's pals with her dad and fearless about weenies" (10).

22. Despite his own MFA, Harrison is consistently critical of the programs and the writers who direct them. The marriage of academia and creative writing has produced only a plague of MFAs who can't write and can't teach literature, an ocean of little books of poems by authors subsidized by grants and teaching positions, published by little presses subsidized by more grants, distributed by independent distributors further subsidized with grants, and praised by grant-fattened colleagues sitting as judges on the panels of subsidized little league

awards and prizes. In 1990 he told Aloysius Sisyphus, "Oh, the poetry situation today is miserable. There's a Red Guard sort of effect in America. There are about 6,000 of these MFA types wandering around muddying the waters of everything, writing their teeny nature poems or their teeny college poems, you know. It's like the civil service, actually, American poetry now, so, I lost interest in it" (DeMott 99). Academia in general strangles the "possible wisdom" of teachers (*True North* 145), and of the writers Harrison knew, early or late, none had college degrees: "Anderson, Faulkner, Hemingway, I didn't notice any B.A.'s attached to their names. . . . None. Hart Crane, Rimbaud, Garcia Lorca. Where are the B. S.'s?" (Reilly 3). In prose, the marriage produced the postmodern academic novel, which "suffocates from ethical mandarinism. It is almost totally white middle class, a product of writer's schools, the National Endowment, foundations, academia. The fact that this doesn't matter one little bit is interesting. Who could possibly give a fuck during this diaspora. The literary world is one of those unintentionally comic movies they used to make about voodoo and zombies" (*Just* 286). Harrison's summary comment on creative writing programs, MFAs, and academic novelists, is a passage in his 1998 novel *The Road Home*, in which John Wesley Northridge II meditates on the relationship between universities and writers: "I've read in *Harper's* that it's fashionable nowadays for universities to acquire living painters, poets, and novelists, to teach the young their craft, which will require of them a great deal of common sense while they drown in the deceitful morass of institutions. May the gods of art take pity on them. Art would have thrived better if they had become beggars or common criminals" (107). In a 1976 interview Harrison told Ira Elliott and Mary Somerness, "The worst thing about academic writers and people who teach writing or live within an academic atmosphere is that it shears them of a base. People think after they teach a while that academic life is a microcosm of the rest of the world, which it very clearly isn't. It's sort of . . . well, do you read Hesse at all? He wrote a book called *Magister Ludi* which is the bead game, a very closed, extraordinarily provincialized atmosphere, which maybe it should be for its purpose, for teaching. But I think that's terribly unhealthy for the writer" (DeMott 11). In *Off to the Side*, he writes, "At one time it was the town against the gown, and now it is closer to the gown against the real world. . . . In university writing programs metaphor can't be taught so it is held in disregard and in the thousand or so galleys I've been sent for 'blurbs' in recent years I've noted a faux Victorian sincerity as the main direction. This misses me as I read for aesthetic reasons and if the writing isn't artful I stop at the end of page one" (309). Harrison himself never took a writing course of any sort in his life (DeMott 36), and he bypassed deconstruction theory because he correctly "thought it was an elaborate plot to make the instructors more important than what they were reading" (DeMott 224).

23. James J. McClintock's "Jim Harrison, Soul-Maker" presents an extended examination of Harrison's relation to Hillman, Keats, and Jungian psychology.

24. Smith calls this "an organic free-form life of their own" (4). Although reviewers complained of the chronological disjointedness of *True North* (2004), that novel was relatively linear.

25. And when it comes to the Baltics, in which Harrison seems to have some odd interest, he's just wrong. He seems to confuse Balts with various other nationalities in Central Europe: "She blabbered on about her lineage, Estonian nobility, who had flown the coop as always on the eve of the Great War . . ., refugees of high birth trotting across the Carpathians through Transylvania, past the ruins of Baron von Frankenstein's castle, always with their pocket stuffed with jewelry and Sèvres eggs" (*Wolf* 75), "a college employee, whom I didn't know, who was a dumpy little parody from the Baltics" (*Julip* 247), "Willa who worked for us, a Latvian woman with a thin chest and a huge butt" (*Road* 184), "Perhaps in Lithuania women like burly men who have a fondness for anchovies and garlic" (*Off* 300).

26. "I wrote a poem in which I said John Calvin's down there under the floorboards telling me I don't get a glass of wine till four o'clock. Not 3:57, but 4:00" (DeMott 30).

27. One can't help hearing an echo of Charley's final assessment of Willy Loman in *Death of a Salesman*: "He was a happy man with a batch of cement."

28. See especially *Wolf*, pages 220 following, and the later novels in which Harrison incorporates long segments of journals, notes, and history: *The Road Home, Dalva, True North*.

29. This novella is generally unconvincing. It seems inconceivable that police—even Iowa police—could not track and find Clare, especially when she builds a fire at night. It seems unlikely that she would be able to build a fire at night after a heavy rain. It seems unlikely that she could wander far in Iowa without coming upon a farmhouse, and it seems unlikely that the night would be balmy enough for Clare to sleep naked at a time in the season when the corn was ripe enough for her to eat it. Iowa is not so far from Michigan that Harrison should not know better. He should also know that the expression—at least in this neck of the woods— is "a fat fuck" not "a flat fuck" (231).

30. McClintock argues that the idea comes from Hillman (201).

31. However in this novel, as Smith points out (41), the river finally becomes an enemy. Strang's life work has been building dams to control the flow of water, and thus metaphorically the changes of time . . . and while this makes him a strong, rooted, purposeful man, it doesn't finally work. In *Sundog, Legends of the Fall*, and other Harrison novels, water can be as ambiguous as it is in Kloefkorn poems and memoirs. The river of life, the salt water of the ocean, the world's seven seas—do they renew or destroy? Both.

Amato, Joseph, and Anthony Amato. "Minnesota, Real and Imagined: A View from the Countryside." *Daedalus* 129 (Summer 2000): 55–80.

———. *When Father and Son Conspire*. Ames: Iowa State University Press, 1988.

Amato, Joseph, Anthony Amato, Richard T. Davies, and David R. Pichaske, eds. *A Place Called Home*. Minneapolis: Minnesota Historical Society Press, 2003.

American Tongues. Dir. Louis Alvarez and Andrew Kolker. Videocassette. New York: Center for New American Media, 1987.

Anderson, Sherwood. *Winesburg, Ohio*. New York: Viking, 1958.

Andrews, Clarence. *A Literary History of Iowa*. Iowa City: University of Iowa Press, 1972.

Barillas, William. "Jim Harrison." *Dictionary of Midwestern Literature*. Bloomington: Indiana University Press, 2001.

Barnett, Mark F. Review of *Welcome to Carlos*. *The Wichita Eagle* 16 April 2000: 4D.

Berry, Wendell. *Sex, Economy, Freedom and Community*. New York: Pantheon, 1992.

Bissell, Richard. *High Water*. Boston: Little, Brown, 1954.

Blei, Norbert. *Adventures in an American's Literature*. Peoria, Illinois: Ellis Press, 1982.

———. *Chi Town*. Evanston, Illinois: Northwestern University Press, 2003.

———. *Chronicles of a Rural Journalist in America*. Ellison Bay, Wisconsin: Samizdat Press, 1990.

———. *Door Steps*. Peoria, Illinois: Ellis Press, 1983.

———. *Door to Door*. Peoria, Illinois: Ellis Press, 1985.

———. *Door Way*. Peoria, Illinois: Ellis Press, 1981.

———. "Echoes of the Berlin Wall." *Crosswinds* (Santa Fe, New Mexico), April 1993: 14.

———. E-mail letter to David Pichaske, 30 June 2000.

———. *The Ghost of Sandburg's Phizzog*. Peoria, Illinois: Ellis Press, 1986.

———. "Hearing Chicago Voices." *Rosebud* 16 (Spring/Summer 1999): 99–103.

———. *The Hour of the Sunshine Now*. Chicago, Illinois: Story Press, 1978.

———. Letter to David Pichaske, 7 July 2000.

———. *Meditations on a Small Lake*. Peoria, Illinois: Ellis Press, 1987.

———. *Neighborhood*. Peoria, Illinois: Ellis Press, 1987.

———. *Paint Me a Picture / Make Me a Poem*. Peoria, Illinois: Ellis Press, 1987.

———. "The Painted Word: The Narration of Images/Writing with a Brush." Lecture. University of Wisconsin: Stevens Point, 9 April 1991.

———. *The Second Novel*. Chicago: December Press, 1978.

———. *The Watercolor Way* (hand-sewn letterpress miniature in slipcase). Browerville, Minnesota: Ox Head Press, 1990.

———. *The Watercolored Word*. Madison, Wisconsin: Quixote Press, 1968.

———. *What I Know by Heart So Far: A Novel*. Appleton, Wisconsin: Page 5, 1995.

———. *Winter Book*. Granite Falls, Minnesota: Ellis Press, 2002.

Blue, Marian. "Jim Heynen." *Twentieth-Century Western Writers*, second edition. Detroit: St. James Press, 1991.

Blum, Etta. "Five Poets." *Poetry* 113 (1967): 340–45.

Bly, Carol. *Letters from the Country*. New York: Harper and Row, 1981.

Bly, Robert. *Iron John*. New York: Addison-Wesley, 1992.

———. "On Being a Lutheran Boy-God in Minnesota." *Growing Up in Minnesota*. Ed. Chester Anderson. Minneapolis: University of Minnesota Press, 1976. 205–19.

———. *Selected Poems*. New York: Harper and Row, 1986.

———. "The Writer's Sense of Place: A Symposium and Commentaries." *South Dakota Review* 13.3 (Autumn 1975): 73–76.

Boudreau, Richard. *The Literary Heritage of Wisconsin*. La Crosse, Wisconsin: Juniper Press, 1986.

Bradshaw, Michael. *Regions and Regionalism in the United States*. Jackson: University of Mississippi Press, 1988.

Bray, Robert C. *Rediscoveries: Literature and Place in Illinois*. Urbana: University of Illinois Press, 1982.

———. "The Regionalist Tradition in Midwestern Poetry." *Studies in Illinois Poetry*. Ed. John E. Hallwas. Urbana, Illinois: Stormline Press, 1989. 117–43.

Brown, Jack. Review of *Covenants*. *Nebraska Territory* (Fall 2000): 25–28.

Brummels, J. V. "An Interview with William Kloefkorn." *On Common Ground: The Poetry of William Kloefkorn, Ted Kooser, Greg Kuzma, and Don Welch*. Ed. Mark Sanders and J. V. Brummels. Ord, Nebraska: Sandhills Press, 1983. 29–33.

Calvino, Italo. *The Path to the Spiders' Nest*. New York: Ecco Press, 1976.

Cather, Willa. *O Pioneers!* Boston: Houghton Mifflin, 1913.

———. *My Ántonia*. Boston: Houghton Mifflin, 1918.

Chatfield, Hale, and William Kloefkorn. *Voyages to the Inland Sea VII*. La Crosse, Wisconsin: Center for Contemporary Poetry, 1977.

Cicotello, David M. "'Stay against Chaos': An Interview with William Kloefkorn." *Midwest Quarterly* (Spring 1983): 274–82.

Clayton, Andrew, and Peter Onuf. *The Midwest and the Nation*. Bloomington: Indiana University Press, 1990.

Contoski, Victor. "Dave Etter: The Art of Simplicity." *Late Harvest: Plains and Prairie Poets*. Ed. Robert Killoren. Kansas City, Missouri: BkMk Press, 1977. 53–70.

Cooley, Thomas. Preface to the second edition. *Adventures of Huckleberry Finn*. By Mark Twain. New York: Norton, 1977. ix–xi.

Crow, Charles L. *A Companion to the Regional Literatures of America*. New York: Blackwell, 2003.

Dagva, Enkhee. E-mail letter to David Pichaske, 8 October 2003.

Dangel, Leo. *Home from the Field*. Granite Falls, Minnesota: Spoon River Poetry Press, 1997.

Danker, Kathleen. "Linda Hasselstrom." *American Nature Writers*. Ed. John Elder. New York: Charles Scribner's Sons, 1997. 337–48.

Davies, Richard O. *Main Street Blues: The Decline of Small-Town America*. Columbus: Ohio State University Press, 1998.

DeLillo, Don. *White Noise*. New York: Viking, 1985.

DeMott, Robert, ed. *Conversations with Jim Harrison*. Jackson: University of Mississippi Press, 2002.

Dillard, Annie. *An American Childhood*. New York: Harper and Row, 1987.

———. *Living by Fiction*. New York: Harper and Row, 1982.

Dylan, Bob. *Writings and Drawings*. New York: Knopf, 1973.

Eliot, T. S. *The Complete Poems and Plays*. New York: Harcourt, Brace, 1962.

Elledge, Jim. "Cornfields Latticed with Railroad Tracks." *Spoon River Quarterly* 8.2 (1983): 52–56.

Engel, Bernard. "Eliot's Contrasts: From the Regional to the Universal." *Exploring the Midwestern Literary Imagination*. Ed. Marcia Noe. Troy, New York: Whitson Publishing Company, 1993. 142–50.

Erdrich, Louise. *Love Medicine*. New York: HarperCollins, 1984.

Etter, Dave. *Alliance, Illinois*. Ann Arbor, Michigan: Kylix Press, 1978.

———. *Alliance, Illinois*. Peoria, Illinois: Spoon River Poetry Press, 1983.

———. "Berryman, John." *Encyclopaedia Britannica*. Chicago: Encyclopaedia Britannica Inc., 1973. 533.

———. *Boondocks*. Menomonie, Wisconsin: Crow King Editions, 1982.

———. *Carnival*. Peoria, Illinois: Spoon River Poetry Press, 1990.

———. *Central Standard Time*. Kansas City, Missouri: BkMk Press, 1978.

———. *Cornfields*. Peoria, Illinois: Spoon River Poetry Press, 1980.

———. *Electric Avenue*. Granite Falls, Minnesota: Spoon River Poetry Press, 1988.

———. *Go Read the River*. Lincoln: University of Nebraska Press, 1966.

———. *Home State*. Peoria, Illinois: Spoon River Poetry Press, 1985.

———. *How High the Moon*. Granite Falls, Minnesota: Spoon River Poetry Press, 1996.

———. *I Want to Talk about You*. Ellison Bay, Wisconsin: Cross+Roads Press, 1995.

———. *The Last Train to Prophetstown*. Lincoln: University of Nebraska Press, 1968.

———. Letter to David Pichaske, 27 March 1999.

———. *Live at the Silver Dollar*. Peoria, Illinois: Spoon River Poetry Press, 1985.

———. *Looking for Sheena Easton*. Granite Falls, Minnesota: Spoon River Poetry Press, 2003.

———. *Midlanders*. Granite Falls, Minnesota: Spoon River Poetry Press, 1988.

———. *Next Time You See Me*. Iola, Wisconsin: Wolfsong Publications, 1997.

———. *Open to the Wind*. Menomonie, Wisconsin: special issue of *Uzzano*, 11 (Fall 1978).

———. *Riding the Rock Island through Kansas*. Iola, Wisconsin: Wolfsong Publications, 1979.

———. "The Road to the Poem: An Autobiographical Fragment." *Spoon River Quarterly* 8.2 (Spring 1983): 15–20.

———. *Selected Poems*. Peoria, Illinois: Spoon River Poetry Press, 1987.

———. *Sunflower County*. Granite Falls, Minnesota: Spoon River Poetry Press, 1994.

———. *Well, You Needn't*. Independence, Missouri: Raindance, 1975.

———. *West of Chicago*. Peoria, Illinois: Spoon River Poetry Press, 1981.

———. "William Kloefkorn: Master Poem Maker on the Great Plains." *On Common Ground: The Poetry of William Kloefkorn, Ted Kooser, Greg Kuzma, and Don Welch*. Ed. Mark Sanders and J. V. Brummels. Ord, Nebraska: Sandhills Press, 1983. 19–21.

Flanagan, John T. "A Soil for the Seeds of Literature." *The Heritage of the Middle West*. Ed. John J. Murray. Norman: University of Oklahoma Press, 1958. 198–233.

Flores, Dan. *Horizontal Yellow*. Albuquerque: University of New Mexico Press, 1999.

Follstad, Steve. Audiotape of radio interview with Norbert Blei and Dave Etter. 2 August 1987. Milwaukee, Wisconsin: WYMS.

Franklin, Wayne, and Michael Steiner, eds. *Mapping American Culture*. Iowa City: University of Iowa Press, 1992.

Frederick, John T. *Out of the Midwest*. New York: Whittlesey House, 1944.

Frost, Robert. *Selected Letters of Robert Frost*. Ed. Lawrence Thompson. New York: Holt, Rinehart and Winston, 1964.

Garland, Hamlin. *Main-Travelled Roads*. New York: Signet, 1962.

———. *A Son of the Middle Border*. Lincoln: University of Nebraska Press, 1979.

Gass, William. *In the Heart of the Heart of the Country*. New York: Harper & Row, 1968.

Gibbons, Reginald, ed. *Chicago*. Special Issue of *Triquarterly* magazine 60 (Spring/Summer 1984).

Gioia, Dana. "Explaining Ted Kooser." *On Common Ground: The Poetry of William Kloefkorn, Ted Kooser, Greg Kuzma, and Don Welch*. Ed. Mark Sanders and J. V. Brummels. Ord, Nebraska: Sandhills Press, 1983. 92–99.

Glaser, Elton, and William Greenway, eds. *I Have My Own Song for It: Modern Poems of Ohio*. Akron: University of Akron Press, 2002.

Greasley, Philip, ed. *Dictionary of Midwestern Literature*. Vol. 1. Bloomington: University of Indiana Press, 2001.

Gruchow, Paul. *Grass Roots: The Universe of Home*. Minneapolis: Milkweed Editions, 1995.

———. *The Necessity of Empty Places*. New York: St. Martin's, 1988.

Guillory, Daniel. "Tradition and Innovation in Twentieth-Century Illinois Poetry." *Studies in Illinois Poetry*. Ed. John E. Hallwas. Urbana, Illinois: Stormline Press, 1989. 43–59.

Hall, Donald. *String Too Short to Be Saved*. Boston: Godine, 1979.

Hallwas, John E. *Illinois Literature: The Nineteenth Century*. Macomb, Illinois: Illinois Heritage Press, 1986.

———. "Introduction." *Studies in Illinois Poetry*. Ed. John E. Hallwas. Urbana, Illinois: Stormline Press, 1989. 1–9.

Hamilton, Jane. *A Map of the World*. New York: Doubleday, 1994.

Hampl, Patricia. "In the Mountain Ranges and Rain Forests of St. Paul." *Imagining Home: Writing from the Midwest*. Ed. Thom Tammaro and Mark Vinz. Minneapolis: University of Minnesota Press, 1995. 123–28.

Hansen, Tom. "Kloefkorn's 'Easter Sunday' and 'Riding My Bicycle without Hands Down Huntington Street.'" *The Explicator* 3 (Spring 2001): 159–60.

———. "Review of *TreeHouse: New and Selected Poems*." *North Dakota Quarterly* 65.2 (1998): 176–79.

Harrison, Jim. *Dalva*. New York: E. P. Dutton/Seymour Lawrence, 1988.

———. *Farmer*. New York: Viking Press, 1976.

———. "Fifty Days on the Water: The Only Answer to an Insane World Is an Insane Amount of Trout Fishing." *Field and Stream* 1 May 2004: 80+.

———. *A Good Day to Die*. New York: Simon and Schuster, 1973.

———. *Julip*. New York: Houghton Mifflin/Seymour Lawrence, 1994.

———. *Just Before Dark: Collected Nonfiction*. Livingston, Montana: Clark City Press, 1991.

———. *Legends of the Fall*. New York: Delta/Seymour Lawrence, 1979.

———. *Off to the Side: A Memoir*. New York: Grove/Atlantic, 2002.

———. "A Really Big Lunch." *The New Yorker* 6 September 2004: 78+.

———. *The Road Home*. New York: Atlantic Monthly Press, 1998.

———. *The Theory and Practice of Rivers and New Poems.* Livingston, Montana: Clark City Press, 1989.

———. *Sundog.* New York: E. P. Dutton/Seymour Lawrence, 1984.

———. *True North.* New York: Grove Press, 2004.

———. *Warlock.* New York: Delacorte, 1981.

———. *Wolf: A False Memoir.* New York: Simon and Schuster, 1971.

———. *The Woman Lit by Fireflies.* New York: Houghton Mifflin, 1990.

Hasselstrom, Linda. "Beauty." *Dakota Arts Quarterly* 12 (Summer 1981): 9–13.

———. "Becoming a Broken-In Writer." *Deep West.* Ed. Michael Shay, David Romtvedt, and Linn Rounds. Cheyenne: Wyoming Center for the Book, 2003. 77–82.

———. *Between Grass and Sky.* Reno: University of Nevada Press, 2002.

———. *Bison: Monarch of the Plains.* Portland, Oregon: Graphic Arts Center Publishing, 1998.

———. *Bitter Creek Junction.* Glendo, Wyoming: High Plains Press, 2000.

———. *The Book Book: A Publishing Handbook (for Beginners and Others).* Hermosa, South Dakota: Lame Johnny Press, 1979.

———. *Caught by One Wing.* San Francisco, California: Julie D. Holcomb, Publisher, 1984.

———. *Dakota Bones.* Peoria, Illinois: Spoon River Poetry Press, 1993.

———. "Everything I Need to Know I Learned from My Horse." *Deep West.* Ed. Michael Shay, David Romtvedt, and Linn Rounds. Cheyenne: Wyoming Center for the Book, 2003. 83–92.

———. *Feels Like Far: A Rancher's Life on the Great Plains.* New York: Lyons Press, 1999.

———. *Going Over East: Reflections of a Woman Rancher.* Golden, Colorado: Fulcrum, 1987.

———. *Land Circle: Writings Collected from the Land.* Golden, Colorado: Fulcrum, 1991.

———. Letter to David Pichaske, 17 December 2002.

———. *The Muse Is Blue.* Vermillion, South Dakota: University Street Press, 1965.

———. "Questions about Linda Hasselstrom." Computer-generated document provided by Linda Hasselstrom, June 2002.

———. "Responsibility." *Orion* (Spring 2002): 32–33.

———. *Roadkill.* Peoria, Illinois: Spoon River Poetry Press, 1987.

———. *Roadside History of South Dakota.* Missoula, Montana: Mountain Press Publishing, 1994.

———. "Why Do I Write about the West?" *South Dakota Magazine,* September/October 1999: 50–51.

———. *Windbreak: A Woman Rancher on the Northern Plains.* Berkeley, California: Barn Owl Books, 1987.

Hasselstrom, Linda, ed. with Gaydell Collier, and Nancy Curtis. *Crazy Woman Creek*. Boston: Houghton Mifflin, 2004.

———. *Leaning into the Wind: Women Write from the Heart of the West*. Boston: Houghton Mifflin, 1997.

———. *Woven on the Wind: Women Write about Friendship in the Sagebrush West*. Boston: Houghton Mifflin, 2001.

Hazard, James. "Dave Etter Interview." *Spoon River Quarterly* 8.2 (Spring 1983): 24–31.

Hemingway, Ernest. *Complete Short Stories*. New York: Scribner's, 1987.

Herbst, Josephine. *Rope of Gold*. New York: Harcourt, 1939.

Herr, Cheryl Temple. *Critical Regionalism and Cultural Studies: From Ireland to the American Midwest*. Gainesville: University Press of Florida, 1996.

Heynen, Jim. *Being Youngest*. New York: Holt, 1997.

———. *The Boys' House*. St. Paul: Minnesota Historical Society Press, 2001.

———. *Cosmos Coyote and William the Nice*. New York: Henry Holt, 2000.

———. "Fifty Hints For Fiction Writers," www.jimheynen.com/bibliography/bibliography.asp?content=10.

———. *The Funeral Parlor*. Port Townsend, Washington: Graywolf Press, 1976.

———. *How the Sow Became a Goddess*. Lewiston, Idaho: Confluence Press, 1977.

———. *The Man Who Kept Cigars in His Cap*. St. Paul, Minnesota: Graywolf Press, 1979.

———. *Notes from Custer*. Ann Arbor, Michigan: Bear Claw Press, 1976.

———. *One Hundred over 100: Moments with One Hundred North American Centenarians*. Golden, Colorado: Fulcrum, 1990.

———. *The One-Room Schoolhouse: Stories about the Boys*. New York: Knopf, 1993.

———. "Sad Hour." *Blink: Sudden Fiction by Minnesota Writers*. Ed. John Colburn and Margaret Miles. Minneapolis: Spout Press, 2001.

———. *Standing Naked: New and Selected Poems*. Lewiston, Idaho: Confluence Press, 2001.

———. *A Suitable Church*. Port Townsend, Washington: Copper Canyon Press, 1981.

———. *Why Would a Woman Pour Boiling Water on Her Head?* Denton, Texas: Trilobite Press, 2001.

———. *Writing about Home*. Portland, Oregon: Northwest Writing Institute of Lewis and Clark College, 1989.

———. *You Know What Is Right*. San Francisco: North Point Press, 1985.

———, ed. *Fishing for Chickens: Short Stories about Rural Youth*. New York: Persea, 2001.

Heynen, Jim, and Michael P. Harker. *Harker's Barns: Visions of an American Icon*. Iowa City: University of Iowa Press, 2003.

Hokanson, Drake. *Reflecting a Prairie Town*. Iowa City: University of Iowa Press, 1994.

Hollinger, Richard. Review of *Sunflower County*. *North Dakota Quarterly* 63.1 (Winter 1996): 154–55.

Holm, Bill. *Boxelder Bug Variations: A Meditation on an Idea in Language and Music*. Minneapolis: Milkweed Editions, 1985.

———. *Coming Home Crazy: An Alphabet of China Essays*. Minneapolis: Milkweed Editions, 1990.

———. *The Dead Get By with Everything*. Minneapolis: Milkweed Editions, 1990.

———. *Eccentric Islands*. Minneapolis: Milkweed Editions, 2000.

———. *The Faces of Christmas Past*. Afton, Minnesota: Afton Historical Society Press, 1998.

———. *The Heart Can Be Filled Anywhere on Earth*. Minneapolis: Milkweed Editions, 1996.

———. *Holmward Bound: An Evening with Bill Holm*. Audiocassette. St. Paul: Big Productions, 2000.

———. "Is Minnesota in America Yet?" *Imagining Home*. Ed. Thom Tammaro and Mark Vinz. Minneapolis: University of Minnesota Press, 1995. 177–90.

———. *Landscape of Ghosts* (with Bob Firth). Voyager Press, 1993.

———. *Minnesota Lutheran Handbook*. Minneota, Minnesota: Westerheim Press, nd.

———. *The Music of Failure*. Marshall, Minnesota: Plains Press, 1985.

———. *Playing the Black Piano*. Minneapolis: Milkweed Editions, 2004.

———. *Warm Spell*. Minneota, Minnesota: Westerheim Press, nd.

———. *The Weavers* (letterpress miniature). Marshall, Minnesota: Ox Head Press, 1985.

———, and Mike Melman. *The Quiet Hours: City Photographs*. Minneapolis: University of Minnesota Press, 2003.

Holman, David Marion. *A Certain Slant of Light: Regionalism and the Form of Southern and Midwestern Fiction*. Baton Rouge: Louisiana State University Press, 1995.

Hoover, Paul, ed. *Postmodern American Poetry: A Norton Anthology*. New York: Norton, 1994.

Hübling, Walter. "From Main Street to Lake Wobegon and Half-Way Back: The Ambiguous Myth of the Small Town in Recent American Literature." *Mythes Ruraux et Urbains dans la Culture Américaine*. Provence, France: Publications de l'Universite de Provence, 1990. 51–66.

Hughes, Robert. *The Culture of Complaint*. New York: Oxford, 1993.

Irving, Washington. *A Tour on the Prairies*. Norman: University of Oklahoma Press, 1956.

Jaffe, Dan. Introduction. *Central Standard Time*. By Dave Etter. Kansas City, Missouri: BkMk Press, 1978. 4–5.

"Jim Heynen." *Contemporary Authors*, http://web3.infotrac.galegroup.com.

"Jim Heynen." Website: http://www.jimheynen.com.

Jones, James T. "Dave Etter." *Dictionary of Literary Biography*. Detroit: Gale Research, 1988: 87–94.

Kazin, Alfred. *A Writer's America: Landscape in Literature*. New York: Knopf, 1988.

Keillor, Garrison. *Lake Wobegon Days*. New York: Viking, 1985.

Kloefkorn, William. *Alvin Turner as Farmer*. Lincoln, Nebraska: Windflower Press, 1974.

———. *Burning the Hymnal*. Lincoln, Nebraska: A Slow Tempo Press, 1994.

———. *The Coldest Christmas*. Lincoln, Nebraska: Platte Valley Press, 1993.

———. *Collecting for the Wichita Beacon*. Lincoln, Nebraska: Platte Valley Press, 1984.

———. *Dragging Sand Creek for Minnows*. Granite Falls, Minnesota: Spoon River Poetry Press, 1992.

———. *Drinking the Tin Cup Dry*. Buffalo, New York: White Pine Press, 1989.

———. *Fielding Imaginary Grounders*. Granite Falls, Minnesota: Spoon River Poetry Press, 2004.

———. *Going Out, Coming Back*. Fredonia, New York: White Pine Press, 1993.

———. "The Great Plains." *The Midwest Quarterly* 36.4 (Summer 1995): 343–44.

———. *Honeymoon*. Kansas City, Missouri: BkMk Press, 1982.

———. *Houses and Beyond*. Lincoln, Nebraska: Platte Valley Press, 1982.

———. Letter to David Pichaske, 21 July 2001.

———. *Let the Dance Begin*. Pittsford, New York: State Street Press Chapbooks, 1981.

———. *A Life Like Mine*. Lincoln, Nebraska: Platte Valley Press, 1984.

———. *loony*. Special issue of *Apple* (10 and 11). Springfield, Illinois, 1975.

———. *Loup River Psalter*. Granite Falls, Minnesota: Spoon River Poetry Press, 2001.

———. *ludi jr*. Milwaukee, Wisconsin: Pentagram Press, 1976.

———. "The Man from Elburn, Illinois." *Zone 3* 3.2 (Spring 1988): 69–74.

———. *Not Such a Bad Place to Be*. Port Townsend, Washington: Copper Canyon Press, 1980.

———. "An Open Letter to the Blue-Eyed Straw Lady on the Front Row, Who Said That She Likes My Poems, Even Though She Understands Them." *Voyages to the Inland Sea*, VII. Ed. John Judson. La Crosse, Wisconsin: Center for Contemporary Poetry, 1977. 33–38.

————. *Platte Valley Homestead*. Lincoln, Nebraska: Platte Valley Press, 1981.

————. *Restoring the Burnt Child: A Primer*. Lincoln: University of Nebraska Press, 2003.

————. *Sergeant Patrick Gass, Chief Carpenter: On the Trail with Lewis and Clark*. Granite Falls, Minnesota: Spoon River Poetry Press, 2002.

————. *Shadowboxing and Other Stories*. Winside, Nebraska: Logan House Press, 2003.

————. *Stocker*. Iola, Wisconsin: Wolfsong, 1978.

————. *Sunrise, Dayglow, Sunset, Moon*. Lewiston, Idaho: Talking River Publications, 2004.

————. *This Death by Drowning*. Lincoln: University of Nebraska Press, 1997.

————. *A Time to Sink Her Pretty Little Ship*. Winside, Nebraska: Logan House Press, 1999.

————. *Treehouse: New and Selected Poems*. Fredonia, New York: White Pine Press, 1996.

————. *Uncertain the Final Run to Winter*. Lincoln, Nebraska: Windflower Press, 1974.

————. *Welcome to Carlos*. Granite Falls, Minnesota: Spoon River Poetry Press, 2000.

————. *Where the Visible Sun Is*. Granite Falls, Minnesota: Spoon River Poetry Press, 1989.

Kloefkorn, William, and David Lee. *Covenants*. Granite Falls, Minnesota: Spoon River Poetry Press, 1996.

Kloefkorn, William, and Ted Kooser. *Cottonwood County*. Lincoln, Nebraska: Windflower Press, 1979.

Knoepfle, John. "Crossing the Midwest." *Regional Perspectives*. Ed. John Gordon Burke. Chicago: American Library Association, 1973. 77–174.

————. *poems from the sangamon*. Champaign: University of Illinois Press, 1985.

Kooser, Ted. *Sure Signs: New and Selected Poems*. Pittsburgh: University of Pittsburgh Press, 1980.

Kowalewski, Michael. "Contemporary Regionalism." *A Companion to the Regional Literatures of America*. Ed. Charles L. Crow. Malden, Massachusetts: Blackwell, 2003. 7–24.

Kunstler, James Howard. *The Geography of Nowhere*. New York: Touchstone, 1993.

Le Sueur, Meridel. "The Ancient People and the Newly Come." *Growing Up in Minnesota*. Ed. Chester Anderson. Minneapolis: University of Minnesota Press, 1976. 17–46.

————. *My People Are My Home*. Videocassette. Minneapolis: Twin Cities Women's Film Collective, 1977.

Levy, Bernard-Henri. "In the Footsteps of Tocqueville." *Atlantic Monthly* May 2005: 54–89.

Lewis, Peirce F. "Axioms for Reading the Landscape." *The Interpretation of Ordinary Landscapes: Geographical Essays*. Ed. D. W. Meinig. New York: Oxford University Press, 1979. 11–32.

Lewis, Sinclair. *Main Street*. New York: Signet, 1961.

Lind, Michael. "Where Have You Gone, Louis Sullivan: Will America Recover from Its Fifty-Year Bout of Europhilia?" *Harper's* February 1998: 53–59.

Lopez, Barry. "The American Geographies." *Finding Home: Writing on Nature and Culture from* Orion *Magazine*. Ed. Peter Sauer. Boston: Beacon Press, 1992. 116–32.

Lorenz, Paul H. "Rethinking Machismo: Jim Harrison's *Legends of the Fall*." *Publications of the Arkansas Philological Association* 15.1 (Spring 1989): 41–51.

Mandat-Grancy, E., Baron de. *Cow-boys and Colonels: Narrative of a Journey across the Prairie and over the Black Hills of Dakota*. Trans. William Conn. London: Griffith, Farran, Okeden and Welsh, 1887.

Masters, Edgar Lee. *Spoon River Anthology*. New York: Macmillan, 1915.

McAvoy, Thomas. *The Midwest: Myth or Reality?* South Bend, Indiana: University of Notre Dame Press, 1961.

McClintock, James J. "Jim Harrison, Soul-Maker." *Midwest Quarterly: A Journal of Contemporary Thought* 41:2 (Winter 2000): 191–207.

McGrath, Thomas. *Letter to an Imaginary Friend: Parts I & II*. Chicago: Swallow, 1970.

McMurtry, Larry. *The Last Picture Show*. New York: Simon and Schuster, 1966.

———. *Walter Benjamin at the Dairy Queen*. New York: Simon and Schuster, 1999.

Meinig, D. W., ed. *The Interpretation of Ordinary Landscapes*. New York: Oxford University Press, 1979.

Mencken, H. L. *Smart Set Criticism*. Ed. William Nolte. Ithaca, New York: Cornell University Press, 1968.

Meyers, Kent. *Light in the Crossing*. New York: St. Martin's Press, 1998.

———. *The Witness of Combines*. Minneapolis: University of Minnesota Press, 1998.

Meyrowitz, Joshua. *No Sense of Place*. New York: Oxford University Press, 1985.

Mohr, Howard. *How to Talk Minnesotan*. New York: Penguin Books, 1987.

Momaday, N. Scott. *House Made of Dawn*. New York: New American Library, 1969.

Montag, Tom. *Concerns: Essays and Reviews 1972–1976*. Milwaukee, Wisconsin: Pentagram Press, 1977.

Morris, Wright. *Wright Morris: A Reader*. New York: Harper and Row, 1970.

Moyers, Bill. *Bill Moyers' Journal: The Poet at Large*. Videocassette. New York: Educational Broadcast System (WNET), 1979.

Mueller, Lisel. "Midwestern Poetry: Goodbye to All That." *Voyages to the Inland Sea I*. La Crosse, Wisconsin: Center for Contemporary Poetry, 1971. 1–10.

———. "Versions of Reality." *Poetry* 117 (1971): 322–30.

Murray, John. "Interview with Linda Hasselstrom." *The Bloomsbury Review* 12.5 (July–August 1992): 1, 20.

Nash, Roderick Frazier. *Wilderness and the American Mind*. 4th edition. New Haven: Yale University Press, 2001.

Nelson, Bruce. Review of *The Plains Sense of Things 2: Eight Poets from Lincoln, Nebraska*. *Nebraska Territory* (Fall 2000): 19–22.

Nelson, Paula M. *The Prairie Winnows Out Its Own: The West River Country of South Dakota in the Years of Depression and Dust*. Iowa City: University of Iowa Press, 1996.

Nemanic, Gerald. *A Bibliographical Guide to Midwestern Literature*. Iowa City: University of Iowa Press, 1981.

Neruda, Pablo. *Extravagaria*. Trans. Alastair Reid. New York: Farrar, Straus and Giroux, 1958.

Noe, Marcia. *Exploring the Midwestern Literary Imagination*. Troy, New York: Whitson Publishing Company, 1993.

O'Brien, Tim. *Northern Lights*. New York: Delacorte, 1965.

Paglia, Camille. *Sex, Art, and American Culture*. New York: Random House, 1992.

Paul, Jay. "Dave Etter's Rural Modernism." *Midwest Quarterly* 33.4 (1992): 384–92.

Phillips, Robert. *William Goyen*. Boston: Twayne Publishers, 1979.

Pichaske, David. "Dave Etter's Alliance, Illinois." *Illinois: The Magazine of Illinois* (September–October 1981): 20–25.

———. *A Generation in Motion: Popular Music and Culture in the Sixties*. New York: Schirmer Books, 1979.

———. "Some Notes on Bob Dylan 'And the Language That He Used.'" *Judas!* 6 (July 2003): 49–59.

———. "Stubby Payne: Stocking Tops." *Indiana Review* 8.3 (1985): 71–81.

Prescott, Peter S. "The Macho Mystique." *Newsweek* 94 (July 1979): 92.

Quantic, Diane Dufva. *The Nature of the Place: A Study of Great Plains Fiction*. Lincoln: University of Nebraska Press, 1995.

Reilly, Edward C. *Jim Harrison*. New York: Twayne Publishers, 1996.

Relph, Edward. *Place and Placelessness*. London: Pion, 1976.

Reutter, Vicki. Review of *Cosmos Coyote and William the Nice*. *School Library Journal*, July 2000: 104.

Review of *Cosmos Coyote and William the Nice*. *Publishers Weekly* (16 July 2001): 73.

Review of *You Know What Is Right*. *Georgia Review* (Winter 1985): 905–6.

Roberson, William H. "'Macho Mistake': The Misrepresentation of Jim Harrison's Fiction." *Critique* 29.4 (Summer 1988): 233–44.

Rolvaag, Ole. *Giants in the Earth*. New York: Harper, 1927.

Roripaugh, Lee Ann. "Poet of the Wind: An Interview with Linda Hasselstrom." *South Dakota Review* 39.2 (Summer 2001): 6–25.

Rotunno, Laura. "A Peopled-Land, A Landed-People: The Nebraska Poetic Voice." *Platte Valley Review* 21.2 (Spring 1993): 15–19.

Ryden, Kent C. *Mapping the Invisible Landscape*. Iowa City: University of Iowa Press, 1993.

Sanders, Mark. "Review of *Going Out, Coming Back*, and *Burning the Hymnal*." *Hurakan: A Journal of Contemporary Literature* 2 (1995): 113–17.

———. "Rocks, Water, and Fire: Kloefkorn's Use of Symbol." *On Common Ground: The Poetry of William Kloefkorn, Ted Kooser, Greg Kuzma, and Don Welch*. Ed. Mark Sanders and J. V. Brummels. Ord, Nebraska: Sandhills Press, 1983. 21–29.

Sanderson, Rena. "Linda Hasselstrom: The Woman Rancher as Nature Writer." *Such News of the Land: U.S. Women Nature Writers*. Ed. Thomas S. Edwards and Elizabeth A. DeWolfe. Hanover and London: University Press of New England, 2001. 170–77.

Sanford, Geraldine. "The Dichotomy Pulse: The Beating Heart of Hasselstrom Country." *South Dakota Review* 20.3 (Autumn 1992): 130–55.

Schlief, Nick. "Norbert Blei: The Quest for Home." Student Paper, 2 May 2005.

Seaton, James. "Afterword—Midwestern Muckrakers." *Exploring the Midwestern Literary Imagination*. Ed. Marcia Noe. Troy, New York: Whitston Publishing Company, 1993. 203–8.

Shea, Henry. "Writer-Teacher Norb Blei Likes the Off-Season Here." *Door County Advocate* (17 September 1970): 11.

Shortridge, James R. *The Middle West: Its Meaning in American Culture*. Lawrence: University of Kansas Press, 1989.

Smith, Patrick A. *The True Bones of My Life: Essays on the Fiction of Jim Harrison*. East Lansing: Michigan State University Press, 2002.

Sobin, A. G. Review of *The Last Train to Prophetstown*. *Quartet* 4.32 (Fall 1970): 27–28.

Sounder, William. "Holm at Last." *St. Paul Pioneer Press Dispatch* (16 February 1990): 1D.

———. "Mr. Big." *Minnesota Monthly* (February 1989): 24–32.

Stegner, Wallace. *Wolf Willow*. Lincoln: University of Nebraska Press, 1980.

Stein, Kevin, and G. E. Murray, eds. *Illinois Voices: An Anthology of Twentieth-Century Illinois Poetry*. Champaign: University of Illinois Press, 2001.

Stern, Frederick C. "What Is 'Regionalism,' and If You Know That, Where Does the Midwest Begin and End?" *Exploring the Midwestern Literary*

Imagination. Ed. Marcia Noe. Troy, New York: Whitston Publishing Company, 1993. 10–26.

Stratton, Russ. "The Poetry of William Kloefkorn." *Elkhorn Review* (Autumn 1986): 8–10.

Stryk, Lucien. *Heartland: Poets of the Midwest*. DeKalb: Northern Illinois University Press, 1967.

Sutton, Kathlene. "Botany and Beef." *South Dakota Magazine* (November 2001): 77–80.

Szymanski, Ronald. *America in Literature: The Midwest*. New York: Scribner's, 1979.

Tammaro, Thom, and Mark Vinz, eds. *Imagining Home: Writing from the Midwest*. Minneapolis: University of Minnesota Press, 1995.

Toth, Susan Allen. *Leaning into the Wind: A Memoir of Midwest Weather*. Minneapolis: University of Minnesota Press, 2003.

Totherow, Barbara. "Family Constellations: Teaching Dave Etter's 'Brother.'" *English Journal* 77.7 (1988): 78–82.

Twain, Mark. *Adventures of Huckleberry Finn*. New York: Norton, 1977.

Utne, Eric. "A Message from Eric Utne." *Utne Reader* (July–August 2004): 47.

Warner, Sam Bass Jr. *The Urban Wilderness: A History of the American City*. New York: Harper and Row, 1972.

Weber, Ronald. *The Midwestern Ascendancy in American Writing*. Bloomington: Indiana University Press, 1992.

INDEX

AMERICAN LAND AND LIFE SERIES

Bachelor Bess: The Homesteading
Letters of Elizabeth Corey, 1909–
1919
Edited by Philip L. Gerber
Botanical Companions:
A Memoir of Plants and Place
By Frieda Knobloch
Circling Back:
Chronicle of a Texas River Valley
By Joe C. Truett
Edge Effects:
Notes from an Oregon Forest
By Chris Anderson
Exploring the Beloved Country:
Geographic Forays into American
Society and Culture
By Wilbur Zelinsky
Father Nature:
Fathers as Guides to the
Natural World
*Edited by Paul S. Piper and
Stan Tag*
The Follinglo Dog Book:
From Milla to Chip the Third
By Peder Gustav Tjernagel
Great Lakes Lumber on the Great
Plains: The Laird, Norton Lumber
Company in South Dakota
By John N. Vogel
Hard Places: Reading the Landscape
of America's Historic Mining
Districts
By Richard V. Francaviglia
Landscape with Figures:
Scenes of Nature and Culture
in New England
By Kent C. Ryden

Living in the Depot:
The Two-Story Railroad Station
By H. Roger Grant
Main Street Revisited:
Time, Space, and Image Building
in Small-Town America
By Richard V. Francaviglia
Mapping American Culture
*Edited by Wayne Franklin and
Michael C. Steiner*
Mapping the Invisible Landscape:
Folklore, Writing, and the Sense
of Place
By Kent C. Ryden
Mountains of Memory:
A Fire Lookout's Life in the
River of No Return Wilderness
By Don Scheese
The People's Forests
By Robert Marshall
Pilots' Directions:
The Transcontinental Airway
and Its History
Edited by William M. Leary
Places of Quiet Beauty:
Parks, Preserves, and
Environmentalism
By Rebecca Conard
Reflecting a Prairie Town:
A Year in Peterson
*Text and photographs by
Drake Hokanson*
Rooted:
Seven Midwest Writers of Place
By David R. Pichaske

A Rural Carpenter's World:
  The Craft in a Nineteenth-Century
  New York Township
  By Wayne Franklin
Salt Lantern:
  Traces of an American Family
  By William Towner Morgan

Signs in America's Auto Age:
  Signatures of Landscape
  and Place
  By John A. Jakle and Keith A. Sculle
Thoreau's Sense of Place:
  Essays in American
  Environmental Writing
  Edited by Richard J. Schneider